ACPL ITEM
DISCARDED

3 1833 00305 6063

Y0-BWS-064

JAN 2 2 '74

ECONOMICS OF AMERICAN AGRICULTURE

THIRD EDITION

WALTER W. WILCOX

Legislative Reference Service
Library of Congress

WILLARD W. COCHRANE

Associate Professor of Agricultural Economics
University of Minnesota

ROBERT W. HERDT

Professor of Agricultural Economics
University of Illinois

PRENTICE-HALL, INC. *Englewood Cliffs, N.J.*

Library of Congress Cataloging in Publication Data

WILCOX, WALTER WILLIAM,
  Economics of American agriculture.

  1. Agriculture—Economic aspects—United States.
I. Cochrane, Willard Wesley, joint author.
II. Herdt, Robert W., joint author.
III. Title.
HD1761.W435   1974   338.1'0973   73-3344
ISBN 0-13-229666-7

To Our Wives,
Pauline, Mary and Lorna,
who helped in many, many ways
in the writing of this book.

© 1974, 1960, 1951 by PRENTICE-HALL, INC.
Englewood Cliffs, New Jersey

All rights reserved.
No part of this book may be reproduced
in any form or by any means without
permission in writing from the publisher.

10 9 8 7 6 5 4 3 2 1

Printed in the United States of America

PRENTICE-HALL INTERNATIONAL, INC., *London*
PRENTICE-HALL OF AUSTRALIA, PTY. LTD., *Sydney*
PRENTICE-HALL OF CANADA, LTD., *Toronto*
PRENTICE-HALL OF INDIA PRIVATE LIMITED, *New Delhi*
PRENTICE-HALL OF JAPAN, INC., *Tokyo*

Contents

1778725

Preface

In 1959 the authors wrote as follows regarding the Second Edition:

This edition is, for all practical purposes, a new book. Besides the usual updating of statistical series and informational materials, this edition has been completely reorganized. The organization of major subject areas and chapters is new. Several new chapters have been added, several old ones have been dropped, and many of the chapters included from the first edition have been completely rewritten. However, the level of analysis, the coverage, and the point of view of this edition are similar to the first edition.

The same statement can be made regarding the Third Edition. The Third Edition builds on the Second, but it is a new book.

In this edition as in the first and second the authors have tried to treat the agricultural sector of the economy in a comprehensive manner. Production activities, marketing activities, the behavior of consumers, the influences of nonfarm agencies and institutions, and the role of government are described and meshed into a total analysis of the economics of the agricultural sector. We continue in this edition to emphasize the role and force of modern technology in the development of the farm economy. But we take a careful look at other important developments in American agriculture: environmental goals and activities and rural development goals and activities, for example. In sum, this volume seeks to describe and to analyze the operating farm economy in the context of a complex, highly dynamic, modern overall economy.

The plan of writing has been, first, to describe each segment or problem area in American agriculture, giving the latest available information, and second, to introduce modern economic analysis as a means of helping the readers understand the forces at work in these areas. Thus, we have sought to strike a balance between factual description on the one hand, and the use of analytical methods and economic analyses on the other. Those who wish to emphasize economic analysis may wish to supplement this volume with readings from intermediate economic theory books. For those who are more interested in descriptive materials, supplementary reading may be done in the current publications of the state agricultural experiment stations and in the publications of the United States Department of Agriculture.

The authors fully recognize and wish to acknowledge the research work of the many professional workers that has contributed to the writing of this book; a listing of the men involved would include much of the profession of agricultural economics. Much has been added to the attractiveness and clarity of the volume by the large number of excellent illustrations obtained from the U.S. Department of Agriculture; and, of course, the statistical and analytical materials obtained from the Economic Research and Statistical Reporting Services of the USDA were indispensable to the entire writing project. Substantial improvements in treatment of certain material were suggested by George E. Brandow of the Pennsylvania State University. Finally, experience gained in using *Economics of American Agriculture* as a text has contributed to revisions in, and we hope improvements in, this Third Edition.

We believe that we have a readable, teachable text for those who seek to understand the economic developments of a highly dynamic agriculture. We hope that students and teachers alike find this to be the case.

Walter W. Wilcox
Willard W. Cochrane
Robert W. Herdt

PART ONE

The Production of
Farm Products

Chapter 1

The Changing Structure

of American Agriculture

American agriculture in the 1970s consists of a tremendously complex set of organizations, including farms, farm supply firms, product marketing firms, public agricultural services, and the people who run, operate, or work in those units. This sector of the economy produces what could be regarded as the absolute necessity of life—food. Most Americans take the food for granted, spending only about 15 percent of their income for it, less than any other people at any other time or place ever. That fortunate state of affairs has resulted from a series of continuing developments. Those developments have favorably affected the mass of Americans, but some groups have suffered from the pace and scope of the changes. Even today, changes are occurring so fast that many of those who are part of American agriculture do not recognize all the dimensions of the developments.

This book is intended to give its readers some insight into the economic aspects of the agricultural system serving the United States. It describes and analyzes the economics of modern American agriculture. It is, therefore, about people—how and why they make economic decisions and the consequences of those decisions. Many noneconomists tend to think of economics as a study of money and industry, but it is much more. In fact, the most central concepts of economics have to do with people. It is useful to quote another economist speaking of this same point to noneconomists:

> Economics, contrary to common usage, begins with the postulate that man
> is the measure of all things...human health and happiness is more directly

"economic," therefore, than...property which is simply an intermediate means to health and happiness. Neither do economists regard "economics" as a synonym for "pecuniary." Rather money is but one of many means to ends as well as a useful measure of value."[1]

Thus, although at times it may appear that we are talking excessively about prices, costs, incomes, acres, and outputs, it should be remembered that we are trying to understand the economic interrelationships that affect the people who are part of modern agriculture.

Modern agriculture is composed of four major components. Farming is the one we normally think of, but the farming operation is supplemented by the farm marketing sector, the input supply sector, and the public agricultural service sector. The farm marketing system involves assembling, processing, packaging, storing, and transporting the farm output from over 3 million farms. The firms in the marketing system gather raw, unprocessed food, much of it during a rather brief period of the year and make it available to over 200 million consumers throughout the year. The system also includes the facilities and knowledge that make the United States a major exporter of food to the rest of the world.

The input supply system is a vital link between farms and nonfarm units producing machinery, fertilizer, power, pesticides, and other inputs. Many of these firms are cooperatively owned by farmers, and many provide inputs or services to parts of the economy in addition to the farm sector. Modern farming is heavily dependent on the inputs that these firms supply, so much so that most farms would come to a rapid halt without such inputs.

The government services provided to agriculture have been a key factor accounting for its development over the past century. Foremost among those services has been research, which had its institutional beginning in the land-grant colleges provided by the Morrill Act of 1862 and was given independent support through the Hatch Act of 1887. The research supported through government funds provided a steady stream of innovations in the early years that has turned into a flood of technological advance in the mid-twentieth century. The Agricultural Extension Service, instituted with the Smith-Lever Act of 1914, provided the means for bringing the new knowledge to the farmer's door. The United States Department of Agriculture supplemented and complemented the research work of the land-grant colleges. It also provided guidelines and regulations to improve the efficiency of the farm marketing system. The Federal Farm Credit System provides credit mainly through a number of self-supporting institutions, which were first set up with government assistance.

Each of these components of U.S. agriculture contributes to the prosperity of our nation. None could do the job alone, and in that sense no

---

[1]M. Mason Gaffney, "Applying Economic Controls," *Bulletin of Atomic Scientists*, June 1965, p. 20.

single one is "most important." In this book, we will examine each, describe its workings, and try to understand how it interacts with other components. We will see how the components have developed and try to look ahead to see how they may change in the future and understand what the consequences of such changes might be.

In the balance of this chapter and the succeeding five chapters, we will examine the farm production sector. Part Two deals with farm product marketing, consumer demand, and the overall price and income trends for U.S. agriculture. Part Three examines the determination and function of farm prices. Part Four discusses how farmers and the farming sector interact with the rest of the national economy and the rest of the world. In Part Five, we look at the inputs used in agriculture, including in one chapter an examination of the environmental effects of agriculture. The last three chapters, Part Six, discuss past, present, and possible future farm policies.

Long-run Changes in American Farming

The farm sector of the United States has experienced constant change since the establishment of the nation. Data reflecting some of the changes since 1870 are shown in Table 1–1. In that year, three-quarters of the

TABLE 1–1

Long-term Trends Related to U.S. Agriculture

	Percentage of Population		Farm Employment		Index of Farm Output	Index of Output per Farm Worker	Number of Farms (millions)
	Rural	Urban	Million	% of Total			
1870	74	26	8.0	50	100	100	
1880	72	28	10.1	49	155	123	4.0
1890	64	35	11.7	42	185	127	4.6
1900	60	40	12.8	37	240	150	5.7
1910	54	46	13.6	31	250	147	6.4
1920	48	51	13.4	27	279	166	6.5
1930	44	56	12.5	22	315	202	6.3
1940	43	56	11.0	17	351	254	5.8
1950	36	64	9.9	12	437	352	5.2
1960	30	70	7.1	9	527	592	4.1
1970	26	74	4.5	4	605	1077	2.9

Sources: Population percentages calculated from *Statistical Abstract of the United States, 1970*, and Series A36–A38 in *Historical Statistics of the United States*. Employment 1870 to 1900 based on Population Series P-9, No. 11, U.S. Bureau of Census. From 1910 to 1960, the figures are from *Average Annual Farm Employment*, U.S.D.A. Agricultural Marketing Service. Other series derived from: *Changes in Farm Production and Efficiency*, 1964 and 1971, U.S.D.A. Statistical Bulletin No. 233.

population lived in rural areas, while in 1970 three-quarters of the population lived in urban areas. Less than one-half of those remaining in rural areas continue to live on farms. This long-term trend underlies many of the concerns that rural people have, but some of the other factors shown in the table are also of concern.

The number of people employed on the nation's farms increased until 1910, when it exceeded 13 million. For four decades after 1910, the number decreased rather slowly, but during the 1950s and 1960s the rate of decline increased substantially so that by 1970 only 4.5 million workers were employed in U.S. farming. With nonfarm employment increasing rapidly during the entire period, the proportion of the labor force employed in farming decreased steadily.

The same period that saw the rapid reduction in manpower also witnessed rapid increases in agricultural productivity. The index of total farm output gradually climbed from one hundred in 1870 to two hundred by the turn of the century, doubled again to over four hundred by 1950 continued its rise to over six hundred by 1970. This rapid increase in output coupled with the reduction of farm manpower has led to very large and rapid increases in output per worker: over the past century output per farm worker has increased tenfold! This increase may be traced to the increased levels of land and purchased inputs per farm worker and to the rapidly changing production technology utilized by U.S. farmers. Each farm worker had nearly three times as much cropland and more than three times as much purchased inputs in 1970 as in 1910. The productivity of those physical inputs, as measured by the U.S. Department of Agriculture, increased by nearly 80 percent over the same period. Further implications of the productivity data will be explored in greater detail in a later chapter, but it is apparent that rapidly increasing productivity has *permitted* the relative importance of farming in the United States economy to decline.

From the data in Table 1–1, it appears that this decline has accelerated in the past two decades. Farmers and rural people are concerned about these changes and what they mean for rural America. Some of the specific questions that concern them are: What has been and will be the impact of continued declining rural population on the quality of life in rural America? What forces are at work reducing the number of farms and when will those forces exhaust themselves? When that day is reached, how many farms and farmers will remain? Who has benefitted from and who has borne the cost of the increased productivity and economic efficiency of American agriculture?

The issues raised by these questions provide the reason for much of the analysis followed in this book. We hope the analysis will help the student begin to answer the questions to his own satisfaction.

Income of Farm People

A useful place to begin is with the income of farm people. The determination of farm income will be considered in detail in later chapters.

As will become apparent from the discussion and data presented, the average income per farm when measured over all farms (noncommercial as well as commercial) reflects the average of a very heterogeneous group of businesses and individuals. One scholar has called it a "meaningless concept."[2] Although this may be true for any single year, trends in average incomes do provide some insight into what is happening to farm income. Figure 1–1 shows that income per capita of the farm population has been getting closer to income per capita of the nonfarm population. In fact, in 1970, income per person in the farm population was 75 percent as large as income per person in the nonfarm population.

What is not clear from Figure 1–1 is that direct government payments and nonfarm sources of income provided a substantial fraction of the income

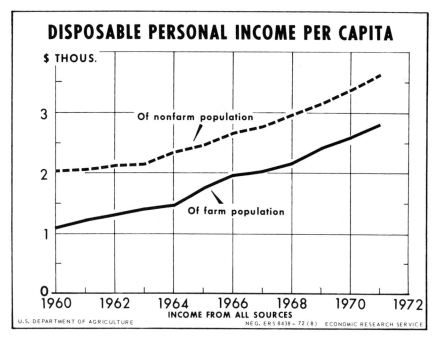

DISPOSABLE PERSONAL INCOME PER CAPITA

$ THOUS.

Of nonfarm population

Of farm population

1960 1962 1964 1966 1968 1970 1972

INCOME FROM ALL SOURCES

U.S. DEPARTMENT OF AGRICULTURE   NEG. ERS 8438 - 72 (8)   ECONOMIC RESEARCH SERVICE

FIGURE 1–1

of the farm population. In 1960, government payments provided 6 percent of realized net farm income, but by 1970 they provided 23 percent. Nonfarm sources provided over half the total income of farmers in 1970 and

[2]Richard J. Foote, "Concepts Involved in Defining and Identifying Farms," *ERS-448*, U.S.D.A., June 1970.

over 80 percent of the income on farms with sales of less than $2500. So although farmers' incomes have been catching up to the rest of the population during the 1960s, this has not been accomplished through reliance on freely operating farm markets.

Income by economic class is a more useful and enlightening concept than average income over all farms. Figure 1–2 shows income for six economic classes of farms in 1970. As would be expected, realized net income per farm is higher for farms with greater value of sales. Farms selling between $2500 and $5000 worth of farm products averaged $2000 of net farm income; farms selling over $40,000 worth had net farm incomes over $25,000 in 1970.

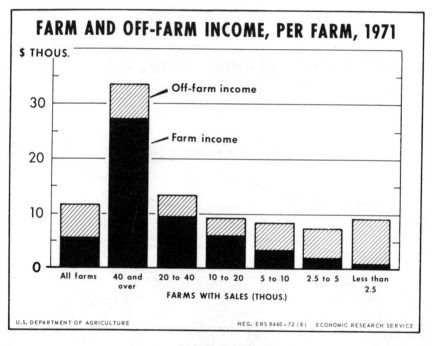

FIGURE 1–2

Nonfarm income was a very significant proportion of total income for all farms with sales less than $10,000. For all farms, this source of income has increased substantially in recent years. One result was that in 1970 the operators of the smallest farms had total incomes greater than the second class and equal to incomes of farmers with sales of $5000 to $10,000. However, Figure 1–2 includes *all* farms with sales of less than $2500 and many units in that group are not commercial farms. In fact, on the average one might consider the operators of all those units with sales less than $10,000 to be nonfarmers because the major portion of their income comes from nonfarm work. However, until modifications are made in the definitions, they will be counted as farmers in all official statistics.

Changes in the Number and Size of Farms

It is useful to look somewhat more closely at the farms that make up U.S. agriculture. This requires a careful examination of data that may appear complex but that can be understood with a little effort on the student's part. The top part of Table 1–2 shows the number of farms that had sales in the indicated sales class for farm census years between 1939 and 1969. The middle section of the table shows the percentage of farms in each size group, and the last section shows the percentage of total sales

TABLE 1–2

Number of Farms in the U.S. by Value-of-Sales[a] Groups, 1939–1969

	Less than $2500		Commercial Farms					
Year	Total	Commer-cial	$2500–$4999	$5000–$9999	$10,000–$19,999	$20,000–$39,999	$40,000 or more	All Farms
	[Number of Farms in Specified Group, thousands]							
1939	3841	2240	1086	600	225	66	29	5847
1944	3264	1661	1044	741	315	93	41	5498
1949	3067	1285	944	739	342	107	48	5247
1954	2606	972	869	725	398	137	63	4798
1959	1922	409	654	693	503	219	106	4097
1964	1544	b	469	533	482	268	146	3447
1969	1216	b	279	385	510	365	216	2971
	[Percentage of All Farms in Specified Value-of-Sales Groups]							
1939	65.7	38.3	18.6	10.3	3.8	1.1	.5	100
1944	59.4	30.2	19.0	13.5	5.7	1.7	.7	100
1949	58.5	24.5	18.0	14.1	6.5	2.0	.9	100
1954	54.3	20.3	18.1	15.1	8.3	2.9	1.3	100
1959	46.9	10.0	16.0	16.9	12.3	5.3	2.6	100
1964	44.9	b	13.6	15.5	14.0	7.8	4.2	100
1969	40.9	b	9.4	12.9	17.2	12.3	7.4	100
	[Percentage Distribution of Cash Farm Receipts (Total Sales)]							
1939	15.8	11.4	22.0	23.2	15.5	8.7	14.8	100
1944	12.4	7.8	17.7	23.9	18.3	9.8	17.0	100
1949	12.6	6.8	14.8	22.4	18.7	10.9	20.6	100
1954	10.0	4.6	12.4	20.2	20.5	13.6	23.3	100
1959	5.9	1.8	7.5	15.5	21.7	18.2	31.2	100
1964	4.5	b	4.9	10.9	19.0	20.0	40.7	100
1969	2.7	b	2.3	6.2	15.9	21.4	51.5	100

[a]Valued at 1959 prices received by farmers.
[b]Not separately identified.

Source: 1964 and 1969 from *Farm Income Situation*, July 1971; other years from Radoje Nikolitch, *The Expanding and Contracting Sectors of American Agriculture*, U.S.D.A. Agricultural Economies Report 74, May 1965.

made by each size group. Some rather rapid changes have occurred in the number of farms in each size class in the period covered. In addition to actual changes, there have been some changes in the definitions of a *farm*.

Intuitively, most people know what a farm is, but precise definitions are another matter. In fact, in the eighteen farm censuses taken since 1850, the definition has changed eight times. Since 1964, the definition has included all places of ten acres or more with at least one of the following specified minimums:[3]

> . . . 2 or more acres of crop failure, 5 or more acres of land in summer fallow, 5 or more acres of cropland pasture or improved other pasture, 10 or more acres of other pasture, 50 or more chickens 4 months old or older, five or more hogs or pigs, five or more cattle and calves, two or more milk cows, 0.2 acre of tobacco, 100 or more pounds of tobacco harvested, 0.5 acre or more of vegetables or berries harvested for sale, 0.5 acre or more in orchards, 3 or more acres of hay, or 2 or more acres of corn if farm had no hogs or pigs.

In addition, the definition included all places of ten acres or less that produced or sold one of the following specified minimum amounts:

> . . . 5 or more acres of crop failure, 100 or more chickens 4 months old or over, 10 or more hogs and pigs, 10 or more cattle and calves, four or more milk cows, 0.3 acre or more of tobacco harvested, 500 pounds or more of tobacco harvested, 2 acres or more of vegetables or berries harvested for sale, 2 or more acres in fruit orchards, or 5 or more acres of corn harvested if farm had no hogs and pigs.[4]

Most Americans would agree that places with as few as 10 hogs and pigs or 4 milk cows or any of the other minimums used in the census definition are hardly what they envision as farms. To separate part-time farms and rural residences from farm businesses, a distinction has been established between *commercial* farms and *other* farms.

Commercial farms include all farms with sales of $2500 or more, plus farms with sales of less than $2500 that represented the main occupation and livelihood for their operators, provided the operators were less than sixty-five years old. *Other* farms include all farms that are not included in the commercial category. This includes farms serving primarily as rural residences for people in predominantly nonfarm occupations. It also includes farms operated by retired or semiretired persons.

Among the commercial farms, six classes are defined by their value of sales. Table 1–2 shows how the number of farms in each class has changed since 1939. The number of commercial farms with sales less than $10,000 is decreasing. That decrease has been more rapid for the smaller economic

---

[3]Information taken from: Richard J. Foote, "Concepts Involved in Defining and Identifying Farms," *ERS-448*, U.S.D.A., June 1970.
[4]Foote, *op. cit.*

classes, and in fact the number of farms with sales less than $2500 decreased from over 2 million in 1939 to four hundred thousand in 1959 and to an insignificant number by 1969. The pattern for the other classes with sales of less than $10,000 is similar, especially the sharp decrease from 1959 to 1969. These farms, along with the group identified as "other," make up what has been called the contracting sector of American agriculture.[5]

The number of farms with sales between $10,000 and $19,999 more than doubled from 1939 to 1959, and since then has remained about constant around one-half million. The number of farms in the largest two farm size classes with sales over $20,000 per year increased sharply from less than 100,000 farms in 1939 to over 550,000 farms in 1969. The three classes of farms with sales over $10,000 make up the expanding sector of American agriculture.

The overall picture, then, shows a rapid decrease in the total number of farms—from over 5 million in 1950 to under 3 million in 1970. Within that total, there has been an increasing number of large farms and a very sharply decreasing number of small farms.

Are the Big Farms Taking Over?

Can we conclude from these data that agricultural production is becoming concentrated in the hands of a very few large farmers? From the evidence available in 1971, the best answer to this question is no. The data in Table 1–2 show that in 1939 about 60 percent of total sales came from about 16 percent of the farms (those in the four largest economic classes). In 1969, the same 60 percent of total sales came from about 20 percent of the farms (those in the largest two economic classes).

M. L. Upchurch comments on what has happened as follows:

> The odd fact is that the average size of all size classes of farms has been moving upward. If you array all farms by size and divide the total into quintiles, you find the upper two-fifths of our farms have produced about 80 percent of total output. The proportion has changed little for many years. The lower two-fifths of our farms consistently have produced about 10 percent of total output. The middle quintile has produced the remaining 10 percent with little change over time. Although farms have become fewer and larger, the relative size distribution among farms remains surprisingly constant.[6]

Thus, even though many fewer farmers remain, agricultural production is not becoming concentrated in the hands of a smaller proportion of farmers. What is happening is that the average sales on the fewer remaining farms are increasing.

[5]Radoje Nikolitch, "The Expanding and Contracting Sectors of American Agriculture," *Agricultural Economics Report 74*, U.S.D.A., May 1965.

[6]"Dynamics of Commercial Agriculture," a talk given at the Annual Agricultural Outlook Conference, Washington, D. C., February 1969.

If we look at the biggest farms, those with sales of $40,000 and over, we see that they are producing and selling an increasing fraction of total output. But most of these are one- or two-man operations. Among the really giant size units, average acreage per farm of all farms with more than one thousand acres fell about 5 percent between 1949 and 1959.[7] These data indicate that the farms in the largest economic class are becoming more common, that the "typical" commercial farm business is now quite likely to have annual sales of $40,000 or more, but not that the big farms are getting bigger.

Corporations Involved in Farm Production. Is the trend to larger farms caused by corporations and conglomerates moving into the farming business at the expense of family farms? This is a question that greatly disturbs rural people and those concerned with agricultural production. It is difficult to answer, but again the best available evidence indicates that the family farm is not losing out to corporation farming.

As with all questions, the words used must be understood before an adequate answer can be given. Many corporations involved in farming are owned by a single individual or a small group of closely related individuals. Although corporations, they have all the characteristics of family farms. That is, the family provides most of the management and most of the labor. (Often a family farm is defined as one hiring less than 1.5 man-years of labor.) The number of such family corporations has been increasing and makes up by far the largest proportion of corporation farms.

A recent comprehensive study of corporate farming in the United States showed that 66 percent of all corporation farms were family owned, another 14 percent were individually owned, and the remaining 20 percent were owned by a group larger than a family.[8] These "other farming corporations" tended to be somewhat larger than the family farm corporations, but not unduly so. The data showed that 17 percent of "other farming corporations" had gross sales greater than $500,000, compared with 11 percent for all farm corporations.

The survey could not directly determine whether the number of corporate farms had been increasing. However, it did indicate that about 8 percent of the firms first began farming in 1967 or 1968, that 46 percent began farming between 1960 and 1966, and the remainder began farming before then. A tabulation of farm income tax returns by William Scofield indicated that the number of corporations filing farm tax returns increased from about 7,000 in 1949 to over 27,000 in 1965.[9] However, corporations

[7]Nikolitch, *op. cit.*

[8]George W. Coffman, "Corporations with Farming Operations," *Agricultural Economic Report 209*, U.S.D.A. June 1971.

[9]"Corporations in Farming," in *Corporation Farming: What Are the Issues*, Proceedings of the North Central Workshop held at Chicago, Illinois, April 1969, Department of Agricultural Economics Report 53, University of Nebraska, p. 7.

receiving the largest percentage of their incomes from nonfarm sources would be excluded from this count of farms.

Scofield concluded that:

> Much of the current concern over the asserted takeover of farm production by large corporations is not supported by the results from the survey. Even allowing for some corporations that were missed, the total number of corporations directly engaged in farming and ranching is probably about 1 percent of all commercial farms. These firms operated about 7 percent of the land in farms and accounted for possibly 8 to 9 percent of the gross sales of all farm products. So-called outside, or nonfamily corporations represented about 0.2 percent of all commercial farms and about 2 percent of gross sales.
>
> The incorporation of existing, larger-than-average family farms appears to be taking place at a substantially greater annual rate than is the entry of newly organized corporations created for the sole, or chief, purpose of engaging in the production of agricultural products. Greater flexibility in estate planning and possible saving in gift and inheritance taxes and other fringe tax benefits appear to be the major incentives for incorporation of family farm businesses.[10]

It is apparent that not all individuals in rural areas are farmers, so that the above data do not reflect the income situation of all rural people, or even of all people dependent on farming for a livelihood. The income status of farm workers and rural nonfarm workers will be considered in later chapters. The important point to understand here is that in 1970 most *commercial farm units* obtained combined farm and nonfarm incomes of over $8,000 per year. However, only farms with sales exceeding $20,000 had realized net farm incomes of over $8,000. The rest of the "farmers" had very large income contributions from off-farm sources. This off-farm income has become much more important in the last few years compared to the middle 1960s.

Capital Invested in Farming

Along with the trends that have been noted above, it is well known that the capital investment in farms in the United States has been rapidly increasing. The aggregate data in Figure 1–3 illustrate the increase for the entire farming sector over the past thirty years. Assets, liabilities, and proprietors' equities have increased sixfold since 1940, and this along with a 50 percent decrease in the number of farms has caused assets per farm to increase more than tenfold. Average equity per farm (including all the small noncommercial farms) has increased from around $7,000 per farm in 1940 to over $87,000 per farm in 1970. During the same period, the rate of return on that equity has dropped from around 10 percent to around 6 percent in 1970 (see Chapter 20 for more on this point).

[10]*Ibid.*

Investment on Typical Farms. The rapid increase in capital
investment per farm is further illustrated by the data in Table 1–3 showing investment and related data on three typical commercial family farms
as reported by the U.S.D.A. in 1957 and in 1968. These are representative
units, so there is a wide range in the actual sizes of each these types of
farms that we do not see in this data. However, we do see very striking
differences in income and investment in the different types of farms and
in the changes that occurred between 1957 and 1968.

TABLE 1–3

Investment, Income, and Production on Three Typical Family Farms,
1957 and 1968

	Dairy Wisconsin		Hog-Beef Fattening Corn Belt		Wheat Southern Plains	
	1957	1968	1957	1968	1957	1968
Investment						
Real estate	$21,810	$ 71,190	$40,990	$126,440	$63,890	$123,840
Machinery	7,120	17,770	6,990	14,070	9,400	10,610
Crops and livestock	7,140	22,650	14,590	35,120	5,070	12,670
Total	36,070	111,610	62,570	175,630	78,360	147,120
Net Farm Income	$3,806	$13,484	$8,116	$12,807	$2,853	$11,240
Livestock Numbers						
Milk cows	20	40	6	—	3	—
All cattle	31	65	52	107	33	71
Hogs	28	—	143	296	4	—
Poultry	102	—	125	—	70	—
Crop Acreages						
Corn	17	47	72	113	—	—
Hays	27	55	30	30	10	35
Small grain	25	30	43	27	100	287
Cotton	—	—	—	—	—	—
Other crops	1	—	—	30	180	30

Source: *Farm Costs and Returns: Commercial Family-Operated Farms by Type and Loca-
tion.* For 1957, Agricultural Information Bulletin 176, U.S.D.A., Agricultural Research
Service, June 1958; for 1968, Agricultural Information Bulletin No. 230, U.S.D.A. Economic
Research Service, September 1969.

Total investment in all three types of farm units increased substantially, with the largest part of that increase traceable to increased real
estate value. Net income increased by the largest relative and absolute
amount on Wisconsin dairy farms. All three types of farms became increasingly specialized as reflected in their corp and livestock data. Although one
might argue that the numbers presented are "too large" or "too small" to
show the "typical" farm of each type, the trend they show is identical to
that shown in Figure 1–3—the capital investment per farm is rapidly increasing. As this has occurred, retained earnings of farmers have become
increasingly inadequate sources of financing farms, making the farm finance

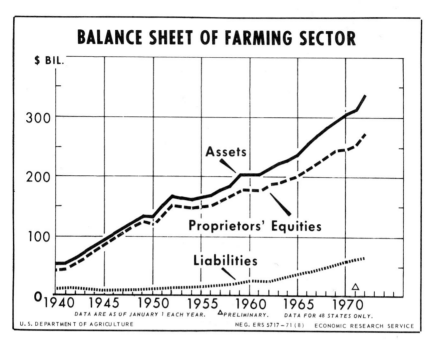

FIGURE 1–3

problem increasingly important. As nonfarm sources of finance are tapped to meet this need, the control of farmers over their own businesses is gradually eroded. This is an issue to which we shall return.

POINTS FOR DISCUSSION

1. Briefly describe the major sectors making up American agriculture.
2. Formulate a working definition of a *farm* that you believe would be more useful than the census definition.
3. Enumerate the major changes taking place in the farming sector.
4. Which problem is more important: the crowding out of family farms by large farming corporations or the continued attempts of many farm families to make a living on inadequate units?

REFERENCES

Changes in Farm Production and Efficiency. Statistical Bulletin 233, U.S.D.A., Economic Research Service, issued annually.

COFFMAN, GEORGE W., "Corporations with Farming Operations," *Agricultural Economic Report 209,* U.S.D.A., Economic Research Service (June 1971).

Corporate Farming and the Family Farm. Iowa State University Press, Ames, Iowa, 1970.

Farm Income Situation. U.S.D.A., Economic Research Service, issued semiannually.

FOOTE, RICHARD J., "Concepts Involved in Defining and Identifying Farms," *ERS-448,* U.S.D.A., Economic Research Service (June 1970).

NIKOLITCH, RADOJE, "The Expanding and Contracting Sectors of American Agriculture," *Agricultural Economics Report 74,* U.S.D.A., Economic Research Service (May 1965).

Chapter 2

Determining What to Produce

Farmers in the United States produce a wide variety of products. This chapter is devoted to an analysis of the economic forces that cause farmers to specialize in the production of a few products, yet seldom to specialize in a single product.

American agriculture is several hundred years old. Farmers in most communities today think they produce what they do because of their fathers' experience and training. Custom is an important factor—too important from an economic point of view. However, it can be overcome by economic considerations. For example, before World War II farmers produced draft horses in most sections of the United States until their production became unprofitable and was stopped because of the general adoption of the tractor. Similarly, thousands of farmers shifted from the production of wheat and other cash crops to the production of more forage crops and livestock as their soil resources became depleted and the demand for livestock increased during the last forty years. On the other hand, in some areas continuous corn has replaced the rotations that an earlier generation thought indispensable.

Two Problems in Determining What to Produce

The problem of determining what to produce has two parts. They are: (1) what particular crops or livestock or combination of them should be produced on a particular farm or in a community; and (2) how much of each of several crops or livestock should be combined on a particular farm. The first part of this problem draws on the principle of comparative advantage. The second part of the problem requires the application of the principles of enterprise combination.

Both these principles imply that farmers manage their business so as to maximize or attempt to maximize their family welfare or the profit from the farm business. The principal explanations of economic phenomena have been developed using this assumption, and although some economists question whether it always holds for all individuals, it holds generally enough to make economic theory useful.

The Basis of Differentiation in Production

Variations in soil and climate from one area to another and distance to consuming centers are the important factors affecting the location of farm production. On some of the western hills differences in altitude and air movements have led to planting oranges near the tops of the slopes, walnuts farther down the slope, and alfalfa and other crops in the valleys. Door County, Wisconsin, is a concentrated red sour cherry producing area largely because of its unique climate. It is a narrow strip of land with large bodies of water on three sides: Green Bay on the west, Lake Michigan on the east, and Lake Superior on the north. The moderating effect of these bodies of water produces a climate unusually well-suited for sour cherry production.

Although fruits are more sensitive to temperature and soil differences than most farm crops, the specialization in the production of other crops is closely correlated with critical climatic and soil resource factors. The large areas of spring and winter wheat in the Great Plains and in the Pacific Northwest, which are described in the following chapter, are areas of productive soils and scant rainfall. Enough rain falls to mature a wheat crop, but not enough to produce the usual Corn Belt feed and forage crops. We find that the dairy regions of the United States are areas where soils, rainfall, and temperatures favor the production of forage crops—hay and pasture. The Corn Belt is limited on the south and east by rough, unproductive soils, and growing season temperatures and rainfall at the northern and western boundaries set the limits of intensive corn production.

Cost of transportation to consuming centers also influences the selection of crops and livestock on farms. Products with a high value per unit of weight tend to be produced in those areas farthest from consuming centers. Farms located adjacent to ocean transportation may be able to purchase certain supplies more cheaply than farms located in the interior. Availability of these cheaper supplies influences the kind and amount of farm products produced with any particular set of natural resources.

The Principle of Comparative Advantage. All these factors play a role in determining the location of production. Their total economic impact is reflected in the comparative advantage of producing one commodity relative to other commodities in a given location. *The principle of comparative advantage states that an area tends to specialize in the production of those products in which its output per unit of input is highest relative to other areas.* Or, stated in an equivalent way, a region will tend to specialize in those products for which its cost per unit of output is lowest relative to other areas.

A good example of this basic principle is the localization of beef cattle and wheat production. Wheat can be grown successfully both in the Corn Belt and in the Great Plains. Farmers can expect to get twenty-five to thirty-five bushels an acre if they grow wheat in the Corn Belt. This same land will produce feed and forage crops for beef cattle. The better land in the Corn Belt will produce feed enough for a beef cow and calf on one to two acres, or produce from 350 to 450 pounds of beef an acre.

Where crops are produced in the Great Plains, wheat yields twenty to thirty bushels an acre. But if this land is used for feed and forage crop production, three to five acres are required to support a cow and calf for a year. Only 80 to 120 pounds of beef are produced per acre.

Suppose the average output per acre of the two products in the area is:

Corn Belt	30 bu. of wheat or 400 lbs. of beef
Great Plains	20 bu. of wheat or 100 lbs. of beef

If labor and power costs of wheat production were the same in the Corn Belt and in the Great Plains (an assumption somewhat at variance with the facts), wheat production costs in terms of land and labor required must be higher in the Great Plains than in the Corn Belt. The Great Plains, nevertheless, must specialize in wheat production. This specialization is explained by the *ratio* of yields (output per unit of input) in the two regions. The Corn Belt can produce 1.5 times as much wheat per acre and 4 times as much beef per acre as the Great Plains, so it has a relative or *comparative advantage* in beef production. On the other hand, the Great Plains produces two-thirds as much wheat but only one-fourth as much beef per acre as the Corn Belt. Because two-thirds is greater than one-fourth, the Great Plains has a comparative advantage in wheat production even though it has an absolute disadvantage in both commodities. Each region specializes in production of one commodity as long as a demand for both exists because the alternative is to leave the Great Plains uncultivated—an alternative clearly inferior to utilizing land in both regions.

The same principle operates to cause the Lake States and the Northeast to specialize in dairy production. In these areas, one dairy cow producing 9,000 pounds of milk requires about three acres of land and the associated labor for crop production and animal care. In the Corn Belt, an equal amount of milk could be produced on two acres of land with the associated labor. But in the Corn Belt, the feed from two acres of land will produce 2,000 pounds of hogs. In the Lake States where small grains and forage crops are relatively more productive than corn, the feed supply is not adapted for hogs. Probably not over 1,200 pounds of hogs could be produced from three acres of land. The student can, using the simplifying assumption that all other inputs are the same in the two regions, show that the Lake States have a comparative advantage in milk production.

Specialization in cotton production in the South is another example of the operation of the principle of comparative advantage. Farmers in the Corn Belt and in the dairy area could produce their own fibers for clothing if necessary. The season is too short to grow cotton, but they could produce their own wool by keeping sheep and they could produce linens by raising fiber flax in some areas. Instead, they specialize in feed and livestock production and buy cotton goods made from raw materials produced by farmers in the Cotton Belt. Here we find that, because of climatic limitations, only one part of the country can grow a particular product.

Substitute products can be produced in other areas, but they are more expensive and less satisfactory for many purposes. Both areas gain by specializing in the products for which they have a comparative advantage and by exchanging them with each other.

Regional specialization in production, following the principle of comparative advantage, occurs not only in the United States but also in other parts of the world where freedom to trade with other areas exists. Thus, we import most of our coffee, bananas, and sugar because the United States farmers cannot profitably produce these products in the quantities desired by American consumers. In contrast, producers in other countries find it profitable to specialize in the production of coffee, bananas, and sugar for export to the United States.

Farmers in one area do not sit down and work out their ratios of advantage or disadvantage as compared with farmers in other areas. Instead, they take their direction from the price system. Farmers in the dairy region find that they can realize a higher income from specialization in dairying, rather than in hogs or sheep. Farmers in the Corn Belt find that they can realize a higher income producing meat animals rather than anything else. Farmers in the Cotton Belt find it more profitable to raise cotton than any other crop.

The Changing Nature of Comparative Advantage. One might think that when farmers in a particular area find which products give them the best returns they have found a permanent solution to their problems of what to produce. Anyone who has studied the history of production in the different areas of the United States knows that this is not so. Comparative advantage is a changing phenomenon. The ratio of advantage or disadvantage in producing a particular product on a particular farm or in an area may change for any one of the following reasons:

1. Changes in natural resources, such as loss through soil erosion
2. Changes in biological factors, such as increased infestations of crops by pests and disease
3. Changes in product or input prices
4. Increased mechanization that is better adapted to level land free of stones than to hilly and stony land
5. Cheaper and more efficient transportation that decreases the disadvantage of areas most distant from markets

Changes under each of these five headings are constantly in process. One can see a pattern in these changes and their effects on regional specialization in production.

Trends in Regional Specialization

Specialization in production, both on individual farms and in particular areas, is increasing. Improved technology and the development of specialized mechanical equipment is the primary economic force leading to increased specialization.

Potato production is an excellent example of this trend. As compared with thirty years ago, potato producers today select a much higher quality seed and use much heavier applications of fertilizer. In areas where rainfall is ample or where irrigation is used, as much as three thousand pounds of fertilizer per acre is applied annually. Potatoes are sprayed several times during the growing season with different spray materials. The hand labor once used to pick up potatoes has been replaced by machines on level, stone-free fields, putting those farms with hilly and stony fields at a disadvantage. In addition to the usual growing and harvesting practices of thirty years ago, potato producers today usually grade and often package their potatoes before selling them.

The requirements for efficient, low-cost potato production can only be met by using the best-adapted lands in combination with modern machinery and specialized sprays and fertilizers. It takes a higher degree of technical competence to organize and manage such a producing unit now than it did in the past when potatoes were produced by planting the potatoes in the spring, keeping the weeds out during the summer, and digging them with horse power and hand labor in the fall. Potato yields have doubled in recent years on the best-adapted lands under good management. Supplemental irrigation is being used to an increasing extent throughout the Eastern states. With no increase in the total demand for potatoes, but with increasingly complex production techniques and specialized grading requirements for processed potato products, farmers who cannot apply the new technology under high-quality management are going out of potato production.

This same tendency toward specialization is in progress for all kinds of farm production. In general, our better land is being farmed more intensively with fewer crops and fewer kinds of livestock than it was twenty years ago. Our poorer land is being used less intensively or shifted to permanent pasture and forestry.

Importance of Alternative Opportunities. It is important to reemphasize that it is relative, rather than total, costs that are important in the interregional competition of farm products. Farms and areas with limited opportunities for shifting to other lines of production will continue specializing in a particular product, even though prices fall below average production costs, and areas with greater opportunities for shifting will change to new lines of production. Thus, in the northern parts of Minnesota, Wisconsin, and Michigan, low productivity soils and the short growing season limit the crops that can be grown in addition to hay and pasturage. The cost of producing one hundred pounds of milk is higher than in the southern parts of the same states and in the Corn Belt. Yet, a drop in milk prices relative to other farm product prices would cause shifts out of dairying in the lower-cost areas farther south, which have the better alternative opportunities, while little change would occur in the production in the northern part of these states.

One of the undesirable social consequences of these economic forces is that farmers with inferior, less-productive natural resources tend to sink to substandard levels of living (see Chapter 18). Technological improvements have increased the relative advantages to farmers with more-productive natural resources, causing the value of the land and invested capital in the areas of inferior resources to drop. Producers in these areas "reduce" their costs by writing down their capital investments. If perfect mobility of human resources existed, undesirable social consequences would not follow. Families would leave the area if they could not earn incomes comparable to families elsewhere and the land would be retired from farming or organized into larger farming units. This has happened on a considerable scale in the New England and eastern states where industrial employment opportunities exist nearby.

More often, families in the densely populated areas of inferior agricultural resources, especially those located some distance from industrial centers, do not find opportunities for leaving the area or are unwilling to do so. They accept the lower standard of living forced on them by their inability to take advantage of technological changes. Their children, reared under conditions of inferior public education, nutrition, health, and medical care, do not migrate as readily as children from the better areas. This is particularly true in some parts of the Southeast.

Principles of Enterprise Combination

We turn now from a consideration of the principles that govern interregional specialization to an analysis of the forces that govern the combination of enterprises on individual farms. On every farm, the activities are directed toward the production of one or more major products and a limited number of related products, managed by the farmer so as to provide the maximum income.

A number of related behavioral rules or principles guide producers in maximizing their incomes. These principles all involve the concept of *marginal returns,* a term defined as *the addition to total returns (or added economic value of the output) due to the last unit of a resource used.* For example, if 199 pounds of fertilizer have been applied to a field, the marginal return to fertilizer on that field is the change in the value of crop that would occur if the application were increased to 200 pounds. That is, the marginal return to fertilizer in this situation is the value of crop produced by the two-hundredth pound of fertilizer.

Nearly every farmer manages more than one enterprise and therefore must decide on the best ratio among the enterprises managed. In this case, *the principle followed to obtain maximum returns is to divide productive resources among the enterprises in such a way that the last unit of resource used for each product brings equal returns.* (This is called the principle of equal marginal returns.)

Joint Products. One of the simplest farm organizations is found on the specialized dairy farms of New York. Their major product is fluid milk for urban consumption. All the feed produced on the farm is fed to the dairy herd. But even on such a specialized farm as this, milk is not the only product sold. Sales of veal calves and cull cows usually average 5 to 15 percent of the value of the milk sold. The veal calf is a joint product in the production of milk. Sale of cull cows is a salvage operation, the farmer recovering as much as possible from worn-out capital assets. Thus, on this very highly specialized fluid milk farm we find joint production of two commodities: milk and calves.

Joint products are two or more products obtained, in relatively fixed proportions, from a single production process. Usually, however, even in the case of joint products, the farmer may vary the output of one product relative to the others. As soon as the calf is born, the dairyman has the alternative of selling it for a nominal sum or feeding it until it reaches prime market condition. Some farmers, with Guernsey and Jersey cows producing milk for high-priced city markets, kill their calves at birth. The calves are too small to have a market value at birth, and the milk is too valuable to feed them until they reach a marketable weight.

This illustrates the principle that when two or more products are produced jointly the joint products should be considered as one enterprise up to the point at which one or more products may be separated in the production process. At this point, the principle of equal marginal returns guides the division of resources. Milk should be fed to veal calves until the value of the added weight on the calves from the last pound of milk fed is just equal to the value of the milk if it were sold for fluid use. The amount of weight to be put on the calves will depend on the price for veal calves and labor, as well as the price of milk. When the marginal returns from resources expended on each product (veal and milk) are equal, total returns will be at their highest.

Many joint products have few competitive relations, either during the joint-production process or after they are separated. Wheat and straw are classic examples of joint products for which most of the economic value is associated with one product. A farmer seldom sacrifices a part of his potential yield of grain to obtain a higher yield or higher quality of straw. After the harvest, the decisions he will make concerning how he will dispose of the straw will not depend on the decisions he makes concerning how he will handle the wheat.

At the other extreme is the case of the joint products of mutton and wool. Animals bred to give the best yields of wool do not produce the best carcasses and vice versa. The sheep raiser must decide how to balance these competing demands in terms of marginal analysis, in which the reduction in prospective wool yield is balanced against the prospective increase in the carcass value of the sheep.

Supplementary Relations Among Enterprises. A farmer may raise more than one crop in order to take advantage of his resources throughout the year. A farmer who produces only cotton has no productive work to do on his farm during the winter months. He has worked long hours planting, cultivating, and harvesting during the growing season and is idle or works away from the farm the rest of the year. Farm power units have similar periods of peak loads and idleness. An enterprise that utilizes the farmer's time when he is not busy with cotton supplements the main cotton enterprise.

American farmers supplement their major enterprise, when they find it possible, with other enterprises in order to use more fully resources, such as lands, buildings, family labor, and equipment, that are relatively fixed and are somewhat of an overhead cost to the business. The size of the supplementary enterprise is set by the scarce or *limiting* resource—by the amount of land that can be spared from the production of food crops or by the amount of labor that is available during the peak planting and harvesting seasons. An enterprise that is primarily supplementary competes for one or more limiting resources with the main enterprise at particular points. *The careful manager meets this situation by developing his supplementary enterprise until the marginal returns to the limiting resources are equal for both enterprises, resulting in the maximum total returns.*

Complementary Relations Among Enterprises. Hogs running in the feed lots with fattening cattle pick up considerable grain that otherwise would be wasted. On farms where separated cream is sold, hogs and chickens utilize the waste skim milk. When two or more enterprises are interdependent so that an increase in the output of one increases the output of the other, as illustrated above, they are said to be complementary. Livestock is supplementary to crops in permitting fuller employment of labor during the winter months. It is *complementary* to crops, however, in utilizing low-quality crops, unmarketable gleanings left in the field, and pasture grasses. Feeding the crops on the farm to well-bedded livestock produces manure, which helps maintain high crop yields.

The complementary relations among the crops, in the usual rotation, are important. The intertilled crops permit weed eradication, beneficial to the close growing legumes in the rotation. Conversely, the organic matter and nitrogen added to the soil by legumes boosts the yields of intertilled crops.

Farmers keep in mind these technical and, thus, economic relations among enterprises. They start with a main enterprise, which has a comparative advantage in the area, and keep adding complementary and supplementary enterprises until the marginal returns from all resources used in farm production are equalized and thus the returns from all enterprises combined are maximized. Any further expansion in the output of one of the joint, supplementary, or complementary products would divert resources from another, more-profitable use. When this point has been reached in the allocation of resources on the farm, the only means of increasing income further is to increase the size of business or, if possible, lower production costs by introducing new lower-cost production practices.

Comparative Advantage of Enterprise Combination. At this point, we should elaborate briefly on our discussion of the principle of comparative advantage. It was inferred earlier that the relative advantage of individual products could be determined directly for each area. Now we see that we must consider comparative advantage between regions in terms of groups of products having joint, supplementary, and complementary relations.

The determination of the competitive position of an area for the production of a particular product turns out to be exceedingly complicated. Probably the simplest and most helpful rule to remember is that areas with resources adapted to the production of a number of different products make the shifts in production that grow out of changing technology and changing demand conditions. Areas with few alternatives, already highly specialized in one product, tend to continue in their specialty, accepting reduced land values and standards of living, if necessary, as the price of their product falls.

Specialization vs. Diversification. The practice of diversification in farm production, that is, developing several enterprises rather than specializing in one or two, has been advocated by farm management specialists for many years. We see the economic basis for this diversification in the joint, supplementary, and complementary relations found among farm enterprises. The land, family labor, and capital equipment on the farm is more fully utilized, and otherwise wasted products are converted into marketable form by the addition of livestock to most crop farms. The total production of the land in most sections of the country is increased when crops are rotated. In addition to promoting efficient use of the farm resources, diversified production reduces the risk in farming. Dangers of serious losses by disease or unfavorable weather are reduced when a number of products are produced. Economic risks associated with price changes also are lower with diversified farming.

The general problem of meeting risk and uncertainty in farming will be the subject of a later chapter. Here, we want to consider the trends affecting the advantages of diversification and specialization on individual farms. Improved technology for the most part favors increasing specialization by individual farms as well as by regions. First, much improved technology requires large capital investments in specialized equipment, which, in turn, requires a large volume of output if costs per unit of output are to be kept low. Second, improved technology has reduced the hazards of disease losses in specialized production of many crops and livestock products. Weather hazards also are reduced by such developments as new frost-resistant seed stocks and mechanical drying equipment. Third, the application of improved technology requires increased specialization on the part of management. A farmer finds it difficult to acquire all the necessary skills and to keep up to date in a number of different fields. Fourth, government price-support programs, marketing agreements, and similar price-stabilization measures have reduced the danger of serious price declines for most major farm products.

Marketing requirements are another factor that cause specialization on some farms. To a certain extent, cooperative marketing associations permit small-scale diversified farmers to market their products efficiently in competition with the specialized larger-scale producers. An examination of the competitive advantage of many large-scale specialized producers, however, indicates that economies in marketing and in furnishing large quantities of uniformly high-quality products are even more important in the success of these farms than their economies in production.

The advantages of extensive diversification under these newer conditions are much less than they were several decades ago. The advantages of specialization are much greater. The trend is toward a greater specialization in a major product and one or two supplementary and complementary enterprises on the more-progressive farms in the community. With farming carried on by several million different entrepreneurs, however, highly specialized farming will be a gradual development.

Regional Specialization and Farm Programs

Although a full consideration of farm programs must be deferred to the last part of the book, the relation between trends in specialization and farm programs should be noted. Price-support programs that require acreage allotments of the crops for which prices are supported tend to slow down adjustments in production in line with changing comparative advantage. Acreage allotments are set largely on the basis of past acreages of the crop grown on the farm. Every producer is required to reduce his acreage by the same percentage. Production changes are "put in a strait jacket." This is one of the most serious charges made against these programs. To the extent that acreage allotments are set at some uniform percentage of previous acreage on the farm, the charge is justified. Thus far, the programs appear to have slowed down the rate of change, but sufficient flexibility has been maintained to permit a continuation of trends that were in progress.

POINTS FOR DISCUSSION

1. What is the most important crop in your home community?
2. Why does it have a comparative advantage over other crops?
3. What other crops and livestock are combined with this key crop on most farms? Explain their joint, supplementary, and complementary relations.
4. Using the data and assumption stated in the text on page 20, show that the Lake States have a comparative advantage over the Corn Belt in milk production.
5. From U.S. Department of Agriculture statistics, determine whether specialization has been increasing or decreasing in your home county.
6. What factors have been responsible for the general increase in farm specialization in the United States?

REFERENCES

CASTLE, E. N., M. H. BECKER, AND F. J. SMITH, *Farm Business Management: The Decision Making Process,* 2nd ed., Chap. 2. New York: The Macmillan Company, 1972.

HEADY, E. O., AND H. R. JENSEN, *Farm Management Economics,* Chap. 5. Englewood Cliffs, N. J.: Prentice-Hall, Inc., 1954.

HEDGES, T. R., *Farm Management Decisions,* Chaps. 1 and 12. Englewood Cliffs, N. J.: Prentice-Hall, Inc., 1963.

SAMUELSON, P. A., *Economics: An Introductory Analysis,* 8th ed., Chap. 2. New York: McGraw—Hill Book Co., 1970.

Chapter 3

Area Specialization
in Production

Farmers, utilizing the principles of comparative advantage and enterprise combination outlined in Chapter 2, have developed distinct patterns of farming in the different sections of the United States. If one travels from New York City to San Francisco, he will find dairying the predominant pattern of farming until he enters western Ohio. From there across Indiana, Illinois, and Iowa, and spilling north and south into Minnesota and Missouri, the Corn Belt supports hog- and beef-feeding operations and production of grain for sale to other regions.

If the traveler goes southwest from Omaha, crossing central and southwest Kansas, he will find highly specialized wheat production covering hundreds of square miles in Kansas and eastern Colorado. This wheat-growing area also extends north into Nebraska. Specialized wheat production gives way to cattle ranching in Colorado. Farther west, in the inter-mountain valleys, one finds farmers growing irrigated crops, often in combination with livestock production. In many of these valleys, especially as one approaches the West Coast, he finds the farmers specializing in vegetable, truck, and fruit crops.

In this chapter, we will systematically examine the major farming regions in the United States and isolate the critical factors that have influenced the development of the patterns of farming prevailing in each region. We then will briefly examine the changes that have occurred in the use of land resources and in regional farm productivity.

Farm-management specialists, after studying the patterns of farming carried on in all sections of the United States, have classified the country into a number of type-of-farming areas with a number of subtype areas within each major area. The location and boundaries of these major type-of-farming areas are shown in Figure 3–1.

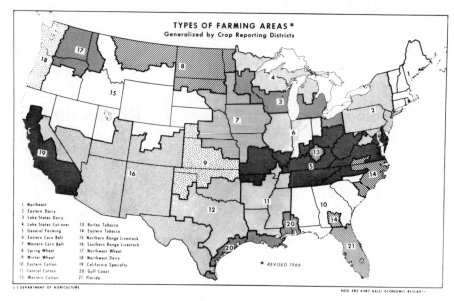

FIGURE 3–1

Many factors influence the type of farming followed in a community. Biological conditions, such as the prevalence of insect pests, weeds, and plant and animal diseases, are important. Economic forces, such as the availability of relatively cheap labor in the South and Southwest or the location of nearby market outlets for perishable products, are the critical influences in certain areas. Institutionalized economic forces, such as tariffs, freight-rate zones, and local sanitary regulations, also influence local production. For example, city sanitary regulations, governing milk sold within the city limits, have directly influenced the location of dairies producing milk for fluid consumption.

But the differences in the *physical factors,* climate, topography, and soils, *dominate* the boundaries of the major farming regions and most type-of-farming areas. This close correlation between variations in physical resources and variations in systems of farming will become more evident as each of the farming regions is examined in detail. Although the identification of the major types of farming was carried out some years ago, the dominance of natural factors in determining regional comparative advantages means that the regions identified twenty years ago are still valid today.

For purposes of statistical reporting, the ten farm production regions

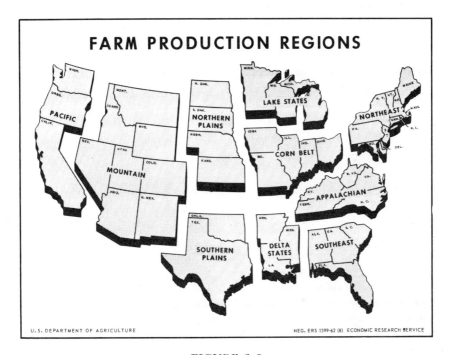

FIGURE 3–2

shown in Figure 3–2 are commonly used. Although the type-of-farming regions and the farm production regions do not correspond exactly, by comparing the two figures we can determine the major type of farming in each production region.

Feed Grain and Livestock Production

This type of farming, including areas 6 and 7 in Figure 3–1, makes up the Corn Belt states. Corn is the key crop because it gives high yields on the deep, warm, fertile soils of the region. Soybeans complement corn and have increasingly replaced oats, wheat, and hay as the secondary crop. Meat producers in the region base their enterprises on the utilization of the dominant feed crops.

Differences in topography and soils within the central section of the Corn Belt lead to three different, characteristic types of farming: (1) Cash-grain production, featuring corn, oats, and soybeans, is found on the most-level areas of the region. (2) Cattle feeding and hog production are found on the wind-blown, loessial soil areas bordering on the Missouri and Mississippi rivers, where the land is more rolling. (3) Hogs are the dominant livestock and soft winter wheat the main cash crop in the east central sections of the Corn Belt, where the soils are lighter and the farms smaller.

The southern parts of the Corn Belt states along with the rest of the general farming area have less-productive soils and hotter summers with more land in pasture than the Corn Belt. Beef-cattle grazing, rather than the beef-fattening and hog production common to the central part, is found here. As rainfall drops off toward the western border of the Corn Belt, the acreage of wheat increases relative to corn and oats. Substantial quantities of wheat and feed grains are sold for cash in the western Corn Belt, partly because of the uncertainty of the rainfall. Farmers understock with livestock to avoid getting caught without feed in dry years.

The Cotton Areas

Cotton production dominates in the three southern farm regions. It is grown up to, but seldom north of, the line of two hundred frost-free days. On the west, the twenty-inch rainfall limits the expansion further westward, except under irrigation. Heavy rainfall during the fruiting and harvesting seasons limits cotton production adjacent to the Atlantic Ocean and the Gulf of Mexico.

Cotton is produced on a wide variety of soils. But differences in soils and topography are largely responsible for differences in the intensity of cotton production in the various parts of the Cotton Belt. Thus, the Delta States, with their large areas of level land near the Mississippi, are important rain-fed cotton areas that have mechanized rapidly over the past ten years. Parts of the Southern Plains region, characterized by large farms and productive soils with level topography, also expanded their cotton production after 1930. These two regions, with the help of mechanization, have become more-intensive cotton areas than the old cotton belt of the Southeast.

Grain sorghums are competitive with cotton in the Southern Plains. In the Southeast, peanuts, corn, soybeans, truck crops, and in some areas tobacco, are grown in combination with cotton. In parts of the Southeast, forage and livestock production are replacing cotton. Partly as a result of increasing the efficiency of cotton production on the high plains of Texas, many of the small cotton producers of the delta and Southeast have lost their comparative advantage and have left agriculture for the urban areas of the North.

Dairy Farming

The Northeast, the Lake States, and the Northwest are the three important dairy areas of the United States. They are characterized by soils and topography that are not as favorable to the production of feed grains as those in the Corn Belt. The cool climate and the ample, well-distributed rainfall in these regions are favorable for hay and pasture. Farms are smaller than in the southern Corn Belt, and they are located nearer the urban consuming centers. For this and other reasons, dairy, rather than beef-cattle raising, is associated with the extensive hay and pasturage production.

In the southern and western sections of the dairy region, where the growing season and the soils permit substantial acreages of feed crops to be grown, hogs, poultry, and some beef-cattle-feeding operations supplement the dairy enterprise. In the northern and eastern sections of this region, silage corn and small grains are the only crops grown in addition to hay and pasture. Dairy cattle are often the only livestock on the farm and a large part of the grain required for the dairy herd is shipped in from the cash-grain areas of the Corn Belt.

Wheat and Small-Grain Regions

The major wheat-producing regions of the United States are the Northern Plains, the northern Mountain region, and northern Idaho and the eastern two-thirds of Washington. The Northern Plains region is characterized by productive soils with level to rolling topography, but with a rainfall too scant for most other crop production. Although grain sorghums and cotton compete with wheat in the Southern plains, in much of the Northern Plains wheat-producing area the only alternative to wheat is to return the land to permanent grazing.

The western boundary of the major wheat and small-grain area is set by limitations in both topography and rainfall that require that the land be kept in permanent range. Much of the land between the winter-wheat area (number *9*) and the spring-wheat area (number *8*) is too rough for crop production. Where it is sufficiently level and rainfall is adequate, corn is often grown in combination with wheat and other small grains. Other small grains and livestock production are more often combined with spring-wheat production than with winter-wheat production.

In the Pacific Northwest area, winter wheat is preferred, although spring wheat often is seeded if winter kills the fall-sown wheat. Rainfall ranges from ten to twenty inches in this area, and the land is rolling. Summer fallowing is practiced in much of this area, as well as in the western parts of both the winter- and spring-wheat areas on the Great Plains. Dry, edible peas are the principal alternative crop to wheat in this area. It is entirely surrounded by lands adapted only to grazing.

Range Livestock Region

Range land, which accounts for more than one-third of the total land area of the country, is the primary use of land in the Mountain region. Rainfall in most of the region is low and uncertain. Some of the land is at altitudes that prevent its use for crops. Other land is too steep and broken.

Differences between cattle and sheep ranges are described as follows:

> Cattle do better than sheep in the rougher and sandy short-grass areas and where few browse plants and annual weeds are found.... Sheep are more likely to be on fine-texture soils or moderately rolling lands where there is a combination of grass, perennial browse and annual weeds....
>
> Sheep are usually grazed on open range throughout the year; but they must be moved, often long distances from one seasonal range to another. In winter many sheep are kept in the desert areas which can be used only when snow is present to furnish stock water....
>
> In general, cattle are grazed on the mountain summer ranges for 3 to 5 months, pastured on hay or crop land during spring and fall or run on spring-fall range, and fed during the winter.[1]

General Farming

Much of the Appalachian region is in general farming. It is characterized by rolling to rough lands of low productivity. Parts of the Corn Belt and Delta States regions are also in general farming, including the Ozark hills of southern Missouri and northern Arkansas and much other semi-mountainous country. General farming predominates in most of these areas because of a relatively dense rural population and the absence of one crop or land use that is definitely superior to others. Hay and pasturage are required in the rotations, hence livestock are an important source of income on most farms, although cash crops, ranging from wheat to fruit, are grown on many of the farms.

In the West, the general farming areas are small and often widely scattered. Most of them are irrigated and their location depends on availability of water for irrigation. Hay, dairy, livestock, potatoes, sugar beets, and dry beans are some of the more important products sold by farmers in these western general farming areas.

Remaining Major Types of Farming

Fruit, truck crops, and special crops are grown in seventeen widely scattered, well-adapted areas throughout the country where their high value can crowd out general feed, forage, and cereal crops. Tobacco production is found in three small subareas and in southern Maryland.

Soils and climate are the dominant factors in the development of small areas of specialized crop production. Thus, we find the soils and climate of Aroostook County in Maine the dominant factors influencing specialized potato farming. Sugar-beet growing areas require special soils and climate, but their localized production is primarily the result of accessibility to sugar-beet factories. The growth of the sugar-beet industry in the

---

[1]"Generalized Types of Farming in the United States," *Agricultural Information Bulletin 3*, U.S.D.A., 1950.

United States has been made possible by constraints on the import of lower-priced cane sugar produced by other countries. The sugar-cane areas of Louisiana and Florida are largely limited by the extent of the flat, alluvial soils adapted to sugar-cane production.

Rice is grown intensively in three areas of the United States: southwestern Louisiana, eastern Arkansas, and parts of the Central Valley in California, where dependable supplies of fresh water are available for irrigation and impervious subsoils reduce water losses from seepage. Specialized vegetable and fruit production characterizes the agriculture of both California and Florida.

Peanuts are grown intensively in three small areas on sandy loam soils with friable subsoils. Substantial shifts have been taking place in peanut production, largely associated with acreage restrictions on cotton and attractive price programs on peanuts.

Regional Farm Productivity Changes   **1778725**

Agriculture in the ten farm production regions has developed and changed at different rates over the recent past as a result of differences in the technological and economic forces that have affected the major types of farming in each region. Table 3–1 shows how selected productivity data for the regions changed between the late 1950s and the late 1960s.

TABLE 3–1

Regional Index Numbers of Farm Output: Total, Per Acre, and Per Man-hour (1960 = 100)

Region	Total Farm Output		Crop Production per Acre		Farm Production per Hour of Labor	
	1958–60	1968–70	1958–60	1968–70	1958–60	1968–70
Delta States	96	133	95	99	93	217
Mountain	100	123	101	115	95	160
Southeast	97	127	93	123	95	165
Pacific	100	119	100	117	97	143
Northern Plains	94	118	93	116	90	158
Corn Belt	98	112	96	128	93	176
Southern Plains	96	110	97	110	92	166
Lake States	100	108	98	122	96	167
Appalachian	98	104	97	107	95	151
Northeast	99	99	96	108	94	158

Source: Calculated from data in "1971 Changes in Farm Production and Efficiency," *Statistical Bulletin No. 233*, ERS, U.S.D.A., June 1971.

During the period shown, farm output increased by about 37 percent in the Delta States, but farm output in the Northeast did not change. The Delta States achieved their output increase with a very small increase in output per acre and a doubling in output per man. In fact, cropland in use increased in the Delta States during this period. Labor declined very substantially, replaced by capital in the form of machines, with the resulting very large increase in output per man.

Output per man-hour gives some indication of the earning power of agricultural workers. It increased by 50 percent or more in all regions except the Pacific. The tendency for capital to replace labor is reflected in these productivity gains. In the Pacific region where fruit, truck, and specialty crops predominate, the relative difficulty experienced in substituting capital for labor kept the increase in output per man-hour to a minimum during the 1960s.

Gains in output per acre have been greatest in the Corn Belt, followed by the Southeast and Lake States. This reflects the continuing yield increases in corn, wheat, and other grains compared to the slower yield gains in tobacco, vegetables, and other specialty crops. The regions best adapted to growing crops in which technological changes have been most rapid have had the fastest rate of productivity changes and in general had a healthy agricultural sector during the 1960s.

Trends in Total Cropland

One of the basic questions regarding American agriculture is its ability to maintain or expand food production as population continues to grow. Will we need to add cropland in the years ahead? Will we "use up" our productive land as population grows?

It may surprise some to know that crop production in the United States today requires approximately the same number of acres as in 1910, when our population was less than half as large as it now is. Table 3–2

TABLE 3–2

Utilization of Land in Farms, 48 States, 1910–1970

Use	1910	1930	1950	1959	1969
Cropland used for crops	324	379	387	359	336
Cropland idle or in cover	23	34	22	33	51
Grassland pasture	284	379	486	532	537
Forest and woodland:					
Pastured	98	85	135	93	62
Not pastured	93	65	86	70	49
Farmsteads, roads and waste	57	45	46	37	24
	879	987	1162	1124	1060

Source: Data supplied by U.S. Department of Agriculture.

shows the census information on farm land utilization. Cropland used reached a maximum in 1950 and has been declining ever since. Most of the land taken out of crops has been put into cover crops or pasture through the encouragement offered by government price support programs. These uses are much more suitable than the intensive production that occurred on marginal cropland brought into production in the 1920s and 1930s. The withdrawal of land from cropping has exceeded the new cropland added by drainage, clearing, and irrigation, although programs of government assistance for these latter activities have been important to many farmers.

It is apparent that land is not presently an important constraint on farm production in the United States. The application of capital in the form of machinery, fertilizer, and farm chemicals has more than substituted for the diminishing number of acres planted and in fact has made many acres surplus. Those who have studied the issue do not expect land to become a constraining factor to agricultural production in the near future.[2] In the event of a sudden sharp increase in demand, two sources of added land could be tapped. A large part of the presently idle cropland could be put back into production within a year, given a change in government policy. Much of the grassland pasture could also be converted to crop production. A longer-run possibility is the extension of irrigation and drainage, which have already added millions of acres of farmland and could add as many as 50 to 80 million more. Thus, there is little cause for concern that we shall run short of productive agricultural land during the present century.

POINTS FOR DISCUSSION

1. From the maps shown in the chapter, identify the type-of-farming area and the farm production region in which you live.
2. What physical or other factors change at the boundaries of your type-of-farming area?
3. What important changes in types of farming are in process today?
4. What developments permitted farm output to increase more rapidly than population without increasing the acreage of crops harvested in the last twenty years?
5. How do you reconcile this with the current statements regarding land depletion and ecological soil damage by agricultural practices?
6. What are the important factors that have caused the changes in productivity that have occurred in your farm production region?

REFERENCES

"Generalized Types of Farming in the United States," *Agricultural Information Bulletin 3.* U.S.D.A., (1950).

[2]*Food and Fiber for the Future,* Report of the National Advisory Commission on Food and Fiber, Washington, D.C., 1967, p. 51.

"Inventory of Major Land Uses, United States," *Miscellaneous Publication 663*. U.S.D.A., (1949).

"Land," *Yearbook of Agriculture.* U.S.D.A., (1958)

"Major Uses of Land and Water in the U.S., Summary for 1959," *Agricultural Economics Report 13*, Economic Research Service, U.S.D.A., (1961).

National Advisory Commission on Food and Fiber, *Food and Fiber for the Future.* Washington, D. C., 1967.

"Soil," *Yearbook of Agriculture.* U.S.D.A., 1957.

Chapter 4

Resource Use
to Maximize Returns

In any particular year, farmers in the United States report a wide range in yields per acre of crops or production per animal. Many factors are responsible for this situation. Some farmers are more skilled than others in using identical production techniques. There is substantial variation in the inherent productive capacity of the land from one farm to another in most communities of the United States. The same holds true for the animals in the breeding herds. Variation in rates of production also results from variations in the weather and from the fact that farming operations are often based on custom.

But each year, an increasing number of farmers consider farming a business; in fact, the farmers who produce the bulk of the market supplies organize their farming operations on business principles. They are interested in maximum net income from their farming operations over a period of years. Given the technology, the machinery, supplies, and seed strains that are currently available, what combination of these and what amount of each will be most profitable to combine with the land and buildings used for crop and livestock production? Important progress has made in recent years in the technical experiments that provide needed information to answer such questions.

The Production Function: The Fertilizer Example

To deal in a rigorous way with the question—How should resources be employed on a farm to maximize returns?—we must first have at our

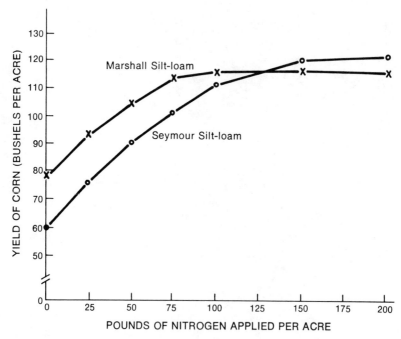

FIGURE 4–1.   Yield of Corn per Acre with Varying Application of Nitrogen;
Missouri, 1961–1967

command physical input-output data, which describe how output changes
as different factor inputs are varied. Sets of input-output data that do this
are called production functions. Such data are available from a Missouri
experiment investigating different rates of nitrogen fertilizer in corn production.[1] Figure 4–1 shows the yield of corn per acre on two silt loam soils
with applications of nitrogen varying from zero to two hundred pounds per
acre and assuming plant population held constant at twenty-thousand
plants per acre. The response to nitrogen on Seymour silt loam was more
pronounced than on the Marshall, although the maximum yields are not
very different for the two soils.

   The response of corn yield to additional applications of nitrogen
fertilizer is illustrated in Figure 4–1. These response curves, or total physical
product curves, are typical of the relationship one finds in all processes
of production as varying amounts of one factor are combined with relatively
fixed amounts of others. *The increased output associated with each addi-*

[1]Dale Colyer and Earl M. Kroth, "Corn Yield Response and Economic Optima for Nitrogen
Treatment and Plant Population Over a Seven-Year Period," *Agronomy Journal*, Vol. 60, No. 5,
September-October 1968, pp. 524–29. Using calculus, the article includes a somewhat more sophis-
ticated analysis than we present here, but the economic ideas are the same.

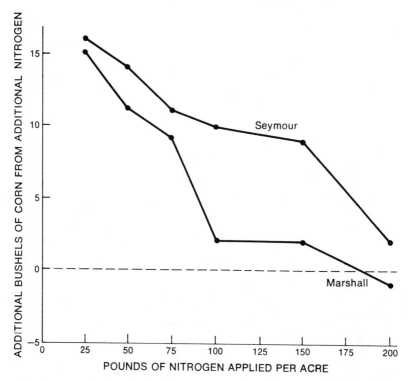

FIGURE 4–2. Marginal Physical Product of Nitrogen on Corn; Missouri, 1961–1967

tional unit of variable input is the marginal product of that input (also called the marginal physical product). As more of the variable factor — fertilizer—is associated with the fixed factor—land, seed, labor, and equipment in this case—output increases but at a decreasing rate. This illustrates *the principle of diminishing returns in production, which states that as units of variable inputs are added to a set of fixed inputs, the marginal product will eventually begin to decline.* The relationship becomes evident when one plots the marginal products obtained in the Missouri experiment (Figure 4–2).

The curves in Figure 4–2 show that 25 pounds of nitrogen on Marshall soils *increased* yields by 15 bushels, and 25 pounds of nitrogen on Seymour soils *increased* yields by 16 bushels. Applying another 25 pounds (50 pounds total), resulted in 11 *added* bushels on Marshall soils and 14 *added* bushels on Seymour soils. If sufficient quantities of the variable factor are added, one reaches a point at which the last unit fails to increase the output or actually decreases it. Increasing the nitrogen used from 150 to 200 pounds an acre actually decreases corn yields on the Marshall silt loam,

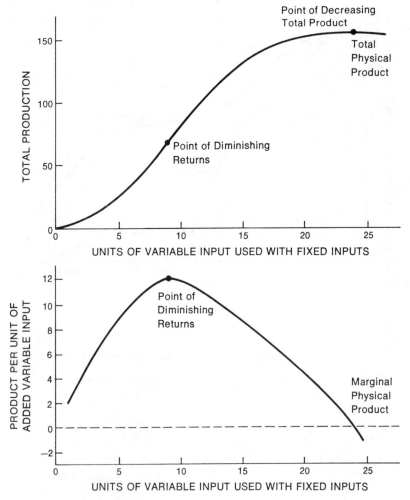

FIGURE 4–3.   Correspondence of Total and Marginal Product Curves

as shown by the negative value of the curve beyond 150 pounds in Figure 4–2.

A generalized total physical product curve and its corresponding marginal physical product curve are shown in Figure 4–3. The initial part of the response function shows total product increasing at an increasing rate (that is, the curve is getting steeper), which means that marginal product is rising. The inflection point, where the total product function goes from increasing at an increasing rate to increasing at a decreasing rate, is often called the point of diminishing returns. Beyond that point, the marginal product declines for added units of variable input. Beyond twenty four units of variable input, the total product declines for added units of variable input, as in the experimental trial on Marshall silt loam.

The important part of these theoretical functions is the portion between the point of diminishing returns and the point of decreasing total physical product. This portion is representative of nearly every production process and in a sense is a diagram of the principle of diminishing returns. The fertilizer experiment showed diminishing returns throughout.

Another illustration of the principle is reflected in fattening hogs or other animals. As they become heavier, they use more feed for maintenance of weight they have already gained and less for additional weight. For this reason, the gains on hogs up to 225 pounds are more economical than they are at heavier weights. In the same way, a 400-pound calf puts on more weight per 100 pounds of feed consumed than a 1,000-pound steer. The same principle also applies to fattening lambs and growing chickens and turkeys.

Most Profitable Combination of Resources. The general application of this principle may be seen by observing that, in farming, many of the resources with which a farmer works each year are relatively fixed. Thus, he can grow only so many acres of corn in his rotation, his barn holds only one hundred cows, or he may have saved only three hundred pigs in any particular year. His general problem is that of adding variable factor inputs to these fixed ones: fertilizer to the corn land, feed to the one hundred cows, and feed to the three hundred pigs, until the most profitable combination of factors is reached. Farmers, in general, are aware of this problem and make their production plans accordingly. When they know the physical production ratios (that is, the input-output ratios), they are able to calculate the most profitable rate of application of fertilizer.

To illustrate this using the fertilizer response data, suppose corn is $1.40 per bushel, nitrogen costs $.11 per pound, and fertilizer can be applied in twenty-five-pound "units." Table 4–1 presents the relevant information. In this case, the most profitable level of fertilizer to apply is one hundred pounds per acre. At that level, the value of the marginal unit of fertilizer is $2.80 (a marginal product of two bushels times a price of $1.40), and the cost of the marginal unit of fertilizer is $2.75 (twenty-five pounds of nitrogen times a price of $.11). At any lower fertilizer rate, the value of the marginal product of another unit of fertilizer exceeds its cost (see Table 4–1 for all rates of nitrogen less than one hundred pounds), so profit can be increased by applying fertilizer up to one hundred pounds. Beyond that level, an additional unit of fertilizer costs more than the value of corn it produces, so it should not be applied.

The principle to follow to find the most profitable level of a variable input is to increase its level of application to the point at which the value of its marginal product just equals its cost.

TABLE 4–1

Economics of Fertilizer Application on Corn Grown on Marshall Soils

Level of Nitrogen	Total Physical Product	Marginal Physical Product	Value of the Marginal Unit of Nitrogen	Cost of the Marginal Unit of Nitrogen	Marginal Revenue of Corn	Marginal Cost of Corn
0	78	—	—	—	—	
25	93	15	$21.00	$2.75	$1.40	$ .18
50	104	11	15.40	2.75	1.40	.25
75	113	9	12.60	2.75	1.40	.31
100	115	2	2.80	2.75	1.40	1.30
150	117	2	2.80	5.50	1.40	2.75
150	117	2	2.80	5.50	1.40	2.75
200	116	−1	−1.40	5.50	1.40	—[a]

[a] Because marginal cost is the cost of an added bushel and because the increased fertilizer caused a decrease in output, marginal cost cannot be calculated.

Another way of looking at this same problem is to ask, with the fixed inputs available, what is the most profitable level of output to produce? The principle stated above may be viewed as saying that inputs should continue to be added in corn production as long as the increased corn obtained is more valuable than the additional cost of the inputs required to produce that corn.

Marginal cost is defined as the cost of producing an additional unit of output. It can be calculated by dividing the cost of the additional input by the additional output obtained. Marginal cost for our example is shown in the last column of Table 4–1. *Marginal revenue is defined as the revenue obtained from producing an additional unit of output,* and under competitive conditions[2] is simply the price at which a unit of output sells. The marginal cost and marginal revenue data for this example are graphed in Figure 4–4. In this presentation of marginal costs, all costs other than nitrogen fertilizer are assumed to be fixed; nitrogen is the only variable input. But fertilizer is one of the few factor inputs that is easily and readily varied in farming operations; hence, the illustration is representative of the actual world situation.

In terms of Figure 4–4, it will pay farmers to apply nitrogen fertilizer to their corn enterprise until the marginal cost of corn is just equal to its marginal revenue. On Marshall soils, they should aim for a yield of 115 bushels per acre, by applying one hundred pounds of nitrogen per acre. At any lower yield, the marginal cost is less than the marginal revenue; at any greater yield, marginal cost exceeds marginal revenue. Thus, we see that *the amount of variable input that gives the output level at which marginal cost is equal to marginal revenue results in the highest possible profit with the available fixed inputs.* We can conclude that, with technical rates of

[2]The economic definition of competition and competitive conditions is discussed in Chapter 12.

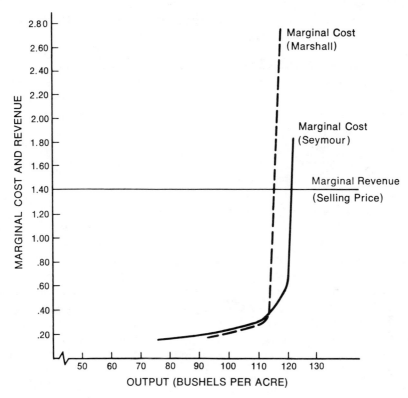

FIGURE 4-4. Marginal Cost Curves on Two Corn Soils

production, cost of the variable factor, and price of the product known, the farmer can determine his most profitable rate of nitrogen application. This in turn determines his most profitable level of corn production under the conditions described above. In point of fact, these physical input-output data are extremely difficult to obtain, and farmers rarely know them with the accuracy suggested here. But given their imperfect knowledge, farmers must, if they are rational profit-seekers, pursue a decision process involving these principles. The actual world problem is—given their imperfect knowledge—how closely can farmers approach the most profitable output positions enterprise by enterprise?

Problems in Achieving the Most Profitable Combination of Resources. The combination of production supplies or factors to produce crops or livestock is seldom easy. We have already noted that the response to nitrogen in Missouri differs on the two soils. Because it does, a farmer with fields of both kinds of soil must apply different rates of nitrogen on different fields. As we saw above, on Marshall soils he should apply 100 pounds of nitrogen per acre, but to maximize his profits on fields of Seymour soil he will aim for a yield of 121 bushels per acre by applying 125 pounds of nitrogen per acre. That is where marginal cost equals marginal revenue on Seymour soil (Figure 4–4).

In setting up the experiment discussed in our example, the scientists knew that plant population would have an effect on yield when fertility was varied. Corn must be planted thicker to produce more plants per acre if the full potential results of heavy fertilization are to be realized. Determining the optimal planting rate is an economic decision, just like determining the optimal fertilizer rate. From the experimental data, we could determine the marginal value product of added plants and the marginal cost of added plants. Because plant population and fertilizer interact (or have a joint response) the analytical technique for simultaneously finding their optimal levels involves mathematics beyond algebra that we will not pursue. However, the principle is the same as that already shown. Plant population should be increased to the point at which the value of the increased yield from a higher population is just equal to the increased cost of obtaining more plants per acre.

Another obvious example of joint response is in the use of fertilizer in potato production. When potatoes are grown without irrigation in the humid sections of the United States, they are commonly fertilized at the rate of 300 to 700 pounds per acre. But supplemental irrigation is being used to an increasing extent in growing potatoes in the humid sections. Where the potatoes are irrigated, applications of from 2,000 to 2,500 pounds of fertilizer per acre are common. Irrigation without heavier applications of fertilizer would not be profitable. Conversely, without irrigation, heavy applications of fertilizer are harmful.

Although the marginal analysis is implicit in all decisions concerning production, the farmer's problem is not so simple that he can vary one factor alone, leaving all others unchanged. Usually, he must change a number of factors. The potato grower in the humid regions, when deciding whether or not to undertake supplemental irrigation, does not balance merely the cost of the irrigation system against an increased yield, with all other factors held constant. He must use more labor to get the water on the land and more seed and fertilizer to take full advantage of the additional water. He must know the functional relationships between these different factors and balance the increased cost of the most economical combination against the value of the increased output. A further refinement is appropriate in the case of potato production. Supplemental irrigation and heavy rates of fertilization not only increase the total output of potatoes but also increase the proportion of No. 1 potatoes. In many cases, the new production techniques involving additional production supplies improve the quality of the output in addition to increasing the quantity. This improved quality must be valued as a part of the increased output.

Budgeting Changes in Production Practices

Because it is extremely difficult to obtain functional input-output data, and therefore equally hard to develop empirical marginal data, most farm-management analyses are made in terms of comparative budgets. These analyses involve the preparation of several budgets: statements of physical supplies used in production, volume of output and expected expenses, and the variation in income that would result from the use of possible different resource combinations. Consider, as a simple example, how the use of an improved variety of oats benefits a Midwest farmer, who grows thirty acres of oats a year. Two and one-half bushels of home-grown seed per acre might cost him $1.50, or $.60 a bushel. Fertilizing and preparing his seedbed as usual, the farmer obtains forty-five bushels of oats for a gross revenue of $27 per acre (forty-five bushels at $.60 per bushel). A new variety of oats that yields fifty bushels an acre costs $1.50 a bushel for seed.

Although this example can be done mentally, setting up the information in the *partial budgeting* format of Table 4–2 illustrates how that technique can be used. Only those aspects of the farm business that change are included in the partial budget, either as income-increasing changes or income-reducing changes. In this example, the total of all the income-increasing changes exceeds the total of income-reducing changes by $.75 per acre. So on thirty acres, using the new oats variety will increase this farmer's income by $22.50. This example is simple because no other changes in farming operations are required to take advantage of the new variety of oats.

Most alternatives are not this simple. Supplemental irrigation, for example, involves a large number of changes in the farming operation. Before undertaking such changes, the business-minded farmer would list all the changes that would occur if he altered his operation through utilizing supplemental irrigation. Because he has installed supplemental irrigation, the farmer may find it necessary to hire extra labor during the watering

TABLE 4–2

Illustration of Partial Budgeting

Income-increasing Changes		Income-reducing Changes	
1. Added returns		1. Added costs	
50 bu/acre new variety oats		2-1/2 bu/acre new variety	
@ $.60	$30.00/A	seed @ $1.50	$ 3.75/A
plus		*plus*	
2. Reduced costs		2. Reduced returns	
2-1/2 bu/acre old variety		45 bu/acre old variety oats	
seed @ $.60/bu	1.50/A	@ $.60	27.00/A
Total increased income	$31.50/A	Total reduced income	$30.75/A

Net income change due to new variety = +$.75/A

seasons; he may find it desirable to change his cropping plans to make more complete use of the new irrigation equipment. By arranging the costs and returns that change in the partial budgeting framework, he can better evaluate the impact of supplemental irrigation on his business. He prepares several alternative budgets and finally selects the operating plan that promises him the best returns. Even though all alternative plans are not worked out on paper, the farmer who is a good businessman goes through such a process when determining his production plans.

Achieving the Most Profitable Combination of Enterprises

Most farmers maintain a cropping sequence or rotation on their land and often have one or more livestock enterprises. The level of output of each crop and livestock enterprise is determined by achieving the most profitable combination of variable factors and fixed factors involved in each enterprise. The operator in his business-management function is thus faced with a series of situations similar to those illustrated in Figure 4–3. Given the state of the arts (that is, the pattern and level of technology) and the fixed production factors in each enterprise and on the total farm, the farmer varies those inputs that can be varied so as to equate marginal revenue and marginal cost in each enterprise. In terms of Figure 4–4, he takes the marginal revenue or price of each commodity as fixed (which is common in agriculture, and the reason the farmer is called a price-taker) and adjusts output in each enterprise to the point where marginal cost in each enterprise equals price. When a producer equates marginal revenue with marginal cost in each enterprise, he is maximizing the profit or net return from the total farm operation. It of course follows that price is not the same in each commodity line: in one it is high, in another low, and so on. It is the task of the manager to adjust resources among the enterprises so that marginal costs and marginal revenue are equal in each.

We can now see why the principle of equal marginal returns discussed in Chapter 2 leads to maximum returns when managing several enterprises. If 100 pounds of nitrogen are applied on corn growing on Marshall silt loam, giving a return of $2.80 to the marginal 25 pounds, then 150 pounds of nitrogen should be applied on corn growing on Seymour silt loam to give the same marginal return, and on all other crops to give the same marginal return. Suppose, in violation of the equal marginal returns principle, the farmer cut back his application to 75 pounds on Marshall and increased his application by 25 pounds to 175 on Seymour. Why would he not be better off since the yield on the Seymour plots is higher (122 bu. vs. 113 bu.)? To answer this, note that the marginal 25 pounds of fertilizer costs the farmer the same amount regardless of where it is applied.

When the marginal cost curve is steeply sloping, so that relatively little additional output is obtained, even with relatively large increases in variable inputs, the marginal cost curve is said to be inelastic.[3] The degree of elasticity or inelasticity depends upon the physical input-output relationship involved. If several important inputs, for example fertilizer or labor, are technically variable and can in the total farm operation be varied, then marginal costs will exhibit some significant degree of elasticity. But if inputs combine in fixed, or relatively fixed, proportions, then costs rise with no appreciable increase in output, and marginal costs are perfectly, or exceedingly, inelastic. The configuration and elasticity of the marginal-cost relation in each enterprise is thus a question of empirical fact and must in each case rest upon research results or judgment.

It can be deduced, however, that the elasticity of the marginal-cost relation will increase as the number of inputs in an enterprise can be and are varied; and the number that can be and are varied will increase as more time elapses. Given sufficient time, the farmer can convert a general-purpose barn to a dairy barn, or vice versa; or given sufficient time, a potato-digger can be traded for a hay-baler. Thus, the marginal-cost curve for a particular farm enterprise becomes more elastic in the long run.

The Supply Curve of the Enterprise. The marginal-cost curve of the enterprise is logically interpreted as the supply curve of the enterprise. This interpretation is evident from Figure 4–5. At any price, say OA,

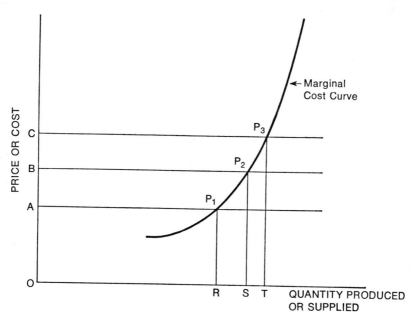

FIGURE 4–5. The Marginal Cost or Supply Curve of the Enterprise

[3]The concept of elasticity is explained and illustrated more fully in Chapter 12.

the manager of this enterprise will produce at the point where marginal cost and marginal revenue are equated. In this case, OR quantity will be produced, or supplied, in order that the manager may maximize his profit. If the price increases to $OB,$ the manager will reallocate resources in order to move along the marginal-cost curve to $P_2,$ or OS amount. At the new price, $OB,$ the marginal cost and marginal revenue are equated at output $OS.$ From this, we see that the marginal-cost curve of the enterprise is the same as the *supply curve of the enterprise; it describes those quantities of the commodity in question that this enterprise will produce and offer for sale at varying prices.*

Included in this concept of supply is the condition that all prices other than that of the commodity being considered are assumed constant. That is, the prices of all other commodities and the prices of all inputs remain fixed. This is called the *ceteris paribus*[4] assumption. Making this assumption is a technique that economists use to analyze the effects of a change in a single variable.

The supply curve of a commodity, say wheat, at the farm level is the summation of all wheat producers' supply curves for wheat. Thus, the elasticity of the commodity-supply relation is dependent upon the elasticity of the enterprise marginal-cost curves. The elasticity of the enterprise marginal-cost curves in the real world are, in turn, dependent first upon the physical production coefficients (that is, the production functions) and second upon the ability and willingness of farmers to substitute one productive factor for another. In other words, the elasticity of the marginal-cost curve, in practice, depends upon the know-how of the farmer to substitute one factor for another, as well as on the physical production coefficients. It also depends on the absence of any strong influence by custom and inertia. Further, when the price, of wheat for example, fluctuates relative to that of oats or barley, farmers are not limited in their operations to varying the application of such inputs as fertilizers and weed sprays; they can and do shift land and labor inputs among farm enterprises. Thus, land and labor, which tend to be fixed inputs for the farm as a whole, are varied among enterprises as the prices of the products vary and as the technical production requirements permit. For example, should the price of wheat rise in comparison to the price of oats or barley, farmers would surely shift some of their land out of oats and barley into wheat, but probably not all of it because of restrictions in the use of labor over the season and of harvesting equipment. In this example, land is the variable input, and labor and harvesting equipment the fixed factors.

---

[4]*Ceteris paribus* is sometimes interpreted to mean "all other things constant," but if this were its meaning, then it would be a useless concept. In the above example, if the only thing that varies is the price, then neither the quantity produced nor the inputs used can vary, so the idea of *all* other things holding constant is too extreme. The more useful concept is that all other prices are constant. See Milton Friedman, *Price Theory*, (Chicago: Aldine, 1965), pp. 23–26.

Commodities with the more elastic supply curves will be those in which the important input factors can be and are varied in production of the commodity. And input factors can be varied *in* one farm enterprise in the following ways: (1) by shifting inputs among enterprises on the same farm, for example, land; and (2) by varying inputs obtained from the nonfarm sector, for example, fertilizer. But our rather limited statistical studies of supply suggest that many short-run commodity supply relations at the farm level are relatively inelastic: wheat and corn have elasticities in the neighborhood of 0.1 to 0.2; cotton, 0.3; potatoes, 0.3 to 0.4; dairy products, 0.1 to 0.2; and hogs, 0.3 to 0.4.

The elasticity of supply is formally defined as the percentage change in quantity supplied resulting from a 1 percent change in price. Thus, a supply elasticity of 0.3 means that the change in supply resulting from a given percentage change in price is only 0.3 as great as the change in price. Or, with an elasticity of 0.3, a 10 percent change in the price will lead to a 3 percent change in the quantity supplied.

The numerical value of the elasticity of supply can be easily calculated. Suppose that according to a supply function at the price p_1, q_1 is the quantity supplied, and at the price of p_2, q_2 is the quantity supplied. The elasticity of the supply curve between the two prices is calculated as:

$$\text{elasticity of supply} = \frac{\dfrac{q_2 - q_1}{q_2 + q_1}}{\dfrac{p_2 - p_1}{p_2 + p_1}}$$

More attention will be given the concept of elasticity in chapters yet to come.

Changing Technology in Agriculture and on the Farm

The discussion of resource use to maximize returns to this point has assumed no change in the state of the arts—has assumed a constant technology. This is the traditional theory of the firm. All factor inputs are assumed to be homogeneous, and all outside conditioning factors (for example, weather, technology) are assumed to be constant, and within this static context the theory of the firm describes how resources are allocated among enterprises as product prices vary to maximize returns for the total farm operation. But technology has not been constant in agriculture over the past fifty years; it has advanced rapidly as hundreds of millions of dollars have been spent by private and government agencies to develop and disseminate new production techniques. New and improved production techniques have, in fact, become the key variable in American agriculture and the principal means for increasing the output of farm enterprises.

Technology and Crop Production. Average production per acre of all crops increased about 30 percent from the pre-World War II period to the early 1950s, jumped 30 percent in the following decade, and another 10 percent in the next five-year period (Table 4–3). These increased yields resulted fundamentally from the investment of increased quantities of capi-

TABLE 4–3

Crop Production and Selected Inputs Used in Agriculture, 1910–1969

Period	Index of Crop Production per Acre	Number of Tractors	Grain Combines, Corn Pickers, and Picker-shellers	Fertilizer, Total Plant Nutrients
	(1957–59 = 100)	(1000)	(1000)	(1000 tons)
1910–14	69	9	—	605
1920–24	68	377	—	654
1930–34	64	995	—	742
1940–44	80	1861	400	1435
1950–54	87	3864	1432	3635
1960–64	114	4715	1706	6711
1965–69	124	4806	1541	10616

Source: *Changes in Farm Production and Efficiency: A Summary Report, 1970,* U.S.D.A. Statistical Bulletin 233.

tal in crop production. This investment has taken several forms, one of the earliest being a substitution of motor power for horse power. As is evident from Table 4–3, this was nearly completed by the 1950s. The tractor has made deeper plowing, fewer delays, and more fully mechanized harvesting possible—all of which would have been uneconomic or impossible with horses. During rainy seasons, although tractor drivers can be switched to keep the power unit in operation whenever soil conditions permit, horses would require twelve to fourteen hours of rest every day. The increase in powered harvesting equipment that closely followed the tractor boom is another manifestation of the rapid substitution of capital for labor in farm production.

The increased use of fertilizer and lime has been even more phenomenal than the increase in tractors. The use of fertilizer nutrients has just about doubled each decade since the 1930s and continued to increase sharply during the last half the 1960s. The use of agricultural lime shot up from 3 million tons before 1940 to between 20 and 30 million tons applied nearly every year since 1950. The increase in yields of such crops as potatoes, vegetables, corn, cotton, and legume hays, which resulted from the heavier application of fertilizer, is another change brought about by the use of increased capital. Other capital investments in drainage and irrigation have produced similar results. Favorable prices for farm products during and following World War II stimulated a large amount of drainage both of land already cropped and of other land not previously used for crop production. Similarly, irrigation brought some new land into crop production and increased yields on existing cropland. Supplemental irrigation is being used to an increasing extent in the humid sections of the United States to increase the yields of such crops as potatoes and truck crops.

Improved seed strains used in crop production today represent another form of increased capital in agriculture. Much of the initial capital investment required in developing these improved seed strains was made by the Federal and state governments in the experimental work carried out at the state agricultural experiment stations. Now, seed companies invest large sums in breeding work and in equipment for producing and processing hybrid seeds. Almost all the farm seeds today have a productive capacity far superior to that of similar seeds used in earlier years. This increased productive capacity is the result of capital investments over a long period of time.

The latest group of capital goods to influence yields are the pesticides, which have been alternately praised and damned for their effects on plants and animal life. There is a lack of long-run data on this input. However, in 1966 farmers spent about $561 million on pesticides.[5] There is little doubt that the increase in use of these pesticides has contributed to the rapid increase in crop yields. The environmental effects of pest control measures are being increasingly examined. It is likely that alternative measures that are environmentally safer, when developed, will be even more costly.

Technology as a Form of Capital. When one reviews the capital inputs now combined with land and labor to produce crops, he notes that most of the capital goods are in a form not available a few decades ago. Wtihout the technical discoveries of the internal combustion engine, the pneumatic tire, the vigor of crossed inbred seed strains, and the lethal qualities of new chemical compounds, there would be little economic basis for the representative farm's increasing its capital investments relative to land and labor in crop production. But new discoveries usually do not just happen. They are the result of months or years of patient experimental work. Improved technology, which has been incorporated in all the production supplies and seedstocks used in farm production, is as much a form of increased capital as are the physical goods one sees in the farmer's buildings.

We can now state a generalization regarding the dynamics of capital use in United States farm production, which has contributed so much to our current high levels of efficiency in agriculture. Progress in technology, either in analyzing the components of the soil or in adapting the capital goods to perform their functions more efficiently, results in a progressively

---

[5]"Quantities of Pesticides Used by Farmers in 1966," *Agricultural Economic Report 179*, Economic Research Service, U.S.D.A., April 1970.

increasing ratio of capital to land and labor in farm production. A later chapter will be devoted to an analysis of the economic problems associated with the introduction of new technology. At this point, it is sufficient to note that most farmers fail to take prompt advantage of desirable new technological developments. The unusual profits of the superior farm managers result, to a large extent, from their ability to discover which are the profitable new techniques or new machines and to adopt them promptly.

Technology and Livestock Production. The upward trend noted in crop yields is even more pronounced in livestock-production rates. Livestock production per animal unit in 1970 was over 50 percent higher than it was forty years earlier. In 1928, the average laying hen or pullet on hand January 1 produced 119 eggs a year. Egg production per layer has increased almost steadily since that time, until by 1970 it was nearly 220 eggs per layer. Milk production per cow has shown a similar increase. In 1928, average milk production per cow in the United States was 4,516 pounds, in 1970 slightly over 9,000. Hog production per sow has increased in a similar manner in the past forty years for several reasons: (1) sows now farrow and save more pigs per litter than in earlier years; (2) more sows now farrow two litters a year; and (3) better feeding and disease control result in more pork going to market per pig weaned. Similar, although less striking, improvements have been made in beef-cattle and sheep production.

Just as increasing yields per acre are a normal development in a progressive economy, we should expect continually increasing livetsock production per breeding animal as a part of economic progress. Much of the upward trend is the result of capital investment. Capital investment in four broad areas has resulted in most of the increase noted to date: (1) improved housing, including brooding equipment for poultry and hogs; (2) improved disease control; (3) improved breeding and selection; and (4) improved nutrition.

As in the case of crop production, however, it is improvements in technology that have formed the basis of the increased use of capital. We have our central-hatching and artificial-brooding developments in poultry, year-round farrowing equipment for hogs, and free-stall housing for dairy cows. Ventilation and cooling of livestock barns in the warmer regions of the country helps increase productivity. Artificial insemination, routine with dairy animals and increasing with other livestock, makes the best genetic material available to every farmer. Studies of the nutritional needs of animals and of the nutritive content of feed have been the basis for improved rations. Increased production of high-protein-content legume hay, the expansion of soybean production, and the routine use of feed additives are the key factors in the better-balanced rations fed to livestock in recent years.

Farm Technological Advance Defined

The foregoing discussion has indicated that capital investment in agriculture and the adoption of new technologies have gone hand in hand. Rarely these days do we get additional capital investment in a farm that does not involve new and improved techniques. And even more rare is the case of the introduction of a new production practice that does not involve the expenditure of more capital of some kind. Thus, the typical development in farm enterprises in recent years has been the additional use of capital, but not capital of a constant quality—not a homogeneous capital. What we have had is the increased use of technically improved capital.

What then do we mean by farm technological advance? We mean a recombination of factor inputs in a farm enterprise such that the output from the enterprise increases with the same total input of factors measured in dollar terns. Stated differently, we mean a shift in the production function such that the output for the enterprise increases for any constant total input of factors measured in dollar terms. The total inputs cannot hold constant in physical terms if there is to be technological advance. The new combination is the essence of the matter. But the new combination must be more productive—must increase output with the same total input, measured in dollar terms—if it is to be defined as a technological advance.

The concept of farm technological advance is illustrated in Figure 4–6. Let us assume that a new type of nitrogen fertilizer is developed, which costs no more per pound and is more easily assimilated as a plant food than

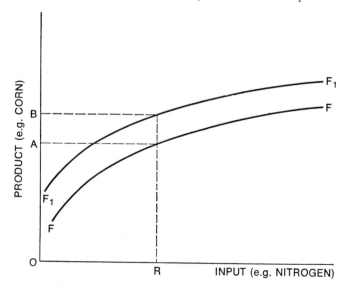

FIGURE 4–6. A Shift in the Production Function with Technological Advance

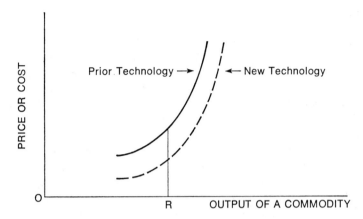

FIGURE 4-7. Marginal Cost Curves Before and After a Farm Technological Advance

was the previous type. Hence, for any given input of nitrogen (OR), the output of corn increases. This increase in output is described by the shift in the production function from FF to F_1F_1, and at nitrogen input OR, the increase is equal to AB. This nitrogen example is highly oversimplified, but it illustrates the nature of a farm technological advance.

Farm Technological Advance Shifts the Supply Curve. The adoption by farmers of a new and improved technology (for example, improved seeds, insecticides, antibiotics) shifts the production function for the enterprise involved as we have observed. This in turn has the effect of lowering the marginal cost of the enterprise (Figure 4-7). Marginal unit costs for any output (OR) are lower after the adoption of the new technique than before. The farmer has made a farm technological advance.

Because the effect of farm technological advance is to lower and shift to the right the marginal cost curve of the enterprise and because, further, the marginal cost in its inclining phase is the supply curve of the enterprise, it then follows that a farm technological advance has the effect of shifting the commodity supply curve to the right. And this has been the overriding consequence of the widespread adoption of new technologies on farms since the middle 1930s—the persistent expansion in supply, commodity by commodity.

Maximizing Returns in a Dynamic World

The task of maximizing total returns on a multiple-enterprise farm in the changing world of today is not easy. The farm operator in response to commodity price changes must do more than vary the inputs of the usual variable factors in the old production functions. He must and does initiate production practice changes that shift production functions and lower cost relations. This action then entails further shifts in resources among enterprises. Factor costs, too, are constantly changing (and usually increased in the 1950s and 1960s) ; this affects marginal costs—it shifts the position of the marginal-cost curve for the enterprise involved. Thus, the farm operator in the fast-changing twentieth century is forever changing his resource mix—as product prices change, as technology changes, and as factor prices change—to obtain profit-maximizing factor combinations in each enterprise. Good management in agriculture now demands a high order of skill, ability, and enterprise.

POINTS FOR DISCUSSION

1. What kind of information does a production function provide? How is this information to be obtained? How is such information used to help determine the proper allocation of resources on the farm?
2. What is meant by *diminishing returns,* or diminishing marginal productivity? What do we mean by *marginal analysis*?
3. How is a marginal cost curve constructed? What does a marginal cost curve describe? In what sense is a marginal cost curve a supply curve?
4. What is a *partial budget*? Why is it used in practice instead of marginal analysis?
5. When are the total returns of a multiple enterprise firm maximized?
6. Determine the profit per acre that would result on each soil if a corn producer applied 75 pounds of nitrogen per acre on Marshall soils and 175 pounds per acre on Seymour soils, given the input-output and price data used in the chapter.
7. What have been the important technological changes in agriculture since the middle 1950s? How have these changes limited the usefulness of static marginal analysis?
8. What is a *farm technological advance*? Define and give some illustrations. Indicate the effect of one of your illustrations on marginal costs and the commodity supply curve.

REFERENCES

BOULDING, KENNETH E., *Economic Analysis,* 4th .ed., Chap. 18. New York: Harper and Row, 1966.

CASTLE, E. N., M. H. BECKER, AND F. J. SMITH, *Farm Business Managent: The Decision Making Process,* 2nd ed., Chap. 2. New York: The Macmillan Company, 1972.

HEADY, EARL O., AND HARALD R. JENSEN, *Farm Management Economics,* Chap. 4. Englewood Cliffs, N.J.: Prentice-Hall, Inc., 1954.

HERBST, J. H., AND R. A. HINTON, "Partial Budgeting—A Shortcut for Estimating Effects of Changes,", FM-25 in the series *Economics for Agriculture.* Department. of Agricultural Economics, University of Illinois, Urbana (1964).

NIKOLITCH, RADOJE, "Family-Operated Farms: Their Compatibility with Technological Advance," *American Journal of Agricultural Economics* (August 1969).

WILCOX, WALTER W., "Effects of Farm Price Changes on Efficiency in Farming," *Journal of Farm Economics* (February 1951).

Chapter 5

Costs, Returns,

and Size of Farm

Cost of production is a much-used and much-abused term. In the previous chapter, we saw how the profitable limits to expanding production were determined by rising marginal costs. In this chapter, we hope to explain the different meanings that are given to the term *cost of production* and show which costs affect farmers' short-run responses to changes in market demand and which affect only their long-run responses. We also will examine the popular dictum "to make higher profits one must 'reduce expenses.'" The way in which costs per unit of output fall as the size of farm is increased also will be noted.

Fixed and Variable Costs

Total costs of farm operation may be grouped in a number of different ways, each method of grouping having its advantages for particular purposes. We are particularly interested in a method that will reflect economic incentives for changing production plans. From this standpoint, two major groups, fixed and variable costs, are particularly significant. The term *fixed costs* is often used interchangeably with *overhead costs* to identify costs that do not vary with the level of output during the time period under discussion, for example, one year. Thus, the real estate taxes are a *fixed cost since they do not change with the level of production* on the farm in any particular year.

Variable costs, on the other hand, as the name indicates, vary with the level of output. As more fertilizer is applied to increase crop yields, total fertilizer costs increase. The significance of this particular classification is evident when one considers why farmers change their production plans. *An especially important concept, marginal cost, consists of the costs of the variable inputs that are used to increase output by one unit.* We found in the preceding chapter that as long as the cost of an additional unit of output is less than its selling price, it pays to continue expanding output. Conversely, whenever marginal costs are not covered by the selling price, profits may be increased by reducing production. Fixed costs do not affect the short-term level of production. The real estate taxes and other fixed costs are incurred, regardless of whether or not any production takes place. Fixed costs per unit of output continue to decline as long as output is expanded, whereas marginal costs and average variable costs first decrease, then increase as output is expanded.

When farming was largely self-sufficient, almost all costs fell into the fixed, or overhead, category. The farmer planted his own seeds, using his own labor and horse power. He increased production by using his labor and horse power more intensively. On the family farm, the living expenses of the family are a part of the overhead costs of the farm business. Family living costs, taxes, and interest on money borrowed were almost all the cash expenses farmers incurred in early colonial days. Obviously, a drop in the price of wheat or hogs had little effect on the farmer's production activities under such circumstances. He could not reduce his cash costs by reducing his output. As farming has become more commercialized, variable costs in farming have increased relative to fixed costs. Variable costs today are a higher proportion of total farming costs than in any previous period.

In the previous chapter, the marginal cost curve for an enterprise was derived directly from input-output and price information. We will use that same example to illustrate the importance of the other kinds of costs and their interrelationships. Suppose a farmer has two hundred acres of Marshall silt loam on which he grows corn. His fixed costs, totaling $10,000, include taxes, interest payments, one hired laborer, and depreciation on machinery. Assume for the illustration that all cropping practices other than fertilization have been determined. The only variable cost is the cost of fertilizer. The input-output information of Table 4–1, the price of fertilizer, and the price of corn are assumed to be known by the farmer.

Table 5–1 shows the calculation of each of the seven principal cost concepts from the input-output function and the prices. Output per acre corresponding to each level of fertilizer times two hundred acres gives total output. Total variable cost is the cost of purchasing and applying fertilizer at the rates shown. Total fixed cost is, by definition, constant for all levels of output. Total cost is the sum of total fixed and total variable cost. *The average and marginal costs are always calculated per unit of output* (for

TABLE 5–1

Production Relationship and Cost Concepts

Total Output	Nitrogen	Total Variable Cost	Total Fixed Cost	Total Cost	Avg. Variable Cost	Avg. Fixed Cost	Avg. Total Cost	Marginal Cost
bu.	lb/acre	$	$	$	$/bu	$/bu	$/bu	$/bu
15,600	0	0	10,000	10,000	0	.64	.64	—
18,600	25	550	10,000	10,550	.03	.53	.56	.18
20,800	50	1,100	10,000	11,100	.05	.48	.53	.25
22,600	75	1,650	10,000	11,650	.07	.44	.51	.31
23,000	100	2,200	10,000	12,200	.10	.43	.53	1.38
23,400	150	3,300	10,000	13,300	.14	.42	.56	2.75
23,200	200	4,400	10,000	14,400	.19	.43	.62	—

this reason, they are sometimes referred to as unit costs). Thus, average variable cost is total variable cost divided by the corresponding units of output; average fixed cost is total fixed cost divided by the corresponding units of output; and average total cost is total cost divided by the corresponding units of output (or the sum of average fixed cost and average variable cost). Marginal cost is the cost of producing one additional unit of output. It is calculated as the *additional* cost of fertilizer from one level to the next divided by the *additional* output of corn. Marginal cost cannot be calculated for output levels greater than 23,400 bushels in the example because with the fixed inputs available 23,400 bushels is the maximum level of output possible. The student should verify his understanding of these calculations by checking one of the rows of Table 5–1.

It is apparent from the unit cost data, which is graphed in Figure 5–1, that average fixed cost declines continuously as output increases. This must always occur because the constant total fixed cost is being divided by a growing number of units of output. Average total and average variable costs typically fall and then rise as output increases and for this reason are called U-shaped curves. The marginal cost curve also is typically U-shaped, but only if output levels below the point of diminishing returns are included. Because that is not the case in our example, marginal cost appears to be continuously rising.

Variable Cash Expenditures Versus Unit Production Costs

The farmer in our example has the choice of producing 15,600 bushels of corn for $10,000 or 18,600 bushels of corn for $10,550 or any of a number of other levels of output with its corresponding costs. The old advice to "keep costs down" may have been valid once. Yet, an examination of the principle that production per acre or per animal unit be expanded until marginal cost equals the value of the marginal unit of output indi-

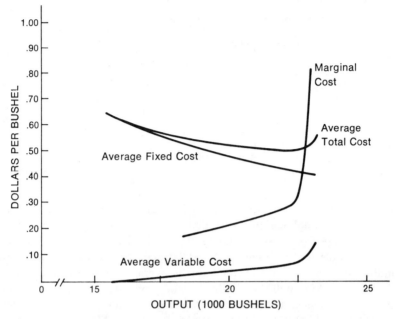

FIGURE 5–1.   Unit Cost Curves for Corn on Marshall Soil

cates that up to this point *profits* are increased by increased cash expenditures. The typical farmer, starting his spring farming operations with his own labor, a fixed acreage of land, and a standard set of machinery, must decide from time to time throughout the season what quantity of variable production supplies to combine with these fixed (or relatively fixed) factors in the year's farming operations. How much fertilizer should he purchase? How much should he invest in improved seeds and breeding stock? How much in insecticides? How much extra labor should he hire to improve the timeliness of his operations or to permit more intensive use of labor and machinery in preparing and cultivating the land? How much should he spend on protein and mineral supplements to improve his livestock rations?

If he followed the old dictum and kept expenses for these items at a minimum, his total production would be low. Total costs, both fixed and variable, would be low, but as long as the value of increased production exceeds the cost of additional fertilizer, net income is increased by increasing expenditures for fertilizer. The farmer who produces under the conditions stated in the example and applies no fertilizer has production costs of about $.64 per bushel and yields of 78 bushels per acre for a total cost of $50 per acre. If his neighbor, with the same production costs other than fertilizer, spends $11 per acre for 100 pounds of fertilizer, his costs are $61 per acre and his yields 115 bushels per acre. The neighbor's total expenses are higher, but his cost per bushel (average total cost) is only $.53.

The returns to an enterprise are never maximized until marginal costs have turned upward. More specifically, *returns to an enterprise are maximized at that point where marginal cost is equal to marginal revenue* (and under competitive conditions marginal revenue is constant and equal to price). These complex relationships are illustrated with the typical cost curves shown in Figure 5–2. Assuming a price of OA, at production levels below point *C*, the cost of each additional unit of product is less than the selling price of the unit of output. Hence, there is an incentive to expand output to point *C*. Beyond point *C*, the cost of each additional unit of product exceeds the selling price of the product. Hence, there is an incentive to reduce output to point *C*. The maximum profit position of the firm at point *C* is described by the rectangle *ABCD* (net return per unit of product *CD* times the number of units of product *BD*). In the common case, then, where the selling price of the product is high enough to cover average total costs, a producer will continue adding inputs of the variable

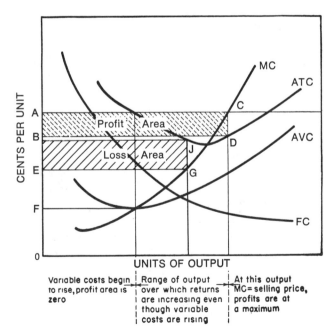

FIGURE 5–2. Determining the Most Profitable Level of Production

factors, thus expanding output, until marginal cost equals the selling price (marginal revenue).

In case the selling price is less than average total costs, a loss will occur on each unit sold. The issue that then must be settled is what level of output will minimize losses? It should be remembered that in the short run fixed inputs are committed to production so the fixed costs must be paid regardless of the level of output. If the price in Figure 5–2 were *OF* or below, then production should be stopped because not even the cost of the variable inputs is being covered. In such a situation, losses are equal to total fixed costs, but they cannot be lowered in the short run. If the price were above *OF,* say at *OE,* then the producer will minimize his losses by operating at the output level where marginal cost equals marginal revenue, *EG* units of output. With this level of output, losses will be equal to *GJ* times *EG* because *GJ* is the loss per unit. This is a smaller loss than would be incurred by stopping production in the short run because the per-unit price of *OE* more than covers the unit costs of variable inputs and thus there is some revenue "left over" from each unit to help pay for fixed costs.

Summaries of farm accounts indicate that cash expenditures are higher on farms with the higher net incomes. All increases in cash expenditures in farming operations do not increase cash income, but in the farming community farmers do not use as much specialized production supplies as would be profitable. When farmers with the highest net incomes from farming in a community are studied, one finds that they have higher cash expenses than the average, with higher expenditures for fertilizer, purchased feeds, insecticides, improved strains of seeds, and similar output-increasing items. The profitable adjustment for most individual farmers is not to reduce expenses but rather to increase those that will bring in even more income.

The advice, "keep expenses down," had more point in the earlier years, when there were few specialized supplies available to increase output per acre or per livestock unit. It also has merit today when applied to some types of farm-business expenditures and when applied to family living. Carelessness in handling farm machinery leads to excessive repair costs. Carelessness in handling the livestock may lead to high veterinary bills and disease losses. Expenses that can be avoided without affecting output are unnecessary expenses. A few farmers in each community fail to make satisfactory incomes because they incur extra expenses from careless management practices.

Unique Character of Farmers' Variable Costs. An analysis of the effect of particular supplies, or expenditures for supplies, on output indicates that there is little possibility for increasing profits by reducing these expenditures under the pressure of lower prices. Production drops so rapidly when expenditures for supplies are curtailed that, even though prices are relatively low, the value of the reduction in output is usually greater than the cost of the supplies.

In our example, on Marshall soils it was most profitable to apply 100 pounds of nitrogen per acre. Another 25 pound application would only increase yields about one bushel. That bushel increase is worth only $1.40, and the 25 pounds of nitrogen costs $2.75. The price of corn would have to increase to $2.75 per bushel to make it profitable to increase fertilizer to 125 pounds per acre. On the other hand, if the price of corn fell below $1.40, even though it would be profitable to cut back application of fertilizer to 75 pounds, output would be reduced only 2 bushels per acre. Cutting back fertilizer application even further to 50 pounds per acre would save $2.75, but would reduce yields from 113 to 104 bushels. This change would be profitable only if the price of corn fell precipitously to below $.31 per bushel. It is apparent that for a wide range of corn prices, the most profitable level of fertilization is close to 100 pounds per acre on this soil, and that there will be no economic inducement to change fertilizer practices unless the price of corn changes drastically.

Similarly regarding other production practices. The good farmer is now using the highest-yielding hybrid varieties; he uses a rotation including deep-rooted legumes to maintain high crop yields and conserve his soil resources; he is practicing modern weed and insect control measures. Guided by the marginal analysis, he equates the cost of each of these specialized supplies, in the amounts commonly used, with the expected value of the increase in yield associated with them. And he finds that, if he plans to grow corn, it will pay him to continue to use each of these specialized supplies in approximately the same amounts as he did before. The explanation for this lack of flexibility lies in the relatively large increases in output that occur up to the usual application levels, and the relatively small increases in output available for higher levels of input use. Graphically, this is reflected in the very sharp increase in the slope of the marginal cost curve that occurs near the most profitable input level (Figure 4–4).

It is possible that, if they had more information on technical responses, farmers would find it profitable to vary fertilizer application rates, the number of applications of insecticides, and similar production practices as the price of the product changes. Until our knowledge of technical production responses increases considerably, however, progressive farmers, following improved practices to obtain high levels of output, will continue these practices, for the most part, irrespective of the price received for their product. If the price of potatoes relative to dry beans or sugar beets drops, they may shift from growing potatoes to growing one of these relatively more profitable crops. If they are livestock farmers, they may change their livestock numbers in response to relative price changes for the different livestock products. But within the limits of practical farm management, they find it profitable to use the improved technology in each line of production undertaken, regardless of price levels.

Average Production Costs Versus Opportunity Costs

We must now examine the nature and significance of average total costs per unit of output, or average unit costs, in contrast to opportunity costs. The U.S.D.A. and the state agricultural experiment stations have made many studies of the cost of producing farm products. These studies were made mostly in the 1920s and 1930s, but a few continue to be made. A condensed statement of the cost of producing corn and oats in Illinois in 1964 is presented in Table 5–2 for illustrative purposes.

TABLE 5–2

Cost of Producing Corn and Oats, Central and Western Illinois, 1964

	Corn	Oats
Growing costs per acre:		
Taxes and interest on land	$ 25.54	$25.98
Labor, direct and indirect	5.13	2.27
Tractor and machinery	7.87	3.16
Seed, fertilizer, other inputs	33.18	8.48
Total growing costs	71.72	39.89
Harvesting costs per acre	8.68	5.19
Storage costs per acre	10.35	2.26
Total costs per acre	90.75	47.34
Yield per acre (bushels)	105	59
Cost per bushel	.86	.80

Source: *Detailed Cost Report for Central and Western Illinois, 1964 and 1965*, AERR-85, Department of Agricultural Economics, University of Illinois, June 1967.

The forty-four farms selected for this study all farrowed eighty or more litters of pigs annually. Half the farms used hog production technology involving slotted floor housing while the other half used older production technology. It is likely that crop production techniques among the sample also represented a heterogeneous mix of technology. Therefore, the average production costs shown have limited significance because of their great variation from farm to farm. From the standpoint of economic analysis, they have even greater limitations. A substantial proportion of the costs of producing a bushel of corn or oats is not cash costs for the period of the growing and harvesting season. For example, interest on land is not a cash cost, for the land that is owned by the farmer. The labor is furnished by the operator and his family. The tractor and other machinery are used for many operations in addition to growing corn and oats each year, and last for five to ten years. Only the seed, fertilizer, and fuel costs are directly chargeable to the corn and oats. In cost-accounting studies, such as that from which the data in Table 5-2 are taken, labor is charged against a particular product at average hired-labor wage rates. Annual tractor and machinery costs are pro-rated to the individual products at uniform rates per hour of use, and taxes and interest on investment in the land are pro-rated on an acre basis to the different crops grown.

This uniform method of allocating total farm costs to individual products has been adopted as an accounting procedure because it is difficult to allocate costs in line with the joint, supplementary, and complementary relationships described in the previous chapters. Using such cost allocations, it is possible to compute the net profit per acre of growing different crops. This has been done in Table 5-3. Without a knowledge of the complementary and supplementary relations among these crops, one would con-

TABLE 5-3

Price, Unit Cost and Profit per Acre and per Unit, Illinois Farm Products, 1964

	Corn	Soybeans	Oats	Wheat
Price per unit	$ 1.17	$ 2.59	$ .60	$1.41
Cost per unit	.86	1.92	.80	1.29
Profit per unit	.31	.67	−.20	.12
Yield per acre	105 bu	32 bu	59 bu	43 bu
Profit per acre	$32.99	$21.38	$−11.85	$5.25

Source: *Detailed Cost Report for Central and Western Illinois, 1964 and 1965*, AERR-85, Department of Agricultural Economics, University of Illinois, June 1967.

clude that farmers would increase their profits by putting all their land in corn. But nothing could be farther from the truth. Profits from corn, in large part, depend on growing corn in rotation with other crops. Unit-production costs, relative to market prices, cannot be used to guide the selection of enterprises because of the accounting procedures used. The average imputed costs do not correspond with the economic motivations. For example, if oats are not seeded in combination with new legume seedings, the farmer gets little or no crop from the land that year. He will grow oats with his legume seedings until he finds another more profitable crop to replace legumes in the rotation, regardless of the relation between computed production costs per bushel and the selling price of oats.

In contrast to these average unit-production costs arrived at by arbitrary allocation of overhead costs, we have a nonaccounting concept of opportunity costs. This concept is particularly useful in analyzing what goes on in a farmer's mind in deciding how much of each product to produce from the group of resources available to the farm. His land, labor, machinery, and breeding stock in any given year are to a large extent fixed, and he must plan his operations within these limitations. If a farmer devotes a greater acreage to soybeans, he has fewer acres to use for some other crop. If he uses more labor and machinery on one crop, he is forced to use less on another. When the resources employed are not purchased in the market, the significant economic cost is the *opportunity cost, or income given up by not using the resource in its next most profitable use.* The cost that a farmer has in mind when he makes his decision to use his labor on one enterprise rather than on another is the cost to him of losing an opportunity to make an income from another, neglected enterprise. Although the loss to the farmer from being unable to exploit all opportunities cannot be measured by accounting methods, except on an individual farm basis, consideration of the loss influences the farmer when he makes managerial decisions. The farmer is using the usual marginal analysis when he arrives at decisions by considering opportunity costs.

Long-Run Costs as Affected by Farm Size

Thus far, we have centered our attention on costs as affected by the level of variable inputs used. Costs per unit of output also are affected by the scale of production. Costs decline as the scale of operations increases, primarily because of the use of larger and more-specialized machinery and buildings. A farmer with five hundred acres of cropland to prepare and cultivate finds it profitable to buy and operate larger tractors and more-specialized equipment than is economical for a farmer with one hundred acres of cropland. However, the farmer with one hundred acres cannot quickly transform his farm business into a five hundred acre unit. The land and machinery necessary to do so are fixed inputs that can be acquired only in the long run.[1] The balance of the discussion in this chapter relates to long-run cost concepts and their relationship to the short-run costs we have just discussed.

Operators of large farms obtain a more efficient combination of labor, power, and equipment than operators of small farms find possible. A detailed analysis of 573 accounting farms in northern Illinois for 1968 indicates that as the size of the farm increases from around two hundred acres up to over eight hundred acres, there are both lower investment and lower production costs per acre (Table 5–4).

A series of studies of farm production costs has shown that the pattern observed in Table 5–4 generally holds. That is, at first costs decline sharply with increasing size, then much less, and at very large sizes costs may actually increase. Van Arsdall and Elder[2] constructed short-run average

---

[1]The *long run* has a particular meaning in economics. It is a period long enough to permit a business to vary *all* resources, including fixed inputs. *Fixed inputs,* in turn, may be defined as goods that provide a stream of income-generating services over several production periods. Thus, land and machinery are fixed inputs, but generally weed spray and labor are not. (See the discussion of the long run in Chapter 6.).

[2]Roy N. Van Arsdall and William A. Elder, *Economies of Size of Illinois Cash-Grain and Hog Farms,* University of Illinois, Agricultural Experiment Station Bulletin 733, 1969.

TABLE 5-4

Selected Investments and Annual Costs of Grain Farms, per Tillable Acre by Size of Farm, High Soil Fertility Rating, Northern Illinois, 1968

	Acres in Farms					
	170–259	260–339	340–499	500–649	650–799	over 800
Number of Farms	90	123	174	106	46	34
Investment: ($)						
Livestock and grain inventory	96.48	90.03	79.99	77.91	83.27	88.21
Buildings and fences	54.35	52.77	46.76	46.87	37.70	49.07
Machinery	44.57	42.44	42.79	39.84	36.80	36.11
Annual Cost Items ($)						
Buildings and fences	7.24	5.46	4.75	4.97	4.63	5.35
Machinery	23.66	22.89	20.73	20.72	19.94	20.56
Labor*	21.01	17.41	13.57	13.27	12.67	12.96

* Includes operator and family labor

Source: *Summary of Illinois Farm Business Records, 1968,* University of Illinois at Urbana-Champaign, Extension Circular 1006, Table 15a.

cost curves for nine types of cash-grain farms with different sets of labor-machinery inputs. Their results, shown in Figure 5–3 indicate that a two- or three-man farm with eight-row equipment achieves the least cost of all sizes, given their assumptions.

The long-run average cost curve shown in Figure 5–3 shows how average total cost changes as the land, buildings, machinery, and livestock are increased from a one-man, four-row equipment farm (about 350 total acres) to a six-man, eight-row equipment farm (about 2000 acres). The long-run average cost curve is sometimes called the *economies of scale curve because it shows how unit costs change as all inputs are increased.* The small curves are short-run average total cost curves that were generated by increasing output while holding labor force and equipment fixed.

In summarizing his survey of fifteen similar studies of scale economies in farming, Madden concluded that "in most of the farming operations examined, a modern and fully mechanized one-man or two-man operation can produce efficiently and profitably, achieving all or nearly all of the economies of size."[3] The units included dairy, grain, and livestock farms.

It should be remembered, however, that modern farming units are engaged in much more than just crop and livestock production. The buying of inputs and the selling of products provide an important opportunity to gain from large volume. When these factors are taken into account, the advantages of "super-big" farming operations become somewhat more apparent.

[3]J. Patrick Madden, *Economies of Size in Farming,* Agricultural Economic Report 107, U.S.D.A., February 1967, p. 35.

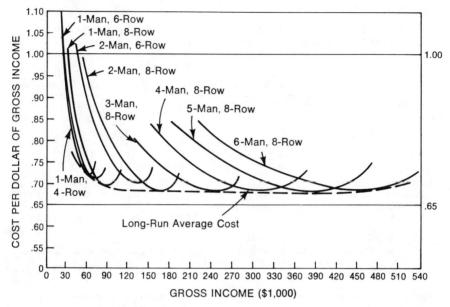

FIGURE 5-3.   Short-Run and Long-Run Average Cost Curves for Cash-Grain
Farms with One to Six Regular Workers and Selected Sizes of
Field Machinery

Krause and Kyle[4] determined the savings and increased costs associated with corn production units of five hundred, one thousand, two
thousand, and five thousand acres. Savings were associated with lower machinery costs and lower input costs per acre while labor, supervision, and
management costs increased for the very large units. In addition, some price
advantage in selling was possible for sizes over one thousand acres. In their
example, they found the five-thousand-acre unit had a $7.30 per acre ad-
vantage over the five-hundred-acre unit, after paying federal income tax
and assuming a 30 percent equity. It would be dangerous to generalize
from one study, but the kinds of advantages they found for large-scale units
may become increasingly important in the future.

Economic Basis of Family Farms

By far, most of the business units in agriculture are family farms. In
most lines of farming, especially those involving livestock production, economies arising from the scale of operation are rather completely realized on
the medium to large commercial family farms. Power and machinery

[4]Kenneth R. Krause and Leonard R. Kyle, "Economic Factors Underlying the Incidence
of Large Farming Units: The Current Situation and Probable Trends," *American Journal of Agricultural Economics*, December 1970, pp. 748–60.

adapted for farm use now permit a family on a farm of one of these sizes to use most of the cost-reducing equipment that a large-scale farming corporation would employ. Large-scale farming operations appear to have been successful where large gangs of hand workers are required, such as in vegetable and sugar-beet production. One-crop farming, such as wheat production, also lends itself well to large-scale units, although it is doubtful if large-scale wheat farms, with several sets of machinery, have any lower production costs than large family units employing one full set of modern machinery. Another example of a large-scale farming unit is the farm that has developed large market outlets for specialized products. In such cases as this, the scale of production is often adapted to supply a uniform product to the market outlets rather than to take advantage of lower production costs. As marketing functions become an increasing proportion of the farm business, very-large-scale units may gain increasing advantages.

Turning our attention to the small farms, we note that the number of small farms declined very rapidly during the boom years of the 1950s and 1960s. In fact, 95 percent of the decrease in the total number of farms between 1939 and 1964 occurred because of the disappearance of 2.3 million farms producing less than $2,500 worth of sales. Still, in 1969 there remained 1.2 million farms with sales of less than $2,500 and 675,000 farms with sales of less than $10,000 but more than $2,500. Why have the operators of these small farms remained? One answer is that for many of these families farming is a way of life, as well as a business. Another answer is that these families rely on the nonfarm sector for the greater part of their incomes. In that sense, they are farmers by definition only. It is likely that the number of small farms will continue to decline through the next decade, if nonfarm employment opportunities are available.

The rapid technological advance in agriculture, including the rapid rise in capital requirements in recent years for efficient, low-cost production, creates real problems for the typical or average farm family. In the 1970s, the family farm will increasingly come to mean a unit with sales of over $20,000, capital investment of $200,000 to $400,000, but with its regular full-time labor and management force of two men drawn from a single family. It seems highly probable that the capital requirement imposed by an advancing technology will increase faster than the capital accumulation of most farm families. It is entirely possible that capital requirements for low-cost farm production, including improved quality control and increased standardization of the products, will become so great that corporations may increasingly replace family farming enterprises in the future. Developments in this area will depend on many factors, including especially the ability of families to obtain and use credit wisely and the ability of families to transfer their farms from father to son as financially solvent and efficient operating units.

POINTS FOR DISCUSSION

1. Make a list of the different cost items in producing the leading farm product in your community. Classify them as either fixed or variable costs.
2. Obtain information from an agronomist in your state on the yield of cotton, tobacco, corn, wheat, or legumes as different quantities of fertilizer are applied per acre. Assume that the cost of the land, labor, and machinery is $25 an acre. Construct a table and chart showing the relation of cost per unit to level of output as the rate of fertilizer application is varied.
3. Make a list of the current farm practices that should be modified and those that should not be modified if the price of the leading farm product in your community drops 33 percent.
4. Give examples of excessive expenditures by farmers in your community. What are the reasons for them?
5. Explain why cost of production cannot be used to determine "fair" selling prices.
6. Using the data in the example on pages 61–63 above, and assuming a price of $1.40/bu. for corn, find the profit per acre for the "farmer" and the "neighbor" being discussed.

REFERENCES

BOULDING, KENNETH E., *Economic Analysis,* 4th ed., Chap. 18. New York: Harper and Row, 1966.

BREWSTER, JOHN M., "Technological Advance and the Future of the Family Farm," *Journal of Farm Economics* (December 1958), pp. 1596–1609.

HEADY, EARL O., AND HARALD R. JENSEN, *Farm Management Economics,* Chap. 15. Englewood Cliffs, N. J.: Prentice-Hall, Inc., 1954.

MADDEN, J. PATRICK, "Economies of Size in Farming," *Agricultural Economic Report 107,* U.S.D.A., 1967.

Chapter 6

The Aggregate Supply Response

in Agriculture

Farmers, in their efforts to maximize returns, have adopted new and improved technologies in one farm enterprise after another. This is clear from the discussions in Chapter 4. These farm technological advances have reduced costs and expanded supply in one enterprise after another during the 1950s and early 1960s. The resulting general picture is one of commodity supply functions shifting to the right under the relentless pressure of farm technological advance. But does this picture of individual commodity behavior properly portray the supply response of the farm firm as an aggregate and of the farming sector as an aggregate? In a way it does, but in another way it is misleading. To understand fully the aggregate supply behavior of the farm sector, one must understand the supply behavior of farm firms, in contradistinction to enterprise behavior, because the industry aggregate is a summation of the firm aggregates. This distinction requires the fullest concentration if an adequate understanding is to be obtained.

AGGREGATE SUPPLY IN THE SHORT RUN

The Aggregate Supply Function of the Farm Firm

The aggregate supply function of a farm firm describes how the total output of all the commodities that firm produces varies as the average com-

modity price (farm price level) varies. Because the typical farm firm is a multiple-enterprise operation, its total output is composed of several commodities, and the relevant measure of price received is a level of prices. Hence, the price-quantity variables in this concept must assume an index-number form. This is necessary to reduce several different commodity prices into a single series and to convert several different commodities into a single measure of output. This statistical problem complicates the supply concept involved, but it in no way invalidates the concept. It is of critical importance to gain a good understanding of the aggregate supply concept.

Understanding the aggregate supply concept in agriculture is furthered by considering the supply behavior of three categories of farms: (1) low-production family farms; (2) commercial family farms; and (3) large-scale commercial farms. We will concentrate on the supply behavior of small farms with inadequate production resources (with gross sales below $2,500) in category (1); of the common family-type farm where the family provides the management and most of the labor required (with gross sales between $2,500 and $40,000) in category (2); and of the large-scale operation largely dependent on hired labor and specialized management (with gross sales above $40,000) in category (3).

Supply Behavior of Low-production Family Farms

The principal productive resources—land and labor—are fixed in the typical low-production farm. Lacking access to sources of financing and having limited contacts with the commercial world, the typical farmer in this category treats land and labor as given, producing as much product as he is able with those given resources. His limited capital resources, too, are typically of a "sunk" type (that is, antiquated machinery and buildings with low salvage values). Thus, we conclude that the typical and principal resource inputs on these farms do not vary in use with the return to them; for practical purposes, the supply of the various inputs is highly or perfectly inelastic.

Because family members on low-production farms often seek and take off-farm employment, it should not be concluded that the supply of family labor is elastic. Off-farm employment does not vary with the return to labor, which is shockingly low at all times on these farms; it varies with off-farm employment *opportunities.* When off-farm employment opportunities of a suitable nature are good, family labor on low-production farms leaves agriculture at a rapid rate. But with any given set of off-farm employment opportunities, the family labor supply on low-production farms is highly inelastic.

A fixed cost, or fixed input, model best describes the supply behavior of low-production farms. The costs of fixed resources run on whether they are used or not, or whether they are used partially or fully. The optimum use of resources on a farm with fixed resources is thus a full use of resources. The farmer produces as much as he can with his often limited managerial ability and with his available resources and there he stops. He does this because the more he produces, the lower his unit costs become. He maximizes his return or minimizes his losses by producing to the limit of his capacity—albeit a limited capacity in this case.

In this situation, the supply function *for each of the enterprises* on a low-production family farm is highly inelastic with respect to price. The farmer is producing to the limit of his capacity, so regardless of what happens to price (within reasonable limits in the short run) he does not change his output. When the farm price level changes, the low-production family farm still has no alternative but to continue full capacity production. The aggregate supply reflects this inability to react, so *the aggregate supply function of the low production family farm is typically completely inelastic.*

Supply Behavior of Commercial Family Farms

We find two classes of inputs on commercial family farms: (1) those that are typically varied; and (2) those that are not. Let us consider the second category first. The most important input that is held fixed for the farm as a whole is labor. Typically, the family supplies all or most of the labor on family farms, as operations on such farms are adjusted to the size, composition, and abilities of the family labor supply. At very high product prices, hence high labor returns, the family labor supply may be augmented by hired labor, and the converse may occur at very low product prices, but over a broad range of product prices and labor returns the supply of labor on commercial family farms is relatively fixed. The family is the labor supply. This is the unique and distinguishing feature of the family farm.

Land inputs on the *representative* family farm are largely fixed. The land area of the representative farm is not easily expanded or contracted. One farm can acquire land at the expense of another, but not all farms (that is, the representative farm) can expand.[1] Many capital inputs—for example, buildings, irrigation structures, orchards, and specialized harvesting equipment—are "sunk" inputs. The salvage value of these capital items is so low once they are committed to production that no thought is given to varying such inputs. Or, stated differently, the salvage value of these capital items is so far below acquisition costs that the marginal value product of such items can vary over a wide range with fluctuations in the farm price level without there being any incentive to acquire more of, or to dispose of, those already acquired. Finally, feed supplies on representative

---

[1]The expansion in the average size of farms operated in the United States in recent years is offset by the fact that there are fewer farms.

farms tend to be fixed in the short run (although intertemporal substitution under government storage programs modifies the fixed input argument somewhat with regard to feeds).

Case A: All Inputs Fixed. We will first derive the aggregate supply function for an extreme situation for a commercial family farm, where the *total* amount of each input available to the farm is fixed but where the manager can vary inputs among enterprises. As we saw in Chapter 4, the supply curve for a *single* enterprise is identical to the rising portion of the marginal cost curve above the average variable cost. Remember though, that this concept held under the condition of *ceteris paribus*—where, in particular, prices of all other commodities were held constant.

However in the aggregate supply problem, by definition *all farm product prices change together,* and therefore marginal cost curves constructed under the assumption that resources will move among enterprises do not describe the output changes of individual enterprises. Because all commodity prices change proportionately (the definition of an increase in the farm price level), the farm firm would gain nothing by switching resources from one enterprise into another. Or stated another way, if a farm is producing two commodities, corn and soybeans, and the price of both increased by an equal proportion, there would be no incentive to increase production of one commodity by taking resources from the other.

In this situation, the firm will gain nothing by switching inputs among enterprises, and because the total inputs available to the firm are fixed, the supply of each enterprise is perfectly inelastic. The aggregate supply relation is the summation in index-number terms of the enterprise curves. In this case when the supply of each enterprise is perfectly inelastic, the aggregate supply function for the farm firm is perfectly inelastic. It will be recognized at once that should the price of one commodity move relative to the others in the total farm operation, then it will be profitable to switch certain variable inputs between enterprises, and the marginal cost curve constructed from the total product function with those inputs variable would be the relevant supply curve for that commodity enterprise. But such would be a relative price change, with individual commodity supply consequences, and we are not concerned with relative price problems in this chapter. We are concerned with the aggregate supply behavior of the farm firm. Thus, we conclude that *the aggregate supply function for a commercial family farm where the total quantity of each input is fixed is perfectly inelastic.*

Case B: Some Inputs Variable. The above case is an extreme. Many inputs can be and are varied on commercial family farms. Typically, they are inputs acquired from the nonfarm sector. Fertilizer is the classic example. Other such inputs might include veterinary services, pesticides, plant disease control, and the repair of machinery and equipment. The use of these resource inputs does vary with the level of product prices. Because these inputs are usually acquired from the nonfarm sector, their prices do not vary directly with farm product prices. What is the nature of aggregate supply under these conditions?

Again, we begin with the single enterprise supply or marginal cost curve discussed in Chapter 4. It describes how output of one enterprise responds to variation in the price of that enterprise, with the prices of all other enterprises and the prices of all inputs held constant. The increased quantity produced with an increased price as reflected in the marginal cost curve results from more inputs being applied to the enterprise. Those added inputs are obtained from two sources: some are new inputs purchased from nonfarm sources; some are switched from other enterprises as the price of the enterprise being considered increases.

In the aggregate supply problem, all commodity prices move together so there is no incentive to switch resources from one enterprise to another. There *is* the incentive to obtain more purchased inputs, and in this case, as contrasted with case A, that can occur. Thus, an increase in the farm price level in Figure 6–1, caused by an increase in both commodity prices, will cause the manager to use more purchased inputs in both enterprises. However, there are still some inputs that the farm firm cannot increase.

For example, contrast fertilizer and land. A rising farm price level may give an incentive to the representative family farm manager to use more fertilizer, and more can be used on all crops. But the total land available on the farm is usually fixed. Because land is fixed, more cannot be applied on all enterprises. Therefore, output of each enterprise will increase by less for a given price rise when that price rise occurs as part of a general farm price level increase than when it occurs for one enterprise alone.

In the aggregate supply problem the appropriate marginal cost curve results from increasing output by increasing the application of purchased inputs. That is, the inputs supplied by the farm (land and family labor) are assumed fixed, whereas those purchased from the nonfarm sector are assumed variable. These are the marginal cost curves in Figure 6–1, which added together result in the aggregate supply curve shown. This aggregate firm supply relation exhibits some slope—nonfarm resources (for example, fertilizer and plant disease control) flow into agriculutre with rising product prices, and out with falling product prices. But it remains a highly inelastic supply relation because many inputs used in commercial family farms (land, family labor, and sunk capital) are not varied with product prices.

Supply Behavior of Large-scale Commercial Farms

This class of farms differs from commercial family farms in one important respect: labor is a variable input factor on large-scale farms. It is hired and fired as profit maximization dictates. When low or falling prod-

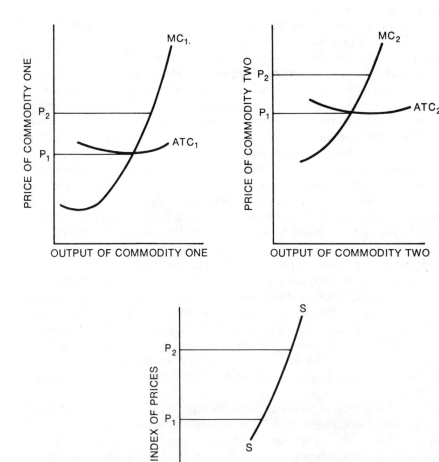

FIGURE 6-1. Derivation of an Aggregate Supply Function

uct prices make the intensive use of labor on a large-scale farm unprofitable, some labor is sent packing down the road. When high or rising product prices render the intensive use of labor profitable, additional labor is recruited from the unemployed, students, or housewives.

Thus, we would expect the aggregate supply function for the large-scale farm firm to be more elastic than that for the family farm firm in comparable situations. In other words, we would visualize the *SS* curve in Figure 6–1 to be more inelastic for the large-scale farm than for the family farm, the reason being that the important input, labor, is varied on large-scale farms.

Certain inputs, however, tend to remain fixed even on large-scale farms. The land area of the *representative* large-scale farm is not readily increased. And numerous capital inputs become sunk inputs and therefore nonvariable on large-scale farms as well as on family farms (for example, buildings, orchards). This tends to reduce the incentive to expand or contract the total output of the firm.

The Aggregate Supply Function for the Farming Industry

The aggregate supply function for agriculture is the summation of all farm firm supply functions. In concept, the industry supply function states how the total output from agriculture varies in response to changes in the level of farm prices, all other influencing factors held constant. The slope and elasticity of this industry aggregate function should be a matter of empirical fact. But problems of statistical estimation make available estimates of its elasticity the subject of considerable controversy. One of the authors' estimation results suggest that the aggregate supply function for agriculture is perfectly inelastic.[2] Estimates by another researcher suggest that the elasticity of this function may approach 0.3.[3]

Theoretically, several kinds of changes associated with the rapidly changing nature of agriculture should seem to have affected the aggregate supply function. The shifting structure of farming, leaving fewer and fewer low-production family farms in existence, is one factor. Because these farms are theorized to have perfectly inelastic aggregate supply functions, their disappearance should have the effect of making the aggregate supply more elastic.

On the other hand, the capital investments in sunk inputs on family and large-scale commercial farms are becoming ever larger, with much of that capital specialized in production of a particular product and the rest useful only in producing a closely related agricultural commodity. Variable costs make up a relatively small proportion of total costs, so the incentive is to produce up to full capacity. For example, a large hog producer may have plant and equipment with the capacity to add five thousand pounds of gain per day on hogs. If that equipment is used at less than full capacity, the forgone income will be substantial. The increasing ratio of fixed to

[2]Willard W. Cochrane, "Conceptualizing the Supply Relation in Agriculture," *Journal of Farm Economics*, December 1955.

[3]Zvi Griliches, "The Demand for Inputs in Agriculture and a Derived Supply Elasticity," *Journal of Farm Economics*, May 1959.

variable inputs on commercial farms will tend to make the aggregate supply functions on those farms more inelastic. Attempts to empirically document[4] a change in the elasticity of the aggregate supply function have been unsuccessful, and perhaps this indicates that the two forces identified above have offset each other.

In 1970, large-scale commercial farms accounted for about 37 percent of the gross sales of agricultural products, and commercial family farms for about 55 percent. Because we have argued that the typical firm supply function in each of these classes of farms is not perfectly inelastic, the industry supply function could hardly be perfectly inelastic. On the other hand, some 55 percent of total market sales are accounted for by firms—commercial family farms—with inelastic aggregate supply functions. Thus, it is the judgment of the authors that the aggregate supply function for agriculture probably has an elasticity falling somewhere between 0.0 and 0.3. The short-run aggregate supply function for agriculture is highly, but not perfectly, inelastic.

AGGREGATE SUPPLY IN THE LONG RUN

Short- and Long-run Considerations

So far, the discussion in this chapter has focused on short-run supply. The relations discussed describe how much the output of the firm or industry may change from one season to the next, or one production period to the next, in response to a given price change. And price change here, although almost impossible to measure, refers to the change in price from the past production period to the forthcoming period. (The price change involved is some sort of expected price change that varies from one farmer to the next, and hence is difficult to quantify.) Thus, changes in firm supply that we have been discussing relate to those changes in resource use that can be made from one production period to the next.

In the long run—that is, in a length of run in which all possible resource adjustments in response to a given price change can be made, but in which all other influencing factors hold constant—the firm supply functions under consideration would probably become more elastic. Particularly at very high and very low product price levels, the relationships would become more elastic. This increased elasticity of firm supply, for the long run, is deduced from the logic that at very high prices capital formation in agriculture would occur more generally and more intensively in the long run

[4]Luther G. Tweeten and C. Leroy Quance, "Positivistic Measures of Aggregate Supply Elasticities: Some New Approaches," *American Journal of Agricultural Economics*, May 1969, pp. 342–52.

than in the short, and at very low product prices some capital that wears out would not be replaced. Some further adjustments in the use of hired and family labor might occur in the long run. But the important long-run adjustments would probably occur through capital formation and destruction.

We should be clear about what we mean by *long run,* however. The long-run concept under discussion here, and common to economic analysis, covers no definite time period. It is an abstraction to permit the analyst to conceptualize and visualize the complete resource adjustments to a given price change, *where all other influencing forces are conceived to be constant.* In the world of reality, the full and complete resource adjustments to a given price change can rarely be observed. All other things do not hold constant in the real world. We get changes in technology, changes in institutions, changes in consumer tastes, war and peace, and so on. The authors therefore are inclined to minimize the implications of long-run economic analyses and to concentrate on the short-run functions, and shifts in those functions, that generate real-world prices, quantities, and incomes.

Output and Inputs in Agriculture—The Historical Record

The total output of agriculture increased slowly between 1910 and 1929, but has nearly doubled in the forty years since 1930, with livestock output increasing somewhat more and crop output slightly less (Table 6–1). A stationary aggregate supply function with an elasticity of less than 0.3 is obviously incompatible with this great increase in farm output. Some part of the concept of supply is missing or incorrect. Some further reflecttions on the concept of supply make it clear that the great increase in farm output between 1930 and 1970 cannot be explained by a stationary aggregate supply relation no matter how elastic it is conceived to be.

Farm product prices did not increase relative to nonfarm prices over the forty-year period in question; so there was no relative price increase to induce greater farm output. The relative increase in farm prices that occurred in the 1940s was entirely lost in the 1950s when farm product prices actually declined relative to nonfarm prices. The only kind of a stationary supply curve that could explain the increased farm output of the 1950s with declining prices is one with a negative slope.

The riddle of agriculture supply, in an aggregate sense, is first deepened and then cleared away by a careful look at resource use in agriculture. From Table 6–2, it is clear that the farm labor force declined significantly and steadily beginning in the middle 1930s. The index of farm real estate has increased very modestly over the past forty years, with much of the increase due to buildings and land improvements. In contrast, inputs of almost every capital item used in agriculture increased rapidly during

TABLE 6–1

Total Output and Gross Production of Livestock and Crops,
United States, 1910–1970 (1957–59 = 100)

Year(s)	Total Farm Output	All Livestock and Livestock Products	All Crops
1910–14	52	51	65
1915–19	55	55	69
1920–24	57	57	70
1925–29	61	61	73
1930–34	60	65	68
1935–39	64	64	72
1940–44	78	81	83
1945–49	84	83	90
1950–54	91	92	92
1955–59	99	100	98
1960	106	102	108
1961	107	107	106
1962	108	108	107
1963	112	111	111
1964	111	114	108
1965	114	111	115
1966	113	114	111
1967	118	117	117
1968	120	117	120
1969	121	118	121
1970	120	124	117

Source: "Changes in Farm Production and Efficiency: A Summary Report," *Statistical Bulletin 233*, U.S.D.A., 1964, 1970, and 1971 issues.

this period. Farmers have substituted all kinds of capital for human labor while holding the overall size of the physical plant constant since the 1930s. This is the picture of resource use in absolute terms. But output has increased since the middle 1930s. Thus, in terms of resources used per unit of output, nonfarm-produced capital has substituted for both land and labor.

One might hypothesize that the increased use of all kinds of nonfarm-produced capital has just about offset the decrease in labor employed in agriculture in an absolute sense, and offset the decrease in *land and labor* used in a per-unit sense. And this hypothesis squares with the best available estimates of the use of total resources in agriculture over the period in question. An index of total farm inputs, developed by the U.S. Department of Agriculture,[5] indicates that total resources used in agriculture increased 7 percent between 1930 and 1960, and another 12 percent between 1960 and 1970 (see Table 6–3). In other words, total inputs in agriculture probably

[5]The index is computed by considering the combined volume of farm labor, land and service buildings, machinery and equipment, fertilizer and lime, purchase of feed, seed and livestock, and miscellaneous production items in constant dollars.

TABLE 6–2

Farm Inputs in Major Subgroups, United States, 1910–1970 (1957–59 = 100)

Year(s)	Farm Labor	Farm Real Estate	Mechanical Power and Machinery	Fertilizer & Liming Materials	Feed, Seed & Livestock Purchases	Miscellaneous
1910–14	217	89	22	14	15	59
1915–19	221	91	28	12	18	64
1920–24	217	90	32	14	25	71
1925–29	220	91	36	19	28	73
1930–34	210	88	35	15	24	76
1935–39	197	90	37	22	30	69
1940–44	191	90	47	35	55	75
1945–49	164	92	66	54	71	77
1950–54	135	99	94	78	79	89
1955–59	107	100	99	96	95	98
1960	92	101	104	111	109	106
1961	88	101	101	117	111	109
1962	84	103	100	125	117	113
1963	81	104	104	141	123	117
1964	77	106	102	155	126	120
1965	73	106	105	162	127	120
1966	69	107	110	182	136	123
1967	68	107	114	204	144	128
1968	66	107	114	214	143	130
1969	64	107	115	224	148	133
1970	63	109	115	231	157	135

Source: Compiled from data in *The Farm Income Situation*, Economic Research Service, U.S.D.A., July 1971.

increased moderately, but did not nearly approach the rate at which total farm output increased.

What did happen between the 1930s and the 1960s is this: output per unit of input in agriculture increased greatly—productive efficiency soared. We see this in Table 6–3. Output per unit of input was nearly constant until the early 1930s. Then, from the early 1930s to the early 1940s productivity increased 22 percent, from the early 1940s to the early 1950s productivity increased 13 percent, and from the early 1950s to the early 1960s productivity increased another 22 percent. Surprisingly, productivity did not change substantially during the decade of the 1960s.

Sources of Increased Productive Efficiency

There are several ways by which output per unit of input could have increased between the early 1930s and the early 1960s: (1) through a tendency for more farm operators to approach the minimum points on their respective long-run planning curves; (2) through increased specialization; (3) through the adoption of improved production practices; and (4)

TABLE 6–3

Aggregate Farm Output, Total Inputs and Output per Unit of Input,
United States, 1910–1970 (1957–59 = 100)

Year(s)	Farm Output	Farm Production Inputs	Output per Unit of Input
1910–14	52	85	61
1915–19	55	90	61
1920–24	57	92	62
1925–29	61	96	63
1930–34	60	93	65
1935–39	64	91	70
1940–44	78	99	78
1945–49	84	100	85
1950–54	91	103	88
1955–59	99	101	98
1960	106	101	105
1961	107	101	106
1962	108	101	107
1963	112	104	108
1964	111	104	107
1965	114	104	110
1966	113	107	106
1967	118	110	107
1968	120	111	108
1969	121	112	108
1970	120	113	106

Source: "Changes in Farm Production and Efficiency, 1970" and *Statistical Bulletin No. 233, 1971,* Economic Research Service, U.S.D.A.

through the increased skill of the labor force. Technically, any one of these avenues to increased efficiency means that the firm's production function shifts, hence the supply curve of the firm shifts. Thus, all these avenues could have contributed to the expansion of the aggregate supply function in agriculture. But some of the ways probably contributed more to increased efficiency than others, and certain interactions were involved, too. Consequently, we will investigate these various sources of increased efficiency briefly.

There is no obvious reason why more farmers should be at the minimum point of their respective long-run planning curves in 1960 than were there in 1930. In fact, there are grounds for arguing that farmers generally may have been farther from such minimum points in 1960 than they were in 1930. These grounds are: the world of production techniques was more dynamic in 1960 than it was in 1930, and the task of effecting optimum long-run adjustments was more difficult in 1960 that it was in 1930. In any event, the authors are not inclined to believe that this source contributed significantly to increased productive efficiency in agriculture.

Regional specialization in agricultural production continued to evolve over the period. Cotton spread onto the High Plains and into the irrigated valleys of the West; potatoes moved out of general farming in the Midwest and into concentrated production areas; and the soybean found a new home in the Midwest. All this certainly contributed to increased production efficiency, but much of this industry relocation and specialization resulted from the availability of new, improved techniques, such as new plant varieties, improved plant-disease control, and new tillage practices. In turn, the adoption of new techniques is associated with the skill and intelligence of the human agent. The effective use of new techniques often requires that highly skilled labor and skilled intelligent operators seek out and adopt improved techniques.

There is interaction all along the line among these three sources of increased productive efficiency. Increased specialization, the adoption of new techniques, and enhanced operator skill combine and interact to increase output per unit of input in agriculture. In the drive to increase efficiency in the dynamic production process in agriculture, it is difficult, if not impossible, to separate these three efficiency-generating forces into separate causal strands; they are inextricably combined in practice. Thus, we are inclined to wrap the total process—*increased specialization, the adoption of new techniques, and enhanced operator skill—into one package and call it farm technological advance.*

Thus, the great increase in total farm output between 1930 and 1960 was fundamentally the result of farm technological advance in the inclusive sense given above. Total farm output increased only modestly, if at all, as the result of the increased employment of resources committed to agricultural production by farmers. And the change-in-scale argument (that is, that there is movement to more optimal positions on long-run planning curves) is not persuasive. The principal explanation for the great increase in total output in agriculture since the middle 1930s must be the occurrence of rapid and widespread farm technological advance. Rapid and widespread technological advance in agriculture has shifted the enterprise production functions on most commercial farms. This in turn has expanded firm supply relations, with the final result that the aggregate supply function for the industry has shifted to the right—has increased.

Of course, farm technological advance, as we shall discuss in Chapter 16, is not a free good. It occurs, and only occurs, as resources are devoted to it. It costs money to develop new techniques through research; it costs money to extend those techniques to farmers through informational services; and it costs money to educate farm workers and improve their productive skills. But the resources employed in the above activities are not committed to them solely by farmers, or solely to maximize profits. Resources employed in research, extension, and teaching that result, in some part, in farm technological advance are committed to those activities by all society and for various reasons. Thus, resources employed in research, extension, and teaching are not expanded and contracted, except indirectly, as farm price levels or general price levels change. The society of the United States has supported and continuously expanded research and educational activities because it places high values on the results of those activities.

The Shifting Aggregate Supply Function

The riddle of the aggregate supply problem is solved. It is possible for the firm and industry supply functions to be severely inelastic and for the total output of agriculture to increase. It can and has occurred through expanding shifts in these functions; farmers in the aggregate have stood ready to offer more supplies on the market at a given price level in almost every year between 1938 and 1960 (this action is illustrated in Figure 6–2). Aggregate farm output has increased through shifts in the aggregate supply function rather than through a movement along such a function. And these shifts in the aggregate supply function have been powered by persistent and widespread farm technological advance.

Our theoretical construct of the aggregate supply function for agriculture is then as follows: *a short-run, highly inelastic function expanding through dated time in an irregular but persistent fashion* (see Figure 6–2). For obvious reasons, the aggregate supply function does not expand in a regular cadence: the chance occurrence of important new technologies for example, the gasoline motor, hybrid seed corn), the bunching of new technologies, and the financial position of farmers all cause the aggregate supply curve to shift in an irregular way. But the outpouring of new technologies in agriculture has been along a sufficiently broad front and the financial position of farmers has generally been sufficiently strong since the 1930s to insure almost continuous and widespread adoption of new techniques through the early 1960s. Hence, the aggregate supply function has shifted to the right in terms of Figure 6–3 during that period.[6] In the 1960s, the aggregate supply function seems to have remained relatively constant.

The financial position of farmers is, of course, related to the level of farm prices. The financial position of farmers generally is strong when the farm price level is high and stable. Thus, we would always expect to find a more rapid rate of farm technological advance with a high and stable level of farm prices than with the converse.

One final point needs to be made with respect to the industry supply function. Logic suggests that the rightward shifting action of the industry supply function is not reversible. Technological advance shifts the indus-

---

[6]For an empirical view of the aggregate supply function for agriculture, refer to Chapter 14.

try supply function to the right, as marginal and average unit costs on individual farms are lowered. It is to the advantage of farmers to hold on to such techniques once adopted, whether prices turn high or low.[7] If prices are falling, the farmer can minimize his losses by continuing to

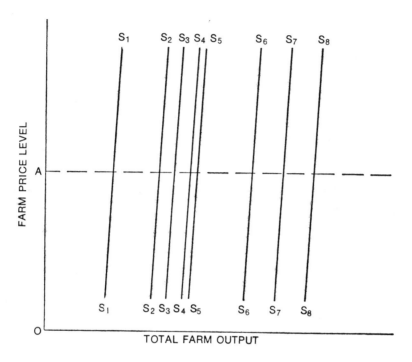

FIGURE 6–2. The Shifting Aggregate Supply Relation in Agriculture

employ the cost-reducing techniques already adopted, and he, of course, can maximize his profits by pursuing the same course of action. Thus, once a farmer has adopted a new cost-reducing technique there is *no* logical reason why he should want to give it up, except to substitute a still better technique for it.

In longer-run situations, if farm prices hold at an extremely low level, fixed capital investments in agriculture may not be replaced as they wear out, and labor-saving equipment may not be substituted for the labor that shifts to other industries. In the shorter-run situations, how-

[7]Typically, the new technique involves a capital investment that, once made, serves for a number of years or involves the use of new output-increasing supplies, such as a feed supplement, which costs so little in relation to its contribution to increased output in the new production function that it is profitable to continue its use as long as the enterprise is continued on the farm.

ever, including periods as long as several years, we find no logical basis for a contracting aggregate supply function of agriculture. Farm operators who fail to replace their worn-out capital investments in these shorter periods of low prices are more than balanced by others who adopt new cost-reducing production technologies in order to lower production costs.

Although there are periods of stability, there is no evidence of a contraction in the aggregate supply function in agriculture going back as far as 1929. The historical data indicate that the aggregate supply function in agriculture did not contract—did not shift to the left—between 1929 and 1932, when farm prices fell disastrously. The aggregate supply function in agriculture appears to have held constant in a perfectly inelastic position from 1929 to 1936. And when the farm prices level fell by about 25 percent between 1951 and 1955, the industry supply did not contract; in fact, the industry supply curve continued to shift to the right in the face of this farm price level decline. Thus, what we seem to have is an industry supply function for agriculture that expands irregularly but persistently over time, *but that does not contract.* At least it has not in modern historical experience.

POINTS FOR DISCUSSION

1. Distinguish between the concept of "fixed costs" and the concept of "sunk costs."
2. How does the concept of a firm supply function differ from that of an enterprise supply function?
3. Compare the supply function with respect to elasticity for different categories of farms: low-production farms, commercial family farms, and large-scale farms. If there are differences in elasticity, explain why.
4. What effect does the length of run have on the elasticity of firm supply?
5. Is the great increase in farm output over the period 1930–1960 incompatible with a highly inelastic industry supply function? Explain how the event and concept can be reconciled.
6. How does the aggregate supply function for agriculture behave through time?

REFERENCES

"Changes in Farm Production and Efficiency, A Summary Report." *Statistical Bulletin 233,* U.S.D.A., annual issues.

COCHRANE, WILLARD W., "Conceptualizing the Supply Relation in Agriculture," *Farm Prices: Myth and Reality,* Chap. 3. Minneapolis: University of Minnesota Press, 1959.

JOHNSON, D. G., "The Nature of the Supply Function for Agricultural Products," *American Economic Review* (September 1950).

JOHNSON, GLENN L., "Supply Function—Some Facts and Notions," in Earl O. Heady, Howard G. Diesslin, Harald R. Jensen, and Glenn L. Johnson, eds., *Agricultural Adjustment Problems in a Growing Economy,* Chap. 5. Ames, Iowa: Iowa State College Press, 1958.

TWEETEN, LUTHER G., AND C. LEROY QUANCE, "Positivistic Measures of Aggregate Supply Elasticities: Some New Approaches," *American Journal of Agricultural Economics* (May 1969).

PART TWO

Marketing
Farm Products

Chapter 7

The Farm Marketing

System—What Is It?

A complex and elaborate set of practices, processing and handling facilities, and commercial "know-how" have come into being over the past hundred years to move the products of our farms to consumers. All this we call marketing, or sometimes distribution when the emphasis in on the broad aspects of the problem. In brief, marketing comprises those business activities involved in the flow of goods and services from production to consumption.

But there is more to the marketing of farm products than the transfer of the raw products of the farm to the consumer. We do not eat wheat; we eat bread. We do not eat hogs; we eat pork chops. We do not wear cotton lint; we wear cotton shirts. Further, we do not consume the entire apple crop at the time of harvest, and we do not smoke up the entire tobacco crop during the months of harvest. Farm products must be processed into a form that consumers can use; the supply of these products must be released to consumers in an even flow, in order to span the interval between one surplus producing period and the next. It is the function of our marketing or distribution system to undertake these operations: processing, storage, orderly dispersement. Thus, we usually say that the act of production creates form utility and the act of marketing creates time and place utility. But this is not strictly correct, for when wheat is processed into flour and cotton fiber is spun into thread, form utility is created.

Developing Needs for a Marketing System

The need for a specialized and, in this case, highly complex system for marketing farm products is very often poorly understood. In the early 1800s, an American farmer hauled his wheat crop to the local miller, had the wheat milled into flour, and hauled the flour back to his farmstead for the use of his family during the coming year. Payment to the miller was probably made in kind, in flour. In this self-sufficient situation, there existed little need for a system for marketing flour; there existed little in the way of a marketing problem. And in primitive societies, in which a few goats (or cows) are driven around the producers' milk route and milked before the door of each customer, the marketing problem is reduced to its simplest form. But we know that self-sufficiency has not been the way of American agriculture. We have seen already how certain areas and farms in those areas specialize in the production of those products for which they have the greatest advantage. And once individual areas and farmers specialize in the production of certain commodities, we have a marketing problem. Producers in one area now have a *surplus* of certain commodities that they *must* trade for the surpluses of producers in other areas in order to obtain the goods that are required to maintain a balanced living.

This tendency toward specialization and production of surpluses for trade, area by area, began early in our national life. Pennsylvania farmers, even prior to 1800, were raising surpluses of rye and corn in the more fertile limestone valleys of the Appalachians, converting these grains into whiskey, and marketing their grain to the outside world in this form. Before the coming of the railroads, settlers in the broad stretches of the Ohio Valley fed their surplus grains to cattle and hogs, sometimes floating their hogs down the Ohio and Mississippi rivers to the New Orleans market, sometimes driving their cattle overland, via the Cumberland and the Mohawk Valley routes, to the eastern markets. And far on the West Coast, surpluses of barley and wheat were loaded into sailing ships and carried around the Horn to English markets before the steamship and the steam locomotive reached that new area of settlement. Out of these early tendencies toward specialization and surplus production grew a need for methods of collecting the produce of many producers and, in turn, dispersing these products in modified form to many and distant consumers. "Middlemen," in the broadest sense of the term, entered the picture to undertake such activities as collection, transportation, storage, processing, and retailing in order to move these surplus products from producing areas to consuming areas.

Marketing Needs of Commercial Agriculture

In the highly commercialized agriculture of the present time, the need for an effective marketing system has reached its greatest intensity. Where wheat production is concentrated on highly commercialized farms on the Great Plains to the extent that not even a garden or chicken or milk cow is maintained in many cases, where fruits and vegetables are produced in "factories in the field" in California and certain southern states, and where corn and hogs have become the dominating enterprises of the rich prairie lands of Iowa and Illinois, it is clear that the organization and services involved in moving those commodities to consumers form an indispensable part of our economic life. For if these area surpluses are not moved to consuming centers, they become almost valueless. What would Kansas do with all the wheat it produces if it could not trade it for goods and services produced elsewhere?

Distribution and Concentration of Population. Marketing problems created by surplus producing areas are intensified by the distribution and concentration of population. The marketing problem is not simply that of trading back and forth between surplus producing areas. We must recognize that our population is not uniformly distributed state by state. Rather, it is heavily concentrated in the industrial states. In 1970, some 36 percent of the total population of the United States was concentrated in the six industrialized states: New York, New Jersey, Pennsylvania, Ohio, Michigan, and Illinois. Into this area of population concentration must move the principal farm surpluses of our specialized producing areas. Another area of population concentration is on the Pacific Coast. Thus, we see the picture: specialized producing areas scattered over the country with the core located in the Mississippi Valley and two centers of population concentration, one in the Northeast and one on the Pacific Coast. In one case, we have surplus farm products; in the other, we have food and fiber deficits. It is the job of the marketing system to move the surpluses to the deficit areas and, in that way, satisfy the needs of producers for a market and the needs of urban consumers for supplies. In the United States, no master planner sits at the head of this system, directing and controlling each individual action in an effort to match demands with supplies. Still, that is the problem that must be solved in our present interdependent, specialized economy, and we rely on the marketing system to do this.

The Complexity of the Marketing System. It is difficult to describe the farm marketing system because of the diversity of activities and complexity of business relations found therein. The variety of services, practices, and agencies found in the marketing of cotton lint is portrayed in Figure 7–1. As complex as Figure 7–1 may appear, however, it is not complete; it does not tell the full story. In the first place, we do not get any picture of the volumes handled. In the second place, we do not get a picture of the number of firms and the size of firms engaged in the various activities. In certain instances, there may be a few firms, in other instances many firms. In some cases, the operation may be dominated by one or two large firms, and in other cases there may be many small firms. All this we do not see. The information that Figure 7–1 conveys is that of the number and type of *activities* involved in moving cotton lint from the producer to spinners' markets.

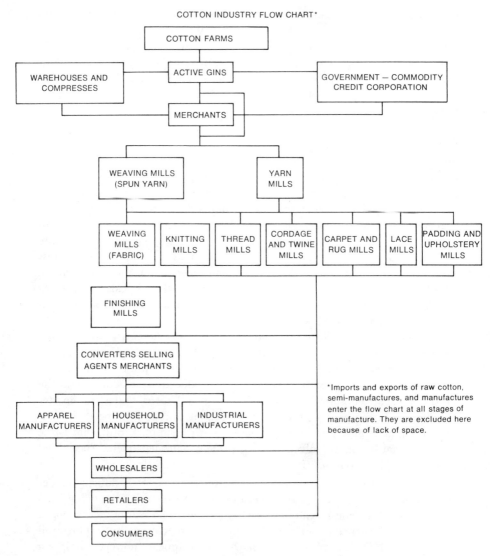

FIGURE 7–1

But even with regard to the presentation of activities, Figure 7–1 is not complete. Certain activities must be imagined. For example, the financing services provided by individual firms in the transfer of the product are not shown. Neither are the informational services of the various government agencies nor the regulatory operations of the various government agencies indicated in Figure 7–1. And, of course, that part of the market from the spinners to the retail outlets is missing.

Marketing Channels

Although it is important to have an appreciation of the complexity of the farm marketing system, the purpose of any field of study is to explain, to point out, the significant relationships hidden in a maze of raw information. Such is our purpose in studying the marketing of farm products. One of the useful ways of describing the farm marketing system is in terms of *flows* of products from producers to consumers. These flow processes may be likened to pipelines conducting food and fiber products from the producer to the consumer. To these pipelines we commonly give the more elegant name *marketing channels*. And these channels, if properly marked out, provide us with information as to the direction of product movement and volume of product movement.

A highly simplified, yet descriptive, flow chart for wheat is shown in Figure 7–2. We see that the principal marketing channel for wheat is to

MAJOR U. S. MARKETING CHANNELS FOR WHEAT, 1963-64

(All movement is from left to right)

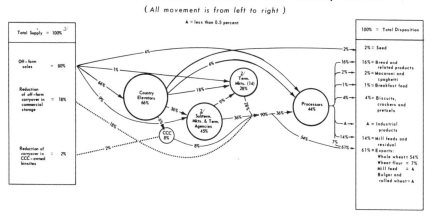

FIGURE 7–2

the country elevators and then to either subterminal markets and terminal agencies or to terminal markets. From there, it either goes to processors or is exported. Although not all marketing activities are shown in Figure 7–2, the proportions flowing through each channel is shown. It is interesting to note that in 1963–64 more than 60 percent of the total wheat produced was exported. The importance of exports to American agriculture becomes more evident the more one learns about agriculture.

Although schematic flow charts describing the principal marketing channels have been worked out for most farm products, we do not have the time to work through the marketing system commodity by commodity. We will point out only that these flow charts describing the principal marketing channels become considerably more complex in the case of livestock. In contrast, the flow chart for the marketing of eggs is a rather simple affair.

The flow of food from producers to consumers in terms of value is shown in Figure 7–3. Domestic agriculture is by far the largest supplier of food, with about 10 percent additional being imported. The expenses involved in marketing (assembling, storing, and processing) more than double the value of food from when it leaves producers to when it reaches consumers. The functions performed in the process are the subject of marketing.

The Concentration and Dispersion Process. We have gained some insight into the complexity and nature of the farm-marketing system in the previous sections. But the bulk of marketing activities, appearing in the graphic presentations between the producer and the consumer, may have warped our perspective. In reality, the marketing system consists of a great concentration process on the one hand and a great dispersion process on the other. Business firms early in the marketing system are engaged in the collection of products from several million farmers; in the next phase, firms are engaged in the concentration of those products at strategic points, such as processing points or car-lot receiving points; and last, firms are engaged in the dispersion of those products to 200 million (and more) consumers.

This total process might be likened to the figure of an hourglass. That is the picture, in any event, that emerges in Figure 7–4, where the concentrating and dispersing processes for a large city are illustrated. Across the upper opening of this hourglass, we must imagine many thousand individual producing units. The products of these units are reduced and moved through the hands of only a few thousand country shippers. The flow is further reduced as the products concentrate into the hands of processors, manufacturers, and car-lot receivers. There, the trend toward concentration is reversed, and the dispersion process begins. The original products, processed, packaged, or broken into smaller lots, are now dispersed to a greater number of wholesalers, jobbers, and manufacturers' representatives. The dispersion process continues as these food products move on to the shelves of many thousand retail stores. And from these numerous stores, these food products move into the many thousand homes of our mythical city.

These processes of concentration and dispersion are highly important for food and agriculture. We say this, first, because farm products are produced in relatively small quantities on many, many producing units; second, because the farm units engaged in producing particular commodities are

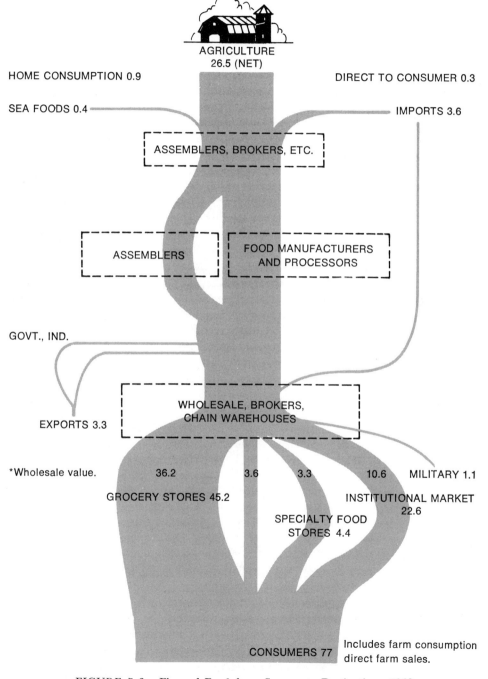

AGRICULTURE
26.5 (NET)

HOME CONSUMPTION 0.9

DIRECT TO CONSUMER 0.3

SEA FOODS 0.4

IMPORTS 3.6

ASSEMBLERS, BROKERS, ETC.

ASSEMBLERS

FOOD MANUFACTURERS
AND PROCESSORS

GOVT., IND.

WHOLESALE, BROKERS,
CHAIN WAREHOUSES

EXPORTS 3.3

*Wholesale value.   36.2   3.6   3.3   10.6   MILITARY 1.1

GROCERY STORES 45.2   INSTITUTIONAL MARKET
                                                 22.6
                                    SPECIALTY FOOD
                                    STORES 4.4

CONSUMERS 77   Includes farm consumption
                direct farm sales.

FIGURE 7–3. Flow of Food from Sources to Destinations, 1963

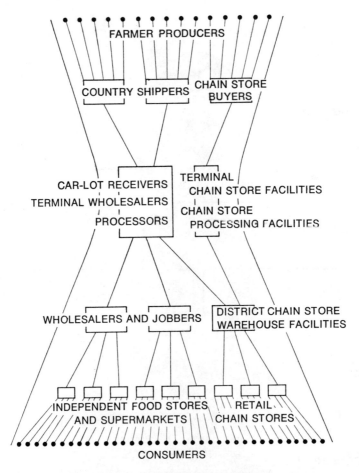

FIGURE 7–4.   The Concentration, Dispersion, and Equalization
Process for Farm Food Products

not distributed uniformly over the country, but rather are to be found in specialized producing areas; and third, because centers of population do not lie close to specialized producing areas. Thus, the problem, which the marketing system solves satisfactorily in most cases, but not so satisfactorily in others, is that of concentrating products from many producing units, directing those products to centers of population, and there dispersing them to many consumer units.

The Equalization Process. What do we mean by equalization? By this, we mean the process whereby the supply of a farm product is fed to consumers as they require that product. It is the adjustment of supply to demand on the basis of time, quantity, and quality. The seasonal flow of farm products to market bears little reference to the continuous needs and demand of consumers. Most farm commodities are produced over a climatically determined period, are harvested at a given time, and come to market in a rush. Even products such as milk and eggs, which are produced the year around, have flush periods of production. In sum, commodities are produced on the farm for the market (in the general sense of the word *market*), not for the filling of orders at the retail level.

Further, farm products rarely come to a specific market in the quantity or quality demanded in that market. For example, the supply of fluid milk forthcoming from the milkshed surrounding a particular city may not be adequate to meet the requirements of that city the year around. Or the supply of wheat from the area around a milling center may be adequate, as far as quantity is concerned, but lacking in the particular types of grain needed to yield the quality of flour in demand. The process of equalizing or adjusting supplies to demand is carried out, for the most part, in wholesale markets. These markets may be looked upon as great reservoirs into which farm products flow in varying amounts and varieties; and here they are held until the demand for them by consumers brings about their dispersion. *Equalization is the great service provided in wholesaling*, involving the acquisition of products of the qualities demanded, the accumulation of products demanded seasonally, the storage and dispersement of products produced seasonally, and the taking up of slack between currently changing volumes of output and consumption.

A Market

We have alluded to the term *market* above, but what exactly is a market? A *market* is not an easy thing to define. It can be a specific place (a meat market, a produce market, a livestock auction), but it need not involve space or occupy a geographic location. It may, for instance, be organized or integrated around the telephone or telegraph. But there is one thing that always occurs in a market, the thing for which a market is organized, namely, *the exchange of title to a particular product*. Markets are organized to facilitate transfers of ownership. Hence, we think of a market as a place or a sphere in which buyers and sellers get together to arrange sales, to effect transfers of ownership.

We find markets in the economic system wherever one group of individuals finds it convenient to dispose of its products and another group finds it convenient to acquire those goods. Thus, at country shipping points we often find a market: a place where producers who do not know how to ship and handle the product efficiently wish to sell, and dealers who do know how to ship and handle the product efficiently wish to buy.

A market is thus a sphere within which price-making forces operate. We have the forces of demand represented by the buyers and the forces of supply represented by the sellers. Out of the interaction of these forces, the price of the product in question is determined. The size of a market is described by the number of firms engaged in buying and selling who are subject to the common forces of demand and supply. In other words, any group of buyers are in the same market when the action of one affects all others; the same is true of suppliers.

Economists once said that the size of a market is limited to that area or sphere in which one price prevails. But where product differentiation is the rule, the single price criterion does not correctly delimit the market. There can be as many different prices prevailing in a market as there are differentiated products in the market. Thus, the criterion of a market becomes the common influence of demand and supply, not a single, uniform price.

Classes of Markets

The markets in which farm products are handled and exchanged in the flow from farm to city may be divided into three principal classes: (1) local markets; (2) central markets; and (3) retail markets.

Local markets lying close to producing areas constitute the first step in the concentration of farm products. These markets provide a convenient place for producers to sell their products; hence, they contribute to the collection of products from many small producers for economic handling and shipment. In the performance of this basic service, local markets usually provide facilities for weighing, storing, grading, packaging, and loading.

Buyers and shippers operating in local markets furnish a ready and, in most cases, a cash outlet for growers. They constitute the link between many producers on one hand, and wholesale markets on the other. It is their task to establish those numerous and intricate business relations with dealers in the wholesale markets on one hand, and with producers on the other. There are four principal classes of middlemen operating in the local markets: (1) private resident buyers; (2) local farmers' cooperatives; (3) traveling buyers; and (4) local auctions. Of course, the proportion of product shipped by each class of middlemen will vary with the market. For example, oranges produced in California typically enter the marketing channel through a farmers' marketing cooperative. Grain more often enters the marketing channel through a private elevator. And an increasing number of meat animals are entering the marketing channel by sale to local truckers who ship them direct to interior packers.

But farmers sometimes dispose of their products through other local outlets. Producers, in some cases, sell directly to consumers, either by peddling their products from house to house or from roadside markets. On occasion, farmers sell directly to chains, restaurants, and institutions. On other occasions, they sell directly to manufacturers or make direct shipments to commission merchants in wholesale markets. Thus, the four classes of local agencies described above do not constitute the only ways by which farmers dispose of their products. To repeat, however, those four types of agencies constitute the principal ways.

Central markets in food and agriculture, sometimes known as terminal markets, are preeminently concerned with the broad processes of concentration, equalization, and dispersion. These are the markets to be found in cities, located strategically between producing and consuming areas, in which the means of transportation converge as in a spiderweb. Chicago, Kansas City, and Buffalo are representative of these important central wholesale markets.

These central wholesale markets must be the focal point of the major transportation facilities. This is clearly the case with Chicago, where most railroads find a terminus, where water transportation meets the rails, and where good highways lead trucks. Here also are to be found the great storehouses, credit agencies, commodity exchanges, and other institutions requisite to successful marketing. Because of their strategic location, their improved facilities, and the large volume of consumption in the immediate area, buyers come to look upon these markets as basic sources of supply. The bulk of some farm products flows through these narrow points; hence, buyers and sellers concentrate at these points to conduct their business. These markets represent the final point of concentration and the initial point of dispersion. And in these markets the basic equalization decisions are made.

In recent years, the terminal markets have experienced a reduction in the proportion of some products handled. For example, in 1925 80 to 90 percent of all livestock was marketed through terminal markets. By 1960, only 30 to 40 percent flowed through terminal markets, and by 1970 it had fallen to 15 percent of calves, 20 percent of hogs and sheep, and 30 percent of cattle. Better transportation, market reporting, and dispersed processing facilities have speeded these trends and made terminal markets for some commodities obsolete.

The retail market forges the final link in the marketing process. The service of retailing is often looked upon from the point of view of the consumer. The retailer, in this view, is the purchasing agent of the consumer. He anticipates consumer needs, assembles the products that the consumer desires, and serves them up in quantities that the consumer can use. The farmer tends to overlook this final act in the flow of products from farm to city. He tends to ignore this step, concentrating his attention on marketing steps closer to him. But to ignore the retailing link may constitute a major error. The cost of retailing is by far the largest single item in the total marketing spread. For some commodities, it absorbs half of all marketing charges, and on the average amounts to nearly 40 percent of total marketing charges.

Commodities may be sold at retail level in several ways: (1) through retail stores; (2) through restaurants and other eating places; (3) through mail-order houses; (4) house-to-house; and (5) by automatic vending. We could discuss each of these ways at some length, but we wish to concentrate on the modern retail food market, whether chain or independent. Private grocery chains grew very rapidly in the 1920s. It is estimated, for example, that the Great Atlantic & Pacific Tea Company increased its number of stores from 5,217 in 1922 to 15,737 in 1931. To survive the intense competition offered by chain systems in the 1930s, independents affiliated with each other in voluntary buying organizations to reap the benefits of large-scale buying and advertising. The growth of affiliated buying organizations and grocery buying cooperatives in the 1930s and 1940s was almost as spectacular as the earlier chain-store development. During the 1950s and 1960s, the affiliated independents and chains continued their growth, so that in 1970 each group had over 45 percent of total sales, with less than 10 percent remaining for the unaffiliated independents.[1]

But the issue is not simply chains versus independents. It is the absolute level of concentration. In 1970, the top ten food chains had nearly 30 percent of the total retail food sales in the nation. The next fifty firms had 17 percent of the sales, and the remaining 53 percent of total sales went to firms operating 88 percent of all food stores. We will discuss this issue in more detail in the next chapter.

MARKETING FUNCTIONS

In the foregoing discussion of markets, we met certain of the functions undertaken in the marketing system. Whatever mention was made of these functions, however, was fragmentary and incomplete. Hence, it seems useful at this point to set forth in outline those services, often referred to as marketing functions, that business firms undertake in the marketing system. Much thought has been given to the analysis of the marketing functions, and it is possible to classify these functions in different ways, depending upon the purpose of the study. In fact, many different classifications may be found in the literature dealing with marketing. But some classification must be settled upon, and the following one would seem to be inclusive and useful for our purposes:

Marketing Functions

A. Exchange functions
   1. Buying
   2. Selling
B. Physical handling functions
   1. Assembling

[1]Data in this and the following paragraph derived from *Progressive Grocer*, April 1971.

    2. Standardizing and grading
    3. Storing
    4. Transporting
    5. Dividing and packaging
C. Facilitating functions
    1. Financing
    2. Risk-bearing
    3. Providing market information
D. Processing[2]

Let us now discuss each of these functions briefly. It is important to see how and where each of these functions forms an integral part of the total farm marketing system.

Exchange Functions: Buying and Selling

One is tempted to say that buying and selling are simply different sides of the same transaction, for in every transaction in which goods and services are exchanged there must be a buyer and a seller. But in marketing, the function of buying differs considerably from the function of selling. Let us consider the case of a small independent grocer in New York City. The function he performs in buying is quite different from that of selling, when he rises early in the morning and goes down to the Hunts Point terminal market to purchase fresh fruits and vegetables to sell in his retail establishment during the day. He goes to Hunts Point, first to purchase fruit and vegetable items that his clientele wants, and second to acquire them at a price that will permit him to make a net return on each item handled. Thus, he moves throught the market looking, selecting, and purchasing in a discriminating way to acquire just those items at the prices that will move them through his store during the day at a profit.

Now, let us observe this independent grocer in his selling function. In the first place, he has acquired a volume of fruits and vegetables that he must sell. He displays these fruit and vegetable items and prices them in such a way as to make them move. Further, he reminds his customers that certain items are in stock, that they are of good quality, and they represent economical buys. In short, he does everything with in his power to move that stock during the day, even to the possible extent of revising prices.

The transaction between wholesaler and retailer and the transaction between retailer and customer each represents an identity: in each case, the seller receives in money exactly what the buyer gives up, and vice versa, for the goods. But certainly, our retailer has performed a different service in his

---

[2]There is some debate as to whether processing should be included here; whether it is, in fact, a marketing function. Perhaps it is not a true marketing function as it is concerned with the provision of form utility, rather than time and place. But we include it here because it plays such an important part in the moving of farm produce from the farm to the consumer.

purchasing operations than he has in his selling operations. In the American economy, the impetus to exchange goods falls, in large part, on the seller. Hence, throughout the marketing process, we find that the selling function assumes an aggressive and driving character, whereas the buying function tends to be selective and discriminatory. At all stages in the marketing process, we find salesmen relentlessly seeking out prospective purchasers and purchasers hanging back, seeking better conditions of sale, better quality at the same price, and lower prices. In sum, different motives are at work in the selling function than in the buying function, and different services are provided.

Assembling

Assembling is concerned with gathering together farm products at a central point, in the country or city. Assembling at country points often occurs because an individual grower does not have enough produce to fill out a freight car or truck. By assembling the output of several farms, cars may be filled immediately and shipped to distant markets. Assembling at country points is also necessary to bring together sufficiently large quantities of a product to interest buyers in coming to that local point. Shipping point auctions, for example, are organized for the primary purpose of collecting at one point sufficient produce to meet buyers' demands, thereby attracting those buyers.

Wholesale markets in large cities require a constant supply of a wide variety of products. These products must be assembled from diverse producing areas to provide retailers with a certain source of supply of the wide variety of commodities demanded by their customers. The process of assembling is also performed by retailers, who assemble a wide variety of food products in one store so that consumers may make all their food purchases in one place. Thus, assembling commodities occurs at all stages of the marketing process, *and we should not confuse the function of assembling with the broader process of concentration and dispersion.* Assembling takes place in the early process of concentration and in the later process of dispersion.

Standardizing and Grading

This function has to do with such activities as the establishment of standards, the maintenance of standards, and the sorting of products into lots conforming to established standards. The latter two of these activities are often referred to as grading. It is evident, however, that all three activities are closely related and have as their objective the realization of those advantages to be derived from marketing standardized products: the marketing of products whose unit characteristics, in a particular lot, are uniform.

When products are graded into uniform lots, in accordance with defined standard grades, they can be bought by sample or even description. In these cases, it is not necessary for a buyer to inspect an entire lot of produce to know what he is getting. Graded products may be sold by description over the phone or by letter, thereby facilitating the marketing process.

Grading also enables agencies and individuals in the marketing process to obtain the grade of products they seek. Some groups may want only high-quality products and are willing to pay for that quality. Others may seek lower-quality products in order to obtain them at lower prices. Graded products make it possible to satisfy both groups, whereas ungraded products would satisfy neither.

Some grading is done for almost every farm product. Produce that is obviously spoiled or is otherwise unfit for consumption must be removed from the lots in which they are found. To be most effective, however, grading must be carried out in accordance with well-established standards. Grade specifications have been established for practically all important agricultural products by the United States Department of Agriculture and the various state departments of agriculture. The grade specifications exist; it is left for the farmer to decide whether or not it will pay to grade his product.

Storing

Wherever farm products are assembled for sale, we find storage facilities. At country shipping points, we find all types of storage facilities: grain elevators, potato warehouses, cotton warehouses, fruit packing warehouses, vegetable packing sheds, and refrigeration rooms in creameries. Wholesale houses must have storage facilities, and retailers of course have their stores in which they stock, display, and move their goods. From one end of the marketing system to the other, we find storage facilities. No other type of facility is so omnipresent. And by reason of these storage spaces, vast and small, the marketing system is able to engage successfully in that complex process of equalization. These storage spaces, which are continuously filled and drained, make possible the physical adjustment of supplies to demand.

Storage permeates every nook and cranny of the marketing system and is involved in practically every operation undertaken in the marketing system. Once produced, products spend most of their time in storage awaiting some new operation: handling, processing, or transporting. Storage is the great matter-of-fact function in the marketing system providing time utility.

Transporting

Transportation provides place utility. By means of transportation, we place products where we need or want them. The development of modern means of transportation has permitted specialization in production. And specialization in production has given rise to the modern, interdependent economy. Thus, we might say that the development of cheap transportation is, in fact, responsible for the highly complex marketing system that we have today.

Railroads have had an important influence on the location of production in agriculture and upon the marketing of farm products. The development of refrigerated railway cars in the 1890s represented a tremendous innovation in transportation, with far-reaching consequences for agriculture. Prior to this, perishable products could be produced only within the immediate areas surrounding large centers of population. With the development and use of refrigerator cars, it became possible to locate the production of perishable products in areas best suited to their production. Tomatoes and lettuce could be produced in the Imperial Valley of California and transported to the eastern seaboard. The location of fruit and vegetable production has moved far from the centers of urban population to the South and Southwest. The development of refrigerator cars also made it possible to establish meat-packing plants in the Midwest, closer to the supply of animals, with the result being that fresh meat rather than live animals is shipped East.

The continued improvement of the highway transportation system and the development of faster, larger-capacity trucks have had a greater influence on the farm marketing system in recent years than any other single factor. Trucks provide low-cost hauling to nearby assembling points and markets. The advent of larger trucks and better roads has enabled farmers to haul their products further distances, thereby leading to the demise of some of the smaller country assembly points. Local livestock shipping associations that assembled livestock for rail shipment have disappeared, and direct trucking to markets and packing houses now flourishes.

Air cargo transportation has just begun to make an impact on agricultural marketing, but it is apparent that with "jumbo jets" and the resulting reduction in costs air transport will have an important future role in marketing. A major part of the California strawberry crop is already moved to eastern cities by air. The change to air transportation will be especially important for high-value, perishable commodities, for which air transport may actually lower net unit transport costs through higher quality and less spoilage.

Dividing and Packaging

It has already been pointed out that products must be assembled at different stages in the marketing system for efficient movement and for the convenience of buyers. The final consumer, in most cases, makes purchases in small lots or quantities. Therefore, the marketing function of dividing and packaging is a counterpart to assembling. Division into wholesale lots, remember, was one of the major services provided by operators in central wholesale markets. And jobbers in smaller markets have as their principal function the breaking down of car-lot shipments into smaller lots that retailers can use. For example, it is the principal function of wholesalers and jobbers in fruit and vegetable terminal markets to divide car-lot shipments into the smaller portions that retailers are able to sell through their stores in one day (or another brief period). Sometimes, the final packaging is done in the stores, but to an increasing extent, for many commodities, it is done in the field by the producer or by the initial assembler. Prepackaging at an early stage of marketing saves time and money at the retail level. Still, retailing firms find their main reasons for being in (1) the purchase of relatively large lots and (2) the sale of relatively small lots.

Financing

From the time products leave the farm until they reach the consumer, someone's funds are tied up in them. Farmers could finance the entire marketing operation by waiting to be paid until after their products were sold to the final consumer. But this is impracticable and undesirable from the farmer's point of view. On sending his product to market, the farmer wants to get his money as soon as possible, and ordinarily he does not have to wait long. The local grain elevator usually pays him in cash, the dairy sends him a check once a month, and he is paid at the time of sale in local livestock auctions.

It is the middleman who bears the brunt of financial operations. It is he who purchases farm products, places them in storage, and feeds them out as demand requires. And it is this accumulation and maintenance of inventory that creates a financing problem. For during the period that stocks are held in storage, the middleman has his funds tied up in those stocks. But middlemen usually do not possess sufficient free funds to finance such inventory operations. They obtain their funds from banks and other sources of credit. Thus, interest on funds tied up in stored products becomes a necessary and unavoidable marketing cost. Financing is a service indispensable to the holding of stocks, but financing is attained only at a cost: the cost of money borrowed to finance the purchase and the holding operations.

Risk-bearing

Whoever takes title to products moving through the marketing processes also takes risks. The farmer runs a risk when he buys livestock to feed, or when he stores potatoes in his cellar. He does not know what will happen to price between the current date and the time of sale.[3] It is possible too, that uncertain weather will interrupt his feeding operations, or that his potatoes will spoil. In short, there are many types of physical risks that the farmer, or any operator who takes title to products in the marketing process,

---

[3]It is assumed here that prices are not fixed or supported by government.

must consider. But it is the price risk that causes the most trouble. This type of risk permeates the entire marketing system. Prices are forever changing or fluctuating, and there is little that any one individual operator may do to influence these price changes, although it should be kept in mind that prices can go up as well as down. During periods of falling prices, middlemen may realize losses that cause them financial difficulty and even bankruptcy. But during periods of rising prices, profits accumulate on goods held in storage through no effort on the part of the middleman.

Various devices are used to shift or spread risk. For certain commodities, such as wheat and cotton, farmers can get government non-recourse (price-support) loans. Here the government bears the full cost of protecting farmers against price declines. Farmers redeem the loans and sell the product when prices are good, but permit the government to take title to the commodity at the loan maturity date when market prices are below the loan rate.

Another device is to sell products for later delivery. A wheat miller may sell flour to bakeries for later delivery at the price prevailing when he bought the wheat. The deferred delivery period might be thirty days to six months, depending on buyers' needs and willingness to run the risk of falling prices.

A more widely used device is the buying and selling of futures contracts on commodity exchanges. All individuals or firms holding agricultural commodities for which futures markets are available may guard—"hedge"—against price changes in that way. Essential marketing services are performed by the people who run a futures exchange and enforce its trading rules, the brokers who act as agents on the floor of the exchange, and the speculators who assume the risks and thus make hedging possible.

Providing Market Information

Decisions to buy and sell are based on market information, good or bad. Thus, an important function in marketing is the collection and interpretation of market information. By this, we mean the collection of information dealing with quantities moving in trade; market price quotations for the previous hour, previous day, previous week, or other periods; weather conditions; government operations; and other factors. Some individuals base their decisions on information collected by themselves or on personal hunches. Some firms pay private agencies to collect information of an exclusive nature for them. But most individuals, farmers, and middlemen operating in the market depend upon the federal government for their basic market information. The United States Department of Agriculture maintains a far-flung system of crop reporting and market news reporting on which almost everyone in the market relies. Periodically, the department issues reports describing the condition of crops and storage holdings on hand, and daily it releases to radio stations and newspapers current information on prices received in the various markets and quantities moved to these markets. This is the basic information used by farmers and middlemen in making their decisions to buy and sell.

Processing

Processing is, in effect, manufacturing. For some reason, we describe those operations in food and agriculture concerned with changing the form of agricultural products by the term *processing,* whereas in other fields we describe the operation that changes the form of the product as *manufacturing.* But in either case, it is the form of the product that is changed. This is in contrast to the functions discussed above. All those were concerned with the movement of farm products through space and time. Processing, in contrast, changes the form of products. Some farm products reach the consumer in much the same form as they were produced on the farm: eggs, apples, and cabbages are examples. But these products, too, may be processed. We now have dried eggs and frozen eggs. Apples are canned, dried, frozen, or processed into cider and other products. And cabbage, we know, sometimes ends up in sauerkraut. Thus, processing is important for even those commodities that we usually do not think of as being processed.

Processing arises, in part, from the obvious fact that we cannot consume most farm products in the form in which they come from the farm. This, clearly, is the case for such farm products as livestock, wheat, and cotton. It is the perishability of farm products, however, that gives rise to much of the processing. It is the perishability of milk, of fruits and vegetables, and of meat products that forces some type of processing in each of these cases. Because farm products often do not come to market at the time when consumers need them, they must be stored and fed into the market as consumer demand develops, which means that perishable food products must be processed. Thus, the characteristic quality of all foods, namely perishability, makes processing an indispensable part of those activities to be found in moving products from farm to city.

THE FIRM IN THE MARKETING PROCESS

The impression may have been formed from the preceding discussion that the marketing system, in some vague way, undertakes to provide the various services necessary to effective marketing. If that is true, we have fostered a false impression. The various services described above must be provided, but the loose structure we call the marketing system certainly does not *undertake* the provision of these services. Individual business firms, operating within the marketing system, *undertake* the provision of these services. The provision of services (perhaps storage, perhaps financing, perhaps selling) represents the "product" of these firms. These marketing services are provided at a cost and, in the usual case, add value to the product. We must remember that the provision of such services as assembly, storage, or transportation create value just as certainly as the original productive act of form creation. Apples grown in the state of Washington are not consumable apples to New Yorkers until they are transported to New York and dispersed to those consumers. So we get the picture: business firms constitute the operating units in the marketing system; it is they who undertake to provide the services necessary to effective marketing; in doing so, they incur costs and create value in the products handled by them.

The analysis of the marketing firm is the same as that presented for the farm firm in Chapter 4. The marketing firm seeks to maximize its profits at all times. To this end, it is continually varying the factors of production under its control in an effort to realize not the least cost output but the maximum profit output. In a rigorous sense, the firm achieves this goal by applying units of a variable factor of production (for example, day laborers) to the fixed combination of factors (such as the building, storage space, equipment and fixtures, business office, management), to that point at which the cost of the added output just equals the selling price of the last unit of product. Or in a more flexible sense, the firm balances off expected increases in cost against expected increases in income from the employment of some variation of past production methods. And when the firm finds the change to be advantageous, it adopts the new practice.

Two dissimilarities between the farm firm and the marketing firm do, however, need to be pointed out. In the first place, as already noted, the "product" of the marketing firm is usually a service. Hence, it is difficult to apply a marginal analysis to the marketing firm, the *output* of which is not readily measurable. The output of the farm is easily measured in bushels or pounds, or some other standard measure, but how do you measure the output of a service, such as selling or storage? Certainly, not in terms of the number of units of product handled. Those units represent the product of the farm firm and a cost to the wholesale firm. The output of the wholesale firm may be measured only in terms of the *value added* to the units handled, for the *services* provided. But this leaves us without a physical measure of output. In the second place, a relatively large proportion of the costs of the farm firm are fixed costs, whereas a relatively large proportion of the costs of a merchandising firm are variable, out-of-pocket costs. Most of the costs of a merchandising firm vary directly with the volume of product handled; labor and inventory charges vary directly with the volume of business. Thus, marketing firms that buy and sell produce tend to have high mortality rates.

Marketing firms operating at the wholesale and retail levels usually apply some "rule-of-thumb" markup to each batch of merchandise purchased. This markup is designed to cover average unit costs, plus some measure of profit, but it cannot be maintained when it comes into conflict with competitive price relationships. If the firm has paid too much for its product or prices fall, the firm will be forced to sell at the competitive price regardless of the desired markup. Thus, one or two bad business decisions or market reverses, which send cash costs soaring above cash receipts, may put the firm out of business.

Our point is that marketing firms constitute the operating units of the marketing system. Through these operating units flow two streams: the product stream and the financial stream. The decision by a wholesale firm to purchase a given quantity of a farm product moving in the marketing channel acts to propel that quantity of product forward to the consumer and money receipts backward to the farmer. The original consumer expenditure becomes cash receipts for the retailer, who holds out a small portion as income for services rendered by him. He, in turn, by the decision to buy inventory from a wholesaler, makes payment to that wholesaler of most of the expenditure made by the consumer. The wholesaler takes a slice of those receipts as income for the services provided by him and by a decision to purchase products from a farmer directs the remaining receipts back to the farmer. So the simple pipeline approach, with a goods stream moving in one direction and a money stream in the other, must be modified. These streams move through operating units—marketing firms—and the flows are maintained only insofar as transactions are made.

POINTS FOR DISCUSSION

1. What do we mean by *marketing*?
2. Why is marketing unimportant in primitive economies?
3. What are the causes of the highly complex farm marketing system in the United States?
4. What do we mean by *concentration, equalization,* and *dispersion*? In what sense are these processes particularly important in agriculture?
5. What is a market?
6. What kinds of markets are encountered in the movement of farm produce from the producers to the consumer?
7. List the principal marketing functions. Are all these functions necessary, or could some of them be dispensed with? If the latter is the case, which ones could best be eliminated? Would you say that storage and transportation, which provide time and place utility, are less important than processing, which creates form utility?
8. Who undertakes to provide these functions in the marketing system? What is the "product" of the marketing firm?

REFERENCES

DOLL, J. P., V. J. RHODES, AND J. G. WEST, *Economics of Agricultural Production, Markets and Policy,* Chaps. 13 and 17. Homewood, Illinois: Richard D. Irwin, Inc., 1968.

Implication of Changes (Structural and Market) on Farm Management and Marketing Research. Center for Agricultural and Economic Development Report 29, Iowa State University, 1967.

KOHLS, R. L., AND W. D. DOWNEY, *Marketing of Agricultural Products,* 4th ed., Chaps. 1 and 2. New York: The Macmillan Company, 1972.

SHEPHERD, GEOFFREY S., AND GENE A. FUTRELL, *Marketing Farm Products,* 5th ed., Chaps. 1 and 2. Ames, Iowa: Iowa State University Press, 1969.

Chapter 8

The Changing Structure

of Farm Markets[1]

The farm marketing system, and the structure of markets within that system, has been changing in America since the earliest colonial times. All the components of economic development—population growth, migration between economic sectors and geographic areas, technological development and adoption, territorial expansion, and changing human wants and the ability to satisfy those wants—acting and interacting have produced a state of continuous change in the farm marketing system. And we can expect the working of most of these same forces to give rise to further changes, probably rapid and dramatic changes, in the farm marketing system in the second half of the twentieth century. Thus, we should not conclude that the institutional and structural changes of the 1940s, 1950s, and 1960s that are considered in this chapter are unusual or unique. They have been and are important, but they are simply the most recent in a continuum of important changes.

It is also difficult to isolate the important current developments and appraise the significance of such developments. Hence, all observers would not describe and evaluate the changing farm marketing system in exactly the same way, or as we have done. But the big issues and the causal forces in the drama of change are laid out for all to see; perhaps the interpretation is open to debate.

[1]This chapter is adapted and updated from the article by Willard W. Cochrane, "Changing Structure of the American Economy: Its Implications for the Performance of Agricultural Markets," *Journal of Farm Economics*, May 1959.

Concentration at the Retail Level

Numerous writers, particularly Mehren, Collins, Mueller, and Davis, have pointed out that some exciting and far-reaching changes have occurred during the past twenty years, and continue to occur, in the farm marketing system. Many of these changes have occurred at the retail level, but certainly not all. And it may be that, after the excitement of current developments has died away, the most dramatic changes will appear to have occurred near the farm level. But it is the thesis of this chapter that the key, causal changes in the food marketing system are occurring at the retail level, and it is the task of this chapter to describe these causal changes at the retail level and trace their consequences through the rest of the farm marketing system.[2]

The large stores or supermarkets,[3] making up some 18 percent of all grocery stores in 1970, made 75 percent of the total sales. Superettes made 13 percent of the sales volume with 16 percent of the stores. This left the remaining 66 percent of the stores—the small ones—with only 12 percent of the market. Concentration of sales in the large stores has increased substantially over the past thirty years. In 1940, supermarkets had 25 percent of sales, in 1952 they had 43 percent of sales, and by 1957 they had 67 percent of sales. Their gains have been slowed since then.

The gains of supermarkets have been slowed since about 1960 by two factors. One is the simple fact that they already have the bulk of the retail food business. The second is the emergence of small convenience stores. These units carry only a few thousand items, have three or four employees, and specialize in frequently purchased items like dairy and bakery products. Although still very small in terms of total sales, convenience stores are the most rapidly growing sector of the food industry.

Prior to 1960, it appeared that the issue of chain versus independents had been settled at a standoff. Chains had 35 percent of the total sales in 1940, 37 percent in 1950, and 38 percent in 1960. However, by 1970 the chains had nibbled another 10 percent of total sales away from the independents (Table 8–1). The big losers have been the unaffiliated independents. They had about one-third of the market in 1940, but this has since declined to about 8 percent. The affiliated independents, which have some of the volume buying and private brand advantages of chains, did well until 1960 but have slipped somewhat since then.

---

[2]Much of the argument and many of the analytical points of this and the following section grow out of the work of George L. Mehren and Norman R. Collins. See particularly the article by Mehren entitled "Market Coordination and Buyers' Requirements," *Policy for Commercial Agriculture,* Joint Committee Print. 85th Cong., 1st Sess.; and the article by Collins and Jamison, "Mass Merchandising and the Agricultural Producer," *Journal of Marketing,* April 1958.

[3]The data on number and sales come from *Progressive Grocer,* April 1971. Their definitions are: Supermarket, any store chain or independent doing $500,000 or more business per year; superette, any store doing from $150,000 to $500,000 business per year; small store, any store doing less than $150,000 business per year.

TABLE 8–1

Number of Stores, Total Sales, and Percentage of Total Sales to Affiliated, Unaffiliated, and Chain Stores, in Retail Grocery Business, 1940–1970

| | | Percent of Total Sales | | | Total |
Year	Total Number of Stores	Affiliated Independents	Unaffiliated Independents	Chain Stores	Sales (million $)
1940	446,350	30	34	35	9,010
1950	400,700	33	30	37	27,090
1960	260,050	49	13	38	51,700
1970	208,300	44	8	48	88,415

Source: The *Progressive Grocer*, April 1971.

It might be reasoned that some sort of oligopsonistic market model,[4] with the resulting less-than-competitive equilibrium prices and quantities for farmers and excessive profits for the buyers (such as supermarkets), could be used to describe the performance of markets between farm and retail. But such a model does not seem to fit the facts of the situation for several reasons. First, the foremost plank in the market policies of large-scale retail grocery firms is *increased volume*—increased volume is viewed as the direct avenue to profit maximization. All readily observable market practices are geared to sales expansion—not to supply control nor to market restrictionism.

Second, although a great concentration process has been going on in the retail food trade in recent years, the market structure of the trade most certainly cannot be characterized as "competition among the few." In 1954, there were some 34,000 retail firms with two or more establishments, and this number has not changed greatly since that year. Furthermore, the relative gains of chains (defined as firms with eleven or more stores) since 1960, in terms of the proportion of total food sales, does not suggest that a few giant chains are about to take over the food trade. In fact, the chains with from fifty to ninety-nine stores experienced roughly twice the increase in sales as did the largest chains (with five hundred and more stores).

Third, the product flows (the marketing channels) from farmer-producer to food-retailer are so complex and so diverse that monopsony power cannot easily be brought to bear on suppliers. The extreme bottleneck situation into which product flows converge, around which a formal market develops and in which implicit or explicit collusion leads to monopsonistic buying practices to the disadvantage of the supplier, is hard to find in the farm marketing system.

The product flow combinations and diversifications that exist in the

---

[4]An oligopsonistic market or oligopsony situation is one in which there are only a few buyers. A monopsony is a market in which there is a single buyer. We will consider these terms in greater detail in Chapter 12.

farm marketing system may be illustrated if we consider what happens to eggs, a relatively uncomplicated product to market. First, some proportion of all eggs produced are consumed on farms. Another small but observable share is peddled by producers directly to consumers. Some eggs move up through dairy and other marketing cooperatives as a side line and are sold to other marketing agencies at various levels of the marketing system. An important share of the supply of eggs moves through egg-marketing cooperatives, sometimes as a differentiated, trademarked item for consumer selection, sometimes to be sold to various marketing agencies at different levels of the marketing system. Some eggs are sold by producers to local, private buyers—often truckers—who in turn sell them to different marketing agencies. Some producers sell directly to retailers or chains. Other eggs go back to hatcheries, and so on. The possible flow and outlet combinations appear to be limitless. In this situation, the large-scale retailer must find it virtually impossible to pursue monopsonistic pricing policies; such policies vigorously pursued over any length of time would eliminate his source of supply.

Retail Procurement Policies and Changes in Market Structure. An independent food retailer with about six supermarkets, each grossing $1 million a year, *does, however, have market power.* And a retail chain with one hundred such supermarkets has even greater market power. This power grows out of the fact that such firms provide an important market outlet for a given product supplier. The supplier *wants* to place his product on, and hold it on, the store shelves of such important market outlets. This is a matter of survival to the supplier in the competitive struggle for product space on the limited shelves of the self-service store. Out of this market situation, the retailer derives power, albeit limited power; and based on this limited power, the retailer develops and pursues independent procurement policies. This, according to Mehren, is the preeminent development in retailing in recent years.[5]

The question before us, then, is: what do such limited market power and resulting policies convert into, with respect to marketing practices? This can best be answered by inquiring into the merchandising goal, or goals, of the food retailers in question. The obvious answer is profit maximization. But this general goal is not analytically helpful; we must be more specific. The overriding goal of modern large-scale food retailers is *increased volume.* The retailer seeks to expand sales as a means of increasing profits, and he seeks to do this in the cultural setting of great consumer mobility, one-stop shopping, self-service, and convenient visual inspection of food products. The means open to the retailer to expand sales in a highly competitive situation, where the possibility of price reductions are limited, are essentially two: (1) to present a product that by its taste, texture, coloring, packaging, or by

[5]*Op. cit.*, p. 291.

a combination of these qualities, impels the consumer to pick it up and place it in her basket; and (2) to present that eye-catching product regularly. A product, though desirable in quality and appearance, is next to worthless from a merchandising point of view if it is not offered to the consumer in a timely context (that is, regularly).

It follows, then, from the nature and objectives of the merchandising operation, that procurement policy must be aimed at acquiring a certain and regular supply of a product with desired quality attributes. The market power of large-scale food retailers is used to gain control over two variables: (1) time and conditions of delivery, and (2) quality and appearance attributes of the product. Food retailers insofar as they are able (that is, insofar as their power in the market permits) specify the content of these two product variables to suppliers.

The brunt of these procurement policies by retailers, of course, falls on the wholesalers with whom the retailers deal most directly. The wholesaling function has in no way been eliminated, or reduced, in recent years, but it has been more closely integrated with the retailing function—usually upon the initiative of retailers. Food retailers have acquired wholesaling facilities, joined cooperative wholesaling groups, and entered into contracts with private wholesaling firms in the furtherance of required procurement policy, namely, control over the product variables—time and conditions of delivery and quality and appearance attributes. The prosperity and adaptability of the "affiliated independent" sector of the retail food business has provided the main demand for the services of wholesalers. Many chain stores manage their own wholesaling. And this, of course, is what we mean by *vertical integration*: the coordination of the decision process in two or more steps of production through management action, rather than through the market.

In the 1940s and 1950s, it appeared that grocery wholesaling and independent retailing might disappear, but the wholesalers met the challenge of vertical integration by adopting many of the chains' marketing techniques. Since then, wholesalers have regained an increasing amount of chain-store business, especially among the regional chains. One reflection of their success is the fact that their sales increased 120 percent between 1958 and 1968, while total retail sales of chains and independents increased only 60 percent.[6]

A great integration battle in the food trade is currently being waged between the large-scale retailers and the national processors and packers. The question at issue is: who is going to integrate whom? There is no question in either camp as to the desirability, or survival value, of product differentiation, quality control, and product eye appeal. The national packers

[6]*Progressive Grocer, op. cit.*

and processors recognize that survival in an independent status rests on their ability to hold their national brands before the consumer. The large-scale retailers, on the other hand, recognize that control of their merchandising policy rests on the establishment of their own private brands and the specification of the quality attributes of their products, which means in turn the reduction of processors to the passive status of present-day wholesalers. Thus, the issue is joined and the outcome is in doubt. And, although it seems to the authors that a strategic advantage lies with the retailers in this power struggle, namely, control over the product outlet to consumers, it is not necessary to the argument of this chapter to pick, or even to know, who the final victor will be. Further, it is possible, perhaps even probable, that the combatants will accept a policy of "live and let live" in order to restrict the range of the battle and limit potential losses. In any event, the remaining large-scale independent marketing agents will push integration, and for identical reasons—the twin imperatives of procurement policy: control over time and conditions of delivery, and control over the quality and appearance attributes of the product.

The question may now be asked: why is the vertical integration of wholesaling and processing activities into the retailing organization essential to the control over the two product variables in question? Why cannot market price effect the necessary integration with respect to these variables? Collins and Jamison provide the answer in general terms:

> ...The complexity of the demand function plus the uncertainty surrounding interfirm relationships in general make it difficult, if not impossible, for the producer to translate a price quotation (particularly if this is only an estimate of a future price at time of harvest) first into the set of product characteristics that is implied and then in turn into a set of production operations to achieve this result.[7]

More specifically, market prices do not, and cannot, effect the integration between production stages required by modern retail merchandising policy first because of the uncertainty that attaches to future farm product prices, second because market prices fail to adequately evaluate and report desired and undesired quality attributes of a commodity, and third because quality and appearance attributes are assessed and valued differently among different retail firms. In other words, the process of acquiring through open markets a product with desired quality and appearance attributes and the required time specifications turns out to be an inefficient, costly business, as far as many agricultural commodities are concerned. Thus, to gain as complete control as possible over the two variables in question, large-scale retailers have acted and continue to act vigorously to integrate the wholesaling and processing functions into the retail organization.

[7]"Mass Merchandising and the Agricultural Producer." *Op. cit.*, p. 364.

Markets, providing a nexus between wholesaler and processor on one hand and retailers on the other, have never been noted for their formal structure or institutionalized procedures, and markets of an informal sort have existed in this marketing area. Wholesalers and processors historically have published price lists, and on the basis of such lists orders have been sought and taken. But even such informal markets are withering away under the impact of vertical integration. Purchase of facilities, merger, cooperative affiliation, and contracts are replacing the order taker. The operator of a few or a chain of supermakets feels that he cannot afford to wait and order what the order taker may have in stock when he comes around. Aggressive merchandising requires that the operator take the initiative to acquire and maintain in stock products that the consumer cannot resist plucking off the shelves and stuffing in his basket. In this milieu, the "open" market is passing out of existence.

Changes in Market Structure at the Farm Level

Let us now inquire into the extent to which retailer-initiated integration is bypassing local farmers' markets, to encompass farmers as well as middlemen. But first, we must recognize that vertical integration has long existed between the processor and the farmer in certain vegetable-canning crops, and it has come into prominence between processors and broiler producers in recent years. In these, and other instances that could be cited, the initiating force has come from the processor, or first-handler, and for the very same reasons as those outlined for retailers. Processors have long felt the need for quality control during the complex production and processing operations and the pressure to acquire a certain and regular source of supply of these products. Control over these variables by processors was a prerequisite to the establishment of national brands, and the widespread distribution of a product of a given quality. Thus, whether the large-scale retailers or the large-scale packers and processors win the integration battle, it seems clear that the production activities of farmer-producers will be increasingly integrated into the processing stage of marketing.

But to return to the question under consideration: is the integration of marketing activities, initiated by retailers, bypassing local markets and reaching farmer-producers? Although the vertical integration process comes unhinged to a great degree at the processing stage, at the present time—with many integration strands running from retailer to processor and fewer, different strands running from processor to farmer—large-scale retailers are beginning to integrate their procurement activities all the way back to the farmer, involving most often fresh fruits and vegetables but also eggs, poultry, and red meats. It is occurring wherever retailers have acquired their own handling or processing facilities, or where they clearly dominate small private processors. And it is facilitated at the farm level by large-scale producers, areas of product concentration, and an effective farmers' marketing cooperative.

The extent to which more farmer-producers are tied to processors and first-handlers through integration and the extent to which the operations of those farmer-producers are more closely integrated into the operations of processors and first-handlers depends upon at least two sets of factors: (1) those on the producer side; and (2) those on the processor-handler side.

The willingness of farmers to work under a contract rather than for an open market will depend upon their need for capital, which in turn will depend upon the general prosperity of agriculture. (It is assumed here that the contracting firm is able to supply the capital because if it could not, it would not be in business.) Also, it will depend upon the effectiveness of the contractual arrangement to reduce, or minimize, price and income risks to farmers. These factors will set the stage and determine the reception that forgers of the final link of integration will receive from farmers.

The initiating forces, as usual, will come from the supply procurement side and in large measure for the same reasons. The imperatives of (1) a certain and regular source of supply and (2) control over quality and appearance attributes will force the issue. And the greater the need to control these variables at the farm level, the greater the push to integrate the production activities of farmers with those of the processor or first-handler.

But other considerations may enter from the processor-handler side. If there are great opportunities to reduce product costs or to produce an eye-appealing product, through fundamental and complex changes in technological or institutional practices, processor-handlers may be expected to initiate such changes through integration. This process is complete in broilers. In recognition of the fact, U.S.D.A. suspended the reporting of live broiler prices in 1965 because the market volume was so small as to be nonrepresentative.

The process of integration has already progressed to the point where more than half of fluid milk, turkeys, vegetable seeds, hybrid seed corn, sugar crops, citrus fruits, and vegetables for processing are transferred under integrated or contractual arrangements. The practice is gaining ground in the meat industry. Meat packers contract with feeders for future delivery as well as buying and managing their own feedlot operations. From the input side, feed manufacturers have the incentive to integrate into the livestock-feeding process to assure themselves a market. In some cases, farmers' cooperative marketing associations may integrate forward to the retailer. In this context, institutionalized auction markets and less-formal local markets will wither away. In the future, farmers typically will not produce a product of uncontrolled quality for uncontrolled delivery to an open market. Instead, most farmers will produce a product to quality specifications for specific times of delivery. It is important to keep this movement in perspective, however. In 1967, less than one-third of farm production was coordinated by contract or integration—the rest still reacted directly to market prices.

Bargaining by Cooperatives and Other Farm Institutions. Farmers have long recognized their lack of market power and have attempted to offset it in part through cooperatives. Cooperative associations have played many roles on the agricultural scene: forcing competition, providing previously nonexistent marketing services, purchasing supplies, and bargaining. Some of these ventures have been highly successful—in those cases where the need was great, adequate financing was achieved, competent management was secured, and farmer-members understood the real problems confronting the association. Where these ingredients in some proportions have been lacking, the ventures have been less successful. But it is possible that farmers' cooperatives have yet to play their greatest role—as the business organizations representing independent farmers in the negotiation of (in the bargaining over) contracts with marketing organizations integrated from retailer down in many cases, and from processor down in still others. We hasten to add, however, that we attach no probabilities to this outcome (that is, the widespread seizure of this bargaining role by farmers' cooperatives). Institutional developments along this line will depend upon the extent to which farmers generally and clearly appreciate the nature of the marketing problem confronting them, and, more importantly, upon the extent and generosity of federal credit policies to farmers' cooperatives in the future. The activity of milk cooperative federations on bargaining for better prices may be the beginning of a trend for other commodities.

Whatever the ultimate success of this institutional development, the cooperative prototype, at first, is likely to be similar to the bargaining association that has been developed to confront sugar-beet processors and vegetable processors. But it is not likely to remain such a simple organization for very long. In some cases, it may develop its own processing facilities as in the case of fluid milk, and in some others it is likely to develop distributive facilities as in the case of the Sunkist Growers, Inc. Negotiation or bargaining may remain a central function of cooperatives, and to negotiate effectively they may have to establish product-handling, storing, and processing facilities.

On what kinds of issues will the cooperative be able to represent independent farmer-members effectively in negotiations with vertically integrated marketing organizations? Unfortunately, for farmers, it is unlikely that cooperatives will be able to effectively bargain about prices except in very special cases. More about those in a moment. There are many other issues, but they group nicely under two headings, our same two variables: (1) time and condition of delivery; and (2) quality and appearance attributes. With respect to the first variable, the following items must go into every contract in some form: the time schedule of delivery, method and schedule of payment, point of delivery, supply of harvesting and cartage equipment, and so on. With respect to the second variable, the following points must be settled: variety of seed or breeding stock, feeding rates and rations, disease and pest control, control of the harvesting schedule, and premium and discounts for variations in quality and appearance.

Negotiation over these variables may seem unglamorous to economists and disappointing to farmers, but there are many points to be negotiated with respect to each, and the *net* effect of these many decisions can be important to the farmer's pocketbook and to his self-respect. And, in theory at least, an intelligently managed and loyally supported farmers' cooperative should be able to negotiate effectively on these issues because no single issue is likely to be as important to the purchasing firm as the continued receipt of supplies from the cooperative in the desired time and quality dimensions. The large-scale retail organization with heavy demands for a product of given quality and delivery specification has an important stake in any particular source of supply that can, in fact, deliver the specified product. The cooperative gains limited power in the market—power to negotiate effectively with purchasing firms over issues of time and conditions of delivery and quality and appearance—as it becomes an important supplier to a purchasing firm of a product with given time and quality specifications. Thus, size achieved through collective action at the farm level brings with it some limited power to bargain. And cooperative marketing organizations are already important for some products. They market 85 percent of citrus and cranberries, 65 percent of dairy products, 40 percent of grain, and 25 percent of cotton, wool, and fruits and vegetables.

Bargaining for Higher Prices. There is another set of issues, however, on which local, state, or even national marketing cooperatives are not likely to be strong bargainers. Those issues relate to prices received by farmers. It is reasonable to assume that every produce buyer comes to the contract negotiation table with an upper price limit in mind—a reservation price based on all known supply and demand conditions. And it is reasonable to assume that a skillful and experienced cooperative negotiator could approximate the buyer's reservation price. But, the moment the cooperative pushes its selling price above the buyer's reservation price, the cooperative will have pushed itself out of that market. This follows from the fact that the purchasing firm can obtain its supplies from another cooperative, a large private producer, or by entering into agricultural production itself. Locating a new, desirable source of supplies would certainly prove annoying, and in all probability would involve some extra costs, but it could be done; that is the important point in this context. A higher-than-going price, or readily acceptable price, can only be made to stick where the purchaser does *not* have alternative sources of supply. And unless some general scheme of supply control is embraced by farmers with the aid of government, the typical integrated buyer will have many sources of supply for many years to come. Thus, the bargaining power of farmers' cooperatives, unless buttressed by state action as in the case of fluid milk, has been and will continue to be weak with respect to price. In the typical case, a farmers' cooperative cannot control supply; it is as simple as that.

Mueller has stated the proposition even more strongly:

> ...Once and for all let us recognize that vertical integration per se does not give a cooperative or any other firm market power. Market power is built of different stuff. It depends upon a high degree of horizontal concentration or product differentiation....[8]

Referring to such vertically integrated associations as Sunkist Growers, Inc., Sun Maid Raisin Growers, and Diamond Walnut Growers, each of which has marketed as much as 70 percent of its industry's supplies, Mueller goes on to say:

> ...None has the essential prerequisite of market power, the ability to limit supply.... Market power depends upon control over the supply of the product passing through the system, not just on ownership of the marketing facilities through which it passes....

The major general farm organizations as well as specific commodity groups are interested in the possibility of raising farm prices through bargaining. Their leaders recognize that the economic imperatives of effective bargaining for higher prices include: (1) effective control over product supply to sustain a higher market price; (2) the inclusion of all major farm commodities so that resource substitution does not weaken prices; and (3) an industry-wide bargaining approach to eliminate possible alternative sources of supply.[9] However, farmers and their organizational representatives have been unable to agree on a common course of action and thus have been unable to devise wide-ranging, effective bargaining procedures.[10] And there is some question whether farmers are ready to give up the personal economic freedom they would have to in order to obtain higher prices.

We have, in earlier sections, been describing a situation in which vertical integration is pushing its way back to the farmer, deriving the strength

[8]"Vertical Integration Possibilities for Agricultural Cooperatives," *The Frontiers of Marketing Thought and Science*, Proceedings of the December 1957 Conference of the American Marketing Association, Philadelphia.

[9]See papers by representatives of the Farmers Union, NFO, and Grange in: Center for Agricultural and Economic Development, *Bargaining Power for Farmers* (Ames, Iowa: Iowa State University Press, 1968).

[10]An interesting picture of the conflicts at work in the attempts to get farm groups to agree to a common course of action from: Randall E. Torgerson, *Producer Power at the Bargaining Table* (Columbia, Missouri: University of Missouri Press, 1970).

to do this from the operational goals and the capacity of large-scale processors or retailers to control the two merchandising variables. In this changing structure, the open, auction type of market is becoming a casualty. Production activities are, more and more, being integrated through contractual and ownership arrangements rather than through open markets. But in the last stage of integration, at the farmers' level, we witness the emergence of a new power, *a countervailing power,* in the form of farmers' joint action. This power is limited, as is the power at the retail level, which, it is the thesis of this chapter, started the whole integration business.[11] Market power is not absolute at either end of the line, nor can the agents involved control price at either end of the line. But farmers, acting through their cooperative associations—associations that we see existing already in fruits and vegetables and being talked about and initiated in hogs and other animal products—can use their limited market power to moderate and blunt, hence influence, actions taken by purchasing firms with respect to the variables of time and conditions of delivery and of quality and appearance attributes of the product.

A new type of market is, thus, beginning to take shape at the farm level—a bargaining market, in which farmers are using in some instances, and are learning to use in other instances, the limited power of cooperative action to countervail against the typically greater, but still limited, power of large-scale, vertically integrated purchasing organizations. It will remain a market so long as farmers remain independent agents. And they will remain independent agents in the tide of vertical integration so long as they manage and run their cooperative bargaining associations wisely.

Some Larger Questions Related to Changing Market Structure

In bringing this discussion to a close, let us touch briefly on two larger questions raised by the broadening and deepening of vertical integration. First, will the rational allocation of resources be impaired by the eroding of open markets and the overt prices generated in such markets. And second, will the farm surplus problem pass away, as a general problem, under the institutional complex envisaged above?

Some kind of a pricing system, market or accounting, that accurately describes the rates at which commodities are being traded one for another, and therefore describes the true alternatives open to the maximizing decision maker, is basic to the operation of a rational economic system. In our economy, market prices generated in open markets have typically provided this basic information. But, where products and services move through an integrated system under contractual and ownership arrangements, open

---

[11]The fact that vertical integration appears on the historical scene earlier at the processor level does not spoil the argument. It occurred at the processing level for the same reasons that it is occurring at the retail level. But integration stemming from retailer action is the general, classic case.

markets disappear, and market prices are not generated. Or they are formed on such a thin portion of the supply that the prices so generated are not representative, that is, they do not describe the true situation. (This has been the case in butter and egg markets for some years.) Hence, it is sometimes concluded that a rational allocation of productive resources is not possible in integrated sectors of the economy.

But this is not necessarily the case; accounting prices can serve as a basis of resource allocation. If, in the integrated farm marketing system, farmers' cooperatives would regularly report their contract prices, they would provide a part of the information required for the rational use of resources. If, further, the government collected and regularly reported supply information, including production, quantities contracted, and inventory data, all the price-quantity information prerequisite to rational resource allocation would be available. In the world of vertically integrated production activities, accounting prices *actually used* must take the place of market prices *actually generated*.

It has been argued on occasion that the general and chronic surplus problem of American agriculture would cease to exist in a vertically integrated farm marketing system. Perhaps so, but probably not. If our picture of the ultimate farm marketing system were one of three or four giant chains doing all the retail grocery business, with clean, integrated strands of productive activity stemming back from each retailer through the wholesaling and processing operation to the farmer in each food line, then, perhaps the surplus problem would be solved. Each of three or four large retail chains in this world could accurately gauge the total market for a food product and its (the firm's) share of the total market, and transmit this knowledge back through the system in the form of contracts to farmer-producers to yield the quantities necessary to fill out their shares of the market. In other words, where a few retailers share the total food market, they can know and stabilize their own shares and contract for just those quantities required to satisfy their shares. In this neat world, there can be no surplus problem; other problems, yes, but no surplus problem.

But is the farm marketing system likely to become so structured in the decade of the 1970s or even the 1980s? It seems doubtful. The farm marketing system seems destined to become integrated to an important degree through contractual and ownership arrangements within a decade or so. But it can remain a somewhat complex, disorderly affair under the dominance of such institutional arrangements. Certainly there are going to be several thousand retail firms for a long time to come. Some of these retail firms are going to integrate back to the farm level, others are not. Some independent processors and packers with well-integrated operations seem destined to stay in the picture. And some farmers' cooperatives are going to push toward the retailer with integrated operations.

In this institutional complex, market shares cannot be known, hence total contracted quantities cannot equal total retail sales in any given period except by chance or through inventory accumulation or de-accumulation. (It is assumed that supply control and sales quotas under governmental sponsorship do not exist.) In the context of market uncertainty with regard to shares of the market at all stages, farmers may be expected to produce on their own account, cooperatives will accept supplies not contracted for, and purchase contracts will remain flexible with respect to total quantities, in the event that sales in a particular commodity, or through a given firm, turn out to be greater than prior operational estimates.

In a context of market uncertainty, all agents in the marketing system will remain flexible in regard to quantities, and farmers will continue to produce in the hope of finding a market outlet. In this context, burdensome surpluses are a distinct probability, where the government seeks to support farm income. And if it does not, returns to farmers can be expected to be disastrously low for a long time to come because one of the important byproducts of vertical integration will certainly be a speed-up of an already revolutionary rate of farm technological advance.

POINTS FOR DISCUSSION

1. What dramatic changes have taken place in food retailing in the last two decades? How have these changes affected procurement policies of retailing firms? What influence have these new procurement policies had on the structure of markets?
2. Why are large-scale retailing firms so anxious to control the merchandising variables: (a) time and conditions of delivery; and (b) quality and appearance attributes of the product?
3. What specifically is happening to wholesalers and wholesale markets?
4. What is the major point at issue in the economic battle between the large-scale processors and the large-scale retailers? How is the battle turning out currently (that is, at the time you are studying the problem)?
5. What new role is being thrust upon farmers' cooperatives by market integration? How well are such cooperatives meeting the challenge?
6. Can comprehensive integration in food production and marketing solve the surplus problem in agriculture?
7. What are some reasons for general farm organizations taking an interest in bargaining in addition to the commodity organizations?

REFERENCES

"Agricultural Markets in Change," *Agricultural Economic Report 95,* U.S.D.A. (July 1966).

Center for Agricultural and Economic Development, *Bargaining Power for Farmers.* Ames, Iowa: Iowa State University, 1968.

COLLINS, NORMAN R., AND JOHN A. JAMISON, "Mass Merchandising and the Agricultural Producer," *The Journal of Marketing* (April 1958)).

"Contract Farming and Vertical Integration in Agriculture," *Agricultural Information Bulletin 198,* U.S.D.A. (July 1958).

Food from Farmer to Consumer. Report of the National Commission on Food Marketing, June 1966.

Progressive Grocer, monthly and annual summary issue.

Chapter 9

Marketing Services and Costs

It is often noted, sometimes with a note of despair but more commonly with implied criticism, that charges for marketing take a large share of the consumers' food dollar—about 60 percent in the 1970s. It is further noted that the marketing and processing charges on a basket of given food items have increased substantially over the past twenty years, while the farm value of those food items has declined. These developments are disquieting to many people—particularly to farmers and farm leaders. In this chapter, we will examine these trends in the context of the total economy and analyze the factors responsible for them.

Employment in Production and Distribution

The expanding role of distribution (marketing and processing) in the economy is reflected in the increased employment of workers in the distributive trades. In 1870, more than three-fourths of the laboring force of 13 million workers were engaged in the production of physical goods, and less than one-fourth was engaged in distribution and service activities. Agriculture alone, at that time, absorbed 7 million workers, or more than one-half the total laboring force.

The number of gainfully employed workers in agriculture continued to rise to about 11 million in 1910, but the proportion declined from 50 percent of the labor force in 1870 to 30 percent in 1910, then to about 5 percent in 1970. The declining relative importance of agriculture as an employer was part of an overall changing pattern of employment in the United States, which is documented in Table 9–1. The proportion of the labor force in the primary sector industries (agriculture, forestry, fisheries, and mining) has declined throughout the past century. The proportion of the labor force in the secondary (manufacturing) sector increased until 1950 but since then has decreased slightly. Thus, the proportion of the labor force employed in the production of physical goods has continuously fallen, while the proportion of the labor force in the tertiary sector (marketing and other services) has steadily increased.

TABLE 9–1

Sectoral Composition of the Labor Force, 1870–1970

	1870	1890	1910	1930	1950	1970
	(percent of those gainfully employed)					
Primary sector						
Agriculture	49.7	42.1	30.8	21.5	18.0	5.2
Forestry, fisheries, mining†	2.0	2.8	3.5	2.7	1.6	0.8
Secondary sector						
Manufacturing	17.4	20.0	22.4	22.7	27.6	26.3
Construction	5.8	6.0	6.2	6.3	4.2	4.4
Tertiary sector						
Wholesale and retail*	6.4	8.4	9.1	13.0	17.0	19.8
Other services	18.6	20.6	27.7	33.6	31.4	43.3
	(thousands of persons)					
Number gainfully‡ employed	12,920	23,740	36,730	47,400	55,148	74,416
Population over 14 years**		41,799	64,601	89,550	109,140	142,365
Total population	39,905	62,948	92,407	123,407	152,271	205,395

† For 1950 and 1970 includes only mining.
* Includes finance and real estate for 1870 and 1890.
‡ For 1950 and 1970 relates to number of employees.
** For 1950 and 1970 relates to population over 16 years.

Source: For years prior to 1950, *Historical Statistics of the Unites States*, Series A22, A34, A35, D1, D57–71, K73; for 1950 and 1970, *Statistical Abstract of the United States*, 1970, Tables 325, 351.

This pattern of change is the result of two forces related to the generally increasing real incomes that Americans have enjoyed over the past century of development. The first force is reflected in one of the "laws" of economics—Engels's law. It says that as real incomes of individuals increase, they will tend to spend a smaller proportion of their incomes on the necessities of life and a greater proportion on less-necessary expenditures. Thus, as incomes have increased, consumers in general have spent relatively less on primary products.

The second force has been the substitution of capital for labor in the primary and secondary sector. As capital is substituted for labor, the same amount of output can be produced with less labor, leading to a relative decline in employment in the sectors where the substitution is taking place most rapidly.

These forces have been especially strong in agriculture, but they have affected the other primary and secondary industries as well. A smaller and smaller proportion of the nation's laboring force is needed to produce raw materials and manufactured products and an increasing proportion is needed in transporting and distributing these goods and in providing personal services.

The Changing Role of the Home

Distribution is more important today than it was in 1870 because so many activities, once carried out in the home, are now undertaken in factories. Spinning and weaving have long since left the home. The ready-made clothing industry has, in large measure, taken the place of home sewing. The canning and preserving of fruits and vegetables and the baking of bread and pastries have been transferred from the home to the factory. The role of the home has changed; factories have replaced homes as producing units. And with this changing role, the number and extent of activities between the farm producer and urban consumer have increased.

Instead of selling the housewife staples, such as flour and sugar, to be processed into bread and pastries in the home, the retail grocer today must carry in stock a wide variety of *finished* products (seven thousand to nine thousand items in a modern supermarket) from which the housewife makes her selections. Most of these finished products, too, are purchased in small quantities by the homemaker. And the cost of marketing a variety of finished products in small quantities is greater than merchandising yard goods or one-hundred-pound sacks of flour.

The crowding of families into small city apartments with little or no storage space has made the dividing and packaging of foodstuffs an important phase of marketing. The emphasis on the hygienic preparation of food has further contributed to the packaging service, hence, to the higher cost. The grocer no longer sticks his hand into the pickle jar and fishes out a dill or two. On the contrary, dill pickles come in pairs, safely encased in a plastic wrapper. Today, then, we find the kitchen cupboard scantily stocked, with neat cartons of rice, sugar, coffee, and macaroni, encased in air-proof wrappings. Beside these cartons, we find the canned goods packed in conveniently small tins. Add to this a refrigerator and freezer stocked with a variety of fruits and vegetables and numerous small cuts of meat, and the picture is complete. But to concentrate this variety of foodstuffs in the home in convenient and attractive packages, merchants and distributors have had to assume new risks, accept new tasks, and incur additional costs.

The Revolution in the Kitchen. As average family incomes in the 1960s have pushed into and beyond the $7,000–$8,000 income range, they have changed their food habits. They spend their food dollars differently. They eat more expensive foods, of course; but what is significant to agriculture and to the marketing system is that they also demand and buy a lot of processing, packaging, and special services in their food. Instead of buying a whole chicken to be cut up and apportioned at home, they buy a package of frozen chicken breasts, or better still, go out for a chicken dinner. And instead of buying a bushel of apples to be stored in the basement, they buy six beautifully colored apples in an attractive carton. The modern American family wants not only good food *but convenience built into that food as well.*

At the same time as convenience foods have eased the housewife's task in the kitchen, more and more meals are being eaten away from home. In 1960, consumers spent $13 billion on food away from home. By 1970, this had increased 75 percent to $23 billion.[1] In the same period, expenditures on food for use at home increased only 58 percent. And that 58 percent increase in spending on food at home resulted mainly from more marketing services and higher prices. Most of the food purchased today is prepackaged. And an important share has been precooked and apportioned as well.

The American housewife substitutes these conveniences built into food items for nonexistent kitchen help and hours in the kitchen. Thus, the purchase of services or conveniences built into food products or meals prepared outside the home is now enabling the housewife to follow the cook and the maid in their flight from the kitchen.

Selling the Consumer

The creation of demand, selling the consumer, becomes increasingly more important as finished goods are produced by mass production. Unit costs of production are reduced through mass production only when large volumes are, in fact, produced and sold. Hence, the incentive to produce in large quantities and to realize low unit costs continually drives the businessman to expand his sales, to enlarge the market for his product, to convince more and more consumers that only his product is good. In broad terms, the consumer has permitted himself to be convinced, with the result that the material level of living has improved, as the fruits of mass production have been realized.

To understand the problems of marketing in a modern, interdependent economy, we must consider not only the *volume* to be marketed but the *nature* of new things to be marketed. The things that people want today are not necessarily things that the consuming public demanded on its own ini-

[1] *National Food Situation*, Economic Research Service, U.S.D.A., August 1971.

tiative. The automobile, color television, elaborately packaged foods, and the current style in women's clothing are not goods that consumers first wanted and that later were produced to their specification. On the contrary, those goods were first conceived and pioneered by producers, and then the demand for them was created by aggressive sales methods. This does not mean that producers can present anything they wish and induce the public to demand those commodities by an aggressive sales campaign. When new products are suited to their times, such as quick-frozen and packaged foods for families in small apartments, they have proved successful. Demand can be created and must be created for new products by selling activities, but success, in the sense of creating and expanding the market for a new product, is not achieved in every case, in fact, in only a relatively few cases.

Someone has to guess what to produce. In the usual case, consumers do not know and are not concerned with what their new wants may be and cannot tell manufacturers and distributors what they are. It is the task of innovators in manufacturing and marketing to seek out new wants and create products and services that satisfy the wants. It is in this sense that demand is created. And for the individual business firm, the problem is not one of filling the demand for cereals, clothes, or detergent, it is a problem of creating demand for a specific kind of cereal, a specific brand of clothes, and a specific kind of detergent. This type of demand creation is necessarily costly, but it goes hand in hand with the development of mass production techniques. Thus, sales promotion becomes an important and indispensable part of marketing when low unit costs of production are dependent on wide markets.

Competition and Service. Competition in production has most often had the effect of decreasing costs. But competition in distribution more often leads to increased costs. Success very often comes to the manufacturer and distributor who spend the most on advertising, packaging, delivery, and other expensive personal services. And efforts to cut costs are restricted by the inherent difficulties of mechanizing and standardizing marketing methods. Thus, competition in the marketing process does not tend to take the form of price competition. Competition in the marketing and distribution process, instead, often takes the form of the provision of additional services. Merchants seek to attract customers by offering additional services.

The consumer is the victim, as well as the beneficiary, of modern merchandizing. He appreciates improved service and is attracted to those retail outlets that provide the greater service, but greater service entails greater costs. Thus, the consumer, as indicated above, is responsible, in part, for the higher distribution costs that have resulted from the competition for his favor. Since about 1965, however, consumers have been acting, not just reacting, in response to marketing services. The retail food industry has been jarred by a wave of "consumerism"—consumer groups insisting on specific quality and pricing practices. Three issues have dominated these demands. Unit pricing, where the price per ounce or cup is posted as well as the price per package, has been advocated. Open dating of perishable products, which tells the buyer the last day the product can be sold and still keep for a reasonable period at home, is a second demand. Greater disclosure of nutritional information (as is now required on cereals) is a third goal of consumer groups.

The food marketing industry as a whole has resisted these moves, arguing that they would confuse rather than inform consumers and that they would raise costs. A few retailers have accepted the first two, and it appears these services will become more widespread. The third depends on the cooperation of processors and packers and may not occur without legislation. Like the added convenience and packaging, they will add to the total marketing costs, but they may prove worthwhile to consumers.

Food Processing

The food processing industry is one of the most technically dynamic components of the food marketing system. Innovations in food processing have transformed the shelves of U.S. supermarkets in the past twenty years, with every indication pointing to continued change. Frozen foods have become as familiar to today's housewife as cans were to her mother. Dehydrated foods are commonplace—dried skim milk, dried soups, and dried fruits. Freeze-dried coffee has taken a major share of the instant coffee market in the past few years.

New methods for processing food are likely to be commercialized during the next ten years. Arthur, Goldberg, and Bird estimate that by 1980 there is an 85 percent probability that food freezing by cryogenics will be in commercial use,[2] there is a 70 percent probability that dehydrofreezing and dehydrocanning will be in commercial use, and there is a 30 percent chance that irradiation sterilization will be in commercial use. And it is practically certain that the food technologists will have developed even newer, more exotic-sounding processes by 1980.

However, it is by no means certain that the new processes will be used simply because they are technically possible. Their cost in relation to the value of the food product to the consumer will be a major determining factor. Thus, freeze-dried coffee is already in high demand by housewives, but freeze-dried meat is sold only to the mountain-climbing backpacker who requires the ultimate in lightness and nonperishability.

Processing costs of four foods as a percentage of the consumer's dollar are illustrated in Figure 9–1. Processing costs for fresh beef are small because processing consists mainly of cutting, and also because some of the processing and packing costs are "hidden" in the retail component. Processed cheese is

---

[2]H. B. Arthur, R. A. Goldberg, and K. M. Bird, *The United States Food and Fiber System in a Changing World Environment*, Vol. IV of the Technical Papers of the National Advisory Commission on Food and Fiber, August 1967.

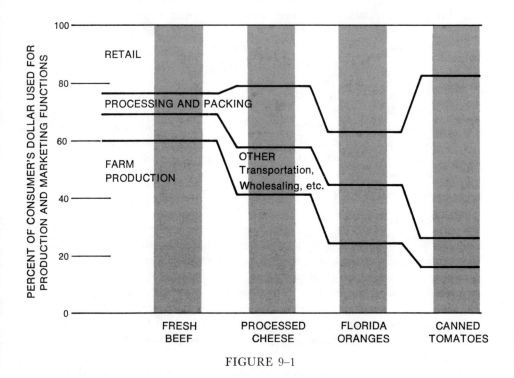

FIGURE 9–1

a somewhat more complex product, requiring relatively more processing. Florida oranges, nearly all made into juice, have about the same fraction of the retail price used for processing as does cheese. Canned tomatoes are at the far extreme—more than half the retail price is used to cover processing, with the farmer receiving a relatively small share.

Price Spreads Between Farmers and Consumers

Processing is but one component of marketing costs. Transportation and retailing are other major components, and as Figure 9–1 shows, the percentage of the consumer's dollar going to each of these differs for different products. In general, processing costs increase with perishability, transportation costs increase with bulkiness, and retailing costs increase with both. These relative differences in marketing costs for various foods are relatively constant, but the marketing costs for food in general do change over time.

In order to measure changes in the spread between retail prices of food, on the one hand, and payments to farmers, on the other, the U.S. Department of Agriculture combines farm products into what is known as the family "market basket." This basket is made up of a combination of food items that remains fixed over a relatively long period of time. The basket presently being used represents the average quantity of domestic food products bought per family by urban wage-earner and clerical-worker families in 1960 and 1961. These families had an average of 3.3 members in that year. With the quantities in this basket fixed, the cost of the basket changes as prices or costs change. Changes in food prices at retail, at farm market levels, in food-marketing charges (that is, the farm retail spread), and in the farmer's share of the consumer's food dollar *of this market basket* over the period 1913–1970 are presented in Table 9–2. A review of the data presented here brings to the fore several interesting relationships. First, the farmer's share of the consumer's dollar changes in a direct relation with fluctuations in business activity. The farmer's share of the consumer's dollar rose during World War I to $.51, dropped during the 1920s and stabilized in the neighborhood of $.40, tumbled again with the onset of the Great Depression,

TABLE 9–2

The Market Basket of Farm Food Products: Indexes of Retail Cost, Farm Value, Farm-Retail Spread, and Farmer's Share of Retail Cost, 1913–1970*

Year(s)	Farmer's Share	Retail Cost	Farm Value	Farm-Retail* Spread
	(percent)	(1947–49 = 100)		
1913–14	46	40	37	44
1915–19	47	60	57	63
1920–24	41	67	54	79
1925–29	42	66	55	77
1930–34	34	69	34	64
1935–39	40	52	40	62
1940–44	47	60	57	64
1945–49	51	90	91	90
1950–54	46	106	98	113
1955–59	40	106	85	127
1960	39	105	82	128
1961	38	106	82	130
1962	38	107	83	131
1963	37	108	80	135
1964	37	108	80	135
1965	39	110	88	133
1966	40	116	95	137
1967	38	115	89	140
1968	39	119	93	144
1969	41	125	103	146
1970	39	130	103	157

* The market basket of food from 1913–1947 is representative of the consumption of all U.S. consumers in 1935–39. From 1947–56, it is representative of products bought by urban families in 1952. From 1956–1970, it is representative of products bought in 1960–61.

Source: Marketing and Transportation Situation, U.S.D.A., ERS, MTS-182, August 1971 for 1960–70; balance from "Farm-Retail Spreads for Food Products," *Miscellaneous Publications* 741, U.S.D.A., Agricultural Marketing Service, Marketing Research Division.

reaching a low of $.32 in 1932, then rose gradually during the 1930s, and hit a new peak of $.53 in the war year of 1945. Thereafter, the farmer's share has declined, leveling off at around $.40 in the late 1950s and 1960s. It would seem that the farmer's share of the consumer's dollar did not trend upward or downward over the period 1913–1970, but simply rose and fell with business fluctuations and with war and peace.

If, however, we examine the data on *Farm Value* and *Farm-Retail Spread,* we obtain additional insight. Marketing charges and farm value rose together from 1913–14 to a peak during World War I. But during the 1920s and 1930s, marketing charges did not fall as much as the farm value of the market basket. In the 1950s and 1960s, the farm-retail spread increased much faster than the farm value of food. In fact, the farm-retail spread has decreased in only two years since 1945, but the farm value declined or was stable in thirteen of the twenty-five years.

Two generalizations emerge from these data. First, it appears that once marketing charges increase, they do not come down easily. Second, although marketing charges do not come down easily, they do seem to rise easily. The farmer's share of the market basket has declined from a World War II high of 53 percent to 40 percent, where it stood in 1940. The fact that the farmer's share of the consumer's food dollar stands at 40 percent once again in 1970 does not prove that the representative farmer is either suffering or prospering financially, or that the whole long development in marketing is either good or bad. It does suggest one important thing, however; the farmer is the residual claimant of the consumer's food dollar.

The Total Marketing Bill

Marketing-bill data are sometimes confused with the market-basket data, but the two sets of data describe different phenomena. Marketing-bill statistics relate to the total quantity of farm foods purchased annually by all civilian consumers, whereas the market-basket statistics describe the average quantity of domestic farm foods bought per family by urban wage-earner and clerical-worker families. The marketing-bill data measure year-to-year changes in the cost of marketing the actual quantities of the various groups of farm products. Market-basket data, in contrast, measure changes in the cost of marketing a constant set of food items.

The total bill for marketing farm food products has increased steadily (see Table 9–3). In 1960, it was $44 billion, in 1970 it was $68 billion. Further increases are in prospect in both the near and distant future. This bill includes charges for processing and distributing to civilian consumers domestically produced farm foods, including food sold in the form of restaurant meals.

Price inflation was the major factor contributing to the $50 billion

TABLE 9-3

The Bill for Marketing Domestic Farm Food Products Bought
by Civilian Consumers, 1929–1970

Year(s)	Civilian Expenditures for Farm Food	Farm Value	Total* Marketing Bill
	(billion dollars)		
1930–34	12.7	4.5	8.1
1935–39	13.6	5.4	8.1
1940–44	20.2	9.0	11.3
1945–49	36.5	16.6	20.1
1950–54	46.6	19.0	27.6
1955–59	55.5	19.7	35.8
1960	65.9	21.7	44.2
1961	67.1	22.0	45.1
1962	69.3	22.4	46.9
1963	71.5	22.6	48.9
1964	74.6	23.4	51.2
1965	77.6	25.5	52.1
1966	82.8	28.1	54.7
1967	84.8	27.3	57.5
1968	90.1	29.0	61.1
1969	95.3	32.1	63.2
1970	101.6	33.1	68.5

* Difference between retail-store cost (or civilian expenditures) and farm value, except that federal processor taxes have been deducted for 1933–35 and allowances for federal government payments to processors have been added for 1943–46.

Source: *Marketing and Transportation Situation*, U.S.D.A., ERS, MTS-182, August 1971.

rise in the marketing bill between 1940 and 1970. It alone contributed $36 billion of the increase. The remaining $13 billion increase was a result of the larger volume of food marketed and the increased services provided by the marketing system. These latter charges include costs and profits to firms providing such increased services as prepared dinners and other built-in maid services.

Components of the Marketing Bill. The bill for marketing farm food products has increased in every year since 1939 as the result of persistent increases in all principal components of that marketing bill. Each of the components—labor, transportation, corporate profits, and other costs—doubled between 1939 and 1950 and doubled again between 1950 and 1960. The changes for recent years are shown in Figure 9–2.

The upward trend in labor costs since 1940 has been caused in part by the increase in the number of persons employed in processing and distribution activities; more workers have been required to handle the increasing volume of products and to provide the additional services required in the processing and distribution of semiprepared and prepared foods. In addition, an increasing number of technical, clerical, professional, and sales

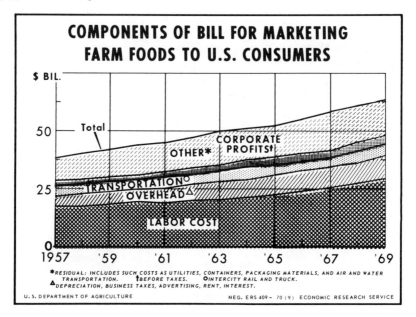

COMPONENTS OF BILL FOR MARKETING
FARM FOODS TO U.S. CONSUMERS

*RESIDUAL: INCLUDES SUCH COSTS AS UTILITIES, CONTAINERS, PACKAGING MATERIALS, AND AIR AND WATER
TRANSPORTATION.   †BEFORE TAXES.   ○INTERCITY RAIL AND TRUCK.
△DEPRECIATION, BUSINESS TAXES, ADVERTISING, RENT, INTEREST.

U. S. DEPARTMENT OF AGRICULTURE   NEG. ERS 409– 70 (9) ECONOMIC RESEARCH SERVICE

FIGURE 9–2

personnel was employed by marketing firms in selling more products. It is
estimated that the number of workers employed in processing increased 33
percent between 1940 and 1956 and since then has continued to increase
at about the same rate.

Since 1940, the spread of unionization in food-processing and distributing industries has led to the establishment of a workday and workweek
with provision for overtime payments, higher wage rates, and numerous
fringe benefits. In addition, state and federal legislation provided for increasing kinds and amounts of fringe benefits. Part of these higher labor costs
has been offset by the greater productivity of labor during the period. From
1940 to 1963, *unit* labor costs increased by about 150 percent, while hourly
labor costs went up more than twice that much. Since 1964, however, unit
labor costs in food marketing have risen steadily, paralleling the rise in
hourly labor cost (Figure 9–3).

Between 1945 and 1958, corporate profits of farm food marketing
firms varied between $1.2 and $1.9 billion before taxes, with highs of $1.7
billion in 1946 and $1.9 billion in 1957 and 1958. During the 1960s, corpo-
rate profits approximately doubled to $4 billion. At the same time, there
has been a tendency for corporate profits to assume a greater importance
in the total marketing bill—rising from about 5 percent in 1960 to over 6
percent in 1970. Although profits as a percentage of invested capital have
been at approximately the same level in the food industry as in all manufacturing, they are not an inconsequential item in the food marketing bill.

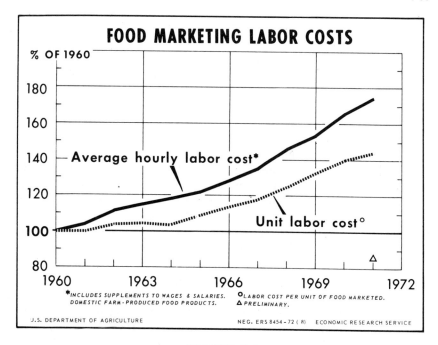

FIGURE 9-3

Does Distribution Cost too Much?

This is a difficult question to answer. A study undertaken by the Twentieth Century Fund back in 1939 concludes that the answer is yes, distribution does cost too much, and because the marketing bill has increased substantially since then, the same individuals would probably still hold the same opinion. The conclusion is also advanced in that study to the effect that:

> ...there is little evidence of general high profits being made in the field of distribution considered as a whole. Some firms, it is true, and some of the newer branches of distribution, have been conspicuously profitable. But for every outstandingly successful and profitable organization there are many that barely break even and some which operate at a loss, even in good years.[3]

The National Commission on Food Marketing came to similar conclusions in its 1966 report, that is, that "profits in the food industry were approximately in line with average profits in the economy at large in 1964."[4]

The basis for the conclusion that distribution (marketing and process-

---

[3]Paul W. Stewart and J. Fredrick Dewhurst, with the assistance of Louise Field, *Does Distribution Cost Too Much?* (New York: The Twentieth Century Fund, 1939), p. 335.

[4]National Commission on Food Marketing, *Food from Farmer to Consumer*, June 1966, p. 99.

ing) costs too much, thus, must rest on grounds other than exorbitant profits. The affirmative conclusion would seem to depend upon such factors as duplication of services and functions and the insidious drive to provide consumers with more and more service. In other words, the basis for the conclusion that distribution costs too much rests upon a second conclusion, namely, that services are provided and costs are incurred, *which really are not to the advantage of the consumer,* to expand sales.

We are inclined to take a somewhat opposing view. We recognize that services are foisted on consumers, in certain cases, and additional costs are incurred when in fact consumers do not want those additional services. But we know that when real incomes of consumers are rising, as they have been in the United States for many years, consumers desire to spend those additions to income, not entirely for new and more products, *but, rather, on additional services.* And the competition for new customers through the provision of greater services, which must add to the cost of distribution, succeeds only because consumers desire to spend their rising real incomes for greater convenience and more service. Thus, we conclude that costs of distribution are high and are rising because consumers seek greater services. Merchants, realizing this, compete to provide these greater services with the result that distribution costs are high and increasing. Consequently, we take the view that distribution does not cost too much. If consumers desire to allocate their incomes in such a way as to spend a larger proportion of their income on service (packaging, credit, delivery, convenience), who is to say that such an allocation is improper or costly?

We are not saying that the food distribution system is perfect or highly efficient. Inefficiencies may be found in the system in almost any direction that we care to look: in the antiquated fruit and vegetable terminal markets of the East, in the shrinkage of livestock on their way to terminal markets, in the inequitable payment practices to be found in country cotton markets. But a comparable list of inefficiencies could be set forth for any sector of the economy: manufacturing, professional services, government administration. We are inclined to doubt that the extent and magnitude of inefficient practices is any greater in food processing and marketing than in other areas that we might care to examine. And we do not feel that the growing list of marketing services, which consumers demand and pay for, should be treated as unwarranted or exorbitant costs. Very simply, consumers are purchasing services as well as products.

POINTS FOR DISCUSSION

1. How did the distribution of the laboring force, as among agriculture, manufacturing, and the distributing trades, change over the long period 1870–1970? What explanation can you offer for the changing proportions?

2. Make a list of the services that were undertaken in the home in 1870 but which now are provided in the marketing system. Does the transfer of these services from the home to the marketing system, with the increased costs of marketing, mean that the economy is more or less efficient?
3. What form does competition most often take at the retail level: price competition or service competition? Why?
4. What has been the long-run trend with respect to the distribution of the consumer's food dollar among farmers, processors, and other middlemen? Do you expect the share going to processors to increase in the future? If so, why?
5. How does the "market-basket" concept differ from the "marketing-bill" concept? What do the marketing-bill data measure that the market-basket data do not?
6. Why has the total marketing bill for domestic food products increased so greatly since 1940? Indicate sources of the increase.
7. Which of the following developments best explains increases in food- and clothing-marketing costs over the last century: (1) excessive profits; (2) duplication and inefficiency; (3) the provision of new services; or (4) greater processing and manufacturing outside the home? Do you think that the trend toward increased marketing and distribution costs is an undesirable trend? If so, what should we try to do about it?
8. Using one farm product of your choice, make a table showing the farm value, retail value and price spread from 1960 to date. What changes do you observe? What explains those changes?

REFERENCES

ARTHUR, H. B., R. A. GOLDBERG, AND K. M. BIRD, *The United States Food and Fiber System in a Changing World Environment.* Vol. IV of the Technical Papers of the National Advisory Commission on Food and Fiber, August 1967.

COCHRANE, WILLARD W., "Some Additional Views on Demand and Supply," *Agricultural Adjustment Problems in a Growing Economy.* Ames, Iowa: Iowa State College Press, 1956.

DAVIS, JOHN H., AND RAY H. GOLDBERG, *A Concept of Agricultural Business.* Boston: Harvard University, Division of Research, Graduate School of Business Administration, 1957.

National Commission on Food Marketing, *Food from Farmer to Consumer,* June 1966.

SCOTT, F. E. AND H. T. BADGER, "Farm-Retail Spreads for Food Products," *Miscellaneous Publication 741.* Economic Research Service, U.S.D.A. (January 1972).

Chapter 10

Consumer Needs,

Wants, and Demands

The consumer has long been eulogized in economics texts. Often we find statements such as: the consumer is the prime mover of the economy; all economic activity is undertaken to satisfy consumer wants; the people who direct business firms only execute what is prescribed for them by demands of consumers. But writers of these statements often have turned their major attention to the complexities of production and exchange. More recently, however, economists have been paying more attention to consumer behavior. As we will see more explicitly in Chapter 15, consumer decisions to spend or save, when lumped together in a national total, have significant implications for the operating economy. Further, the manner in which consumers allocate their limited incomes between different lines of expenditure has important price-output consequences for the goods and services involved. Here we will discuss the role of the consumer in shaping farm production and marketing activities.

The Consumer in the Marketing Process

As suggested in Chapter 7, it is sometimes useful to take a channel or "pipe line" approach to the marketing process. Let us, therefore, visualize the marketing process in food and agriculture as a broad channel carrying food and fiber along from farm-producers to consumers. And within this broad channel, we may picture many smaller channels carrying this particular farm product and that. But this flow of food and fiber is not forthcoming automatically. Neither are the total flow and its component parts fixed and unvarying in size. It is the consumer, injecting purchasing power at the end of the channel, who *pulls* farm products along through the marketing channel. It is, further, the behavior of consumers, in the allocation of their purchasing power between different food and fiber products, that causes a strong pull to be exerted in one line and a weak pull in another.

This mechanistic view of the marketing process is, however, rather complicated. We have food and fiber products flowing toward the consumer, and purchasing power flowing toward the producer; a goods stream, on one hand, and a purchasing power stream, on the other. And neither of these streams flows automatically. The purchasing power stream grows out of the consumer's income, which is injected by him in the act of making purchases for food and clothing. In the other stream, the goods stream, food and fiber products move toward the consumer only as a result of initial purchases by consumers and secondary purchases by handlers in the marketing channel.

Now, it may be argued that all important changes in the goods stream do not result from consumer action. This we do not deny. Innovations, such as the development of new products (freeze-dried coffee), or the development of cost-reducing techniques (computerized inventory control), are usually initiated by producers or business firms. Changes in the method of handling or in the form of a product are almost always pioneered by enterprising businessmen who have studied the market and believe a new product or a new marketing service will better meet the needs of consumers. Nonetheless, it is the consumer at the end of the marketing process, who, by making purchases or withholding them, makes the final decision as to the acceptability of a new product or service.

CONSUMER NEEDS AND WANTS

Physiological Requirements

We first consider an explanation of the behavior of consumers in their strategic position at the end of the marketing process. It seems useful to begin with a discussion of the basic needs of consumers. By *basic needs* we mean that consumption necessary to life itself; that consumption rooted in the physiological requirements of the human body. This physiological drive plays an important role in the consumption of food and fiber products. We must eat regularly, or we starve, and in many climates, we must wear clothing, or we freeze. With respect to food consumption at least, the basic physiological requirements of the body lend themselves to scientific inquiry wherein the needs may be tested and measured. As a result of much scientific research into basic food needs, there have been established certain objective standards (or dietary allowances) necessary to the maintenance of good health.

The Food and Nutrition Board of the National Research Council issues reports from time to time, setting forth in precise terms the amounts and kinds of nutrients required by the human body to maintain the body in good health. We present in Table 10–1 the recommended daily dietary allowances specified by the National Research Council for selected age and weight groups. A quick glance at the table makes it clear that these recommended dietary allowances are not set forth in measures common to everyday living. These requirements are presented in terms of the kinds of nutrients that the human body assimilates out of foods consumed. For example, the human body requires, according to the age of the person and his weight, a certain amount of food energy measured in terms of calories. But calories, fuel that motivates the body, are not enough. We require other types of nutrients: protein, calcium, iron, and various types of vitamins.

Three points should be made regarding Table 10–1. First, it is clear that persons in different age and weight groups require different amounts of the various nutrients. For example, a moderately active woman who is twenty-five and weighs 128 pounds requires 2,100 calories a day to maintain her health, whereas a man who is twenty-five and weighs 154 pounds requires 2,900 calories. Growing boys in the age group twelve-to-fifteen-years old require seventy-five grams of protein a day, whereas a moderately active woman only requires fifty-eight grams. Second, although the data presented in Table 10–1 appear fixed, they should not be considered the ultimate in dietary requirements. These recommended allowances have changed over the years as the state of nutritional knowledge has advanced, and we must expect them to change in years to come, as the state of nutritional knowledge continues to advance. Third, these recommended allowances are designed to provide the human body with quantities of nutrients well above minimal requirements. It is perhaps too strong to say that the recommended allowances represent optimal quantities, but they are designed to support desired body growth and repair, and good health.

Science has provided a guide to good nutrition in terms of calories, proteins, minerals, and vitamins. These allowances are in terms of the nutrients that *need to be ingested daily*. But in our daily lives, we do not consume nutrients as such; we consume foods that provide our bodies with nutrients. A real problem arises in translating these nutrient requirements into the kinds and amounts of specific foods that, in fact, satisfy those requirements. Many different combinations of foods will satisfy the basic requirements set forth by the National Research Council and, of course, many combinations of foods that we might wish to consume do not satisfy these requirements. It is possible, for example, to specify a nutritionally adequate diet plan composed largely of wheat flour, navy beans, cabbage, and evapo-

TABLE 10–1

Recommended Dairy Dietary Allowances*

	Calories	Protein	Calcium	Iron	A	Vitamins B₁	B₂	Niacin	C	D
		gm	mg	mg	units	mg	mg	mg	mg	units
Children, 1–3 yrs (29 lbs)	1300	32	800	8	2000	.5	.8	9	40	400
Boys, 12–15 yrs (98 lbs)	3000	75	1400	15	5000	1.2	1.8	20	80	400
Girls, 12–15 yrs (103 lbs)	2500	62	1300	15	5000	1.0	1.5	17	80	400
Men, 18–35 yrs (154 lbs)	2900	70	800	10	5000	1.2	1.7	19	70	
Men, 35–55 yrs (154 lbs)	2600	70	800	10	5000	1.0	1.6	17	70	
Women, 18–35 yrs (128 lbs)	2100	58	800	15	5000	.8	1.3	14	70	
Women, 35–55 yrs (128 lbs)	1900	58	800	15	5000	.8	1.2	13	70	

* Intended to meet the needs of moderately active, healthy individuals living in the United States.

Source: *Report of Food and Nutrition Board*, National Academy of Sciences, National Research Council, Publication 1146 (rev. ed.), Washington, D. C., 1964.

rated milk, which no one would want to eat. It is also possible to suggest a combination of high-cost foods, heavily weighted with sugars and fats, that do not satisfy the requirements stated in Table 10–1. Consumers, then, are confronted with a continuing problem of translating basic nutrient requirements into the kinds and quantities of foods that, in fact, satisfy those requirements.

The U.S. Department of Agriculture has converted these physical requirements into realistic diet plans at several levels of cost. In Table 10–2, the kinds and quantities of foods that satisfy the nutrient requirements of Table 10–1 are presented at three levels of cost for identical age and weight groups.

As the plans appear in Table 10–2, we cannot see the extent to which higher priced cuts of meat are included in the liberal-cost plan as compared to the economy- and low-cost diets. We can, however, see how quantities vary by food groupings. For example, under the economy plan, a twenty-five-year old man consumes 2 pounds of meat per week, compared to 3.75 pounds under the low-cost and 6 pounds under the liberal-cost plan. In the case of citrus fruits and tomatoes, we see that the twenty-five-year old man would consume 1.75 pounds under the economy plan, 2.25 under the low-cost, and 3.00 under the liberal-cost plan. The same man would reduce his consumption of potatoes from 4.25 under the economy plan to 2.75 under the liberal cost plan.

Thus, it is clear that the combination of foods consumed can vary considerably and still satisfy the basic nutrient requirements. The suggested quantities of specific foods in the diet plans under consideration are quite different. And diet plans for families not restricted in the amount of money that they can spend on food could change still further. More liberal plans with respect to cost would include larger quantities of meat, dairy products, and fruits and vegetables. Although a family may have an unlimited amount of money to spend for food, this is no guarantee that it will have an adequate diet. Care must always be taken to include sufficient quantities of such foods as milk and fruits and vegetables.

We have dwelt at some length on physiological needs as a factor determining the selection and consumption of food. We have done this because much nutritional information is available in an objective form. But when we turn to fiber products, we cannot be so specific and so definite. It is clear that in extremely hot climates the body needs to be covered to prevent heat exhaustion and a burning of the skin. It is even more evident that in cold climates man must protect himself from freezing and frostbite by covering his body in some way. It is difficult, however, to develop objective standards and measures of the amount of covering that man must have in these varying situations. It is technically possible to specify weights and kinds of clothing that best satisfy physical need, and, in fact, such is common

TABLE 10-2

Master Family Food Plans at Three Expenditure Levels (pounds per week except as noted)

	Milk, Cheese, Ice Cream	Meat, Poultry, Fish	Eggs	Dry Beans, Peas, Nuts	Flour, Cereal, Baked Goods	Citrus Fruits, Tomatoes	Dark Green, Yellow Vegetables	Potatoes	Other Vegetables	Fats, Oils	Sugar, Sweets
	(qts)		(nos)								
Children (1–3 yrs)											
Economy	5.0	0.75	4	0.06	1.50	1.00	0.25	1.00	2.00	0.25	0.25
Low cost	5.5	1.25	5	0.06	1.25	1.50	0.25	0.75	2.25	0.25	0.25
Liberal	6.0	2.25	7	0.06	1.00	1.75	0.25	0.75	2.75	0.25	0.25
Women (20–34 yrs)											
Economy	3.0	1.25	4	0.25	3.00	1.75	0.75	3.00	3.00	0.50	0.75
Low cost	3.5	2.50	5	0.25	2.50	2.00	0.75	2.00	5.00	0.38	0.62
Liberal	4.0	4.75	6	0.06	2.00	3.00	0.75	1.25	6.25	0.50	1.12
Men (20–34 yrs)											
Economy	3.0	2.00	5	0.62	4.75	1.75	0.75	4.25	3.50	0.90	1.12
Low cost	3.5	3.75	6	0.38	4.25	2.25	0.75	3.25	5.50	0.75	1.00
Liberal	4.0	6.00	7	0.25	3.75	3.00	0.75	2.75	7.75	1.00	1.50

Source: *Family Food Budgeting, Home and Garden Bulletin No. 94*, U.S. Department of Agriculture, November 1969.

practice in military organizations in which the wearing of clothing is uniform. But in everyday life, we do not do this. The most we can say is that some clothing is necessary.

Consumer Wants and Desires

Consumer wants and desires are more inclusive than physiological need. This was evident in the discussion of translating a schedule of nutrient requirements into diet plans. We do not consume nutrients as such. We do not consume food as such. We want and select specific kinds of food to satisfy the basic needs of our bodies. In some way, wants and desires for specific things come into being. These wants and desires are broader than need, but, in the case of food and fiber products, they grow out of physiological need.

In broad outline, wants, the variation in wants, and the almost unlimited aspects of these wants come into being: (1) because of personal characteristics, some physical, some psychological; and (2) because of the nature of the social and physical environment. In other words, a person wants (or doesn't want) a particular food because it *tastes* good (or bad) to him and because it *looks* good (or bad) to him. And a person wants a particular food because it is customary in his society to eat that kind of food. Or he may want a wide variety of foods because this is customary. It is customary, for example, in America, to want a variety of foods on the table. It lends prestige to the family to have out-of-season foods on the table. It widens the experience of the family to have exotic foods on the table. And because prestige and wide experience are valued in our society, a basis is established for wanting a variety of foods. In another direction, it has, in the past, been sociably acceptable and even socially desirable among certain peoples for one man to eat another. The willingness, yes, desire, to consume human flesh in one society and the repugnance of the idea in another illustrates forcefully the power of social environment in determining food wants. The physical environment, too, influences wants. In South China, people learn to eat rice as children and continue to eat rice throughout their lives because rice grows well in South China. In North China, people want wheat products because wheat grows well in North China. So, many things contribute to the diversification of wants.

We cannot live in any social group without feeling the need for a tremendous number of goods and services that are not necessary for bare existence but that are, nonetheless, important to our happiness and welfare. Although we need clothing, in some form, to protect us from the elements, our desires for such protection are more often dominated by cultural conditioning than by the demands of the season. In short, it is the ornamental value of clothing that usually determines the nature of a selection made. We conclude, therefore, that the culture in which we live is most important in determining the structure of the individual's wants. But we must recognize that wants take a personal twist because each individual is a personality unto himself. The average individual wishes to conform to socially accepted patterns of conduct, but he also wishes, by reason of his distinct personality, to vary in some degree from socially accepted norms. Thus, the total environment imposes on each of us a structure of wants that are more or less accepted. But each individual continuously nibbles away at socially accepted patterns of conduct as he varies his consumption from those patterns. Hence, in time, the structure of wants changes.

The changing pattern of crop and livestock product consumption by United States consumers is illustrated in Figure 10–1. Data for a longer period would, of course, show more dramatic changes in consumption patterns, but eating habits have changed substantially even over ten years. More fruits and vegetables are being consumed as processed products than as fresh products. Poultry consumption has increased by 50 percent per capita over the period. Consumption of dairy products, eggs, pork, and grain products have slowly declined. Many reasons account for the changing consumption patterns; changes in food production and processing, changes in the state of nutritional knowledge, changes in the real income of consumers, and changes in food superstitions all contribute.

THE THEORY OF DEMAND

The Central Problem of Choice

The elements of the central problem confronting every consumer begin to emerge. First, the consumer has almost an infinite number of wants, conditioned and created by physiological need, personal characteristics, and social and physical environment. Even when we narrow the area of discussion to food and fiber products, consumer wants are varied and numerous. Second, the consumer has only a limited income with which to satisfy this myriad of wants. It is a rare consumer indeed who has sufficient income to satisfy his many and varied wants, either in total or in the narrower field of food and fiber consumption. Consequently, each consumer is faced with the problem of choosing from his list of wants those that he must or that he will satisfy through the purchase and consumption of specific goods and services. His is a continuing problem of choice—choice among many alternative lines of consumption, where personal income is limited.

The question arises: how does the consumer make his choices? Is consumption a purely random process, or can one discern some motivating

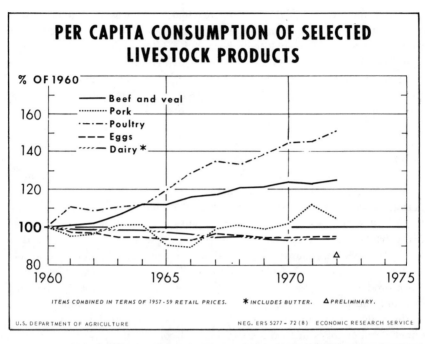

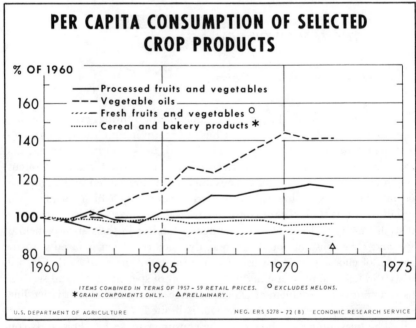

FIGURE 10–1

principle that consumers follow? Economists have postulated, perhaps partially on the basis of personal insight, that consumers try to maximize their total satisfaction or well-being. This satisfaction or well-being is called the consumer's *utility,* and like the assumption that a business maximizes profits, in the theory of consumption, *consumers are assumed to maximize their utility.* In the farm-business firm, resources are combined and recombined, always with the goal of maximizing total profits. The consumer unit or household is comparable, in many respects, to the farm-business firm. The consumer unit or household is not engaged in maximizing profits. Its activity leads to spending income, not acquiring it. But the consumer unit or household is engaged in maximizing total satisfaction. Each of its decisions in choosing and spending is taken with the objective of increasing its total utility.

This concept of total utility is a little hard to understand, because satisfactions are not measurable. Still, the concept is useful. In the selection of goods and services, each consumer unit or household seeks to maximize its total satisfaction. If a dollar spent for milk today provides more satisfaction, all things considered, than a dollar spent for bread, consumers will purchase milk instead of bread. For by adding the quarts of milk that a dollar will purchase, total satisfaction will be greater than by adding the loaves of bread that a dollar will purchase. But as more and more milk is purchased, the usefulness of the additional milk falls; its capacity to satisfy wants falls. We might arrange the wants for milk in a descending order: to drink, to use in cooking, to feed to the cat. In this scheme, we see that milk wants are limited, and some are lower than others. Thus, consumers do not indefinitely expand their consumption in any one line.

Even though the utility derived from a dollar spent on milk exceeded that derived from a dollar spent on bread at one point in time, continued purchase and consumption of milk leads to smaller and smaller increases in satisfaction. Continued consumption in one commodity line must, assuming that consumption in other lines is constant, lead to diminishing marginal utility for the consumer with respect to the commodity in question. Hence, in the milk-bread example, we reach a point at which the satisfaction derived from a dollar purchase of milk is no greater than that to be derived from a dollar purchase of bread. At this point, the consumer ceases to expand his consumption of milk because further milk consumption now provides less satisfaction than a dollar purchase of bread.

From the reasoning above, we can set forth an economic principle: the *equimarginal principle.* Consumers, in dividing a fixed quantity of income among different lines of expenditure, will apportion that income among different uses so as to cause the gain involved by transferring a unit of income into one use to be just equal to the loss involved in the use from which the unit of income is withdrawn. Here we have a principle of great importance. The ideal apportionment of consumer income is clearly that in which there is nothing to be gained by transferring a marginal unit of income from one use to another. Because if some additional satisfaction could be gained by such a transfer, the previous situation would not have been ideal. Total satisfaction could and would be increased, for example, by taking $.35 out of milkshake consumption and adding $.35 to hamburger consumption, when $.35 spent for hamburgers provides more satisfaction than $.35 spent on milkshakes.

The way in which consumers allocate their scarce funds at different levels of income may be seen in Table 10–3. Many important relationships are revealed in the data presented there, but we will point out only a few. First, food and housing expenditures make up the largest proportion of total expenditures for all income groups. The average family with income less than $3,000 devotes about 60 percent of its expenditures on these two items, while the top income group devotes only about 40 percent. Low-income families also devote a larger proportion of their incomes to medical care than do high-income families. On the other hand, higher-income families allocate a larger proportion of their incomes to clothing, transportation, recreation, and education than do lower income families.

TABLE 10–3

Proportion of Total Expenditures Devoted to Various Consumption Items, U.S. Nonfarm families, 1960–61

	Annual Income					
Consumption Item	Under $3000	$3000– $5000	$5000– $7500	$7500– $10,000	$10,000– $15,000	Over $15,000
	(percent of total)					
Total food	29	26	25	24	23	20
Tobacco and alcohol	3	3	4	4	3	3
Housing and household operations	30	25	24	23	22	22
House furnishings and equipment	4	5	5	6	5	5
Clothing and accessories	7	9	10	11	12	12
Transportation	9	15	16	16	17	15
Medical care	9	7	7	6	6	6
Personal care	3	3	3	3	3	2
Recreation and equipment	2	3	4	4	5	5
Reading and education	1	1	2	2	2	3
Other	2	2	2	2	2	4

Source: *Expenditure Patterns of the American Family,* prepared by the National Industrial Conference Board, based on a survey conducted by the United States Department of Labor, 1965.

We see in some detail the food choices of consumers in Table 10–4. It will be observed that consumers at low levels of income use relatively large quantities of sugar, fats, flour and cereals, dry vegetables and fruit. And they go easy on fresh fruits, milk, meat, and eggs. In short, they fill up

TABLE 10–4

Per Capita Weekly Consumption* of Selected Food Groups U.S., by Family Income Class, 1965

Food Item	Family Income: Under $1000	$1000–$2999	$3000–$4999	$5000–$6999	$7000–$9999	$10,000 and over
Milk or equivalent	3.49	3.63	3.77	3.89	4.36	4.43
Meat, poultry, fish	3.86	4.04	4.36	4.67	4.66	5.12
Eggs	0.61	0.60	0.58	0.56	0.52	0.53
Dried vegetables and fruit	0.27	0.27	0.19	0.11	0.08	0.07
Other processed vegetables and fruit	1.96	2.50	2.95	3.45	3.87	4.32
Fresh vegetables	2.17	2.19	2.04	2.14	2.31	2.74
Fresh fruit	1.66	2.15	2.11	2.49	2.69	3.32
Potatoes, sweet potatoes	1.43	1.53	1.73	1.66	1.68	1.44
Sugar, sweets	1.26	1.25	1.26	1.09	1.06	0.95
Fats, oils	0.84	0.86	0.84	0.82	0.81	0.78
Flour, cereal	2.38	2.10	1.64	1.28	1.13	0.97
Bakery products	1.90	1.96	2.20	2.38	2.56	2.52
Total except milk and eggs	17.73	18.85	19.32	20.09	20.85	22.23

* In pounds except for milk, which is in quarts, and eggs, which are in dozens.

Source: *Household Food Consumption Survey 1965–66,* U.S.D.A., Agricultural Marketing Service, 1968.

on cheap, energy foods. They choose those cheap foods where their funds go farthest, in terms of quantity. But as consumer incomes rise, consumers are inclined to, or more properly can afford to, satisfy more and more varied food wants. The pattern of food choices reflecting the pattern of income allocation is modified as incomes increase. The consumption of flour and cereals actually declines; the consumption of such foods as sugar and fats changes little, but the consumption of meat, milk, and fresh fruits and vegetables increases in important proportions.

We conclude then, that when incomes are low, consumers maximize their total satisfaction by purchasing and eating large quantities of cheap, low-resource-using foods. When incomes are high, consumers maximize their total satisfaction by consuming less of these low-resource-using foods and by expanding their purchases and intake of high-cost animal products and fruits and vegetables.

Consumer Demand

Demand is used in everyday language to refer to the quantity of a good that a consumer purchases. However, in economics its meaning is much narrower. *The demand for a commodity is a function or relationship showing the quantities of that commodity that consumers stand ready to purchase at various prices, with all other factors held constant.* Demand is thus a paired set of prices and quantities, often shown on a graph. In Figure 10–2, a consumer demand curve (*DD*) for chicken is presented. This curve is constructed from the following hypothetical, but nontheless realistic information:

Price Per Pound	Per Capita Consumption (in pounds)
$.65	18
.55	23
.45	30
.35	40
.25	50

This curve (*DD*) states a relation between the number of pounds of chicken consumed per year per person and the price of chicken per pound. This measure tells us how the average per capita consumption of chicken might be expected to vary as the price of chicken varies.

It will be observed that the demand curve for chicken is negatively inclined; it slopes downward and to the right. When the price of chicken rises, the number of pounds consumed declines, and when the price falls, the number of pounds consumed increases. This is a perfectly logical relationship, and one we would expect to find for most food items. As more and more of a product is consumed, the amount of utility or satisfaction derived from additional amounts of consumption declines. The willingness of consumers to pay for additional amounts of that commodity falls. Hence, increased amounts of a particular commodity may be sold to a consumer only at lower prices.[1]

Demand Elasticity

The relationship between price and quality along a demand curve is of interest, especially to the sellers of a commodity. To illustrate, if you were selling chicken at a price of $.50 per pound, you would probably like to know what would happen to the quantity demanded if price were to fall by 10 percent. Specifically, would consumption increase more than 10 percent, in which case your total revenue would rise, or less than 10 percent, in which case your total revenue would fall.

This relative reaction of consumption to a price change is measured by the price elasticity of demand. Often called simply the *elasticity of demand, it measures the percentage change in quantity purchased that results from a 1 percent change in a product's price.* Figure 10–2 provides an illustration.

When price goes from $.50 to $.45, quantity consumed goes from twenty-six to thirty pounds per year (assuming *DD* is the relevant demand curve). Thus, a 10 percent price fall leads to a 15 percent increase in consumption, implying a 1.5 percent increase in consumption for every 1 percent

---

[1]The rationale for the demand curve sloping downward and to the right can be presented in strictly behavioristic terms (rather than in utilitarian terms), as will be done in Chapter 12.

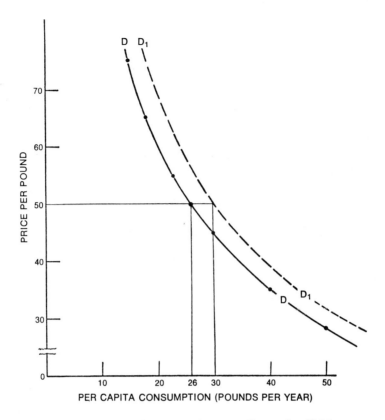

PER CAPITA CONSUMPTION (POUNDS PER YEAR)

FIGURE 10–2. Consumer Demand Curves for Chicken

decrease in price, an elasticity of −1.5. A rise in price from $.45 to $.50 per pound would result in a reduction of consumption from thirty to twenty-six pounds. Because this is the exact reverse of the price decrease, it should have the same elasticity, but because the starting points for price and quantity are now different, it is actually a 13 percent change in quantity arising from an 11 percent change in price. To avoid these arithmetic difficulties when calculating an elasticity along a curve, the following *arc elasticity* formula is used:

$$\text{demand elasticity} = \dfrac{\dfrac{q_2 - q_1}{q_2 + q_1}}{\dfrac{p_2 - p_1}{p_2 + p_1}} \text{ or, in our example for the price fall,}$$

$$\dfrac{\dfrac{30 - 26}{30 + 26}}{\dfrac{45 - 50}{45 + 50}} = \dfrac{4}{56} \Big/ \dfrac{-5}{95} = \dfrac{-19}{14} = -1.36$$

The reader can verify that the same elasticity results for a price rise from $.45 to $.50 using this formula.

A little reflection makes it apparent that demand elasticities will always be negative because consumers stand ready to purchase more of a good at a low price than at a high price. A price decrease brings forth an increase in quantity demanded, and a price rise brings forth a decrease in quantity demanded. This relationship, sometimes known as the law of demand, insures that demand elasticities are always negative.

The demand for a good is said to be *inelastic* or not very responsive to price changes if the absolute value of its elasticity of demand is less than 1.0. A good has an *elastic* demand if its elasticity has an absolute value greater than 1.0. A good with *unitary* elasticity has, as the term implies, an elasticity of exactly -1.0.

The relation between the elasticity of demand for a product and the effect of a price change on the total revenue received for the product is critical, especially for agricultural products. This relationship is illustrated in Figure 10–3 for a hypothetical product. The table below shows the total revenue corresponding to four points on the demand curve.

| | Demand | | Total |
Point	Price	Quantity	Revenue
A	8	20	160
B	5	40	200
C	4	50	200
D	2	70	140

For this product, if price is lowered from $8 to $5, quantity demanded increases from twenty to forty units. Calculation shows that this portion of the demand curve has an elasticity of $-13/9$, that is, it is elastic. Notice that total revenue increases with a decrease in price. Between points B and C, a price reduction from $5 to $4 causes an increase in quantity demanded from forty to fifty units, but total revenue remains unchanged. The average percentage change in quantity is exactly equal to the average percentage change in price over this range, that is, demand is unitary. A further price reduction from $4 to $2 again causes an increase in quantity demanded, but this portion of the demand curve is inelastic and the total revenue falls. It follows from the definitions that *a price fall will cause total revenue to increase along an elastic demand curve, to be constant along a unitary demand curve, and to fall along an inelastic demand curve.*

At this point, it would seem wise to distinguish between two commonly used phrases: *change in demand* and *change in the quantity demanded.* By a *change in demand,* we have in mind a shift in the demand curve itself: a shift from position DD to D_1D_1 in Figure 10–2. By reason of that

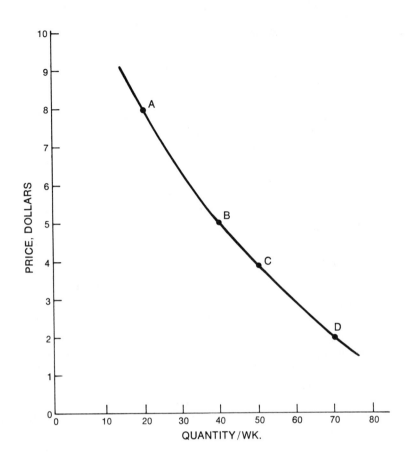

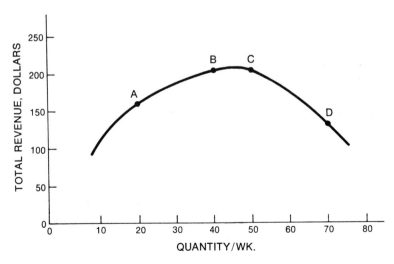

FIGURE 10–3. Relation of Elasticity and Total Revenue

shift, the consumption of chicken increases from twenty-six pounds per year per person to thirty pounds at the price of $.50. And that is what we mean by a change (in this case an increase) in demand. If *at any given price,* the consumer stands ready to buy more chicken, the demand for chicken may be said to have increased. With a decrease in demand, the consumer stands ready to buy less chicken *at any given price.*

By a *change in the quantity demanded,* we mean a movement along one curve, along curve *DD* in Figure 10–3. When the price of chicken falls from $.55 to $.45, we read off curve *DD* and discover that the consumption of chicken increases from twenty-three to thirty pounds. And this is what we mean by a change in the quantity demanded.

Changes in Demand

Changes in a consumer's demand for a product arise from three basic sources: changes in income, changes in the prices of related goods, and changes in tastes and preferences. In addition, changes in the aggregate demand for a product occur with population growth.

Consumers will often purchase more of a particular good at a given price when their income increases. This is reflected in the greater consumption of meat by high income families that is evident in Table 10–4. The relationship between income and the quantity of a commodity consumed is the income-consumption curve. Such curves for three food commodities are shown in Figure 10–4. The income-consumption curve for any one of these commodities states a relation between pounds of that commodity consumed and average incomes of United States families in 1965. The measure tells us how the consumption of beef, for example, might be expected to vary as family income varies.

The curves in Figure 10–4 illustrate the different income-consumption relationships to be found in agriculture. The consumption of beef increases at a decreasing rate with rising incomes, the consumption of white flour falls sharply and then levels off with rising incomes, and the consumption of pork is not influenced much one way or another by changes in income. The consumption curve for white flour illustrates the case of an *inferior good*— one whose consumption decreases with rising incomes. Relatively few foods are consumed in smaller amounts by consumers with high incomes than by those with low incomes. The typical curve will assume a shape falling within the limits of the two commodity-consumption curves for beef steak and pork. Goods within this range are known as *normal goods,* and their consumption increases with rising incomes. It is important to notice, however, that the consumption of each of the three commodities shown in the figure changes only modestly in amount once the middle-income class is passed.

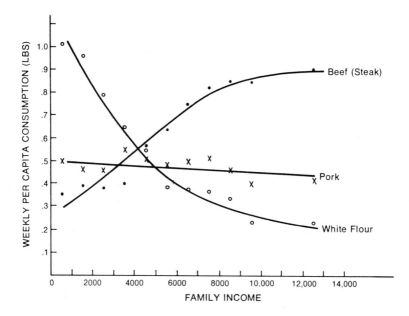

FIGURE 10–4. Food Consumption for Selected Commodities, U.S., 1965

Changes in income, once the upper-income brackets are reached, usually have only a small effect on the amount of food consumed.

The income elasticity of demand is a measure of the relationship between consumption and incomes. Commonly called the *income elasticity*, it *measures the percentage change in the quantity purchased of a commodity arising from a 1 percent income change.* Its formula, given below, is similar to the formula for the price elasticity (y_1 being the first income level, and y_2 the second income level).

$$\text{income elasticity} = \frac{\dfrac{q_2 - q_1}{q_2 + q_1}}{\dfrac{y_2 - y_1}{y_2 + y_1}}$$

A little thought will show that normal goods have positive income elasticities and inferior goods have negative income elasticities.

Increased income will shift the demand curve for a normal good such as chicken from DD to D_1D_1 in Figure 10–2. That is, an increase in demand occurs because with a higher income the consumer stands ready to buy more chicken at each price than he would have with his old income.

A similar shift in the demand for chicken may occur because of a change in the price of a related product like pork or beef. Suppose the price of other meat falls; it seems likely that consumers will buy more of the other meat, and, because of limited income and stomach size, less chicken. That is, chicken and other meats are *competitive products in consumption.* In contrast, corned beef and cabbage are *complementary products in consumption,* because consumption of more of one is usually accompanied by greater consumption of the other.

An increase in the price of a competitive product will cause the demand for the product in question to increase, whereas an increase in the price of a complementary product will cause the demand for the product in question to decrease. This is the second important cause of shifts or changes in demand, and its importance to agriculture is obvious from such examples as that of butter and margarine. The demand for butter has shifted as a result of lower margarine prices and better margarine quality.

The effect of changes in prices of related goods is expressed in the cross-elasticity of demand between commodities. The *cross-elasticity measures the percentage change in the quality of one good demanded as a result of a one percent change in the price of the related good.* Its formula is:

$$\text{cross elasticity of chicken with respect to the price of beef} = \frac{\left[\dfrac{q_2 - q_1}{q_2 + q_1}\right]_{\text{chicken}}}{\left[\dfrac{p_2 - p_1}{p_2 + p_1}\right]_{\text{beef}}}$$

The idea of cross elasticity is illustrated in Figure 10–5. Suppose the price of beef falls from \$.80 to \$.60, causing an increase in quantity demanded of beef from 2 to 3 pounds per week. The consumer will be less willing to buy chicken, even though its price has not changed. Thus, the reduction in the price of beef causes a reduction in the demand (that is, a shift in the demand curve) for chicken. The *cross elasticity between chicken and beef is positive, as it is for all substitutes,* and the *cross elasticity of complements is negative.*

Providing nothing disturbs the income-consumption relationship as shown in Figure 10–4, we know what consumption response to expect from a change in family income. But these curves can and do change in configuration and position with the passage of time. Changes in taste, changes in fashion, and changes in knowledge commonly influence these income-consumption relationships. A growing preference for beef, for example, would have the effect of raising the curve presented in Figure 10–4. And an upward shift in the curve would mean that, for any given income class, more beef would be consumed than now is indicated. These modifying influences do not render the concept of a consumption curve useless; they simply mean that we must make costly and inclusive budget studies periodically.

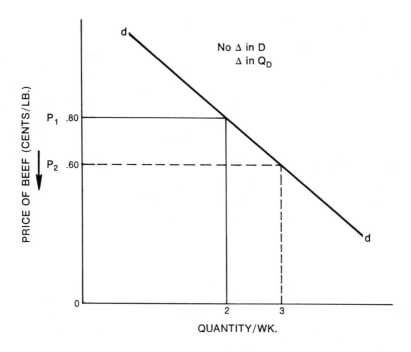

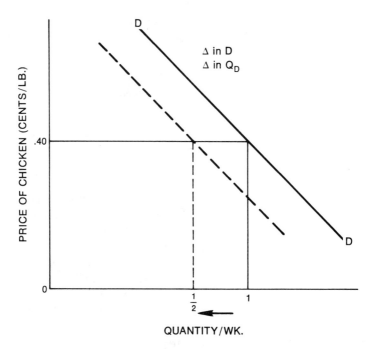

FIGURE 10–5. The Effect of a Change in the Price of Beef on the Demand for Chicken

A word or two about the hypothetical character of the demand curves presented here, such as the curve for chicken, is perhaps in order. The demand curve DD does not represent an actual measurement; it is illustrative only. We did not present a statistically derived consumer demand curve because such curves are terribly hard to come by. It is difficult to obtain a measure of the quantities of chicken (or any other commodity) that a particular consumer stands ready to take at varying prices, at any one time. Hence, the statistically derived demand curves that we do have are complex, sophisticated, and difficult to present. But the concept of a consumer-demand curve is straightforward and highly useful, so we have illustrated the concept with realistic, yet hypothetical, data.

Market Demand

The market demand for a particular commodity is the summation of all individual demands for that commodity. The market demand curve sums up the amounts that individual consumers stand ready to take at each price in the price-quality schedule. The individual consumer demand curve DD for chicken in Figure 10–3 may be converted to a market demand curve by assuming the individual portrayed is an "average" consumer and multiplying consumption at each price by the total population. Assuming the population of the United States to be 200 million, we obtain the following price-quantity schedule:

Price per Pound	Total Consumption (in millions of pounds)
$.65	3600
.55	4600
.45	6000
.35	8000
.25	10,000

The market demand curve is an analytical tool of great power. It tells us how much of a commodity, chicken in this case, all consumers will purchase at varying prices. If, then, we are able to derive statistically the demand curve for a *given commodity*, we are able to predict how much of that commodity will move into consumption at a particular price, or with a change in price. The idea of consumers exerting a pull on particular goods in the marketing channel now gains in precision. We do not visualize consumers aimlessly tossing coins down the marketing channel. On the contrary, we have a precise concept of demand that tells us how much consumers will spend on a commodity, on chicken, at various prices. Thus, our measure of the pull exerted by consumers on a specific good in the marketing channel is the market demand curve for that good.

We should never forget, however, that our measure (the market demand curve), can shift;—expand or contract. And real world market demand curves are constantly shifting as tastes and preferences, consumer incomes, and prices of related goods changes. These shifts do complicate the problem. An expansion in market demand, for example, means that all consumers stand ready to take more at the same price. So, our measure is not easily derived and is not to be used carelessly. But when properly applied, it is most useful.

POINTS FOR DISCUSSION

1. In what sense is the consumer sovereign?
2. Why are we able to state precise, physiological requirements with respect to food, but not with respect to fiber? How do these requirements vary with respect to sex, age, and weight?
3. What problems are encountered in the conversion of nutrient requirements into kinds and quantities of food? How do tastes and preferences enter into the problem?
4. What do we mean by the central problem of choice? How does the limitation of income act to create a problem of choice?
5. By what principle do consumers allocate their income between different lines of expenditure? How does the concept of diminishing marginal utility relate to this principle?
6. What is an income consumption curve? What variables are related in the income consumption curve?
7. What is a demand curve? What variables are related in the demand curve? What is the difference between a change in demand and a change in the quantity demanded?

REFERENCES

Cochrane, Willard W., and Carolyn Shaw Bell, *Economics of Consumption: Economics of Decision Making in the Household,* Chaps. 5, 7, 10, 16, and 17. New York: McGraw-Hill Book Co., Inc., 1956.

Expenditure Patterns of the American Family. National Industrial Conference Board, 1965.

Samuelson, P. A., *Economics,* 8th ed., Chap. 22. New York: McGraw-Hill Book Co., Inc., 1970.

PART THREE

Toward an Understanding
of Farm Prices

Chapter 11

The Price-income Structure

of Agriculture

Farm prices are constantly on the move, and that movement is often extreme in character. This we must recognize. Farm people often have the idea that there is such a thing as a normal price or a just price. The price they usually have in mind is a pleasant recollection from some favorable historical period. But farm price behavior is not one of stability. Rather, it is one of change, fluctuation, and sharp movement. It is this evolving pattern of farm prices in the United States, sometimes called the *structure* of farm prices, that we wish to portray.

The Farm Price Level

It is often useful to speak of a price level, for example, the general price level, the farm price level, or the retail food price level. When we speak of a price level, in this case the farm price level, we have in mind an average of the prices of all farm commodities. Such an average, with its changes from month to month or from year to year, that sums up the behavior of all farm prices is useful in situations in which we wish to speak of total agriculture. Now it may be readily seen that this device is a meaningful one if all farm prices move up and down together. But if some prices are rising, some falling, and others holding stable, the concept becomes devoid of meaning and may even convey a false impression. Fortunately, because prices of individual farm products tend to move up and down together, the concept of the farm price level is a handy one.

The Use of Index Numbers. To measure changes in the farm price level, or any other price level, we make use of a concept known as an index number. An index number measures the level of farm prices at any one time, not by measuring any particular price, but by representing the whole structure of prices. If, for example, a large number of prices are plotted over a series of years, one gets the impression of a badly frayed, raveled rope (see Figure 11–1). There are many loose strands, *yet a central core* exists, and the whole pattern follows the bends of that core. The index number becomes our measure of that central core, rising and falling with it through time.

An understanding of the computation of index numbers helps in understanding the meaning of an index number. Suppose we want to determine how much the level of farm prices has increased since the 1957–1959 period. Then, 1957–59 is called the base period and serves as a reference for prices in other years. To simplify the problem, we assume that there are only three farm commodities: wheat, hogs, and milk. We start with the following price information:

Commodity	U.S. Price, 1957–59 Average	U.S. Price, 1970
Wheat	$ 1.80 per bu.	$ 1.24 per bu.
Hogs	17.00 per cwt.	21.00 per cwt.
Milk	4.15 per cwt.	5.50 per cwt.

First, the price of each commodity in 1970 is expressed as a percentage of its average price in 1957–59. This percentage is sometimes called a *price relative*. The three price relatives can be averaged for a measure of the level of farm prices in 1970 compared to their level in the base period.

Commodity	Price Relative in 1970
Wheat	69
Hogs	124
Milk	133
Simple average	109

Thus, the price of wheat in 1970 was 69 percent of its 1957–59 level, that is, it fell, but the price of hogs and milk rose, so that the simple average of price relatives rose by nine percent.

This measure gives equal importance to each commodity, but in reality one commodity may be more "important" (in some sense) than another. One way (out of many) to correct this obvious imperfection is to weight each commodity by its proportional contribution to gross income of farmers in the base period.

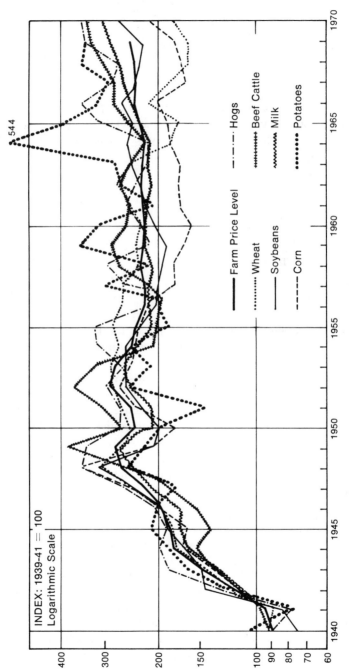

FIGURE 11-1. Indices of Prices Received by Farmers for All Commodities and for Selected Commodities, 1939–1970

INDEX: 1939-41 = 100
Logarithmic Scale

Farm Price Level ——— Hogs ——·——
Wheat ·········· Beef Cattle ++++++++
Soybeans ——— Milk ∿∿∿∿∿
Corn ——–——– Potatoes ●●●●●●

Commodity	Gross Income, 1957–59	Percentage of Gross Income
Wheat	2,122,339	20
Hogs	3,343,923	32
Milk	5,080,604	48

Because milk is the most important source, contributing 48 percent of gross income in the base period, the price of milk is given the most weight in the index of prices, and wheat, the least important source, is given the least weight. The weighted index of farm prices is computed by multiplying the price relative times its weight and finding the weighted average of price relatives as below.

Commodity	Weight	Weight × 1970 Price Relative
Wheat	20	20 × 69 = 1380
Hogs	32	32 × 124 = 3968
Milk	48	48 × 133 = 6384
		11732

Dividing the weighted total by the sum of the weights, we get *117*.

Thus, the weighted index of farm prices for 1970 is 117 rather than the simple average of 109. The weights provide a way of reflecting the relative importance of each commodity.

The index of 117 says that the average price of farm commodities increased 17 percent from 1957–59 to 1970, assuming that agriculture produced only three commodities. (In reality, the index of farmer's prices received takes into account all farm commodities.) It should be remembered that this farm price index does not tell us anything about the price level of the total economy, on the one hand, nor anything about the price of No. 2 hard winter wheat, on the other. It tells only what is happening to all farm prices on the average.

Long-run Price Trends

The only information we have that describes price-level movement over a long period of time in the United States is that for wholesale prices. We have a measure (index numbers) of the wholesale price level extending back to 1800 and broken down between farm and nonfarm products (see Figure 11–2). Surveying wholesale price-level movements from 1800 to 1960, we can observe some interesting developments. We have experienced four great price peaks, the first reaching its high point in 1814, the second in 1864, the third in 1920, and the fourth in 1951. A fifth peak in 1971 appears possible, although prices may continue to rise beyond that year. In

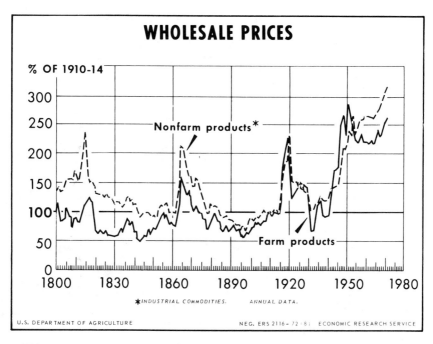

FIGURE 11–2. Wholesale Prices and Farm Prices as a Percent of Nonfarm Prices

every case, the peak in wholesale prices is associated with war or its aftermath. It would seem that wars and price inflations go hand in hand. Between these precipitous price peaks, we have had long, troughlike periods of low prices. From this, it becomes exceedingly clear that wholesale prices (whether farm or nonfarm) have not been stable. Price fluctuations have been the normal thing.

Another interesting trend emerges from Figure 11–2. We see that the amplitude of farm price swings has become greater over the years. In the early 1800s, the wholesale price level for farm products exhibited greater stability than the nonfarm price level. But in more recent years, the wholesale price level of farm products has shown the greatest variation. In the long run from 1800 to 1920 farm prices increased relative to nonfarm prices at the wholesale level (see the ratio of farm to nonfarm prices at the bottom of Figure 11–2). Finally, we observe that farm prices in the last two decades, even though supported by government action, have once again sagged.

In Figure 11–3, two well-known and commonly used farm price series appear: (1) the index of prices received by farmers, and (2) the parity index, which is an index of prices paid by farmers including interest, taxes, and farm wage rates. The index of prices received tells us the level of prices farmers received for the products they sold over the period 1910–71, relative

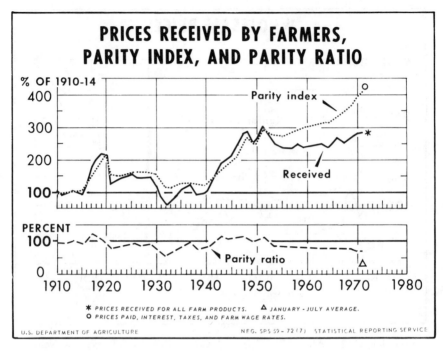

PRICES RECEIVED BY FARMERS, PARITY INDEX, AND PARITY RATIO

FIGURE 11–3

to the level of farm prices in 1910–14. The parity index tells us the level of prices farmers had to pay for production supplies and consumer goods over the period 1910–71, relative to what they paid for these supplies in 1910–14. And because the two series have the same base period, 1910–14, a comparison of them in the form of the parity ratio, for any given year, tells us whether farm products have a lower or higher purchasing power in terms of farm supplies as compared with 1910–14.[1] This comparison is made in the lower chart, where the parity ratio is below the 100 percent parity line whenever the prices-paid index exceeds the prices-received index. It needs to be pointed out carefully, however, that the prices received by farmers and the prices paid by farmers were not identical in 1910–14. As in our index problem, we simply let both the prices received and the prices paid in that period equal 100. Incidentally, the prices farmers received then were relatively high: 1910–14 is often referred to as the "golden age" of American agriculture.

It will be observed from Figure 11–3 that the prices received by farmers moved up to high levels during and immediately after World War I and then fell, in one swift movement, in 1921. Farm prices steadied in 1922 and remained on something of a plateau during the glittering 1920s, although

[1]The meaning and significance of the parity ratio is explained in greater detail in Chapter 23.

not too high a plateau. They broke again with the onset of the Great Depression and remained at relatively low levels during the 1930s. The prices that farmers had to pay for the things they purchased also fell in 1921, but not nearly to the extent that the received prices fell. Hence, the position of two series is reversed, and, for the next twenty years, the price level for those things that farmers bought remained substantially above the farm price level, the index of prices received by farmers. Now this does not mean that the price of a cookstove was greater than the price of one hundred pounds of hog, or that the price of butterfat was less than the price of gasoline. These index values tell us nothing about prices of specific items, and such information would be meaningless if it did, for the commodity units are not comparable. We learn from Figure 11–3 that, over the twenty-year period, 1921 to 1941, the prices paid by farmers were high, relative to the prices they received.

In 1942, prices received by farmer-producers began to rise in absolute terms, and they rose spectacularly over the period 1942–1948. Prices received by farmers also rose relative to prices paid by farmers. The prices-received series shot past the prices-paid series in the early years of World War II and held that preferred position down to 1949.

The 1950s and 1960s are suggestive once again of the 1920s and 1930s as far as farmers are concerned. Prices received by farmers thrust upward sharply in 1951 in conjunction with the Korean conflict. But they did not hold. After 1952, prices received by farmers began to decline. Furthermore, relative to the index of prices paid, the index of prices received was low and depressed throughout the 1950s and 1960s, even though there was an upward movement in both sets of prices during the late 1960s.

Because most of us have an interest in a particular crop or livestock product, let us look at some of the component items of the prices-received index (see Figure 11–4). Surveying the price behavior of the commodities presented, feed grains and hay, meat animals, cotton, oil-bearing crops, poultry and eggs, and dairy production, one point is made indelibly: the similarity of commodity price trends. Only two important exceptions to the overall pattern stand out: (1) cotton prices, in the early 1920s, rose strikingly above the general price trend; and (2) meat-animal prices, in the late 1920s and again in the late 1950s, ran counter to the general trend. The cotton exception may be explained by a very short crop in 1921 and below average crops in 1922–23, which had the effect of reducing the total world supply. The rise in meat-animal prices between 1925 and 1929, the very high meat-animal prices in 1951, and the upward trend during the 1960s would seem to stem from the great prosperity of those periods. When workers have spare money, they switch from bread and potatoes to pork chops and beef steaks, or perhaps, they just eat more chops and steaks. But it takes time to increase livestock numbers; supply was limited during the early

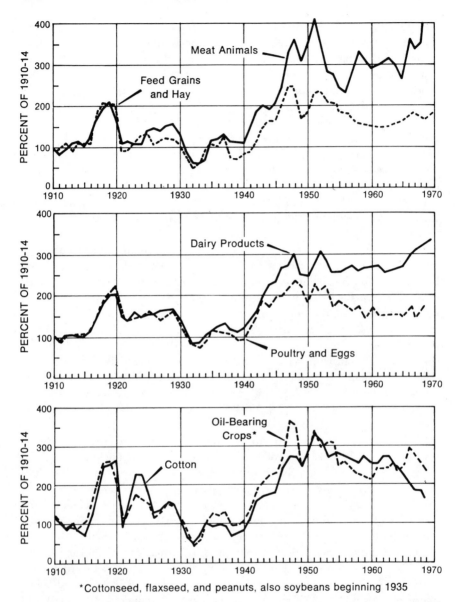

FIGURE 11–4.   Prices Received by Farmers for Selected Commodity Groupings, 1910–1970

phases of those periods, hence livestock prices advanced sharply. These variations are important, as are the multitude of smaller variations that escape us in these sweeping trend-like movements. The central and important point to be made, however, is the similarity to be found in commodity price movements in the long run. The structure of farm commodity prices trends up and down in the extreme, but the individual commodity prices maintain a rather uniform pattern within that structure.

Influencing Factors

We have observed the wide swings in the farm price level since 1910 and the tendency for farm price-level movements to be of greater magnitude than nonfarm price-level movements. We will now look at some of the more important forces or factors that have been at work over the years influencing, actually causing, these dramatic price-level swings. A first step in any analysis of prices, whether it be hog prices at a local livestock auction, the world wheat price, or the farm price level, is to sift out the various influencing factors and place them under two principal headings: *demand* and *supply*.

On the demand side of the price problem, there are several factors to be considered. The income of consumers is an important consideration, perhaps the most important. The tastes or preferences of consumers is another. And the ability of consumers to substitute one product for another must also be considered. In other words, these forces are always at work, influencing the amount of total food and the various kinds of food that consumers demand.

The farm price level, as measured by the index of prices received by farmers, moves up and down with any measure of consumer or national income we wish to take. Referring to Figure 11–5, we see that personal incomes in the United States fell in the early 1930s, rose modestly in the late 1930s, turned up sharply during the war years, and advanced persistently in a great period of national prosperity from 1945 to 1970. With the exception of the 1941–1947 period, which reflects the effects of World War II, expenditures on food have claimed a continuously decreasing proportion of consumers' disposable income, although the volume of expenditures continues to change in the same direction as disposable income. A brief reference to Figures 11–3 and 11–5 indicates the close correlation that exists between movements in income and the farm price level. We do not say that changes in income alone caused those price movements. We cannot say that because other factors must be considered, the supply of farm products for example. But it is obvious that the personal incomes of all people in the United States provide the bulk of the purchasing power out of which farm products are purchased. Hence, changes in the income received by individuals influence expenditures for food and in turn the demand for farm products and the prices at which they sell.

The total amount of food consumed by individuals and all consumers together changes very little with changes in tastes and preferences. We require so much food to ward off hunger and maintain a good state of health; those requirements are physiological. But within the total basket of

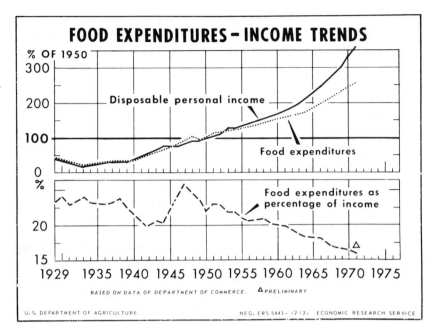

FOOD EXPENDITURES - INCOME TRENDS

Disposable personal income

Food expenditures

Food expenditures as percentage of income

1929   1935 1940 1945 1950 1955 1960 1965 1970 1975

BASED ON DATA OF DEPARTMENT OF COMMERCE.   △ PRELIMINARY

U. S. DEPARTMENT OF AGRICULTURE   NEG. ERS 5443- 72 (2)   ECONOMIC RESEARCH SERVICE

FIGURE 11–5

food demanded, consumers prefer this food item to that; they prefer beef steak to navy beans, for example. Consequently, changes in tastes and preference influence the demand for individual commodities in the total basket.

When consumers come to care less for a particular commodity than previously was the case, their expenditures for that commodity are likely to fall and the price of that commodity falls. Potatoes are a case in point. Consumers steadily cut down on their consumption of potatoes over the long period between 1900 and 1965—a clear case of reduction in the demand for potatoes from a change in tastes that resulted in a secular downward trend in potato prices. However, since 1965, per capita consumption of potatoes has increased, due to another change in consumer tastes brought about by the development of appealing forms of processed potatoes. In contrast, consumer preference for oranges increased over the period 1920–1970. This change in preference, in itself, acted to strengthen the demand for oranges and to strengthen orange prices. So we find in this determinant of demand (changes in consumer tastes and preferences) a reason for commodity price trends changing their position relative to one another in the structure of commodity prices.

But potato prices do not fall indefinitely and orange prices do not rise indefinitely. They do not for one very important reason. When potato prices fall, consumers tend to eat more potatoes and less of other kinds of

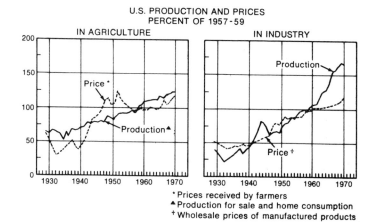

U.S. PRODUCTION AND PRICES
PERCENT OF 1957-59

* Prices received by farmers
▲ Production for sale and home consumption
† Wholesale prices of manufactured products

FIGURE 11–6

food halting the downward slide in potate prices. With oranges, we have the opposite situation: As the price of oranges rises, some people find oranges too expensive and substitute other fruits and/or vitamin pills for orange juice with the result that the price of oranges stops rising.

It is on the supply side of the price problem that we unearth some unusual relationships. We are aware that *total* agricultural output has increased steadily over the years (see Figure 11–6). But if we were to remove the upward trend from the agricultural production series, we would discover that *total* output does not change much from year to year. When farm prices were shooting skyward during World Wars I and II, total agricultural production increased but not much faster than the long-run trend. And when farm prices fell sharply and remained low during the interwar period, total agricultural production leveled off but did not decline. This behavior on the part of agricultural production is in sharp contrast to the behavior of industrial production. On the nonfarm side, production varies directly with changes in the price level. When industrial prices move up, so does total output, and when prices move down, so does total output.

This relationship in industry and the lack of relationship in agriculture has important implications for the price-level movements. The expansion in total industrial output associated with a price rise tends to modify that rise; more goods come off the assembly lines to ease the pressure on prices. And the contraction in total industrial output associated with a price decline tends to modify that decline; the fewer goods on retail shelves act to strengthen prices. But in agriculture, we do not find this price-dampening influence of output. Total output pours forth largely without regard to price-level movements. This pouring forth of a relatively constant volume of food and fiber products when the price level is falling simply acts to push prices to lower levels. Carry-overs pile on top of average crops and the combined supplies provide a persistent downward pressure on farm prices. In an upward price movement, just the opposite occurs. Greatly expanded supplies of food and fiber do not materialize even though demand is increasing and prices are rising; hence, consumers bid wildly for what they believe are short supplies and prices keep rising; total agricultural output, like "Old Man River," just keeps rolling along.

Cyclical Price Movements

Although the long, wide price swings that we have been considering are undoubtedly of the greatest importance to them, American farmers are confronted with other types of price movements that also are important to them. In the day-to-day and month-to-month operation of the farm, producers are faced with short-run price movements that are more or less regular in character and that last more than one year. These we call cyclical price movements.

Both the production and prices of some types of livestock move up and down in a somewhat regular, cyclical pattern. In Figure 11–7, we see this wave-like price movement for hogs: the hog price cycle. We observe a fairly regular cyclical pattern that takes between four and five years to complete itself. Hog prices go up for about two years and down for about two, and this cycle repeats itself over and over again. Sometimes the number of years required to move from one price peak to the next extends to five or six years and sometimes drops to three. And some cylical movements are more intense than others; some are deep and some are shallow. But a persistent, wave-like movement of about four years in duration emerges, that is clear.

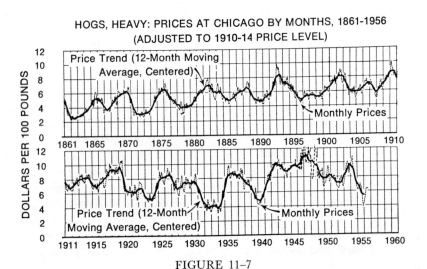

HOGS, HEAVY: PRICES AT CHICAGO BY MONTHS, 1861-1956 (ADJUSTED TO 1910-14 PRICE LEVEL)

FIGURE 11–7

Two forces generate the hog cycle. One is the supply of corn. When the supply of corn is large, the farmer's best alternative use for most of it is feeding hogs. When it is short, a decrease in the number of hogs fed is required to make the available corn go around. The second force is a change in the price of hogs and the farmer's attempt to respond to that price change. Farmers try to expand production when hog prices are high and contract production when prices are low. (Although we have observed that the total output of agriculture is stable in the short-run, the production of individual commodities often varies and importantly so, from year to year.)

The hog-corn ratio puts these two forces in one formula, and helps explain the cyclical movement in hog production and prices. The ratio is computed by dividing the price of one hundred pounds of hog by the price of a bushel of corn. The ratio tells us how many bushels of corn are required to buy one hundred pounds of hog. A high ratio means that hogs are high-priced in relation to corn, that putting corn into hogs is a profitable way to market corn. But it takes time to raise hogs, hence, an increase in the market supply of hogs does not occur until more than a year after farmers first started to expand production. And one year later, the situation is likely to be changed: hog numbers will have outrun corn supplies and corn prices will be high, whereas hog supplies will have increased and hog prices fallen. Thus, the hog-corn ratio falls, and producers contract production. This sequence of events gives rise to the hog price cycle.

The effect of changes in the hog-corn ratio on the number of hogs marketed is shown in Figure 11–8. The upper part of the chart shows hog-corn ratios as they move above and below the average line of slightly over twelve. The lower part of the chart shows the cyclical movement in hog slaughterings. Comparing the upper chart with the lower, we see that the number of hogs slaughtered always reaches a peak about two years after the hog-corn ratio has reached a peak. We see, on the other hand, that a low hog-corn ratio, when the ratio falls below the average, causes a decrease in marketings a year or two later. And even though the average price ratio seems to be increasing over time, the cycle still seems to hold.

Beef cattle also exhibit a cyclical pattern with respect to prices and production. A market cycle, averaging about fourteen years in length, is apparent with respect to both the number of beef cattle on farms and the prices received for beef cattle. Although somewhat irregular in length, the cycle is smoother and more pronounced than that for hogs.

Fluctuations in feed supplies and attempts by farmers to respond to price changes generate a beef cycle. The lapse of time between breeding and marketing is, however, much longer for beef cattle than for hogs. Cattle are not as prolific as hogs. Considering that cattle have a longer life cycle as well, this means that it takes longer to increase and decrease beef production. When farmers start to increase production, they first hold back breeding stock. This reduces the numbers marketed and market prices rise. These

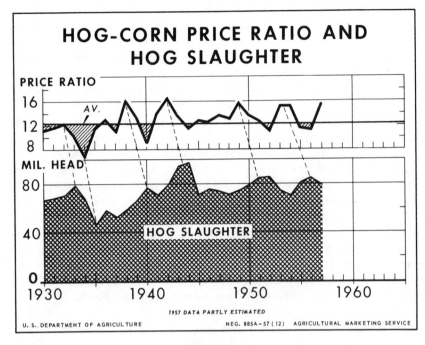

FIGURE 11–8

higher prices encourage a further expansion in numbers. When increased supplies of beef cattle eventually do come to market, prices drop, and farmers begin to liquidate breeding stock. Thus, we have a cycle for beef cattle with respect to both prices and numbers that is similar to the hog cycle, except that a greater number of years is involved for the beef-cattle cycle.

Seasonal Price Movements

We now want to look at those time-price movements, occurring within one year, to which we give the name of *seasonal* price movements. The prices of most farm products do not remain constant throughout the year; they follow some seasonal pattern. Usually prices are lowest during harvest and immediately thereafter (or during the period of flush production), and then they rise throughout the remainder of the year, reaching their highest point just prior to the period of harvest or the period of flush production. This is the common seasonal pattern, although exceptions may be found for particular commodities and for particular years.

This seasonal movement in farm prices does not result from any imperfections in, or manipulation of, the market. The price of a farm product can be expected to rise over the year as costs of storage and handling accumulate, or as current supplies are reduced because production of such commodities as eggs and milk slacken off in the winter months. On the other hand, we would expect prices to be lowest in that period of the year when agricultural products come to market directly and costs of storage and handling are at a minimum.

The seasonal pattern in prices and production is highly pronounced for eggs, as may be seen in Figure 11–9. It will be observed that the production of eggs reaches a high point in March, April, and May and reaches the low in September, October, November, and December. Egg prices move directly opposite to the seasonal production pattern. When farm production is high, prices received for eggs are low, and when production is low, prices received for eggs are high. A large proportion of the eggs produced during the flush season moves into storage and then moves out during the slack season. This tends to even out the supply over the season and modify the seasonal price movement. We would not, however, expect the seasonal pattern in prices to be eliminated, even with a perfect storage program because costs of storage must increase as the season advances.

Seasonal patterns in production and prices are important for such other commodities as butter, corn, hogs, lambs, cattle, fluid milk, and fruits and vegetables.

Daily Price Fluctuations

In addition to the seasonal, short-run, and long-run price fluctuations, certain farm prices fluctuate a good deal from one day to the next. This fluctuation is of concern to sellers of these commodities like livestock. They may hear one price quoted by a market news service, but by the time they market their livestock the price has changed (and it seems to them that it always moves down!).

Figure 11–10 shows the daily prices and quantities of hogs sold at eight terminal markets in 1964. The analysis of those daily price data revealed that the important factors influencing prices on a particular day were lagged price, season of the year and day of the week.[2] Somewhat at variance with popular belief, the analysis showed that daily prices generally respond very little (percentage-wise) to changes in the quantity supplied. On the other hand, the study showed that supplier of hogs to the terminal markets respond sharply to price fluctuations by varying their shipments following price changes. In fact, the quantity shipped increased 8.5 percent for every 1 percent increase in the previous day's price.

Commodities like hogs whose prices are determined in auction markets all experience daily price fluctuation, but it is clear that such daily

[2]Raymond M. Leuthold, "Economic Analysis and Predictions of Short-Run Hog Price and Quantity Fluctuations," AERR-104, Dept. of Agricultural Economics, Agricultural Experiment Station, University of Illinois at Urbana-Champaign, June 1970, p. 13.

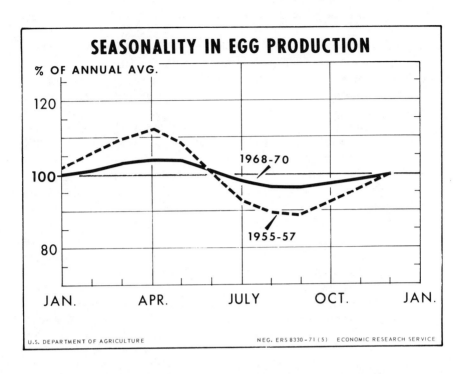

U.S. DEPARTMENT OF AGRICULTURE

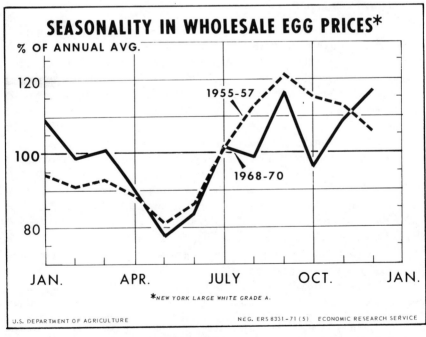

U.S. DEPARTMENT OF AGRICULTURE

FIGURE 11–9

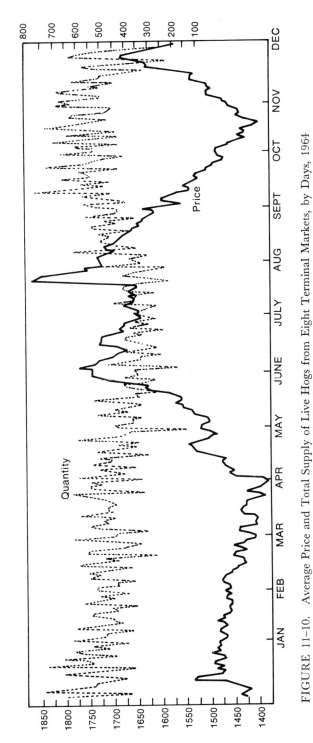

FIGURE 11–10. Average Price and Total Supply of Live Hogs from Eight Terminal Markets, by Days, 1964

fluctuations are of much smaller magnitude than the seasonal and cyclical price movements. The causes are different for different commodities and an understanding of these causes are most valuable for sellers and buyers of the commodity.

Farm Income

Farm prices are important because they reflect the cost of producing farm commodities to consumers and thereby guide consumers in the allocation of their incomes. Farm prices also guide farmers in the allocation of their productive efforts. However, farm prices are more than management guides. They are vital components in the determination of farm incomes, but the correspondence between farm prices and incomes is far from direct.

Gross farm income in 1970—the sum of cash receipts from farm marketings, the value of food produced and consumed on the farm, the rental value of farm dwellings, and direct government payments—is estimated at $56 billion (Table 11–1). This was the highest level gross farm income had ever reached and was the result of a steady increase since the middle 1950s.

TABLE 11–1

Gross and Net Income of All Farm Operators from Farming,
United States, 1910–1970

Year(s)	Realized Gross Farm Income	Production Expenses	Realized Net Income
	($ millions)	($ millions)	($ millions)
1910–14	7,592	3,789	3,802
1915–19	13,055	5,354	6,870
1920–24	12,458	7,312	5,146
1925–29	13,533	7,498	6,035
1930–34	8,362	5,167	3,195
1935–39	10,473	5,744	4,728
1940–44	18,281	9,610	8,671
1945–49	31,313	16,286	15,044
1950–54	35,190	21,418	13,772
1955–59	35,621	23,817	11,804
1960	38,088	26,352	11,736
1961	39,771	27,125	12,646
1962	41,258	28,639	12,619
1963	42,271	29,688	12,583
1964	42,567	29,481	13,086
1965	44,926	30,933	13,993
1966	49,740	33,406	16,334
1967	48,998	34,775	14,223
1968	51,038	36,012	15,026
1969	54,598	38,444	16,154
1970	56,188	40,423	15,765

Source: *The Farm Income Situation*, U.S.D.A., (issued four times each year).

The long-term pattern of gross income follows the same general movements as prices—up between 1910 and 1920, stationary during the 1920s, then down during the Great Depression, and recovering its earlier peak during the war years of the early 1940s. Gross farm income was nearly constant during the 1950s before renewing its upward trend in the 1960s. However, farmers have not realized income gains of the same magnitude.

Total production expenses have more than kept up with increases in gross income since the middle 1940s. In fact, 1970 realized net farm income was very close to the 1945–59 average. Between 1960 and 1964, gross income increased about $1 billion a year while net income barely changed. In 1965 and 1966, realized net income increased substantially, but in 1967, net income fell because gross income decreased while production expenses increased. This brings to light an important income relationship in agriculture: net farm incomes are at the crack end of the whip. Production expenses tend to be sticky: rising more slowly than gross farm income and falling more slowly. Consequently, net farm income rises rapidly in good years, as in 1951 and 1966, but in the bad years a squeezing action comes into play as production expenses remain high and relatively constant and gross farm incomes decline. This is the cost-price squeeze so common to American agriculture, which has been experienced by farmers throughout the middle 1950s and the 1960s.

Net incomes of farm operators have fluctuated in the extreme—from $1.9 billion in 1932 to $17.3 billion in 1947. But when we compare variations in net income with farming's share of the national income, the latter has fluctuated much less (Table 11–2). That is, farming's share has decreased steadily since 1935–39, with the exception of the years during World War II, but the trend has been a fairly stable one. Farming generated somewhat more than 8 percent of the national income during 1950. By 1970, farming was producing only about 3 percent of the national income, reflecting the rapid growth of the nonfarm economy and the rather stable demand for food.

Income Comparisons

The average income of the farm population has been consistently below that of the nonfarm population, but as shown in Figure 11–11, in recent years the farm population has been "catching up." In 1957–59, per capita income of farm people (from both farm and nonfarm sources) was about 50 percent of the nonfarm level, but by 1970 it had increased to 75 percent of the nonfarm level. Tempering this improvement, as we saw in Chapter 1, is the fact that a significant part of the income of the farm population is beginning to come from off-farm employment.

Not all the interesting income comparisons are to be made between the farm and nonfarm sectors of the economy. There is a great deal of variation

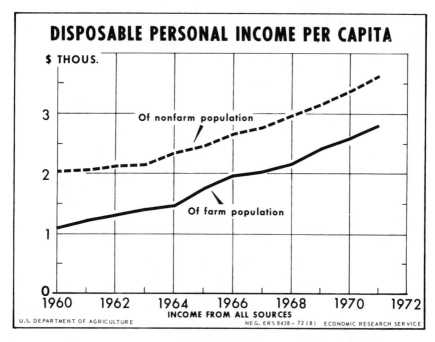

FIGURE 11–11

of incomes by size of farm and location. Although average incomes of the farm population are lower than the nonfarm population, those commercial farmers with sales over $20,000 have maintained a relatively satisfactory income position, as shown in Figure 11–12. It is the farmer with sales under $10,000 per year, and to some extent those with sales between $10,000 and $20,000 per year, who have unsatisfactory incomes.

Annual net farm income per farm in 1971 varied from $34,616 in Arizona to $334 in West Virginia, with a U.S. average of $5,581 (Figure 11–13). No other state approaches Arizona. California is second at $20,000 followed by Florida at $16,000 with fourteen other states over $7,000. At the low end, New Hampshire, Virginia, Tennessee and West Virginia all averaged realized net farm income per farm at less than $3,000.

Price and Income Problems

We have not as yet inquired into how farm prices are determined. We have been preoccupied with a presentation of the structure of prices and incomes in agriculture, with a presentation of a setting for questions and problems to come later. Now, one of the important questions that we want to develop thoroughly in Chapter 12 is that dealing with the determination of farm prices. Why is one price high and another price low? And what

TABLE 11–2

Relation of Total Net Income From Farming to National Income,
United States, 1935–1970.

Year(s)	Total National Income	Total Net Income from Farming	Farm Income as a Percentage of National Income
	($ millions)	($ millions)	
1935–39	60,929	6,232	10.2
1940–44	124,192	10,872	8.7
1945–49	183,219	17,591	9.6
1950–54	266,389	17,270	6.5
1955–59	348,019	15,121	4.3
1960	398,665	15,857	4.0
1961	410,443	16,898	4.1
1962	440,386	17,301	3.9
1963	464,523	17,404	3.7
1964	501,415	16,653	3.3
1965	544,706	19,630	3.6
1966	599,402	21,183	3.5
1967	633,496	20,084	3.2
1968	690,715	20,425	3.0
1969	740,752	22,908	3.1
1970	773,372	22,550	2.9

Source: *The Farm Income Situation* U.S.D.A., annual July issues. The data on total net income from farming include farm wages, interest on farm mortgages, rent to nonfarm landlords in addition to the realized net income shown in Table 11–1.

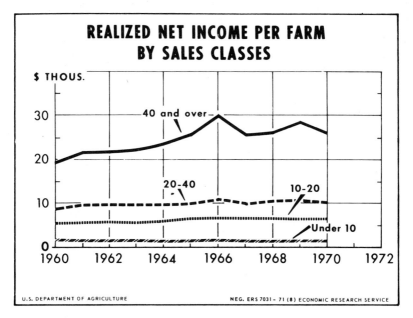

FIGURE 11–12

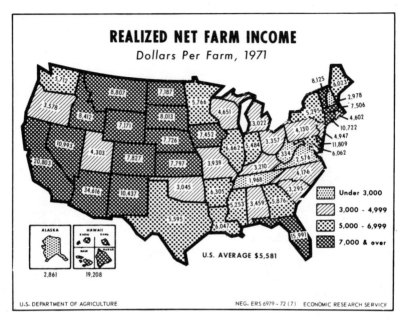

REALIZED NET FARM INCOME
Dollars Per Farm, 1971

U.S. AVERAGE $5,581

Under 3,000
3,000 - 4,999
5,000 - 6,999
7,000 & over

U.S. DEPARTMENT OF AGRICULTURE   NEG. ERS 6979 - 72 (7)   ECONOMIC RESEARCH SERVICE

FIGURE 11–13

causes one commodity price to rise and another to fall? These are questions to which we must provide answers, for we have seen that farm prices do rise and fall, often in an extreme fashion. But we do not want answers so narrow in scope that they fit only the one situation under investigation. We want to develop a method for analyzing the price-making process that can be used in any situation.

Probably the most important question asked by producers and consumers is: what functions do prices perform in a dynamic society? We are all familiar with and we have seen, in the recent discussion, how prices influence the incomes received by farmers. But is this the only role that prices are expected to play, or do farm prices play other and more-complicated roles in the operating economy? These are not idle questions. Farm people, working through the federal government, have been tinkering with the pricing system for years, and they seem determined to continue to do so. But to tinker without an appreciation of the consequences involved is dangerous. Thus, a thorough understanding of the function performed by prices becomes imperative.

After we understand how the price of a particular commodity is determined and what the function of commodity prices are in the operating economy, we must inquire in more detail into an explanation of farm price-level movements in the United States. Why is it that all farm prices seem to travel the same tortuous road together? What is the explanation for the extreme movements in the farm price level? We have observed the extreme behavior of the farm price level, and we have seen some of the implications for farm incomes. But what can be done to reduce the amplitude of these price-level movements? What can be done to prevent the level from fluctuating so widely? Here is the heart of the farm price problem.

After we have built, bit by bit, an understanding of farm price behavior —commodity prices and the price level—we will analyze current government programs and alternative proposals for dealing with the problem. For we must provide some help in trying to answer the question: how may we best support farm prices and farm incomes? But, it is vital to understand the functioning of the price system before trying to answer this important problem.

POINTS FOR DISCUSSION

1. What do we mean by the general price level and farm price level?
2. How do index numbers measure a price level?
3. Construct an index of food prices for these items on sale in your local grocery store: bread, fluid milk, round steak, eggs, oranges, and coffee. What weights will you use?
4. How do farm prices behave in wartime? What are the important causes of this behavior on the demand side? On the supply side?
5. How does the process of substitution operate to moderate commodity price movements?
6. What is the hog price cycle? How is the hog-corn ratio related to the hog price cycle?
7. Does net income from agriculture fluctuate in a more extreme fashion than national income? What has happened to agriculture's share of the national income in recent years?
8. Do farm workers or urban workers on the average receive the higher incomes?
9. In which geographical areas of the United States are farm incomes the highest? The lowest? What was the range in incomes in 1969?

REFERENCES

Agricultural Outlook Charts. U.S.D.A. (annual issues).

COCHRANE, W. W. *Farm Prices: Myth and Reality,* Chap. 2, Minneapolis: University of Minnesota Press, 1958.

The Farm Income Situation. U.S.D.A. (July issue of each year provides a summary).

Report of the Governor's Study Commission on Agriculture, The State of Minnesota, 1958, pp. 97–150.

WAITE, WARREN C., AND HARRY C. TRELOGAN, *Agricultural Market Prices,* 2nd ed., Chaps. 2, 9, and 10. New York: John Wiley & Sons, Inc., 1951.

Chapter 12

How Farm Prices
Are Determined

We inquired into the nature and problems of agricultural production in Part I. From that discussion, we gained some insight into the way in which the supply of a commodity is determined: how farmers decide what and how much to produce and at what cost. In Part II, we inquired into the nature of demand: how consumers decide what food and fiber products they want and in what quantities. Further, the movement of farm products to the consumer through the complex marketing system was investigated. Now, we want to bring these ideas together in an explanation of how farm prices are determined. The economic forces arising in the household, under the category *demand*, and on the farm, under the category *supply*, command our attention in the price-making process.

Price, that is, the price of a particular farm commodity, provides a neat focal point for studying the economic system. Most of the important economic forces come into focus in a study of the price-making process. Thus, we seek a full explanation of price determination, not only to understand how the price of a bushel of wheat is arrived at but also to provide an explanation of the operating economy.

Demand

The *demand* of an individual consumer for a particular product is defined as the amounts of that product that the consumer stands ready to take at varying prices (refer to the discussion of demand in Chapter 10).

The market demand for a particular product is the sum of the individual consumer demands. Thus, the *demand* for a product in a particular market is defined as the quantities of that product that all consumers stand ready to take at varying prices.

The demand for pork in the United States' market is illustrated in Figure 12–1.[1] We see at once, in this hypothetical but nonetheless realistic example, that the amount of pork demanded increases as price declines: at a price of \$.53, all consumers stand ready to take 10.8 billion pounds of pork; at a price of \$.45, they stand ready to take 11.9 billion pounds, and so on down the scale. For a century or more, economists have explained this phenomenon by using the concept of utility as discussed in Chapter 10. As each consumer purchases additional pounds of pork, the utility derived from each additional pound consumed declines, *when all other things remain constant, unchanged.* Or to take a more exciting example, the satisfaction

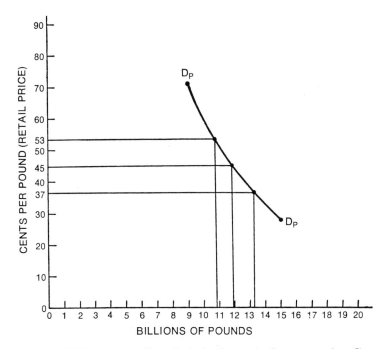

FIGURE 12–1. Hypothetical Demand Curve at the Consumer Level for Pork, by Carcass Weight Equivalent in the U.S. Market

[1]To simplify the discussion, we treat the United States as one market, which, in fact, it is, but we assume away geographic price differentials arising out of different transportation costs. Further, we assume that pork is one homogeneous product. And last, we ignore foreign trade in pork products.

(the utility) derived from a piece of pie, say the tenth in a pie-eating con-
test, is somewhat less than that derived from any of the previous pieces and
much less than that derived from eating the first. And perhaps, the twelfth
piece has a negative utility, that is, it makes us sick. Now this explanation
as to why we value additional units of a product less and less is a useful and
meaningful explanation. But it has certain limitations. This concept of
utility is a nebulous thing. It cannot be measured directly; and whether the
utility of the second piece of pie was greater for you than me, we have no
way of knowing.

Economists have extended theory to include a second way to explain the
downward slope of the demand curve. It is a more behavioristic explanation;
one that says less about why and more about how. The consumer will take
more pork at a lower price for two reasons: (1) when the price of pork
goes down and the prices of other food products do not, pork has become
relatively cheaper, hence, it pays to substitute pork for other food commodities; and (2) when pork is an important item in the budget, a decline
in the price of pork increases the real income of the consumer, and out of
this increase he may buy more of all products including pork. The first of
these reasons is known as the *substitution effect,* which describes the behavior
of consumers in substituting lower-priced food items in the diet for more
expensive items. The second reason is known as the *income effect,* which
describes the behavior of consumers in purchasing more goods and services
when their real income has been increased by a price decline in one of the
principal items of their budget. The advantage of this explanation exists,
then, in the fact that we can observe these actions and measure them. The
two explanations, the old and the new, complement one another and render
more complete our understanding of the concept of demand.

As we saw in Chapter 10, the price elasticity of demand provides a
measure of the relative change in quantity demanded that occurs as a result
of a price change along the demand curve. Using the arc elasticity formula,
the elasticity of demand for pork between the prices of $.45 and $.37 is
−0.53. (The reader should verify this calculation.)

The concept of elasticity, strictly interpreted, refers to infinitesimally
small changes from point to point along the demand curve.[2] But in the
economic world, price-quantity data most often occur in discrete jumps, as
indicated by the points along the demand curve in Figure 12–1. Therefore,
the arc elasticity formula is commonly applied. This measure of elasticity
($E = -0.53$) means that the rate of increase in the amount of pork pur-

---

[2]The point elasticity formula (as distinct from the arc elasticity formula given in Chapter
10) is given by:

$$\frac{dq}{q} \div \frac{dp}{p} \text{ or equivalently, } \frac{dq}{dp} \frac{p}{q}$$

where q = quantity, p = price, dq = infinitesimal change in q, and dp = infinitesimal change in p.

chases is 0.53 of the associated rate of decrease in the price of pork. Stated approximately, the percentage increase in the quantity purchases is one-half the percentage decrease in price. And the minus sign before the esti-mate −0.53 indicates that the demand curve is negatively inclined, as all good demand curves are supposed to be.

As we pointed out in our earlier discussion of demand, the three classes of forces that can change the position of the demand curve in the short run are: changes in tastes and preferences of consumers, changes in consumer incomes, and changes in the prices of competing commodities.

When a change in tastes and preferences is running against a com-modity, as would seem to be the case with pork, we would expect the demand curve to shift to the left, to contract. By contract, we mean very specifically that the quantity taken *at any given price,* say $.45, is reduced. In contrast, an expansion in consumer incomes would have the effect of shifting the demand curve for a normal good to the right. The third determinant is the most difficult to measure and handle. The prices of close substitutes are changing all the time, and the combinations are almost limitless. But we must recognize that a change in the price in some commodity, such as beef or chicken, will have an important influence on the quantity of pork de-manded.

Our analytical tool, the demand curve, is forged. We have an explana-tion for its slope, and we have a method for measuring that slope. Finally, we know what factors determine the position of the demand curve and cause it to shift.

Supply

The *supply* of an individual producer of a given product is defined as the amounts of that product the producer is willing to produce and sell at varying prices (refer to the discussion of commodity supply in Chapter 4). Thus, we have a supply curve for an individual producer comparable to the demand of the individual consumer. It happens that the supply curve of a producer of a particular commodity, say pork, is identical with the marginal cost curve of the pork enterprise of that farm firm. This is so because the marginal cost curve describes the additional costs associated with the pro-duction of one additional unit: the cost of producing the sixty-ninth pig over the sixty-eighth. Now, if we know the cost of producing the marginal pig, the sixty-ninth, we know the price that the farmer must receive to call forth the extra production (that is, a price that covers the cost of producing the sixty-ninth pig). Hence, the marginal cost curve of the individual pro-ducer is, in fact, the supply curve of the hog-pork enterprise on his farm.

Very simply, the market supply for a particular product, in this case, pork, is the sum of the individual supplies. Thus, the *supply* in a particular

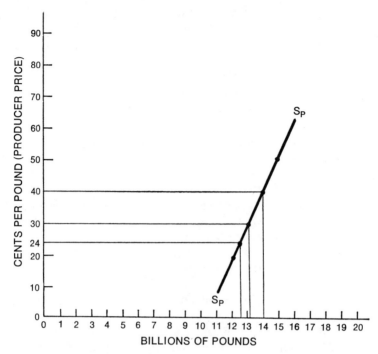

FIGURE 12–2.   Hypothetical Supply Curve at the Producer Level for Pork, by Carcass Weight Equivalent in the U.S. Market

market may be defined as the amount of that product that all producers in that market are willing to produce and sell at varying prices.

A hypothetical representation of the supply of pork in the United States' market is illustrated in Figure 12–2. We see that the supply curve is positively inclined—slopes upward and to the right—which tells us that amounts offered on the market increase as price increases. Reading off the supply curve, S_pS_p, in Figure 12–2, we obtain the following information: at a price of $.24 (producer price), farmers will supply the market with 12.6 billion pounds of pork; at a price of $.30, a supply of 13.1 billion pounds is forthcoming; at a price of $.40, a supply of 14 billion pounds is forthcoming, and so on. In other words, *when all other things are constant, unchanged* (for example, prices of competing products, costs of production), we can set forth the general principle that producers will produce and sell a larger volume as the price of that product rises. And that, of course, is what the hypothetical supply curve, S_pS_p, describes.

This relationship between price and amount offered should not come as a surprise. It squares with our everyday experience. To induce most people to put forth more effort and produce a greater supply, a greater reward must be offered. In most cases, they will produce more at higher prices. In a more rigorous sense, the supply curve slopes upward and to the right because it represents the sum of the marginal cost curves of all firms producing hogs. And as we already know, the marginal cost curves will be rising in each instance, indicating the additional costs involved in producing one more pig, or one hundred additional pounds of pork. The commodity supply curve may, however, be more gently sloped than the marginal cost curves of individual firms because new firms enter production at higher prices. At higher prices, the outputs of newly attracted producers of hogs must be added to the market supply. Thus, the market supply curve may possess some slope, as in Figure 12–2, even when the marginal cost curve of the hog-producing enterprise is highly inelastic (nearly vertical in position).

The relative responsiveness of quantity to price changes along a supply curve is measured by the supply elasticity, calculated by the formula stated in Chapter 4. The price elasticity of supply between $.24 and $.30 along the curve shown in Figure 12–2 is, as the reader can verify, 0.17. This measure of elasticity ($E = 0.17$) means that, relative to the existing price and quantity, the increase in the amount supplied is only 17 percent as great as the increase in price. Over this price range, the hypothetical supply curve for pork may be described as highly inelastic.

As in the case of the demand curve, the supply curve can and does shift positions. Even if the hypothetical supply curve, $S_p S_p$, is properly constructed and positioned as of, say, 1960, there is little reason to assume that it had the same position in 1965, or that it had that position in 1955. But the determinants of the position of the supply curve are not the same as those determining the position of the demand curve. In fact, the determinants of the supply curve, the factors that fix its position and cause it to shift, are of an altogether different nature than those discussed in connection with demand.

The position of the supply curve is determined by *cost* relationships. Money costs of the agents of production combined in the production of hogs influence the position of the marginal cost curve, as do technological innovations. A technological innovation that increases the productivity of the hog enterprise or reduces the money prices of productive agents has the effect of lowering marginal costs, which, in turn, cause the supply curve to expand to the right. This follows from the fact that hog formers may now produce any given volume of hogs at a lower cost than before, which is the same thing as saying that producers may now offer the same amount at a lower price. The latter condition describes and defines an expansion in supply. In the opposite direction, when the prices of productive agents rise, we find that marginal costs rise and the supply curve shifts to the left; that is, it contracts.

A Purely Competitive Market

Before we come to grips with the problem of price determination, we need some knowledge of the market in which price is to be determined, and of the behavior of individuals in that market. We could describe the nature and operation of some specific market, as for example a terminal livestock market or a local livestock auction. We will not follow that procedure, however. We will abstract from our knowledge of and experience with the operation of *competitive* markets and define the conditions that must be satisfied in order that a market be purely competitive. It is the determination of price in a *purely competitive* market that we will inquire into first.

The concept of a purely competitive market is a stilted concept, and certainly most markets do not satisfy the rigorous conditions imposed by this concept. But we make use of it because the price-making process can most clearly be described in such a synthetic market. Later, we can relax some of the conditions imposed by the concept of a perfectly competitive market.

The nature of pure competition may be described by four conditions:

1. The sales and purchases of individual firms and households are so small, relative to the total volume of transactions in the market, that each exerts no perceptible influence on the price of the product it sells or purchases.
2. The products of all firms in the industry are homogenous and indistinguishable, so that the product of a single firm cannot be identified after it is sold.
3. There are no restraints to the free operation of the market, and the mobility of resources is not restricted in any way.
4. All units operating in the market have equal access to information, and that information adequately describes the operation of the market.

We must consider one more element: the behavior of individuals or economic units operating in the market. We make the fundamental assumption that every individual or economic unit in the market behaves *rationally*. Rational economic behavior implies that the individual in his economic action seeks to "maximize his gains and minimize his losses." In other words, the individual undertakes those activities that increase his net income, or net return, or material well-being, and refuses to engage in activities that decrease them. Critics often claim that this maximizing assumption is unrealistic and point out that individuals often behave irrationally in the economic sense; they are often careless, charitable, or listless, rather than vigilantly acquisitive. And insofar as these criticisms are valid, our theoretical explanation of price determination does not hold. Still, an appeal to personal experience reveals the general validity of this assumption: as producers and consumers, we seek, in general, to maximize our gains and minimize our losses. As we shall see, this assumption regarding the behavior of market participants proves most useful in developing a theory of prices.

Derived Demand and Supply

The reader may have observed that our market-demand curve for pork exists at the consumer level: quantities demanded are related to retail prices. The market supply for pork exists at the producer level: quantities supplied are related to producer prices. Thus, for mechanical reasons, we may not combine on the same chart the demand and supply curves in their present forms. They do not have common vertical axes.

If, in this pork example, it is our decision to explain the determination of price at the consumer or retail level, we must *derive* a supply curve that incorporates marketing and processing charges. Such a derived supply curve we may then relate to the presently constructed demand curve. However, if we wish to explain the determination of price at the producer level, we must *derive* a demand curve for pork out of which marketing and processing charges are subtracted. Such a derived demand curve we may then relate to the supply curve at the producer level. Technically, either method is correct, and we could apply either with propriety. We will not, however, use either method. Rather, we will derive both the demand and the supply curves to obtain schedules representative of those existing in the central wholesale markets for hogs. In Figure 12–3, the derived demand and supply curves for hogs (carcass-weight equivalent), both at the wholesale level, are presented. With the aid of these derived demand and supply curves, we will inquire into the price-making process at the wholesale level.

We follow this mechanical procedure for good, analytical reasons. The source of demand is to be found in consumer decisions. The source of supply is to be found in producer decisions. But original consumer demand rarely meets original producer supply to determine price; the marketing system intervenes. The basic determination of price takes place somewhere within the marketing system, and, in this hog-pork example, we place it at the wholesale terminal market. The basic determination of the price of pork occurs through the competitive action of producers and producer representatives, on one side, and packers and packer representatives at the wholesale level, on the other.

It would be a mistake to regard this pork example as an exception. Producers and consumers rarely come into direct contact in the modern, interdependent economy. There are about a million commercial producers of farm products and some 200 million consumers of them. In this context, most transactions involving producers and consumers are negotiated with intermediaries in the marketing system, and it is to the wholesale markets that we turn to observe the price-making process. Changes in consumer demand and/or producer supply work themselves out in the central markets and result in changed central market prices. The initiating price-making forces grow out of the decision of consumers and producers, but the tangible results, as far as prices are concerned, first appear at the wholesale level.

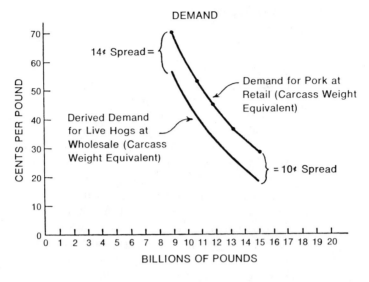

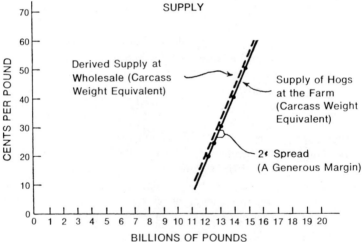

FIGURE 12–3.   Derived Demand and Supply Curves for Pork
in the Wholesale Market

For example, an increase in the demand for pork first manifests itself
at the retail level in an increase in sales. The local supermarket usually will
not mark up its price. If its competitor down the street has not done so, the
first store would cut its sales by increasing its price. Thus, retail store
operators generally prefer to follow a safe course and sell more at the same
price. In this way, they realize an increased return from an increased volume
of turnover. But when all retailers increase their orders for pork products,

dealers in the central market feel the increased demand and compete more vigorously for supplies. The competition for hogs drives the price upward at the wholesale level, and when the supermarket receives its next delivery of meat it discovers that the price of pork has gone up. Now, the local supermarket and its competitors add their customary margin to the new, higher, wholesale meat price with confidence, and consumers reap the consequences of their increased demand for pork: higher retail prices.

Price Determination in the Wholesale Market

When the schedule of demand and the schedule of supply are given for a particular product, as in Figure 12–4, the theoretical determination of price is easily accomplished, although the actual process in the market may be involved and somewhat indeterminate. In Figure 12–4, the derived demand curve, DD_p, intersects the derived supply curve, DS_p, at the price (wholesale) of $.275. We call this price the equilibrium price. It is the only price that is stable, showing no tendency to move. It is the only price that clears the market. At a price of $.275, the quantity demanded is equal to the quantity supplied. At $.275, buyers in the market will take 12.8 billion

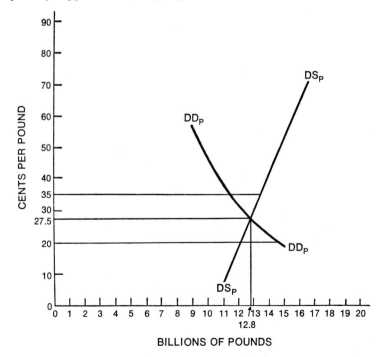

FIGURE 12–4. Determining the Price of Pork at Wholesale under Competitive Conditions

pounds of pork and sellers will supply 12.8 billion pounds of pork. The price is stable, and the market is in equilibrium.

But these conclusions are in the nature of assertions. Can we demonstrate that with a price of $.275 and a quantity of 12.8 billion pounds "the price is stable, and the market is in equilibrium"? We think we can. A price of $.35, for example, is not stable. At $.35, the quantity supplied exceeds the quantity demanded: 13.4 billion pounds are supplied and 11.4 billion pounds demanded. In a free market, where men are motivated by profit (income maximization) and information concerning the market situation is adequate and widely distributed, a price of $.35 cannot hold. Buyers will hold off, waiting for the price to fall. Sellers will be forced to lower the offering price in order to make sales. Thus, the price will be driven toward the equilibrium price of $.275. A price of $.20 is also unstable. The quantity demanded exceeds the quantity supplied at a price of $.20. In this situation, sellers will hold back and buyers will bid up the price in an effort to obtain supplies. Hence, the price will be driven toward equilibrium price, $.275. Competitive forces are continuously operating in a free market to drive the actual price toward the equilibrium price.

Does this mean that every transaction in a market will take place at the equilibrium price? No. At a price of $.35, for example, buyers demand 11.4 billion pounds of pork. Now, if market information is imperfect or inaccurate, or possibly for other reasons, some of these buyers may enter into transactions to buy pork at $.35 a pound. This price is sometimes called a false price. But we should not get the idea that only a few transactions are negotiated at a false price of say $.35 or $.30 or $.29. The more closely we approach the equilibrium price, the more transactions will be entered into. This occurs because market information is not perfect. We must remember that dealers operating in the market are not so fortunate as we. They do not have a neat chart, as that in Figure 12–4, telling them the exact level of the equilibrium price.

Dealers are feeling their way toward equilibrium by adroit and artful higgling in the market. As the price declines from $.35, in our example, many buyers may enter the market and purchase supplies of hogs at $.29, thinking that equilibrium had been reached. Hence, a large volume of transactions takes place at $.29. But the price does not stablize there; it must fall on to $.275 to clear the market. For at $.29, all the hogs offered on the market will not be taken. The final, firm price is $.275, but in the wake of this equilibrium price, we have a series of false prices. In practice, then, we would expect to find a cluster of prices, ringing the equilibrium price, where transactions actually took place. These transaction prices are the market price quotations that we read in the newspaper and hear on the radio. And the more nearly perfect the information in the market, the tighter the cluster of transaction prices we would expect to find ringing the equilibrium price.

The price of $.275 is determined by the well-known forces of supply and demand. The determination of this price has taken place at the terminal wholesale market for hogs, where the forces of consumer demand and producer supply are given expression in the decisions of dealers in the market. The price in the retail market now becomes this $.275, plus the marketing margin, which in this example is $.115. Thus, the price of pork to the consumer is $.39 per pound, and at this price all consumers in the United States take a total 12.8 billion pounds (see Figure 12–1). To obtain the price received by producers at the farm level, we subtract the margin of $.02 from the wholesale equilibrium price of $.275, which yields a price of $.255.

These prices, at the producer level and consumer level, will hold until the wholesale price changes once again, and it *changes because at the producer price of $.255, and the consumer price of $.39, producers and consumers make decisions that cause the amount demanded and the amount supplied at wholesale to change, consequently changing the equilibrium price.* The forces that change the equilibrium are thus initiated at the consumer and producer levels, but when the marketing system intervenes, the price-making process occurs at the wholesale level and the price changes effected there will naturally reverberate forward to the consumer and backward to the producer.

A Price Change

The equilibrium price at the wholesale level will change whenever consumer demand changes (*the curve shifts*), or whenever producer supply changes (*the curve shifts*). The derived curves at the wholesale level change correspondingly, and we obtain a new equilibrium price. Thus, to explain a change in the equilibrium price at wholesale, and with it, the whole structure of pork prices, we must explain the causative shift in either the consumer-demand curve or the producer-supply curve. Happily, we have already provided this explanation. Shifters of the demand curve are to be found in the determinants of demand: (1) incomes of consumers; (2) tastes and preferences of consumers; (3) prices of close substitutes; and (4) size and composition of the population.

When one (or some combination) of these determinants changes, the demand curve shifts. Shifters of the supply curve are to be found in the factors that determine the position of the marginal-cost curve: (1) price of productive agents; and (2) introduction of new technologies. When one of these factors changes, the supply curve shifts.

Certain of these determinants operate slowly and others quickly. Changes in the tastes and preferences of consumers, size and composition of the population, and introduction of new technologies usually take place slowly. In contrast, changes in the prices of close substitutes and productive agents take place quickly and fairly often. And, as we know, changes in consumer incomes occur cyclically and secularly.

In the hog-pork example that we have been using, one determinant on the supply side, the price of productive agents, is particularly volatile. The total production of corn, the principal raw material of pork, varies considerably from year to year. And in a free market, the price of corn varies inversely with the total supply. Hence, we have changes in the price of corn that influence the supply of hogs (the hog-corn cycle).

We see the effect of these year-to-year changes in pork production on pork prices, illustrated in Figure 12–5. A 15 percent reduction in per capita pork production in 1960 resulted in nearly a 40 percent increase in price. The same pattern occured in 1964 and 1969, with the opposite effect of greatly increased supply apparent in 1961, 1966, and 1970.

On the consumption side, the price of beef and other protein foods, relative to pork prices, has an influence on the amount of pork demanded at any particular price. The state of consumer incomes, however, is probably the most important determinant of the demand for pork. When consumer incomes are high, the demand for all meat (including pork) is large, but when consumer incomes are depressed, the demand for meat falls off rapidly.

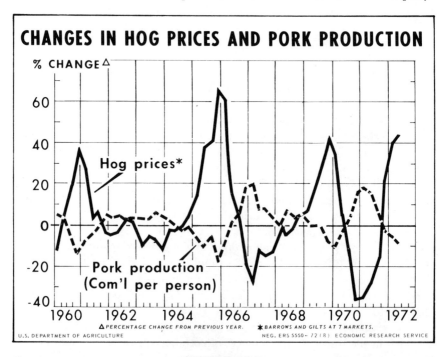

FIGURE 12–5

In Figure 12–6, the effects on price of a change in (1) consumer incomes and (2) tastes and preferences are illustrated. Here we see the derived demand curve, DD_p, and the derived supply curve, DS_p, the intersection of which yields an equilibrium price of $.275 and a quantity of 12.8 billion pounds (the same as in Figure 12–4). Now, let us assume that (1) the incomes of all consumers increase as the national income expands; and (2) the preference of consumers for pork over beef, or beef over pork, becomes less pronounced (consumers become increasingly indifferent as to the type of red meat consumed). The effect of the increase in income is that of expanding the demand for pork. At any price, consumers will stand ready to take more pork than previously. The effect of the change in preference is to make the demand curve more elastic. Because of the increased indifference on the part of consumers as between pork and beef, when pork prices fall consumers more readily substitute pork for beef, and when pork prices rise they more readily substitute beef for pork. The greater willingness

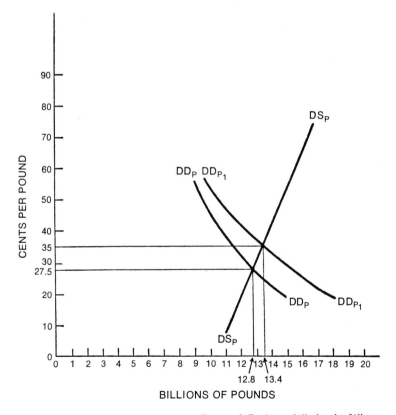

FIGURE 12–6. Determining the Price of Pork at Wholesale When the Demand Increases

to substitute gives rise to a more gently sloping demand curve. The result of these influences is to push the demand curve for pork to the right and into a more elastic position, as indicated by the curve, DD_{p1} in Figure 12–6.

The intersection of the expanded demand curve, DD_{p1}, with the old supply curve, DS_p, yields a new price-quantity solution. The new equilibrium price is $.35; the new equilibrium quantity is 13.4 billion pounds. We see clearly the consequence of the expansion in demand: more is taken and at a higher price than was previously the case. Of course, a contraction in demand has the opposite effect.

The new equilibrium price of $.35 will soon make itself felt throughout the marketing system. Deliveries made to retailers after this price rise are marked up accordingly. Hence, the consumer finds that the price of pork has risen by approximately $.075. Producers, too, feel the effects of the price rise. In a perfectly competitive market, which is still our assumption, competition among packers for hogs will drive up the price at the farm level by approximately $.075. So the price changes, which came into being at the wholesale level, reverberate through the marketing system, affecting all concerned: producers, middlemen, and consumers.

Imperfect Competition

The discussion of price determination, to this point, has been in terms of a perfectly competitive market. But the rigorous requirements of perfect competition are not easily satisfied in the business world. In the first place, the imperfect state of knowledge in most markets goes a long way toward making those markets imperfect. But a more critical element is that of the number of buyers and sellers in the market. If the number of buyers or sellers in a market are few, the action of any one will have a discernible influence on price. In this context, a dealer can no longer assume that a purchase or sale action by him will have no influence on market price; on the contrary, he must consider the price consequences of his action and the possible retaliatory action of competitors. Clearly, when this condition prevails, we have passed out of the realm of pure competition. We have passed into that broad area variously described as imperfect competition or monopolistic competition, lying between pure competition at one extreme and pure monopoly at the other.

Monopoly is a market situation characterized by a single seller, and is actually very rare at the national level in the U.S. The maker of "instant" photography film is a monopolist for that particular product, and the U.S. postal service is a monopolist for long distance first class mail delivery, but these are exceptions. Monopoly in the delivery of electricity to a city or state is common, and this kind of public utility monopoly is regulated. Other forms of imperfect competition are much more common. They are defined as markets in which the rigorous requirements of a perfectly competitive market are not met in full, but where some competition exists, where the market is not monopolized by one buyer or one seller.

Now, this concept of imperfect competition may lack precision, but this lack of precision does not stem from the fact that it is an exceptional case. *On the contrary, the vagueness of the concept grows out of the multitude of cases that exist, each different in some respect.* Practically all durable goods, household appliances, clothing, and personal effects are sold under brand names. Each firm produces and sells a differentiated product, a product differentiated by appearance, name, and advertising. Hence, we no longer have a situation in which many firms produce and sell the same product; rather, we have as many products as firms. For each product, we have a market demand, and this demand confronts the single firm producing the product. Competition takes place through the substitution of one differentiated product for another. This is the classic case of monopolistic competition.

But a growing number of imperfect markets are to be found in food and agriculture; most processed foods are now branded. We do not think of oatmeal; we are conditioned to think of *Quaker Oats*. We do not think of frozen spinach; we think of *Birdseye Frozen Spinach*. And at the wholesale level, there are the imperfectly competitive conditions in the fluid milk and livestock markets, specifically, and all of agriculture, insofar as governmental price-supporting operations are engaged.

But what is the point of all this for our discussion of how farm prices are determined? The point is this: when the market is imperfectly competitive, the equilibrium price will differ in some respect from the solutions shown in Figures 12–4 and 12–6. We cannot make a general statement as to the nature of the difference, for the imperfections take many forms and may occur on the buying side, the selling side, or both. But let us examine some possible cases under our hog-pork illustration.

If the market imperfection takes the form of imperfect knowledge, we would expect to find an expansion of the cluster of false prices around the equilibrium price. Further, the tendency for transaction prices to move toward the equilibrium price would be weakened. If the market imperfection should take the form of a national cooperative marketing organization that controlled the total supply of hogs moving to market, we might find the supply curve contracted in certain situations, to support prices, and expanded in others, with the result that wholesale prices would fluctuate less than in a perfectly free market.

Or, if the market were an *oligopoly with the sellers consisting of a very few large firms and many smaller firms* as was once the case in meat packing, we might find that market price would be determined by the largest packer (the price leader), and it and the remaining three large packers would take their "fair" and constant percentage shares of the volume offered by all producers at that price. In support of this practice, George E. Putnam of Swift and Co. had this to say:

> ...It should be observed that the general practice among intelligent competitors of respecting one another's position need not be a matter of "tacit understanding." *In the case of Swift and Company it is an individual, common-sense policy arrived at independently, not to invite retaliation and trade wars by using overaggressive tactics.* [Swift] has deliberately tried to avoid cut-throat competition wherever it was legally possible to do so.
>
> The same policy will always be followed by intelligent men. Purely as a matter of self-interest, no intelligent and successful business man wants to destroy his competitors. He knows that he himself may not survive the competitive struggle. Or if he should survive that struggle and become a monopolist, he knows that private monopoly, in these days of democratic government, will invite public ill-will and destructive legislation. It is clearly a matter of sound business policy to avoid cut-throat competition, but, unfortunately, there are times when the tactics of a competitor may become intolerable and in the interests of self-preservation one must have recourse to the same tactics. Thus a trade war may be provoked by an over-aggressive policy on the part of one competitor.[3]

The situations mentioned above illustrate certain of the imperfections to be encountered in price-determining markets. But we should be clear on the fact that the number and variety of situations to be encountered in the area of imperfect competition are almost infinite. It needs, also, to be pointed out that the basic forces of supply and demand are not altered significantly by different forms of market organization. The force of demand arises out of decisions of consumers, and the force of supply arises out of decisions of producers. Dealers in the market, few or many, must operate within the conditions of that demand and supply. In our case, for example, consumers have, in a general way, decided how much pork they will take at various prices, and producers have decided how much they will supply. If there were but one meat packer, the perfect monopolist, he could not ignore these determining forces. He might manipulate them a bit to his advantage, but he could not control them in a free society.

A continuing force of imperfection in agricultural commodity markets is the action of government in restricting supply by means of acreage controls. This kind of program, as well as the support of farm prices by government purchases, means that market prices will differ from equilibrium prices. The forces that we have grouped under supply and demand do not cease to operate; government counteracts the operation of those forces by reducing supplies, in the usual case, by the amounts necessary to hold market prices at

[3]George E. Putnam, *Supplying Britain's Meat* (London: Geo. G. Harrap & Co., 1923), pp. 124–26.

the announced support prices (the methods and consequences of price-supporting operations will be treated thoroughly in Part Six).

What we have here is price-making in political markets, rather than in economic markets. What prices of farm commodities *ought to be* are determined by political action in the Congress, rather than by economic action in markets. We do not say that such a development is bad, but it does represent a market imperfection in the technical sense.

A Generalizing Statement

We have developed only one commodity illustration in this chapter. We have followed this technique to maintain the continuity of the discussion in a difficult and vital area of economics. But is the price-making process that we have described applicable to other agricultural commodities? In a broad and general way, the answer is yes. We have outlined the process and the principal determinants within that process whereby a commodity price is determined. And the broad outline is as applicable for cotton and potatoes as it is for pork. But each commodity has peculiar and differentiating characteristics of its own. Hence, an analysis of cotton prices will take a somewhat different form than an analysis of potato prices, and the latter analysis will vary in some degree from the hog-pork case. The over-all framework of analysis is established, but the form of the analysis will vary commodity by commodity, as the market organization varies and as the supply-price and demand-price relationships vary.

POINTS FOR DISCUSSION

1. How do the twin concepts of the *substitution effect* and the *income effect* explain the negative slope of the demand curve?
2. What do we mean by the elasticity of demand? Derive a measure of the elasticity of demand for pork when the price rises from $.45 to $.53 per pound and the quantity purchased declines from 11.9 billion pounds to 10.7 billion pounds. Is the demand for pork over this price range elastic or inelastic?
3. How do we derive the market supply curve for any commodity, say pork? What basic principle explains the positive slope of the supply curve? Why does it slope upward and to the right?
4. How do we define a *purely competitive market*? Why do we make use of such an unreal, abstract formulation?
5. Demonstrate that the price indicated by the intersection of the demand curve with the supply curve is stable, that it shows no tendency to move.
6. Assume that consumer incomes rise: what will happen to the demand for pork; what will happen to equilibrium price?
7. Suppose the price of corn rises: what will happen to the price of hogs? Why?
8. What do we mean by *imperfect competition*? Where in the agricultural industry are we most likely to find examples of imperfect competition? What form will these "imperfections" most likely take?

REFERENCES

BOULDING, KENNETH E., *Economic Analysis,* 4th ed., Vol. I, Chaps. 7 and 10. New York: Harper & Row, 1966.

SAMUELSON, PAUL A., *Economics,* 8th ed., Chaps. 20 and 21. New York: McGraw-Hill Book Company, Inc., 1970.

WAITE, WARREN C., AND HARRY C. TRELOGAN, *Agricultural Market Prices,* 2nd ed., Chaps. 3, 4, and 5. New York: John Wiley & Sons, Inc., 1951.

Chapter 13

The Role Farm Prices Play

Everyone is interested in farm prices: the farmer, the economist, the politician, and the consumer. To appreciate this continuing interest, we must understand what farm prices do, the role that they play. In some cases, this role is so obvious that economists are prone to overlook its importance. In other cases, it is so complex that laymen and economists alike find it difficult to understand thoroughly. Our goal here, then, is to describe clearly the role (or roles) that farm prices play.

The Overall Integrating Role of Prices

Every economic society, whether it be a military dictatorship, a communistic dictatorship, free and perfectly competitive, or mixed capitalism (compounded of perfectly competitive markets, imperfectly competitive markets, and governmental intervention, as represented by the United States), must meet and solve in some way four fundamental economic problems:

1. What goods and services shall be produced and in what quantities?
2. How shall those goods and services be produced, that is, by whom, with what resources, and in what technological manner?
3. For whom are they to be produced, that is, who is to consume and enjoy the goods and services produced?
4. How shall changes in the underlying determinants of the economy be transmitted so that adjustments in production and distribution may take place?

These four questions are fundamental and common to all economies and to every segment of each economy. For as a rereading of these questions will indicate, their solution determines how well each of us lives, how each of us is employed, and what each of us lives by. These are determinations that vitally concern people everywhere. It should not be inferred that these are the only economic questions of importance confronting society. The employment problem and the growth problem are both problems of great importance not included here.

Important for this discussion is the fact that the automatically operating pricing system in a free and perfectly competitive society solves, or tends to solve, the four questions simultaneously. In such a competitive system, no individual or organization is consciously concerned with the solution of these four questions. Thousands of different kinds of goods and services, produced by millions of geographically scattered workers are moved around and distributed to millions of other consumers in a relatively orderly fashion, under the unconscious direction of the pricing system. In a mixed capitalistic system, the automatic price mechanism continues to provide this basic integrating function, but not perfectly, and it gets some help from the government. In other words, business firms, when they can, and government, when it intervenes as with the price freeze and the price and pay boards of 1971–72, provide conscious price control and administration. Still, under normal conditions in the U.S., the automatically operating price system carries the main load. In this overall integrating role, farm prices, of course, play their part. They knit the various parts of food and agriculture together in a whole fabric, and they integrate agriculture with the rest of the economy in an organic fashion.

We have worked through the theory and mechanics of price determination for a single farm commodity (Chapter 12). The question now arises: how does the automatically operating price *system* integrate the total economy; how does it fit all the parts of the economy together in a meaningful and effective pattern? In the first place, everything has a price: each consumer good has its price, each service has its price, each producer good has its price, each kind of labor has its price (wage rate), and even the commodity money has its price (the interest rate). Everyone receives a money income for what he sells: the producer, a gross income on the product sold; the laborer, a net income (wages) for services rendered; the stockholder, a net dividend on funds invested. And each recipient of this money income, in a free society, uses it to purchase what he needs or wishes. If all consumers demand more lettuce, orders at retail and wholesale rise, market price rises, and eventually more is produced. In contrast, if there are more eggs supplied than consumers will take at existing prices, the prices of eggs are forced down through competitive action. At lower prices, consumers will consume more eggs, and, when the market is perfectly competitive, producers will reduce their production of eggs. Thus, there is a tendency for equilibrium to be restored between the quantity demanded and supplied, in the case of the two commodities mentioned and in the case of the many others that could be mentioned. In the movement toward equilibrium, the public gets the kinds and quantities of products desired, although complete equilibrium is probably never achieved, for prices are forever changing in response to changes in the desires and plans of consumers and producers. The whole problem might be likened to a dog chasing a rabbit. Equilibrium is realized when the dog catches the rabbit, but when the dog (transaction price) reaches the point at which the rabbit (equilibrium price) was when the dog started, the rabbit has hopped to a new position.

These adjustments toward equilibrium take place in markets for factors of production, just as they do in consumer-goods markets. If peach pickers, rather than cow milkers, are needed, job opportunities will be more favorable in the former field. The price of peach pickers (their hourly wage) will tend to rise, while that of cow milkers will tend to fall. All other things equal, this shift in relative prices (wage rates) cause a shift of labor resources into the desired production. As mechanized peach pickers and milking parlors have been developed, and wages for farm labor have risen, the tendency has been to substitute mechanical devices (that is, capital) for labor. Thus, the demand for farm capital increases, leading to greater utilization of mechanized devices. At the same time, there is a decrease in the demand for farm labor, wages fall, and the number of farm workers available is reduced. The adjustment toward equilibrium goes on at all levels and for every unit in society that commands a price.

The process of adjustment through successive approximation goes on until demand and supply are simultaneously satisfied. Thus, prices provide for *adjustment* of the economic system to changes, and when exchange takes place the other three economic problems are solved. *For whom* goods and services are produced is determined by demand and supply, in the markets for productive services, by wage rates, land rents, interest rates, and profits, which add up to total personal incomes received. *How* things are produced is determined by the competition of different producers. The low-cost method, at any one time, based upon technical efficiency and a combination of low-priced inputs, will displace a high-cost method because the only way a high-cost producer may maximize his profits (particularly when prices are falling) is to adopt the more efficient methods. *What* things will be produced is determined by the choices of consumers in decisions to purchase this product and not that. And the expenditures that consumers make, the money they pay into business establishments, ultimately provide the wages, rent, dividends, and profits that they (consumers) receive as income. The circle is complete and, in the total complex of decisions and actions that we term the *economy,* prices have provided the basis for making decisions and taking actions that fit together in an integrated whole.

Income-producing (Using) Role

Abstracting from the overall, integrating role of prices presented above, we wish to analyze in some detail two specific functions that price performs. The first of these is the income-producing (using) function of price. This is the obvious role and, to the worker, the farmer, and the retailer, the all-important role that price performs. Assuming, for the time, a full use of resources, the money income of a steel worker depends upon the hourly wage rate received by him, the cash receipts of a corn-hog farmer depend upon the price received by him for hogs, and the cash receipts of the retailer depend upon the price of the goods sold by him. This is so obvious that the man in the street and the men who represent him in local, state, and federal government find it hard to attach any importance to other roles. It is so obvious that the economist often forgets the importance of this role. But we must never lose sight of this obvious relationship: *where quantities are unchanged, the income of a productive agent depends upon the price it receives for its service.*

Now, dissatisfaction with the income received by productive agents through the automatically operating price system has led, in many, many cases, to tampering with the price system. Productive agents, in most cases, are unwilling to accept the income verdict of an automatically operating pricing system when that verdict is a low price for their service. We know something of the story in agriculture. Farm people have banded together and requested the federal government to support the price of their products, hence, their gross incomes. This is not a unique or exceptional experience. Labor has combined in unions to protect and support wage rates. Business concerns have amalgamated and formed associations that have sometimes illegally controlled the prices of their products. So, we find the incentive to discard the automatically operating price system and to substitute for it a system of managed prices. This incentive exists in the dissatisfaction of producer groups with the income-producing role of prices in perfectly competitive situations. An automatic pricing system in a perfectly competitive economic society *may* be best for all of us, but rarely is a particular group willing to accept the income consequences of such a system if it can avoid it. We have, therefore, metamorphosed into a mixed capitalistic system, with government *intervention* and *private price management.*

Upon this point, we should be clear. The drive toward a mixed capitalistic economy has not come from government. The drive grows out of individual producer groups seeking to enhance and protect their incomes.

We have corporations administering prices, unions bargaining over wage rates, and farm people invoking the power of government to support farm prices.

The income-using role of prices is the converse of the producing role. When consumer incomes are fixed, the higher the prices of consumer goods, the lower the purchasing power of incomes, and vice versa. Very simply, if food prices rise, we have less money income to use in purchasing other goods and services; if food prices fall, we have more money to use in purchasing other goods and services.

Resource-allocation Role

This is the role that intrigues economists, but to which the man in the street pays little attention. In this role, prices serve as signals. When egg prices are high, relative to the prices of products that are close substitutes, egg producers are likely to take one or more of the following actions: cull laying hens less closely, increase the care of the laying flock, buy more baby chicks to increase the size of the laying flock, or build more houses to handle a larger flock. And new producers may be attracted into egg production. In brief, the economy is allocating more resources to egg production. On the other hand, the increased price of eggs has flashed a signal to the consumers, too. Consumers realize that eggs are more expensive and that they had better substitute other foods for eggs whenever possible.

In the other direction, should egg prices fall, relative to other farm prices, producers would first cut output by employing fewer resources in egg production, perhaps by reducing purchases of feed or by culling more severely. But in the longer run, producers would be induced to employ new methods and reduce their costs. So, we see that this allocating role is a highly important one. Price changes direct consumers to use more of one product and less of another, and direct producers to use more resources here and less there, as well as new methods whenever they are cheaper. Hence, we obtain a solution to the questions: *what* commodities, and in *what* quantities, and *how* shall they be produced? In a perfectly competitive economic society, and even in a mixed capitalistic economic society, *relative prices*, the price of one commodity relative to another, tell producers how to combine resources to produce the kinds and quantities of products demanded.

No wonder economists are impressed; this is no little achievement. But this process of resource allocation does not work timelessly or instantaneously. Some resources may be added to a production process quickly and effectively, whereas others take much time. So, it is customary in economic analyses to study production changes, made in response to price changes, by time periods.

The time periods that we shall consider are as follows: the market day, a period so short that supply may not be altered; the short run, a period in which supply may be varied as inputs like labor, feed, and fertilizer are varied in productive combinations; and the long run, a period in which supplies may be varied importantly as all resources are varied (for example, the size of barn, number of acres, arrangement of ditches, number of producers). In all this, we make one important assumption. We assume the state of technology is constant—unchanged. This simplifying assumption helps considerably. Later when we see where we are going, we can drop it.

The Market Day. Let us assume that our market is a large city and that our product is broilers. In the market day, the supply of broilers in the market is fixed. At extremely low prices, dealers might hold back some portion of the day's supply, and at extremely high prices, they might be able to divert some additional supplies into the market. But on an average market day, the total quantity of broilers offered on the market is a fixed amount. The marketing channel leading into the city is emptied in any one day, and the amount flowing in must sell at whatever price clears the market.

This situation is illustrated in Figure 13–1. The fixed supply of broilers in the market day is indicated by the vertical line *FS*. That line tells us that, regardless of the price, 750,000 pounds of broilers are offered on the market. That was the amount that moved up through the marketing channel during the night, and now there is little or nothing that can be done to alter that supply. The demand in the wholesale market on this given day, derived from the demands of consumers, is indicated by the curve DD_c. In the very short run of the market day, the equilibrium price is determined at $.28, which is determined by the intersection of the demand curve DD_c and the supply curve *FS*.

But what if demand should change? The consequence of an increase in demand is illustrated in Figure 13–1. When the demand for broilers expands from DD_c to DD_{cl} and the amount supplied is fixed at 750,000 pounds, the equilibrium price rises from $.28 to $.33. Price rises by the full amount of the expansion in demand. Or, stated differently, the full force of the expansion in demand is absorbed in the price rise. So in the market day, when the amount supplied is fixed, we say that price is determined by and varies directly with the conditions of demand.

The Short Run. The short-run situation grows logically out of the market day. The expansion in demand from DD_c to DD_{cl} in the very short run of the market day forced the wholesale price of broilers up to $.33. These higher prices were transmitted back through the marketing system to take the form of higher producer prices. Higher producer prices are a signal to the production system to devote more resources to the production of broilers. Spurred by the incentive of selling a greater quantity at the existing

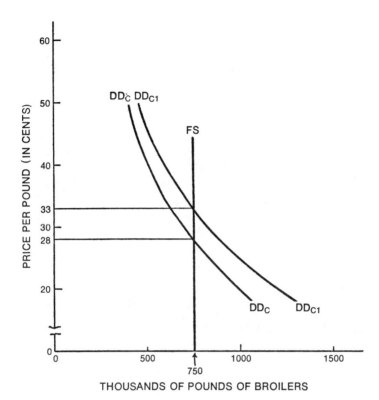

FIGURE 13–1.   Derivation of the Price of Broilers in the *Market Day*, Wholesale Level

higher price, producers take those actions open to them in the short run to expand their production.

Now what can producers do in the short run to expand their production and sale of broilers? They can market broilers earlier, at lighter-than-optimum weights. But probably producers would attempt, through increased care and control over feeding operations, to put meat on their birds more quickly. Or, if the short run is long enough (and the length of each of these periods is relative), producers could expand output by raising more chicks and raising more broilers in their existing buildings.

In the short run, then, there are several ways a producer could expand his output. But additional output, without an improvement in technology, entails additional cost. To illustrate what may happen, we show the unit cost curves of a representative producer in Figure 13–2A, and its correspondence to the market situation in Figure 13–2B, assuming away for present purposes the marketing margin. In response to the somewhat higher price,

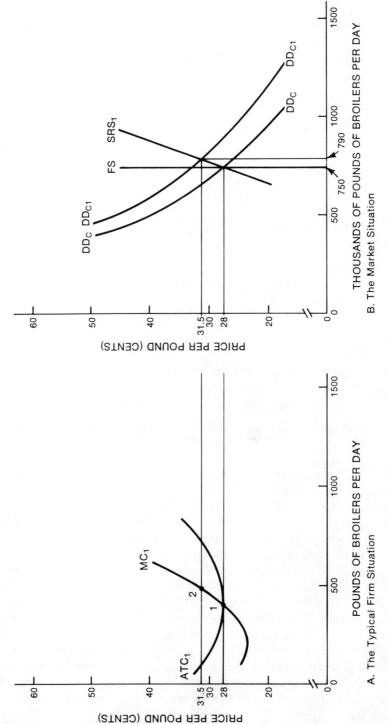

A. The Typical Firm Situation

B. The Market Situation

FIGURE 13–2.   Derivation of the Price of Broilers in the *Short Run*, Wholesale
Level

the representative producer moves from point *1* up his marginal cost curve to the new $MC = MR$ position at point *2*, producing more broilers by using more variable inputs. The summation of marginal cost curves, for all producers, yields the short-run supply curve SRS_1 in Figure 13–2B. This curve describes how the quantity offered increases as price rises. But we should appreciate that increases or decreases in quantity, associated with price changes, take time; in this case, they take place over the short run.

Induced by the high market price of $.33 (Figure 13–1), producers expand output as described by the curve SRS_1 (Figure 13–2B). The intersection of the supply curve SRS_1 with the expanded demand curve results in the short-run equilibrium price of $.315, when 790,000 pounds of broilers are cleared through the wholesale market. In the short run, then, price falls from the *responsive* price of $.33 to the new equilibrium price of $.315. This price decline results from the production adjustment process whereby producers intensify their productive efforts. In this process, they supply a greater quantity of broilers; but the additional quantity is forthcoming only at a higher cost, $.315 per pound to be exact.

Two points need to be made regarding this short-run equilibrium price of $.315. First, it does not grow out of an actual market situation; it is a normal concept. In any market day following these short-run developments, a fixed quantity of 790,000 pounds would be offered on the market, and the equilibrium price for the market day would be determined by the intersection of a vertical supply curve, at a quantity of 790,000 pounds, with the given demand curve DD_{c1}, which yields the identical price of $.315. And, of course, actual transaction prices would cluster about the equilibrium price of $.315. To repeat, the supply curve SRS_1 indicates the supplies forthcoming at various prices, when a short period of adjustment is permitted. But for any one market day, when transactions occur and transaction prices emerge, the supply offered is fixed in amount. Second, we see that the explanation of price determination, in the previous chapter, was really oversimplified. The case we described there was this short-run case, in which the supply curve represents the sum of the marginal cost curves for all firms. But at that point, we said nothing about time. We ignored it. Now, we see that the quantity supplied may vary only as producers are able to vary the units of resources employed, *which takes time*.

The Long Run

We have seen that the equilibrium price of broilers falls over the short run (from $.33 to $.315) due to the greater quantity induced by the price of $.33. But the short-run equilibrium price of $.315 continues to exceed the market price of $.28, which existed prior to the expansion in demand for broilers. Hence, there remains an incentive to increase supplies, because individual producers are making good profits (marginal costs are equal to price, but average unit costs are less than price). In the long run, the total output of broilers may be increased in several ways not feasible or possible in the short run, for it will be remembered that the long run is a period of sufficient length to permit any type of production adjustment. Nothing is fixed in the long run. Plant capacity may be expanded or reorganized (that is, new buildings may be constructed, the layout may be rearranged). Induced by the remunerative price of $.315, existing producers enlarge their plant capacity. This expansion shown by the change from ATC_1 to ATC_2 in Figure 13–3A, we assume, causes an increase in unit cost of production in the representative firm; but with a greater volume, the enterpreneur *expects* continued profits at a price of $.315 operating at point *3* (where $MC = MR$).

But high prices and high profits also attract new producers. And in the long run, there is time for new producers to enter the field of broiler production. In general terms, the favorable price signal is directing (allocating) more and more resources to the production of broilers. The automatically operating pricing system is working as it is expected to work. The higher prices attract additional resources: more labor, more feed, more capital in the form of buildings and equipment. And these additional resources turn out more product, which, in the long run, causes the price of broilers to fall still further.

This situation is portrayed graphically in Figure 13–3. Over the long run, new producers have entered the industry and old producers have expanded their plant capacity. Hence, we obtain a new short-run supply curve, SRS_2, for broilers. This curve, as previously defined, sums up the marginal cost curves of all producers in the industry. But we now have more producers and larger producers. Consequently, the short-run supply curve shifts to the right and takes up the new position SRS_2. The intersection of the supply curve SRS_2 with the demand curve DD_{cl} determines the long-run equilibrium price of $.295, when a quantity of 850,000 pounds clears the market. And at this price, the representative firm ends at point *4* in Figure 13–3A, with a larger volume, but with a price that just equals its average total unit cost.

The industry producing broilers in this illustration, is one of increasing cost. The long-run curve LRS_1, in Figure 13–3, describes this condition. In response to the increase in market price, growing out of the expansion of demand, producers in this example have adjusted their broiler enterprise, first, in the short run, and second, in the long run, to increase production. Output has expanded, but, after complete adjustment in the long run, supply has not increased sufficiently to bring the price of chicken back to or below the starting price of $.28. The economy has allocated additional resources to the production of broilers, but the allocation is not sufficiently

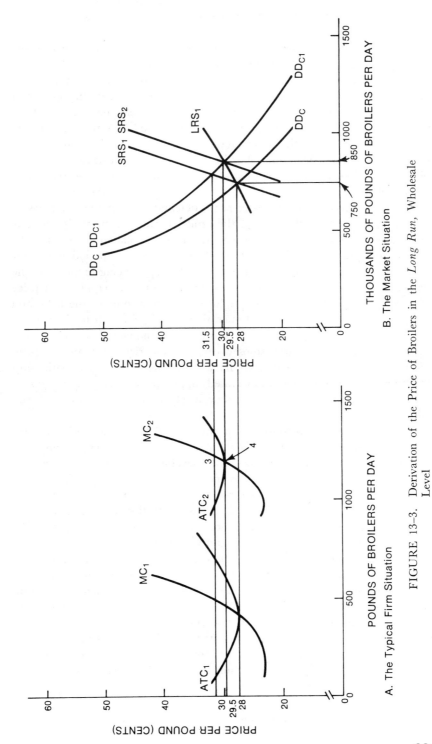

FIGURE 13–3. Derivation of the Price of Broilers in the *Long Run*, Wholesale Level

generous to bring the price back to the starting point. In the long run, the price of broilers increased as shown by the curve LRS_1.

Why should this be? In the first place, we need to recall that advances in technology were ruled out of this analysis. We are analyzing price-cost relationships when the state of technological development is constant. Granted this simplifying assumption, what happened? New resources do not automatically flow into the broiler industry, in either the short run or long run. New resources—feed and labor in the short run, and construction supplies and equipment in the long run—must be bid into the industry. In this process of bidding new resources into broiler production, the prices of the productive agents involved increased as the demand for those agents increased.

In this situation, the costs of the broiler production must rise. At any given level of output, marginal costs and average total unit costs for the typical enterprise are higher at the end of the long-run period than they were at the beginning. The average unit costs of producing broilers for the typical enterprise are, in fact, equal to the new long-run equilibrium price of $.295 per pound because new producers continue to enter the field, and old producers continue to expand operations, until price falls to the level of average unit costs of production. At this point, individual producers stop expanding, the supply curve stops drifting to the right, and the long-run normal price stabilizes at $.295. We have something of a scissors relationship here: price is falling because of increased supplies, costs are rising to produce the increased supplies, and, when they meet (as at $.295), the long-run adjustment is final and complete.

The long-run normal price, in this case $.295, is the price toward which the broiler industry is *tending,* but which it never reaches. This long-run equilibrium price is not realized in a developing, changing economy for at least two main reasons: first, and most obvious, the demand for broilers is not going to hold constant in the position DD_{c1} for say, one, two, or three years. Some determinants of demand, in this illustration, caused the demand for broilers at the wholesale level to increase from DD_c to DD_{c1}. We can be certain that the determinants of demand will continue to change, and, with those changes, the demand curve shifts into new positions. Because price changes every time the demand curve shifts, producers never have the opportunity to *fully* adjust their plans to a stable price. Before long-run production plans are executed in full, the price relationships that brought those plans into being change with changes in demand.

So, the long run, and to some extent the short run, is an abstraction from the economic world that permits economists to trace the consequences of a given price change on production responses. The concept of the long-run normal price is not, then, a price that we may expect to meet in the real world.

The above conclusion is buttressed by another reason, one that helps explain why food costs, outside of wartime, do not tend to rise as total output expands. To this point, we have assumed no change in the state of technology. We made this assumption to simplify the analysis. But in the dynamic economy in which we live, technological advance is rapid and widespread. Almost every day, we read of some new method of processing food, controlling insects and weeds, and enticing Mother Nature to give forth more abundantly. And when the demand for a particular product is strong and its price high, that is the time when farmer-producers adopt new methods, the time of innovation.

In our example of the broiler industry, producers would be inclined to try new methods—new feeding techniques, new breeds, new equipment—when demand is strong and the price is high. During such periods, producers have the necessary bright expectations to invest in new and, for the moment, costly methods. In Figure 13–4, the process of long-run adjustment is portrayed in which technological advance takes place. As in the previous case, high broiler prices and high profits attract new producers, and old producers are induced to expand their operations. These actions have the effect of raising the prices of productive agents, hence, raising average costs of production. *But in this case, there is a difference.* Producers, new and old, adopt a new production technique that, in itself, lowers costs of production, as reflected in ATC_2, shown in Figure 13–4A. Under the new technology, producers have a new lower minimum average total cost, $.27.

The net effect of these opposing influences is assumed to be that of modestly reducing the average total unit costs for typical producers. In this context, the short-run supply curve of the industry shifts to the right until it reaches the position SRS_3, where the long-run equilibrium price is determined at $.27, and a quantity of 930,000 pounds clears the market. It will be observed that the supply curve SRS_3 shifts farther to the right than in the case of the supply curve SRS_2. This occurs because costs have not risen; on the contrary, they have fallen modestly, and the only way that the profit gap may be closed when price exceeds average unit costs is for supply to increase. And supply does increase, by the action of new producers entering the field and old producers expanding, until we obtain the supply curve SRS_3. At the new wholesale price of $.27, prices received by producers equal average unit costs of typical producers. At this price, a long-run price equilibrium is established because producers no longer have any incentive to expand their individual outputs or to contract them.

In all this, our industry has metamorphosed into a "decreasing cost industry": the long run curve LRS_2 slopes downward and to the right. This occurred because producers took advantage of new production techniques; they devised means of producing the same quantity with fewer inputs, or a larger quantity with the same inputs. They reduced the cost of producing a pound of broilers.

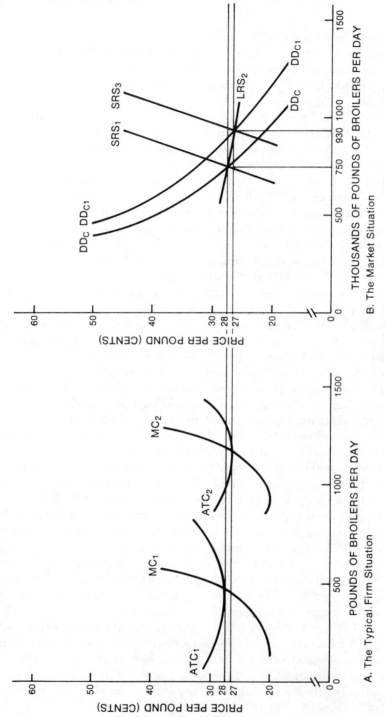

FIGURE 13-4.   Derivation of the Price of Broilers in the *Long Run*, when Cost-Reducing Technologies are Introduced, Wholesale Level

A. The Typical Firm Situation

B. The Market Situation

Some Dynamic Considerations

We have discussed at some length the allocative role of prices and analyzed the way in which this allocative role unfolds itself through time. Yet, perhaps, the most exciting role of prices in the allocation of resources remains to be discussed. We have in mind the role of expected, future prices. What decisions we make today depend, in large measure, on what we expect the price of our product to be next month, next year, and five years from now. This is particularly true in respect to investment decisions, decisions to make expenditures now that will influence costs and output in the future.

The decision to buy a farm, for example, is a tremendously important one that depends, or should depend, on expected future price relationships. If the prices of farm products are expected to fall over the long run, a farmer would be ill-advised to purchase high-priced land in the current period. If, on the other hand, farm prices are expected to rise over the long-run future, high-priced land in the current period may, in fact, represent low-cost land. The decision to plant a commercial orchard is not of the same importance as a decision to buy a farm, but the problem is similar. The decision turns, or should turn, on expected price relationships over the forthcoming five to ten years. If fruit prices are expected to fall, the farmer may find it to his advantage to use his land for other purposes.

So, we see that decisions to combine resources, one way or another, or to allocate resources, do not depend solely on current prices. Resources are allocated by producers, through time, in accordance with the dictates of *expected prices*. Expected prices provide the grist out of which investment decisions are ground.

The problem of entrepreneurship in the *static state* is the selection and combination of various agents to yield a maximum surplus of receipts over costs. And the selection and combination of productive agents is based upon current price relationships. This is the case we analyzed earlier in this chapter, under the allocation of resources in the market day and in both the short run and the long run. In that *static theory,* we recognized that time is required in the adjustment of productive agents to current prices. *But in all cases, the adjustment of resources was made relevant to current prices.* The problem of entrepreneurship in the *dynamic state* (one step nearer the real world) is the selection of a certain production plan, from among many alternatives, to yield a maximum surplus of receipts over costs throughout the expected life of the enterprise. The formulation and selection of a specific plan is based upon *expected price relationships*. The dynamic problem is, then, the organization of resources through time in such a way as to obtain the greatest net return to the enterprise over its lifetime.

But how is a preferred production plan to be selected? In the dynamic situation, it is clear that a chicken, hog, or wheat producer is not looking only at the possible surplus of receipts over costs in the current season. It is a stream of surpluses going on from season to season that occupies his attention. If two alternative streams were such that every surplus in one stream was greater than the corresponding surplus in the other stream, then there would be no question as to which was the larger and which the producer would select. But the alternatives are rarely so clear-cut.

Let us consider a rather typical example. A producer has two production plans under consideration: (1) the development of a turkey enterprise on his farm; or (2) the employment of approximately the same quantity of resources in a hog enterprise. This producer expects future prices for these two products to be such that, in the turkey-producing enterprise, the stream of surpluses is small to begin with, but becomes larger and larger over the years; whereas for hogs, the stream of surpluses is large to begin with and becames smaller and smaller over the years. Which will he choose? We cannot say exactly because we have not assigned values to the alternative surplus streams. But we can suggest a basis for ascertaining the preferred stream: the choice between the alternative production plans, with their attendant surplus streams, will be made on the basis of the *present value* of the two streams. The expected surplus in each year for each stream is discounted by the current and going rate of interest to obtain the present values of each of those expected surpluses.[1] The present values of the stream of surpluses, under one plan, and the present values of the stream of surpluses, under the other, are then summed to obtain the present values of the two production plans. And whichever plan yields the greater net return, discounted to present value, is the preferred plan.

The preferred production plan can be determined easily when product and resource prices are anticipated with some certainty. But therein lies the rub. How can we know the future with certainty? Most of us judge the future by past experience, and the most recent past experience usually dominates our judgment. Thus, each of us, including the farmer trying to decide whether to equip his farm to produce turkeys or hogs, probably projects the pattern of prices existing over the past year into the short-run future with little modification. We may vary the pattern modestly, as a hunch or a bit of recent information suggests, but in the main, our short-run forecast mirrors the recent past.

Long-run price forecasts by the producer and consumer alike are even less well-grounded. About all that any of us can do is guess. It is true that some of these guesses represent informed opinions. But it is equally true

---

[1]The present value of one dollar payable at some time in the future, say t years, is calculated by applying the formula: $pv = \$1/(1 + r)^t$, where $r =$ the chosen rate of interest. Thus, the present value of $100 due in 5 years at a 7 percent interest rate is $\$100/(1.07)^5 = \$71.29$.

that expected prices are not scientifically determined values. Expected prices are vague things, ranging from crystal ball projections to elaborate statistical extrapolations. And the individual producer (and consumer), who must make decisions involving the future, probably does not *expect* in any absolute sense. More probably, he conceives of the expected price of his commodity, at some specific date, in the form of a range of possible prices, each with some degree of probability. For example, the uncertain producer, whom we have been considering, *might* view hog prices one year from his day of decision in the following way:

1. There is one chance in ten that the price will be $.25 per pound.
2. There are four chances in ten that the price will be $.20 per pound.
3. There are four chances in ten that the price will be $.15 per pound.
4. There is one chance in ten that the price will be $.10 per pound.

The mean expected price is $1/10 \times \$.25 + 4/10 \times \$.20 + 4/10 \times \$.15 + 1/10 \times \$.10 = \$.175$. The price of $.175, expected one year ahead, represents a weighted average of this particular producer's range of price expectation and hence may be interpreted as the most probable price expectation of this producer. But producers do not formulate the probabilities so precisely. In some vague way, each producer formulates the most probable price out of a range of possibilities and then acts, making production decisions on the basis of that probable expected price.

This much seems clear. The further into the future that a price forecast is made, the wider will be the range of price possibilities. This follows from the obvious: the more distant the future, the more uncertain the future. The mean expected price, or the most probable expected price, becomes less reliable as a basis for planning.[2] Hence, producers plan less rigorously and formally as the planning dates project into the future. In short, the entrepreneur cannot plan when the principal elements of the problem—prices—cannot be anticipated.

In the short-run future, then, production plans are rather concrete affairs, based upon price relationships expected with a relatively high degree of probability. But as we move further into the future, these production plans merge into dreams, hopes, and, at best, flexible plans. And as production plans become more indefinite, so does the process of resource allocation because the use of resources is determined by the production plan (or plans) and, when plans become vague, so does the allocation of resources.

In this dynamic setting, the entrepreneur comes into his own. The man who judges the future reasonably accurately and who formulates an effective production plan to exploit that future, will reap the large rewards. The

---

[2]The variance of the probability distribution becomes greater and greater.

Johnny-come-latelies, attracted by large profits, rarely enjoy such success. But most people will agree that price expectations are rarely realized in full, and if they are, more luck than skill may be involved. The second test of an entrepreneur is, then, his ability to reformulate plans as expected prices go awry. The successful farm operator modifies his production plan as quickly as possible when his expectations of the future turn out to be wrong. But such adjustments are not easily made. In the first place, it is easier to operate by habit than by conscious adjustment. In the second place, investments already sunk into items such as barns, dairy equipment, and irrigation systems do not fit into a changed plan on a moment's notice. A great deal of skill is required to modify long-range production plans quickly and efficiently. But change they must, for price relationships are forever changing, and only the omniscient producer could foresee and create a plan to exploit all possible price changes over long periods of operation.

Production Responses to Price Changes

Throughout this chapter and the previous one, we have held to the assumption that farm operators behave in a rational way, that is, they make those adjustments in production plans, in response to price changes, that maximize the profits of the farm operation. In a general way, this assumption does not seem to contradict past experience. Certainly, few farmers take actions aimed at lowering profits. But we must recognize that habit and custom play an important part in the determination of producer behavior. Many farmers become accustomed to feeding dairy cows a certain ration and continue to feed them that ration regardless of price changes. It has long been the custom in Pennsylvania to raise winter wheat, and farmers continue to produce that wheat regardless of current cost-price relationships. And many farmers in the South prefer to raise only one crop, cotton.

These customary practices and many more are not undertaken to reduce the return to the farming operation. As the term *custom* implies, they were acquired over a long period of time, perhaps in a period when they represented efficient practices, and farmers continue to apply them without any conscious consideration of their consequences. *The effect of custom is, then, to slow down production adjustments in response to price changes.* The regrouping of productive agents into new and more efficient combinations, in response to price changes, takes place slowly as customs and habits are modified.

This does not mean that the price system has failed in its resource-allocation role. If only 5 to 10 percent of the farmers change their production plans in response to a change in price relationships, that is enough to keep the allocation process in motion, and studies indicate that just this happens. A small percentage of the producers affected by a price change, usually those who can most easily shift into an alternative enterprise, modify their production plans and bring about, in most but not all cases, the desired change in output. The total output of a particular product expands a little in response to a price rise and contracts a little in response to a price decline.

If we think about this lagging in the allocative process, we will see the advantage (and the disadvantage) involved. Custom, habit, and the limitation of technical possibilities prevent farmers from moving from one extreme to another. Hence, custom and habit help protect the economy against an "explosive" type of behavior where all resources are first devoted to the output of one commodity and then are all shifted into the production of another. Take the case of potatoes and sugar beets in the irrigated valleys of the West. If, in response to a rise in sugar-beet prices, all producers moved out of potato and into sugar-beet production, consumers would find their food supply disrupted in the extreme. But some shift from potatoes to sugar beets is called for by the rise in sugar-beet prices, and the usual modest output response is sufficient to bring the price disparity between sugar beets and potatoes back into line.

But there are times when widespread production adjustments in agriculture are called for, and in those times custom and habit do interfere with effective resource reallocation. In some areas, custom and habit are so ingrained, so crusted over, that we get almost no output response to price changes. There, custom and habit interfere. In most cases, however, the modest total adjustment in the production plans of from 5 to 10 percent of the farmers affected by a price change serves to allocate resources *within* agriculture, in accordance with the needs and demands of consumers.

POINTS FOR DISCUSSION

1. How does the automatically operating price system integrate the economy?
2. What do we mean by the income-producing (using) role of prices? How has dissatisfaction with this role of prices led to governmental intervention in the private economy?
3. In what sense do prices direct the use of resources? How does this direction or allocation take place?
4. What is the elasticity of supply in the market day? How is supply modified in the short run? How is supply modified in the long run? How do these changes in supply through time influence price?
5. How does the adoption of new technologies on farms influence supply?
6. How do price expectations influence the current use of resources? What type of resources would you expect to be allocated primarily on the basis of current prices? What type of resources primarily on the basis of expected prices?
7. How do habit and custom influence producer behavior? Is the role of prices in resource allocation impaired by this behavior?

REFERENCES

HEADY, EARL O., *Economics of Agricultural Production and Resource Use,* Chaps. 15, 16, and 17. Englewood Cliffs, N. J.: Prentice-Hall, Inc., 1952.

SAMUELSON, PAUL A., *Economics: An Introductory Analysis,* 8th ed., Chaps. 2 and 3. New York: McGraw-Hill Book Company, Inc., 1970.

SCHULTZ, T. W., *Redirecting Farm Policy,* pp. 1–38. New York: The Macmillan Company, 1943.

STIGLER, GEORGE J., *The Theory of Price,* rev. ed., Chaps. 9 and 10. New York: The Macmillan Company, 1952.

Chapter 14

Two Farm Price Problems

A review of the behavior and structure of prices in Chapter 11 indicates that there are two kinds of price variability in agriculture: (1) wide swings in the farm price level; and (2) year-to-year, even within-the-year, variations in commodity prices around the moving farm price level.

The complex of lines running across Figure 11–1, which looks something like a frayed rope, illustrates the two different types of price variability found in agriculture. The heavy line at the center of the frayed rope in Figure 11–1 describes movements in the farm price *level*. The differently labeled lines, or frayed rope strands, describe variations in commodity prices around the moving farm price level (for seven of the more-important farm commodities).

The farm price level is unstable, moving through time in broad and dramatic sweeps (Figure 11–2). The upswings are associated with economic recovery and wars; the downswings with economic depressions, postwar periods and chronic overproduction in agriculture. For example, the level of prices received by farmers fell 43 percent between 1919 and 1921, fell another 56 percent between 1929 and 1932, rose 185 percent between 1940 and 1948, fell by 22 percent between 1951 and 1955, and rose 25 percent between 1955 and 1971. Fluctuation has continued, even though since the late 1930s the changes have been moderated by various price- and income-supporting actions of the government. In sum, the farm price level fluctuates in the extreme, but it does not fluctuate in a regular, or rhythmic, pattern.

A different story emerges with respect to the year-to-year variations in individual commodity prices around the moving farm price level. Some commodity prices move in close harmony with the overall level; others fluctuate wildly about it. This can be seen in Figure 11–1. Whole milk prices, for example, tend to move closely with—parallel with—the farm price level; potato and hog prices, in contrast, fluctuate around the price level in a sharp and uncertain fashion. Measures of the year-to-year *percentage* variations in the prices of selected farm commodities around the moving farm price level for the long period 1920–1955 are as follows:[1]

Whole milk	6.1%
Beef cattle	9.7
Wheat	13.7
Corn	17.8
Hogs	15.3
Soybeans	19.2
Potatoes	48.7

In general, what we observe from these estimates and other available data is a continuum of commodity price variability around the farm price level, ranging from modestly variable for commodities such as milk and eggs, to substantially variable for cotton, corn, wheat, and hogs, to very greatly variable for potatoes. When this pattern of year-to-year commodity price variability is superimposed onto the farm price level, which does, in fact, move through time in wide and dramatic swings, we obtain a vivid picture of the jumbled, gyrating price structure confronting farmers.

Two Economic Problems

These two characteristic movements of farm prices give rise to two important but distinctly separate economic problems. The wide swings in the farm price level give rise to even wider swings in aggregate net farm income. *This is the price-income problem.* The fluctuations of commodity prices about the farm price level give rise to uncertainty with regard to the planning of future farm operations. *This is the resource-allocation problem.*

To illustrate the price-income problem; in 1970, realized gross farm income for the nation amounted to $56.2 billion, of which 72 percent, or $40.4 billion, was used to meet production expenses, and $15.7 billion represented realized net farm income. If farm prices had been 10 percent lower for some reason, in the absence of government programs gross receipts would have been reduced to $50.6 billion. And with expenses unchanged, this would have represented a decline of $5.4 billion or about one-third in

---

[1]Individual commodity prices were deflated by the index of prices received by farmers for all commodities. Estimates were derived by computing link relatives, then computing the reciprocal of the link relatives below 100, and taking the unweighted arithmetic mean of the resultant numbers, all of which are 100 or more. An index of 100 represents no variation under this computation; hence, 100 is subtracted from these results to obtain the percentage estimates presented above.

realized net income of farm families. And because we have assumed that all farm prices have declined—the level has declined—the individual farm operator cannot protect himself by shifting enterprises; in one of these price-level downsweeps, the income problem becomes general. The individual farmer, efficient or inefficient, can find no place to hide. Of course, the great price-level upsweeps turn out to be a pure joyride for farmers, as the efficient and inefficient experience rising incomes whichever way they turn.

This is *the* paramount problem of food and agriculture that terrifies farmers in the downswings and send them scurrying to government for income protection, and that terrifies consumers in the upswings and sends them scurrying to government for cost-of-living protection. The general price-income problem of food and agriculture is the problem above all others that demands an adequate explanation and ultimately an adequate solution.

But if there were no general price-income problem in agriculture (that is, if the farm price level were perfectly horizontal), there would still remain the resource-allocation problem. It arises because individual commodity prices fluctuate, often sharply as well as irregularly, around the farm price level. It arises out of the fact that, to the farmer-producer, next year's price is *uncertain*. Confronted with this kind of uncertainty, the farmer plans next year's production without knowing what price he will receive. Instead, he probably uses a planning price. We saw in Chapters 4 and 5 that a profit-maximizing farmer will adjust his output to produce where marginal cost just equals price. In reality, we now see that farmers must make thesse adjustments on the basis of a planning price. And if the planning price differs from the price received six or eight months later, the farmer will not have allocated his resources optimally. In short, his planned production rarely turns out to be right. In other words, an inefficient use of resources occurs among commodities and on farms when farmers fail to use their productive resources in their most advantageous enterprise alternatives. This is a general occurrence in agriculture because before the fact of sale, which may be three months or three years hence, farmers cannot know their most advantageous enterprise alternatives.

An Analysis of the Resource-allocation Problem—the Cobweb Analysis. In the late 1930s, Mordecai Ezekiel formulated the Cobweb Theorem to explain commodity price-output sequences in agriculture.[2] We shall make use of it here to explain year-to-year commodity price gyrations. The cobweb analysis is an equilibrium type of analysis, making use of the traditional concepts of demand and supply. But, whereas the typical demand-and-supply analysis is static (see the analysis in Chapter 12), the cobweb analysis is semidynamic; it is concerned with price-output sequences *through time* where the relevant demand and supply relations *do not shift* during the

[2]Mordecai Ezekiel, "The Cobweb Theorem," *Quarterly Journal of Economics*, February 1938, pp. 255–80.

span of time under consideration. This partially dynamic analysis facilitates the formulation of an explanation of price-output behavior in agriculture where a *growth period,* often a season in length but perhaps longer, separates the decisions to produce and the decisions to sell a finished product.

Not so generally recognized, but central to the cobweb analysis, are two different but related concepts of supply. It takes two concepts of supply, related in a time sequence, to make the analysis valid. First, we have a supply relation that describes those quantities of a commodity that farmers plan to produce at varying prices. It is a planning curve, to which we give the name *schedule of intentions to produce.* Second, we have a supply relation that describes at the end of the growth or production period those quantities of a commodity that farmers stand ready to offer on the market at varying prices. And because it is assumed: (1) that most farm products are perishable; and (2) that farmers have poor storage facilities; it is further assumed that this second supply relation, to which we give the name *market supply curve,* is severely or perfectly inelastic. Given these concepts of supply, let us take a trial spin around the cobweb.

Two cobweb models are presented in Figure 14–1; later we will draw certain comparisons between these models, but for the present let us concentrate on model *I.* To get under way in this analysis, we must arbitrarily break into the continuing price-output sequence at some point in time, and this we do at price P_0 in year *0.* Price P_0 in year *0* induces farmers to plan to produce quantity Q_1 in year *1.* This quantity information we read off the schedule of intentions to produce curve S_1S_1, which describes those quantities of this commodity that farmers intend to produce at varying prices.

Now let us assume that the farmers' intentions to produce are just realized, and that quantity Q_1 is forthcoming in year *1.* This quantity comes to market in a rush—is dumped onto the market—because it is assumed that the commodity is perishable and farmers lack adequate storage facilities. Thus, in fact, the market supply curve in year *1* is perfectly inelastic and is described in model *I* by the line Q_1S_m. The market supply curve intersects the demand curve for the commodity at price P_1; this intersection point provides the price solution for year *1.* Farmers receive price P_1 for an output of Q_1 in year *1.* Price P_1 in year *1* now induces farmers to *plan* to produce Q_2 in year *2.* This quantity sells in turn at a price P_2 in year *2.* The cobweb is forming, and will continue until something comes along to break it.

It will be observed that the price-output path of model *II* differs markedly from that of model *I.* Model *II* is convergent; model *I* is explosive. Now, why does the price-output path of model *II* converge on its equilibrium position, and the price-output path of model *I* explode? The answer is to be found in the relative slopes of the demand relation and the schedule of intentions to produce. Whenever the slope of the schedule of intentions to produce exceeds (that is, is steeper than) the slope of the demand relation,

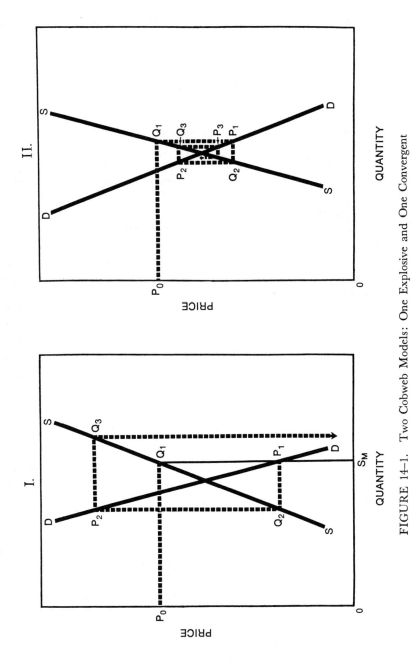

FIGURE 14–1. Two Cobweb Models: One Explosive and One Convergent

the price-output path converges; and, of course, whenever the slope of the demand relation exceeds that of the schedule of intentions to produce, the opposite is true. Finally, in that unlikely case where the slopes of the two curves are identical, the cobweb action goes on endlessly in the same track.

In the real world, it seems reasonable to assume that most commodity cobweb patterns are of the model *II* type. This must be the case; otherwise, agriculture would be flying apart. True, price variability is extreme for certain agricultural commodities, but to date agriculture has not exploded. And this would be the tendency if commodity patterns were generally of the model *I* type.

If we superimpose, in our thinking, the cobweb model onto the farm price level, we have an explanation for year-to-year commodity price variations about that level. Assuming the demand- and supply-cross (that is, the equilibrium position) is at or near the price level, the cobweb interaction can and does generate individual commodity movements about that level. Where the demand for the commodity is highly inelastic but the schedule of intentions to produce is also inelastic, the cobweb model generates extreme year-to-year price fluctuations; this situation applies to the commodity potatoes. If the elasticity of the schedule of intentions to produce is observable less than the elasticity of demand, the year-to-year price variations dampen down rapidly as the model converges on its equilibrium position; this is clearly the case with fluid milk. Figure 14–2 illustrates the effect of the cobweb model in eggs. The year-to-year fluctuation in prices that results from first an increase and then a decrease in production is characteristic of the time path of observations that would be generated by the cobweb models of Figure 14–1. In sum, the cobweb model explains how we get continuing commodity price variability around the price level and explains further why in some cases that variability is extreme and in other cases it is mild.

But it may be observed that the cobweb models generate smooth, rhythmic patterns of price behavior, whereas commodity price variability in the real world is jagged and irregular. Even in the example of eggs, although the fluctuation is very regular, changing direction nearly every year, the magnitude of price fluctuations changes. How are these real-world phenomena to be explained?

It is probably true that no situation can be found in agriculture that fits perfectly the neat cobweb pattern of either model *I* or model *II* of Figure 14–1. In other words, it would be difficult if not impossible to find a commodity situation where: (1) last year's price is always used as the planning price in the current year; (2) actual production never differs from planned production; (3) conditions on farms and in the market are such that the market supply curve is always perfectly inelastic; and (4) most important, the demand relation and the schedule of intentions to produce hold fixed, unchanging, positions for many years. For a countless number of specific reasons, the above conditions are violated in practice, and the regular price-

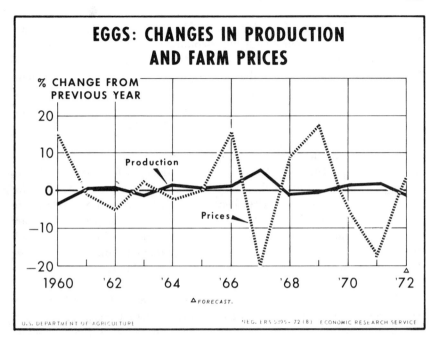

FIGURE 14-2.

output path of the cobweb is broken. Demand changes with changes in consumer tastes; the schedule of intentions to produce expands with technological advance; and weather and other natural conditions bring about, in time, discrepancies between planned production and actual production in most agricultural commodities. The occurrence of any one of these developments breaks the regular price-output path around the cobweb and gives rise to a price irregularity. The changing world breaks down the classic cobweb model and yields irregular commodity price patterns and hence price uncertainty to producers.

It would be wrong, however, to ignore or deprecate the cobweb framework of analysis in developing a general explanation of farm price behavior. *The principal features of the cobweb model are inherent in the structure of most of agriculture.* The use of prices received in the past to arrive at current planning price, the disjointed and recurring growth period in agricultural production, and the tendency for finished agricultural products to come to market in a rush following the growth period are all typical structural features of the agricultural economy. Thus, an analysis that purports to explain *commodity* price-output behavior in agriculture must assume some sort of cobweb form.[3]

---

[3]For a more complete treatment of the cobweb framework of analysis in explaining commodity price variability, see Willard W. Cochrane, *Farm Prices—Myth and Reality* (Minneapolis, Minn.: University of Minnesota Press, 1958), Chap. 4.

The General Price-income Problem of Agriculture. Because we have gained some experience with single-commodity analysis in the preceding two chapters, and we have just inquired into the causes of individual commodity price variability about the price level, let us introduce this analysis of the general price-income problem in agriculture by way of a single-commodity analysis—for instance, hogs. The prices received by farmers for hogs have fluctuated extremely since 1920 (see Figure 14–3). An explanation for these wide swings in hog prices can be set forth in terms of a single-commodity supply-and-demand analysis. The prices received by farmers for hogs fell between 1926 and 1931 because the demand for hogs, relative to the supply, was weak during that period. And prices received by farmers for hogs rose between 1940 and 1947 because the demand for hogs, relative to the supply, was strong. Further, the short-run, saw-tooth price effects are explained by the workings of the cobweb. But this explanation, although correct in itself, is not very satisfying. A full explanation should provide more insights into the kind of farm economy that is capable of generating such wide swings in hog prices.

Let us expand the analysis by looking at the relation of hog prices to other agricultural commodity prices. We observe that the prices received by farmers for beef cattle (a close substitute for hogs on both the production and consumption sides) fluctuate in much the same pattern as hog prices. If, further, we compare the movement of hog prices between 1921 and 1970 with the index of prices received by farmers from all commodities (Figure

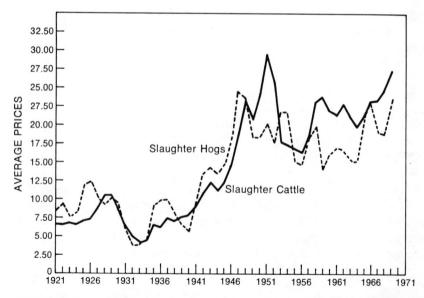

FIGURE 14–3. Average Prices Received by Farmers for Hogs and Beef Cattle, 1921–1970

11–3) and with the various commodity groupings (Figure 11–4), we see that all farm prices, and particularly the prices of close substitutes for hogs, move up and down together in a discernible pattern.

Dairy-product prices, meat-animal prices (including hogs), poultry and egg prices, and grain and hay prices tend to parallel one another for one important reason: resource substitution. If, for example, hog prices rise, relative to the general pattern of prices for these product substitutes, producers devote more feed, more building space, more time to hog production and less to beef-cattle production, butterfat production, and egg production. The result of these shifts, the substitution of resources into hog production, is that of increasing the supply of hogs and reducing the supplies of beef cattle, butterfat, and eggs. The increased supplies of hogs act to pull down hog prices, and the decreased supplies of the other commodities act to pull up their prices. The original price relationships between the product substitutes thus tend to be restored. We do not mean to imply that all the price humps shown in Figure 14–2 are ironed out, or that the short-run, saw-tooth price effects resulting from the workings of the cobweb are eliminated; we mean only that resource substitution operates to keep hog and beef prices moving in a roughly parallel fashion. Stated more generally, when resources may be freely substituted among different productive enterprises, the prices of the commodities involved will hold their relative positions in the general pattern with some precision.

An Industry Analysis: Agriculture

Broadly speaking, we say that all commodity prices in agriculture move up and down together. But this is not quite correct. We observed (Figure 11–4) that cotton prices rose above the general contour of farm prices between 1920 and 1925, and between 1935 and 1940 cotton prices failed to rise to the extent that animal product prices did. We also find similar deviations from the general contour of farm prices for meat animals and certain minor crops—citrus fruit, for example. One important reason that we get these deviations from the average pattern of farm prices is to be found in the breakdown of the substitution process between these product enterprises and the rest of agriculture.

As noted in the last chapter, custom and habit may act to deter production adjustments. The immobility of resources is another important deterrent to adjustment. In the case of livestock, it is not easy to transfer resources into such enterprises and increase supply. It takes time to increase cattle numbers, for example, and in the early phases of the build-up, beef production declines as breeding stock is withheld from market. Thus, the length of the reproduction, hence expansion, process can force cattle prices away from the level of farm prices for extended periods.

In the case of a commercial fruit enterprise, it is obvious that the substitution of resources between enterprises is reduced to a minimum. It takes a long time to bring a grove into bearing, and growers do not pull up their trees at the first price decline. Resources devoted to fruit production are sunk for long periods of time. There is no quick, easy way for fruit growers to respond to price changes in the way of shifting resources from one enterprise to another. Hence, fruit prices may get out of line and stay out of line for a considerable period of time.

In these illustrations, we find a clue to the farm price problem. When the process of resource allocation among enterprises, which occurs through substitution, does not or cannot work, the price of a single commodity or the prices of a group of commodities can get out of line and stay out of line. When we say that a price gets out of line, we mean that the price (or a group of prices) breaks away from the general level and goes off on a tangent— perhaps up, perhaps down. This, we suggest, is what happens between the smaller agricultural segment of the economy and the larger nonagricultural segment. Farm prices fluctuate to a greater extent than nonfarm prices because labor and capital resources do not readily move back and forth across the rural-urban line in response to the greater price movements in agriculture.

The Aggregate Output Problem in Agriculture. The farm segment and the nonfarm segment of the economy are sometimes compared to separate, watertight compartments, between which there is a connective valve that works poorly in the long run and not at all in the short run, *in response to price-level changes.* Because the separate tanks contain water, movement within the tanks is easy. This analogy is meaningful when we consider the nature of the substitution process. Farmers shift readily between potatoes and sugar beets, between the cash sale of corn and the feeding of corn to hogs, and between the production of butterfat and whole milk, but not between farming and banking and farming and manufacturing. There is some degree of resource substitution between individual farm enterprises within most agricultural areas and a significant degree at the extensive margin of all areas, in response to commodity price changes, but not between farm and nonfarm enterprises.

We have not said that farm people do not migrate to the city and vice versa. Except for two brief periods, there has been a net migration from farms to urban areas since 1920. Since 1950, the rate of migration out of agriculture on a net basis has been very heavy—averaging nearly 1 million persons per year. But the net movement seems to be more closely associated with job opportunities in industry than with fluctuations in the farm price level, relative to the nonfarm price level. In fact, one of the two historical periods of net movement from the city to the farm (1932–33) coincides with extremely low prices in agriculture. Hence, we conclude that labor resources leave agriculture as population pressure builds up in agriculture and as job opportunities open up in industry and service trades, but not readily in response to low farm prices relative to nonfarm prices.

What are the consequences, for aggregate farm output, of this failure to get labor and other resources to shift back and forth across the rural-urban line in response to price-level movements? The consequences in the aggregate are nearly the same as for a single commodity. When resources do not, or cannot, shift in response to price changes, output does not change. The price of a commodity, or the price level for a composite of commodities, may go up or go down; but if that price movement has no effect on the number and quality of resources at work, the output of those resources will not change. And that, in broad outline, is what we have in agriculture. In the short run, aggregate output is constant, or nearly so.

The story changes when technological advance on farms is rapid and widespread. But putting aside that complication for the moment, we conclude, on the basis of the empirical analysis that follows, that the aggregate supply curve for agriculture is highly inelastic. This conclusion was arrived at in the theoretical analysis of Chapter 6 and is supported by the elasticities of the empirical supply curves presented below, which vary from completely inelastic to relatively inelastic.

In any event, the industry supply relation for agriculture is given statistical expression in Figure 14–4. In Figure 14–4, an index of aggregate food production[4] is related to an index of *responsible prices* (the prices in existence when the production decisions for the forthcoming production period were made). In other words, the aggregate food output for any given year, say 1960, is related to the level and composition of prices (responsible prices) that were in existence at the time when the production decisions for 1960 were made. The points that relate the index value of responsible prices to the index value of aggregate output for each year over the period 1912–1970 fall into four obvious patterns indicated by the lines *AA, BB, CC,* and *DD.* In the periods covered by each of these lines, farm food prices fluctuated substantially while farm food output changed only modestly. Between 1945 and 1950 (curve *CC*), responsible prices rose from 170 to 270 and then went back down to 245, but the index of output stayed very close to 135. Between 1965 and 1970 (curve *DD*), the index of responsible prices increased from 216 to 280, but the index of output went only from 180 to 190. In a similar way, substantial changes in food prices between 1912 and 1920 and between 1923 and 1936 occurred with very little change in the aggregate production of food.

The period 1923–1936 was one in which farm technological advance was at a minimum; output per unit of input for agriculture as a whole showed no upward trend. In this context, the unresponsiveness of total

---

[4]The food component of the *Index of Farm Marketings and Home Consumption* (published regularly by the U.S.D.A., Economic Research Service).

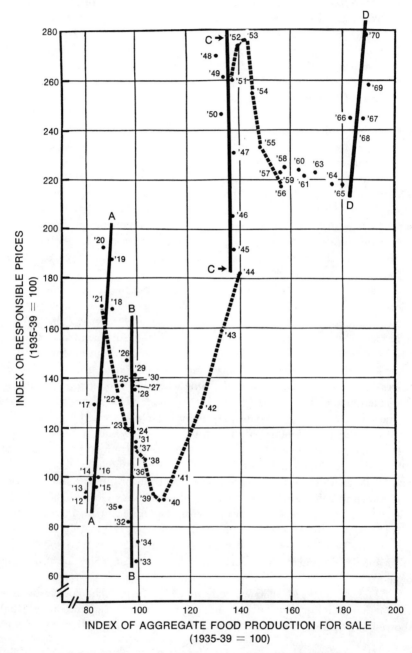

FIGURE 14-4. The Aggregate Supply Curve for Food

farm output to farm price-level changes is illustrated beautifully. The total resources—land, labor, and capital—committed to agriculture production by farmers held almost constant, whereas the farm price level changed dramatically. Hence, the total output from farms in the United States did not change. (The small varition from year to year is explained by variations in the weather.) When, therefore, we fit a line to the price-quantity points for the period 1923–1936 in Figure 14–4 to derive the aggregate supply curve for food, it turns out to be perfectly inelastic—the vertical line *BB* in Figure 14–4. And the line *BB* is a legitimate supply curve because it is derived for a period in which the index of farm efficiency, as an indicator of farm technological advance, is constant.

The dashed line running from *1937* to *1944* in Figure 14–4 brings out a new set of relationships. This was a period of rapid technological advance. Hybrid seed corn swept through the Corn Belt. A tremendous investment was made in tractor power and farm machinery. This was the time when farmers greatly increased their applications of commercial fertilizers. Hybrid seed corn increased corn yields by 20 percent. The substitution of tractor power for animal power released millions of acres from feed production to food production. The increased use of tractor power also greatly improved the timeliness of farming operations. Considering all factors, however, none was more important in the expansion of total food output than the increased use of lime and commercial fertilizer.

What we have, then, between 1936 and 1944 is a shifting of the short-run aggregate output curve to the right as output per unit of input increased by some 40 percent. (The action here in the aggregate is similar to movement of the commodity supply curve for chicken in Figure 13–3.) The dashed line running over the period *1937–1944* is not a short-run supply curve; it is a long-run supply curve, a trend line, similar to that developed in the last chapter. It traces out the intersections of the short-run aggregate output curve with the aggregate demand curve, as the curve *BB* drifts to the right taking up successively more productive positions.

We do not get any movement along the short-run aggregate supply curve during this period in response to price changes. Producers were not varying the variable factors of production (labor, feed) to obtain more output at higher cost from old combinations. They were innovating, combining resources in new ways, to obtain a greater output. And this action, in the aggregate as for a single commodity, resulted in an expansion in supply.

But by 1944, the postdepression, wartime spurt in farm technological advance seemed to have spent itself. Spectacular price increases between 1944 and 1948 failed to induce the adoption of more cost-reducing, output-expanding innovations. Either important new technologies were not coming along, their adoption was being held up by the war effort, or some other factors were operating. In any event, worker productivity temporarily ceased increasing around 1944–45. As a result, the expansion in aggregate output, based on technological advance, came to an end.

The aggregate supply curve for food, *CC*, for the period 1944–50, like the similar curve *BB* for the period 1923–36, is perfectly inelastic. It indicates that all farm producers, regardless of the farm level, kept using the same total number of resources in the same ways to obtain the same total output. In the aggregate, sustained output was the norm for the period 1944–50. And because output per unit was also constant over this period, the aggregate curve does not shift to the right. This supply behavior is baffling to us. Why should farm technological advance slow down and come to a halt during these six years? We need more and better data and more powerful analyses to answer this question. But the quandary is short-lived; the aggregate supply curve *CC* began its rightward drift once again in 1951 and continued at a rather steady rate until 1964, when productivity reached its present level. Another period of rather constant technology during the 1960s resulted in the supply curve *DD* that appears to be somewhat less inelastic than the others. However, it does show a slight response of output to price between 1965 and 1970 similar to that observed during other periods of constant technology.[5]

From this discussion of aggregate output, we have uncovered some interesting relationships, but we have not provided a complete explanation for the wide price swings in agriculture. The breakdown of the substitution process across the rural-urban line explains, in large measure, how the farm price level gets out of line and stays out of line. *But what starts all farm prices up or down in the first place?* Where does the initiating force come from?

A close observer of the behavior of the aggregate output curve, in Figure 14–4, might say that the expansion in supply between 1937 and 1943 could provide the unbalancing action. But an even closer inspection of Figure 14–4 indicates that there is something wrong with this explanation. It is true that the level of responsible prices fell between 1937 and 1940 with the expansion in output. But it is also true that prices rose between 1940 and 1943 with a much greater expansion in output. And we know that an increase in supply, *when demand is unchanged,* leads to a price decline.

Even more to the point, the level of responsible prices rose between 1923 and 1929, fell between 1929 and 1934, and then rose again between 1934 and 1938, when aggregate output clearly was unchanged. Changes in supply could not have initiated the price changes during this period. These price changes were initiated by changes in the aggregate demand for food.

---

[5]It appears that aggregate supply during this most-recent period is more elastic than during the earlier periods. However formal analysis has failed to substantiate this impression. See L. G. Tweeten and C. L. Quance, "Positivistic Measures of Aggregate Supply Elasticities: Some New Approaches," *American Journal of Agricultural Economics*, May 1969.

What we need, then, to complete the explanation of farm price-level changes is a description of the behavior of aggregate demand. For demand is the restless, unbalancing force in the picture.

The Aggregate Demand for Food. The aggregate demand for food, just as in the case of a single commodity, states a relation between price and quantity. In the short run, the principal determinant of demand, the shifter of demand, is income. When consumer incomes are high or expanding, consumers allocate more dollars to the purchase of all foods, and this shifts the demand curve for food to the right. In the opposite direction, when consumer incomes are low or contracting, consumers allocate fewer dollars to the purchase of all foods, and the demand curve for food shifts to the left. As consumers' preferences and styles of living change, their demand for food may also change. Thus, the passing of time may result in a rightward or leftward shift in the demand curve for food.

What, then, does the demand curve for food look like? One formulation is presented in Figure 14–5. The line *AA* shows the aggregate demand between 1929 and 1942, the line *BB* shows aggregate demand between 1947 and 1960, and the line *CC* shows aggregate demand between 1961 and 1970. Each relation describes the aggregate quantity of food consumed per person at different levels of retail food prices, all other influencing factors held constant within each period. That is, each curve is a conventional demand curve, with a price elasticity of about -0.2 and an income elasticity of about $+0.2$.

The functions shown in Figure 14–5 are average relations—for the average consumer and the average income and trend for each period. The demand for food has shifted to the right with the large increase of incomes between the first and second period. Between the 1950s and 1960s, however, the rightward shift induced by rising incomes was offset by a leftward shift apparently due to changing preference patterns. Thus, the difference between curves *BB* and *CC* is much less than between *AA* and *BB*.

For any single curve, the statistical analysis removes the influences of changes in income, and, it is hoped, changes in tastes and preferences, through the trend factor, to enable us to estimate an aggregate demand relation for food for the *average consumer* for the period in question. We are not saying that income and preferences were actually constant during the years between, say, 1947 and 1960, but that the statistical analysis used allows us to remove the effect of those changes. In fact, demand was shifting a bit each year, and the differences between each curve reflect the differences in the *average level* of demand between periods.

The estimates of the aggregate demand curve for food are highly inelastic $(-0.17$ to $-0.32)$. Consumers vary the quantity and quality of food consumption very little as food prices vary, relative to nonfood prices. This fact should not surprise us; it squares nicely with personal experience.

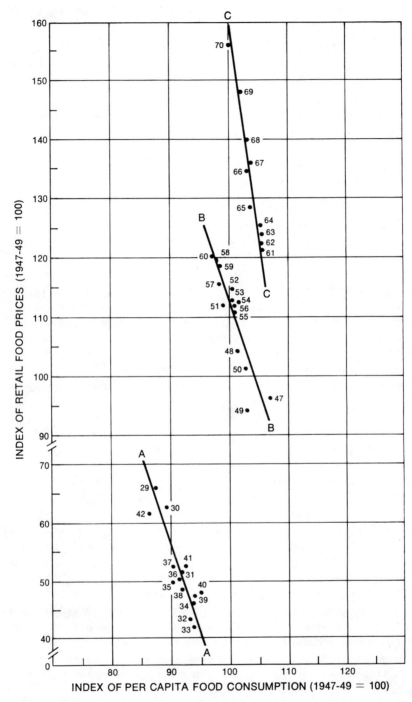

FIGURE 14–5.   The Aggregate Demand Curve for Food

The human stomach is limited in capacity, and most of us fill it several times every day. It requires so much food and we supply it with that amount. When food prices are rising, we may eat a few more beans and a little less red meat, a little more bread, and fewer dairy products. The substitution process is at work on the consumption side, too. But in the United States, we do not vary the poundage intake of food much from year to year. We keep eating about the same amount of the same kinds of food regardless of price. When the family budget is squeezed, we may drop an insurance policy, put off buying a new car, or go without another TV set, but we keep eating. In short, the food needs of the human body, together with food habits, conspire to make the aggregate demand for food highly inelastic.

We have one more link in the explanation of the extreme behavior of farm prices. Consumers, too, find it difficult to adjust the *total amount of food consumed or taken* in response to price changes. So, we have a situation in food and agriculture in which, excepting these spurt-like periods of technological advance, (1) the aggregate output of agriculture is fixed in quantity (sustained in flow); and (2) the aggregate amount demanded varies little with changes in prices. The first condition exists because farm operators cannot, in the aggregate, readily adjust the number of resources employed in agriculture in response to price changes. The second exists because consumers cannot adjust their intake of food in response to price changes. Consequently, when consumer incomes change, let us say decrease, and the aggregate demand for food declines, we get very little adjustment on either the production or the consumption side to act as a brake on the falling food prices.

In the single-commodity analysis, a fall in the price of pork acts to reduce the output of pork and to increase the amount demanded. These adjustments act to stop the price decline. *But in the aggregate, we simply do not get these adjustments in production and consumption;* hence, we get extreme price fluctuations. In one sense, this is a fortunate occurrence. The health and working efficiency of members of society would certainly suffer if they curtailed their consumption of food every time food prices rose and if producers curtailed their output every time food prices declined. We want a continuing and certain supply of food. But we must recognize that a sustained flow of food products accentuates the farm price-level problem.

The General Price-income Problem in Agriculture

We now have at hand the principal elements of the general price-income problem in agriculture. Most farm products move up and down together over the same tortuous road because changes in consumers' incomes shift the demand for most foods in the same direction and because producers can and do substitute resources between enterprises, as prices and profits dictate. If prices and profits are relatively high for a particular type of enterprise, producers shift more resources (land, labor, and capital) into that enterprise. This process acts to pull the price of the product involved back into the average pattern. Hence, we are justified in using an aggregative type of analysis in which all foods are treated as one commodity to be related to the food price level.

The extreme movements in the food price level (farm price level) grow out of the peculiar relation of aggregate supply to aggregate demand. In the short run, the total resources employed in agriculture do not change readily in response to price level changes. When farm prices are high, we generally find that urban incomes are also high, growing out of a high level of employment in industry and the service trades. Hence, agriculture cannot readily attract labor and capital resources from the nonfarm segment of the economy. When farm prices are low, farm operators keep right on producing with the resources already sunk in farming. And in such situations, unemployment in urban areas often slows down, or cuts off, a shift of labor away from agriculture. Thus, because the total resources employed in agriculture do not change readily in response to price level changes, aggregate output tends to hold constant.

The aggregate demand for food is similar in one respect to the aggregate supply of food: the amount demanded is unresponsive to variations in price. But it is dissimilar in another respect. Aggregate demand varies directly and continuously with variation in personal disposable incomes. Shifts in aggregate demand usually are not great because consumers try to maintain the consumption of food when their incomes fall. Increases in aggregate demand represent, for the most part, attempts to shift from cheap energy-producing foods to more expensive protein foods, not attempts to eat more of all foods. *But a shift in aggregate demand does not have to be great to initiate an important price change. That is the principal point of this aggregative analysis.* Because farmers cannot shift out of farming and consumers cannot consume more total pounds of food in response to a decline in food prices, *any small contraction in aggregate demand* leads to a large price decline. An expansion in aggregate consumption and a contraction in aggregate output do not come into play in response to a decline in the farm price level, to place a brake on that decline.

In Figure 14–6, four basic models portray different historical phases of the fluctuating farm price level. A panorama of farm price-level behavior emerges in Figure 14–6. In each of these models, an inelastic supply curve, *SS*, is related to a highly inelastic demand curve, *DD*—a demand curve with an elasticity approximating -0.2 at the base point, price = 100, quantity = 100. The supply curve *SS* is given some slope because the logic of farm firm behavior suggests that the aggregate supply curve does have some slope (see Chapter 6). In these highly simplified models, the marketing system is

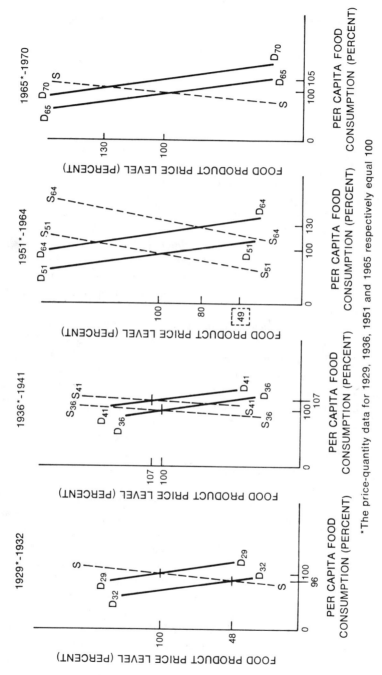

FIGURE 14-6. Farm Price Fluctuations, Basic Models

*The price-quantity data for 1929, 1936, 1951 and 1965 respectively equal 100

assumed not to exist, as the farm level supply curve is related directly to the consumer demand curve. This is a heroic assumption, but it does not invalidate the analysis, and it permits us to avoid a maze of statistical manipulations. In any event, the empirically based, although not derived, models of Figure 14-6 illustrate the basic concepts developed in this chapter and place them in an historical setting.

In the 1929–32 model, demand contracts, and the supply curve is positionally fixed and severely inelastic. In this context, the food price level falls precipitously, from *100* to *48* on the index. But the quantity adjustment is small, from *100* to *96*. This is the case that farm people dread: the situation in which the individual producer is helpless. Hence, farm people have requested and obtained from government price floors, below which the price of some farm commodities may not fall.

In the 1936–41 model, demand expands modestly, but, in this case, *the supply curve shifts to the right, along with the demand curve.* Thus, the price level holds fairly constant as output expands. This is the happy case. The nation needs more food, as the expansion in demand indicates, and farmers are able to satisfy that need through the adoption of new methods and new practices.

In the 1951–64 model, demand expands modestly, but the supply curve out-races demand. The technological revolution in agricultural production pushes the aggregate supply curve out ahead of the modestly expanding demand curve and holds it there. This is the case of chronic overproduction in agriculture in an advanced economy. The price level falls from *100* to *80* on the index, and at that level is supported by government action. Without programs of price support, acreage restriction, and demand expansion, the farm price level would fall to *49* on the index. In this case, rapid and widespread farm technological advance has converted the problem of price-level instability into one of chronic overproduction and a persistent downward pressure on farm prices.

In the 1965–70 model, supply is fixed while demand expands, pushed by the real and inflationary income increases of that period. Food prices rise rapidly while quantity remains relatively unresponsive. Farm incomes, however, are not raised because inflation increases farm costs as rapidly as receipts. Thus, farmers are no better off than in the previous period.

Two final and summary points need to be made with respect to the models in Figure 14-6. First, the steep slopes (that is, the extreme inelasticity) of the aggregate curves are such that any small shift in one curve relative to the other gives rise to a relatively small response along the quantity axis and a relatively large response along the price axis; and the nature of the curves is such that this leads to wide price-level fluctuations. Second, in no case does the aggregate supply curve shift to the left; it holds constant or it expands, but it does not contract. This is the law of agricultural production in the United States.

A Final Note

A theoretical explanation of farm price behavior has been formulated in this chapter. It builds on a conventional demand-and-supply type of analysis, it is sufficiently general to have widespread application, and it meets the test of historical fact. Further, it provides a framework of analysis for considering future developments. *But as a predicting device, it is no better than the judgments and expectations that may be interjected into it.*

Whether the farm price level will fall in the future or rise depends on a host of considerations: the rate of technological advance; personal disposable incomes; the rate of population growth; peace, limited mobilization, or war; and so on. On certain of these items, it is possible to hold informed opinions; on others, we can only guess. But even if we cannot predict with certainty, we can understand, hence, contribute to a solution of current problems. The latter has been the objective of this chapter.

POINTS FOR DISCUSSION

1. What kinds of price instability do we find in agriculture? What kinds of economic problems result from price instability?
2. What is the cobweb theorem? How is it used to analyze price behavior in this chapter?
3. Why is the aggregate output curve so very inelastic when such is not the case for single commodities?
4. What causes the aggregate output curve to shift to the right, to expand? Does it ever shift to the left, contract? If not, why not?
5. What is the configuration of the aggregate demand curve for food? What explanation do you have for this configuration?
6. Relating the aggregate supply curve to the aggregate demand curve, how is the level of farm prices affected by any small change in either curve?
7. What type of force generally initiates a price rise? What type of force generally initiates a price decline? What types of information must the analyst have at his command to use these tools of analysis as predictive devices?

REFERENCES

"Changes in Farm Production and Efficiency," *Statistical Bulletin 233*, U.S.D.A., Economic Research Service (July 1971).

COCHRANE, WILLARD W., *Farm Prices—Myth and Reality*, Chaps. 1–4. Minneapolis, Minn.: University of Minnesota Press, 1958.

SCHULTZ, T. W., *The Economic Organization of Agriculture*, Chaps. 5, 11, 12, 13, and 14. New York: McGraw-Hill Book Company, Inc., 1953.

TWEETEN, L. G., AND C. L. QUANCE, "Positivistic Measures of Aggregate Supply Elasticities: Some New Approaches," *American Journal of Agricultural Economics,* Vol. 51 (May 1969), pp. 342–52.

APPENDIX TO CHAPTER 14

The empirical aggregate demand and supply functions shown in Figures 14–4 and 14–5 were calculated by the authors using conventional economic-statistical methods. A brief description of the methodology and some of the decisions made in the process of the analysis is included here for the interested student.

The index of "responsible prices" used in the supply functions is an index of prices that cause farmers to make production decisions and as such are prices prior to the sale period. In the case of crops, they may be simply the price existing when the previous year's crop was sold; in the case of livestock, they may be prices occurring as much as two years prior to sale. The index of responsible prices used here was constructed with the following price leads: (1) lambs, chickens, and hogs, average monthly prices from July of the previous year to June of the current year; (2) beef cattle, average price for the current year and previous year; (3) eggs, average price for the current year and the previous year; (4) dairy products, average price for the current year and previous two years; (5) crops, average monthly price from July to December of the previous year. Prices used were average United States prices as reported by the U.S.D.A.

The index of productivity is obtained as the ratio of the index of farm marketing and home consumption divided by the index of total agricultural inputs multiplied by 100. It was used to judge whether technology was changing or constant over a period. The index of food marketing and home consumption was taken as the measure of quantity.

Responsible prices and resulting output quantity were plotted and a judgment made as to which years fell into each pattern in conjunction with the index of productivity. For example, one might wonder whether 1951, 1952, and 1953 should be a part of curve *CC* or of the indicated dotted line, but the index of productivity increased steadily beginning in 1951 indicating a shifting supply situation. Similar judgments were made for the other curves. This approach was possible because only one factor other than price and quantity was involved (technology).

The demand analysis was somewhat more complex because three factors other than price enter the demand curve—income, tastes, and population. Population was eliminated by changing quantity consumed to a *per capita* basis. No adequate measure of tastes exists, but it is common practice to simply include time as a variable, assuming that tastes change slowly enough to be reflected in a trend. Income was also adjusted to a per capita basis. Because of the two factors in addition to price, it was decided to use least squares regression[1] to find an equation

---

[1]See J. Johnston, *Econometric Methods* (New York: McGraw-Hill Book Company, Inc., 1963), Chaps. 1 and 2, for an explanation of regression.

describing the relationship between price and quantity. The equations corresponding to the three curves in Figure 14–5 are:

$$1929\text{–}42\text{:} \quad Q = 88.5 - .319P + .397I + .045Y$$
$$(11.5) \quad (.193) \quad (.138) \quad (.222)$$

$$1947\text{–}60\text{:} \quad Q = 137.2 - .310P + .290I - .728Y$$
$$(25.5) \quad (.115) \quad (.187) \quad (.778)$$

$$1961\text{–}70\text{:} \quad Q = 134.8 - .140P + .167I - .714Y$$
$$(40.4) \quad (.138) \quad (.091) \quad (.668)$$

where Q = index of quantity, P = index of price, I = per capita income, and Y = year. The numbers in parentheses are the standard errors of estimate of each coefficient. Several forms of each equation were fit, and the data were separated at several different years. For example, a single demand curve was fit for all the data,

APPENDIX TABLE 14A–1

Data Used in the Supply Analysis

Year	Index of Responsible Prices (1935–39 = 100)	Index of Aggregate Output	Index of Productivity (1957–59 = 100)	Year	Index of Responsible Prices (1935–39 = 100)	Index of Aggregate Prices	Index of Productivity (1957–59 = 100)
1912	92	80	65	1941	100	115	75
1913	94	78	58	1942	128	126	82
1914	99	81	62	1943	159	134	79
1915	96	84	65	1944	182	140	82
1916	100	81	58	1945	192	140	82
1917	129	82	62	1946	205	138	85
1918	168	90	60	1947	236	138	82
1919	188	90	60	1948	271	134	88
1920	193	87	63	1949	262	135	86
1921	169	84	59	1950	246	135	86
1922	132	92	62	1951	260	137	85
1923	120	95	63	1952	279	142	88
1924	118	97	62	1953	281	145	90
1925	132	93	62	1954	255	146	92
1926	147	97	63	1955	237	149	94
1927	137	97	64	1956	217	156	99
1928	136	100	65	1957	225	151	98
1929	141	97	63	1958	230	156	101
1930	139	98	63	1959	223	160	101
1931	114	100	69	1960	229	162	103
1932	83	96	69	1961	224	166	106
1933	66	97	65	1962	224	166	106
1934	74	100	59	1963	225	171	106
1935	88	93	69	1964	216	177	110
1936	100	97	62	1965	218	180	111
1937	112	101	73	1966	245	182	109
1938	107	103	74	1967	245	187	109
1939	93	106	72	1968	243	187	108
1940	91	111	72	1969	257	190	109
				1970	278	191	108

but it did not provide an adequate explanation of the actual events. It seemed most logical to break the post-World War II period into two parts because from 1947 to 1960 the rate of growth of per capita income was rather modest, but it was much faster during the 1960s. Changing the data to logarithms to relate percentages changes in a linear way did not improve the explanatory power of the equations.

APPENDIX TABLE 14A–2

Data Used in the Demand Analysis

Year	Index of Retail Food Prices (1947–49 = 100)	Index of Per Capita Food Consumption (1957–59 = 100)	Index of Per Capita Disposable Income (1947–49 = 100)	"Adjusted" Per Capita Food Consumption
1929	65.6	91.1	55.1	87.1
1930	62.4	90.7	48.8	89.1
1931	51.4	90.0	41.6	91.3
1932	42.8	87.8	31.5	93.0
1933	41.6	88.0	29.4	94.0
1934	46.4	89.1	33.2	93.6
1935	49.7	87.3	37.1	90.2
1936	50.1	90.5	41.8	91.4
1937	52.1	90.4	44.5	90.3
1938	48.4	90.6	40.9	91.8
1939	47.1	93.8	43.5	94.0
1940	47.8	95.5	46.5	94.4
1941	52.2	97.5	56.3	92.5
1942	61.3	96.7	70.4	86.1
1947	95.9	102.2	94.6	106.9
1948	104.1	98.9	103.6	101.7
1949	99.9	98.9	101.6	103.0
1950	101.2	100.2	109.6	102.7
1951	112.5	98.4	118.0	99.2
1952	114.5	100.3	122.0	100.7
1953	112.7	101.3	127.2	100.9
1954	112.5	101.2	127.4	101.4
1955	110.9	101.9	133.9	101.0
1956	111.8	103.1	140.1	101.1
1957	115.4	101.0	144.7	98.4
1958	120.2	99.7	147.1	97.1
1959	118.4	101.8	153.1	98.2
1960	119.7	101.3	155.7	97.7
1961	121.1	100.9	159.4	105.5
1962	122.3	101.2	165.9	105.4
1963	124.0	101.6	171.7	105.5
1964	125.6	102.6	183.2	105.3
1965	128.4	102.2	195.4	103.6
1966	134.8	103.3	208.9	103.2
1967	135.9	105.1	220.5	103.7
1968	140.8	106.4	236.2	103.1
1969	148.1	106.7	249.8	101.9
1970	156.1	107.7	267.9	100.6

Once the equations had been determined, the actual values of I and Y in each year were used to determine an "adjusted" value of per capita consumption corresponding to the quantity that would have been demanded at the prevailing price *if* income (I) and tastes (Y) had been constant at their average value in each subperiod. These adjusted quantities are plotted against the index of retail prices in Figure 14–5. The apparent shift in the demand among the three periods is due to differences in the *average* value of I and Y in the three periods, not to annual changes.

The data used are shown in Appendix Tables 14A–1 and 14A–2. The supply analysis includes all years between 1912 and 1970. The demand analysis begins with 1929 because that is the first year for which national income accounts are available and hence is the beginning of a consistent time series on per capita disposable income. The World War II years of 1943–46 are omitted from the demand analysis because the rationing and price ceilings of that period mean that the prices and quantities observed do not reflect market conditions.

PART FOUR

Farmers in the National and World Economies

Chapter 15

Business Fluctuations and

Agriculture

Good business conditions may exist in one industry or area like an island in a sea of depressed economic activity (or conversely). But usually, the more dynamic conditions, good or bad, spread throughout the national economy to assume the *general condition* of either prosperity or depression. Thus, business fluctuations tend to be general in scope, encompassing the entire economy. The impact of business fluctuations on different segments of the economy is, of course, different. It is the primary objective of this chapter to describe and analyze the ways in which changes in overall business conditions affect farmers and their farm businesses.

First, however, let us take a look at the most disrupting influence, hence the most critical problem of modern economics, the business fluctuation.[1] With broad sweeps of the brush, we will describe the ups and downs of business conditions since 1929, point out the symptoms and forces involved, and set forth a method for analyzing such fluctuations. Once the nature and magnitude of business fluctuations have been established, we shall turn to a study of their consequences on agriculture in terms of (1) the structure of the industry, (2) investment in agriculture, (3) labor mobility, and (4) the operation of the farm firm. The impact of business fluctuations on farmers can be appraised rather completely under these four headings.

---

[1]A term more often used is *business cycle*. We avoid the use of that term wherever possible in discussing the ups and downs of the total economy because we do not find a regularity or periodicity in these phenomena that the word *cycle* connotes.

THE NATURE AND MAGNITUDE OF
BUSINESS FLUCTUATIONS

Prosperity and Depression in the United States, 1929–70

A panorama of business conditions and business fluctuations over the 1929–70 period may be seen in Figure 15–1. The top line shows the Gross National Product (GNP), the most commonly used indicator of the health of the national economy. The GNP is a measure of the money value of all final goods and services produced by the economy. It measures only *final* goods so that double counting is avoided. For example, a loaf of bread is counted, but the flour used to make the bread and the wheat used to make the flour are not counted. It is an imperfect measure because some goods and services that are produced and consumed by the same economic unit are not measured and so are not included, for example, a beef steer produced and consumed on a farm, or a housewife's work in keeping house. Despite this and other imperfections, the GNP is a valuable concept. Figure 15–1 shows two characteristics of the GNP since 1929: (1)

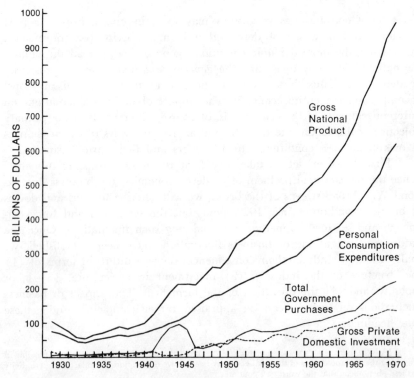

FIGURE 15–1.   Gross National Product and Expenditure, U.S., 1929–1970

the frequent fluctuations, and (2) the impressive secular growth since 1940.

From 1929 to 1933, the GNP fell by nearly 50 percent from $104 billion to $56 billion. The Great Depression had all the aspects that have come to be associated with a business downtown. Leading the fall in over-all economic activity was the precipitous decline in private investment, from $16.2 billion in 1929 to $.9 billion in 1932. (Fluctuations in private investment do not stand out in Figure 15–1 because of the compressed vertical scale.) Private businessmen almost stopped purchasing the mate-rials, machines, and equipment out of which to produce consumer goods, and there was no expansion in expenditures by the government to offset the contraction in private investment expenditures. In fact, expenditures of all units of government fell off somewhat.

By 1933, unemployment had risen to alarming proportions, to be-tween 13 and 15 million. Prices generally, and farm prices particularly, had fallen to very low levels. Social unrest was widespread, and pleas for relief poured into the Federal government from laborers, farmers, and businessmen alike. In this chaotic situation, businessmen were unwilling to invest in new plants and equipment. Hence, plants and equipment simply wore out without being replaced. Investments by manufacturing firms fell short of depreciation charges by approximately $2 billion over the period 1930–32.

But growing out of this latter circumstance and in conjunction with increased federal expenditures, revival at long last got underway in 1933–34. If the economy and the society were to survive, that is, meet the essential needs for food, clothing, and shelter, the productive capacity of the na-tional economy could not be allowed to drop further. Inspired, then, with the efforts of government in 1933–34 and backed by the knowledge that new machines and equipment were sorely needed, businessmen began to take hope and risk investment in producer goods. But the recovery from 1933 to 1937 was never full or complete. Unemployment in the peak year of this upswing, 1937, was estimated at between 8 and 9 million. In addition, inventory accumulation and government expenditures dominated the in-vestment scene in this period, whereas housing and plant construction played more dominant roles in recovering from earlier depressions.

Inventory accumulation, which was taking place at a rapid rate in 1936 and the first half of 1937, dropped off sharply in the later half of 1937. Hence, we have another inventory-induced recession in 1937. But this recession did not last long; it could not. Increased expenditures by government, first in rearmament and mobilization and second in World War II, created a total demand for goods and services beyond anything we had ever before experienced. Expenditures by the government in 1944 approximated the Gross National Product of 1929. (Note the bulge in government expenditures between 1940 and 1946, Figure 15–1). The expansion in total goods and services produced and the rise in the price level between 1940 and 1946 were such as to make all previous efforts look picayune.

Since the end of World War II, the national economy has experienced some sharp but brief periods of unemployment—in 1946, 1949, 1954, 1958, 1961, and 1971—with the unemployment rate rising to 6.8 percent of the labor force in 1958 and 1961 and to over 6 percent in 1971. But in none of the post-World War II business contractions has the GNP fallen by more than a few percentage points, and in none have personal consumption expenditures declined. The flow of income and expenditures has leveled off in these business recessions, but has not declined substantially. These interruptions in the growth of the economy, for that is what they have been, have been brief and moderate, coinciding with slack periods in business investment in plants and equipment and inventories.

The big picture that emerges from Figure 15–1 is one of substantial, sustained growth between 1940 and 1970. There is some price inflation in the GNP figures over the 1940–70 period, but the total output of *real* goods and services increased importantly between 1940 and 1970. In real terms (constant 1958 dollars), the Gross National Product increased over 220 percent between 1940 and 1970, that is, the total real product of the economy more than tripled. Per capita GNP in real terms doubled during this period. Thus, the overall picture for the period 1940–70 is one of rapid growth and prosperity, marred by several minor business recessions.

A Generalized View of Business Fluctuations

It is clear from the 1929–70 experience that no single cycle, from peak to peak or trough to trough, is similar in all details to any other. Each has some peculiar characteristic of its own, for example, first point of weakness, segment of the economy most affected, length of time elapsing from peak to peak, and so on. Yet, it is important to have a picture of the forces at work on, as well as the overt symptoms of, the various phases of the business fluctuation. That is what we want to provide here.

Let us begin this description at the bottom of the trough, in the pit of a depression. At such a time, business firms (farm and nonfarm) have reduced their orders for equipment, land, buildings, and other producer goods to the minimum, possibly below the replacement rate. Business firms are delaying decisions to invest as long as possible because they fear the future. Businessmen do not feel certain that the bottom has been reached, and they do not want to sink their scarce funds in heavy equipment if conditions are going to get worse. Foreign demand for goods is usually low in such a period. Government purchases may be greater than usual but not large enough to offset the decline in investment by private firms. Inventories of retail, wholesale, and manufacturing firms are being depleted, perhaps at a rapid rate. Interest rates are likely to be low, prices may or may not be falling (there is an increasing tendency for nonfarm prices to be sticky—not to fall), and unemployment in the urban areas is large and perhaps still mounting.

Expectations of businessmen are likely to be pessimistic in the type of situation that we have been describing. But there are some favorable elements in the situation: (1) inventories cannot be depleted indefinitely if businesses are to live; (2) the cost of new capital goods is likely to be low, relatively at least; and (3) in time, individuals with funds to lend become venturesome, credit becomes available on easier terms. Thus, conditions eventually become favorable to entrepreneurs with a production plan and an investment program.

When the decline in retail sales comes to an end (or even slows down), profit expectations are raised, and orders are increased all along the line to maintain or perhaps increase inventories. Next, orders for producer goods must go up, first, to keep machinery and equipment from going into further disrepair and, second, to undertake new production plans growing out of rising profit expectations. This expansion in investment brings about an increase in consumer purchases; consumer purchases increase with expanding payrolls. So, all this makes the situation look even more hopeful. Further expansion in investment now becomes profitable and the process becomes cumulative. New investment creates new activity, new jobs, greater product, and higher prices. Out of this combination of circumstances, the purchasing power of consumers expands, and so the spiral grows.

It is difficult to see why or how this joyful cumulative process ever comes to an end. But there are some disquieting elements in the picture, too. Interest rates probably will be rising (or, if interest rates are pegged by the government, sources of credit will be drying up). Prices, hence costs, of producer goods will also be rising. But most important, the investment in new, additional producer goods is building up *the stock* of new machines, equipment, and buildings. This growing stock acts as a brake to further investments in capital goods. The increasing cost of investment, taken in conjunction with the saturation of investment opportunities and the tendency for consumers to save increasing proportions of their rising incomes, causes entrepreneurs to become cautious and less optimistic about the future. At this point in time, the total economy ceases to expand and begins to contract.

The turning point comes when it no longer *appears* profitable to add to stocks of inventories and producer goods—when the rate of investment falls off. With this decline in investment, unemployment in producer goods industries increases, and aggregate consumption falls off. This decline in consumption accelerates the contraction in investment. Thus, the bubble of prosperity is pricked, and optimistic profit expectations give way to pessimistic expectations. This shift in the state of expectations may lead to panic selling, a break in the stock market, and a loss of confidence on the part of banks and other lenders. Credit is restricted, sales fall, unemployment rises, and the gloom deepens. Now, the cumulative process is driving the economy into a depression.

The Income-expenditure Approach to Business Fluctuations

We cannot enter into a full and detailed account of business fluctuations here. We are primarily concerned with the economics of agriculture, and with changes in overall business activity only as they affect agriculture. But that effect can be great, and although the income-expenditure approach does not in itself provide answers as to what caused a downturn here and upturn there, it provides a useful framework for considering the various factors at work. So, we spend a short time describing a framework for analyzing business fluctuations—the income-expenditure approach of macroeconomic theory.

In this approach, we use the same categories that we have been using to describe business fluctuations: income, consumption, savings, investment, and government purchases. Now, consider the GNP from two viewpoints: the *income* generated and the *expenditures* made. Obviously, all the income generated is either saved or spent. The three economic units that spend (or save) are consumers, business, and government. It is convenient to group total spending into three classes: consumption (C), investment (I), and government (G). Although the student should be forewarned that there is *not* a complete one-to-one correspondence between the spending units and the kinds of spending, it is nonetheless convenient for analysis to assume such a correspondence.

Consumption expenditures of a family are closely related to the income earned by that family, but as personal experience will show, the two are not always equal. Low-income families tend to spend more than they earn, financing the difference by borrowing and transfer payments. Wealthy families spend less than they earn, engaging in savings. The aggregate of all consumers behave in somewhat the same way. In a period of economic downturn, consumers tend to spend more than they earn by drawing on savings or borrowing, that is, dissaving. In a period of economic expansion, when incomes are rising, consumers tend to increase their consumption less than their income, thereby resulting in savings. This behavior is reflected in curve CC in Figure 15–2, the consumption function, which shows the desired level of consumption corresponding to each level of income.

In Figure 15–2, we have plotted income on the horizontal axis and consumption on the vertical axis. A line joining all the points at which consumption exactly equals income results in a line at 45 degrees above

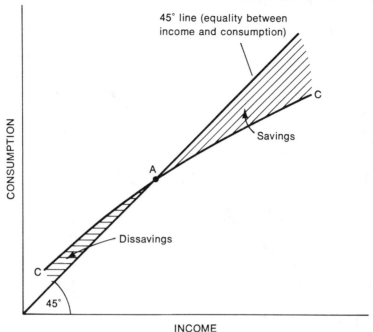

FIGURE 15–2.   The Consumption Function

the horizontal axis. We see that there is only one point of intersection between the consumption function and *45° line,* point *A.* These two concepts, the consumption function and the 45-degree line, form the basis for a geometric intrepretation of the theory of income determination and should be carefully studied by the student.[2]

Investment is defined as expenditures made in the acquisition of producer goods, goods used to produce consumer goods and services. In addition, housing is considered an investment good because it provides its stream of services over a long period of time. Investment expenditures are thought to respond partly to interest rates but primarily to the level of confidence that businessmen have in the economy. Thus, investment is, to a large extent, controlled by noneconomic variables. Government expenditures are those made by the government to purchase goods (as for example, defense material) or services (as for example, teachers). The level of government expenditures depends partly on what goods and services are desired, but as we shall see, an equally important determinant is the effort government makes to preserve the health of the economy.

We can add the three classes of expenditures to one another to get total expenditures, which, ignoring any time dimension, must equal the

[2]A much more comprehensive treatment of these concepts may be found in Chapters 11, 12, and 13 of Paul Samuelson's introductory textbook, *Economics* (New York: McGraw-Hill Book Company, Inc., 1970).

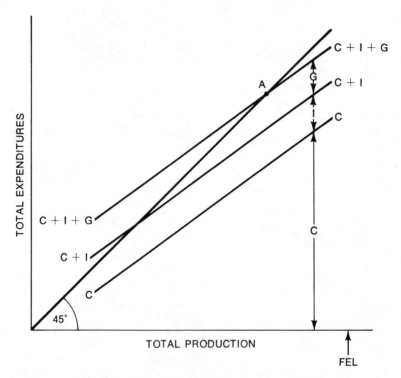

FIGURE 15–3. National Income Determination

value of total production. Thus in Figure 15–3, total expenditures, plotted vertically, equal total production on the 45-degree line at point *A*. Point *A* is an *equilibrium* point for national income. This can be shown as follows: suppose the economy were producing at some point to the left of *A*. The *desired* total expenditures $(C + I + G)$ would be above the 45-degree line and thus would exceed the available production, tending to push prices up, thereby tending to bring forth greater production. Suppose, on the other hand, output was at some point to the right of *A*; then total expenditures $(C + I + G)$ would be below the 45-degree line and thus less than total production. Inventories would build up, prices tend to fall, and producers would tend to reduce production, thereby moving back toward point *A*. Thus, point *A* is the equilibrium level of production (or GNP) in the economy.

The theory thus far shows only an equilibrium point, but we are more interested in the dynamics of how income changes. To explore this issue, consider what would happen if the level of government spending increased. According to Figure 15–3, the equilibrium level of production would also increase. The same thing would result if the consumption function shifted upwards. Implicit in these statements is the assumption that that economy *can* produce a greater quantity of output, and here we get into a second major concern of national income analysis—the level of employment.

If all resources in the economy are fully employed, then increased spending by government or consumers would tend to push prices up but no increased production could occur. Thus, the full-employment level of the economy is an important concept. Suppose, as shown in Figure 15–3, full employment (FEL) is at a higher level than the equilibrium level of output: unemployment exists. Under such conditions, economists and politicians who understand the theory of income determination would call for greater investment and greater government spending. On the other hand, if the full employment level is very close to being attained, restraint in spending and investment is appropriate because inflation would otherwise result.

We earlier saw that individuals may consume or save from their income. To the extent that they save, they do not demand products, and thus the economy tends to slow down. Offsetting this tendency, investors borrow savings to purchase capital goods as investments. To the extent that the desired level of investments equals the desired level of savings, the savings action of consumers has no effect on the level of economic activity. However, when desired savings exceed desired investments, a build-up of unused buying power occurs, inventories accumulate, and a downward pressure is exerted on economic activity.[3] When desired savings fall short of desired investment, an upswing can occur if the economy has unused productive capacity.

The important role of the government in the economy can now be made clear. If the economy is operating at less than full employment, men are out of work, but wages do not fall—there is no self-regulating mechanism to correct the situation. Equilibrium may be established at a less-than-full-employment level. Government then has the task of trying to estimate the amount of added expenditure required to get the full-employment level. It also has the task of "cooling down" the economy when too high a level of spending pushes economic activity above the full-employment level, resulting in inflation.

We have touched on the high points of the modern theory of income determination. Many refinements of the approach have been omitted. But we do see how an unbalancing can occur in our economy. Or more properly stated, we see why economic stability at full employment is not *automatically* achieved. And we have hinted at ways in which the government affects the level of operation of the economy.

[3]This is the same event described as when production was to the right of point *A*, except that now we focus on savings rather than consumption.

THE EFFECTS OF BUSINESS FLUCTUATIONS ON AGRICULTURE

The Agricultural Industry and Business Fluctuations

The agricultural segment of the economy does not behave in a fashion similar to the nonfarm segment in the various phases of business fluctuations. A quick look at Figure 11–6 establishes that fact. During the years of the Great Depression, total production in agriculture was almost constant, in contrast with the sharp decline in total output of industry. During World War II, agricultural production increased in a persistent fashion but not in the spectacular fashion observable for nonfarm industry. In response to the needs of war and a modest price rise, the total output of manufacturing rose nearly 130 percent between 1939 and 1944, in comparison to an increase in agricultural output of 21 percent for the same period. The output of industry oscillates in the extreme, from very low levels in the trough of a depression to very high levels at the peak of prosperity. The total output of agriculture contracts little if at all in depressed periods, and it expands, in a relentless fashion, in periods of prosperity.

The price response in the two segments of the economy is just the converse of the production response. In agriculture, prices fall precipitously in a downswing in economic activity, whereas industrial prices hold fairly constant. On the other hand, prices of farm products shoot skyward in periods of great prosperity, whereas nonfarm prices move upward less dramatically.

The point we wish to underscore is the following: *when aggregate expenditures increase, something must give, must expand, in both the farm and the nonfarm segments.* In the farm segment, prices customarily break loose as production advances slowly, whereas in industry the greater response comes in output as prices advance slowly. An upswing in business activity brings increased incomes in manufacturing and the service trades, by reason of increased employment, and in agriculture, by reason of rising prices. In the downswing, just the opposite occurs. Something must give, as total expenditures decline, and, in agriculture it is price that declines, whereas in industry it is production and employment.

Dale Hathaway has investigated in detail the effects of business fluctuations on agriculture.[4] Based on his analysis of ten business cycles between 1910 and 1954, he concluded that:

1. Severe business cycles have a direct, similar effect on agricultural production, income, and asset formation.

---

[4] Dale E. Hathaway, "Agriculture and the Business Cycle," *Policy for Commercial Agriculture,* Joint Committee Print, 85th Cong., 1st sess. (November 22, 1957), pp. 53–55.

2. Mild business cycles have a moderate effect on agriculture, manifested mainly in the increased rate of outmigration from agriculture during expansions of the general economy.
3. Prices paid by farmers are affected more by mild business fluctuations than are prices received by farmers.

Hathaway noted the possibility of a change in the relationship between agriculture and the general economy following World War II. This possibility has recently been investigated by another analyst[5] using the same methods as Hathaway but separating the observations into pre- and post-World War II periods of expansion and contraction as established by the National Bureau of Economic Research (NBER). Table 15–1 shows the percentage changes that occurred in the variables measuring general and farm economic activity during each period.

As you would expect from the earlier discussion, during most periods of contraction GNP declined, at least when measured in real (constant dollar) terms. Unemployment generally increased during periods of contraction and decreased during periods of expansion. However, these tendencies were much stronger before World War II. The 1945–48 expansion is a good example of inverse movements in real GNP and unemployment in an expansionary period of adjustment from a war-based to a peacetime economy.

Gross farm income, farm production expenses, and net farm income show rather mixed relationships with both expansions and contractions. For example, in the seven pre-World War II contractions, gross farm income increased three times, and in the five post-World War II contractions, gross farm income increased three times. The direct relation between business fluctuations and *net* farm income is much clearer, at least prior to World War II. However, in the postwar period, net farm income seems to have moved in the opposite direction from general business activity as often as it has moved in the same direction.

Prices paid, prices received, and average per capita income of farmers show the same kind of ambiguous relationship with business fluctuations in the post-World War II period as does net farm income. The number of farm workers fell in nearly every period, reflecting the secular changes occurring in the farming sector, but the rate of emigration seems to have been faster in periods of more vigorous business expansion.

Investment in Agriculture

Farm businessmen, like other businessmen, invest heavily in machines, equipment, plants, and buildings when prices are high, receipts large, and expectations bright. In other words, the investment decisions of farmers

[5]Earl D. Kellogg, "The Changing Relationships Between Business Fluctuations and Agriculture," unpublished paper, Department of Agricultural Economics, University of Illinois at Urbana-Champaign, 1971.

TABLE 15–1

Percentage Changes in Selected Measures of Economic Activity During Periods of Business Expansions and Contractions, 1910–68

Periods of Business	Current GNP	Real GNP	Unemployment	Gross Farm Income[1]	Farm Production Expenses	Net Farm Income[1]	Received by Farmers	Prices Paid by Farmers	Paid for Items Used in Production	Average Per Capita Net Income of Farmers[1]	No. of Farm Workers[1]
Pre-WW II											
Contraction											
1910–1911	+ 2.7	+ 2.6	+ 0.8	− 3.9	+ 1.4	− 8.7	− 9.6	+ 1.0	+ 1.0	− 17.7	− 0.1
1923–1924	+ 1.7	− 0.24	+ 2.6	+ 5.1	+ 5.5	− 4.5	− 0.7	+ 0.6	+ 1.4	− 2.7	− 1.0
1926–1927	− 1.4	− 1.0	+ 1.5	+ 0.3	+ 1.2	− 0.8	− 3.4	− 0.6	0	− 2.3	− 2.6
1912–1914	− 2.4	− 3.5	+ 3.3	+ 0.7	+ 5.1	− 3.7	− 2.0	− 2.0	0	− 5.8	+ 0.2
1919–1921	− 6.3	− 12.7	+ 10.3	− 41.0	− 20.4	− 59.1	− 42.9	− 21.3	− 34.4	− 59.9	+ 1.2
1937–1938	− 6.3	− 5.1	+ 4.7	− 12.0	+ 4.5	− 21.5	− 20.5	− 5.3	− 7.6	− 26.1	+ 3.0
1929–1932	− 43.7	− 29.2	+ 20.4	− 53.9	− 41.3	− 69.3	− 56.1	− 30.0	− 32.2	− 65.2	+ 0.4
Expansion											
1927–1929	+ 7.7	+ 7.3	− 0.1	+ 4.5	+ 2.6	+ 7.0	+ 5.7	+ 0.6	+ 3.5	+ 7.0	+ 1.0
1911–1912	+ 8.7	+ 5.7	− 2.1	+ 6.7	+ 7.0	+ 6.3	+ 5.3	+ 3.1	+ 4.1	+ 27.3	+ 0.1
1924–1926	+ 11.5	+ 14.8	− 3.2	+ 4.1	+ 1.1	+ 11.3	+ 1.4	0	+ 0.7	+ 20.09	+ 0.4
1921–1923	+ 16.5	+ 29.8	− 9.3	+ 15.2	+ 6.2	+ 30.5	+ 14.5	+ 2.6	+ 7.8	+ 45.0	− 1.8
1932–1937	+ 55.9	+ 40.9	− 9.3	+ 72.2	+ 36.6	+ 155.3	+ 87.7	+ 17.0	+ 33.3	+ 158.8	− 6.5
1914–1919	+ 116.8	+ 16.6	− 6.5	+ 131.0	+ 106.8	+ 157.4	+ 114.9	+ 91.3	+ 91.2	+ 122.1	− 2.5
1938–1944	+ 148.1	+ 87.3	− 17.1	+ 144.0	+ 109.3	+ 196.7	+ 103.1	+ 46.8	+ 41.8	+ 224.8	− 12.1
Post-WW II											
Contraction											
1959–1960	+ 4.2	+ 2.5	0	+ 1.6	+ 0.9	+ 3.3	− 0.4	+ 0.7	− 0.4	+ 18.4	− 0.7
1957–1958	+ 1.4	− 1.1	+ 2.5	+ 11.6	+ 8.5	+ 19.1	+ 6.4	+ 2.4	+ 2.7	+ 6.2	− 2.1
1944–1945	+ 0.9	− 1.7	+ 0.7	+ 5.9	+ 6.0	+ 5.8	+ 5.1	+ 4.4	+ 1.7	+ 2.1	− 2.5
1953–1954	+ 0.05	− 1.4	+ 2.7	+ 4.1	+ 1.4	+ 12.8	+ 3.5	0	− 0.4	+ 25.8	− 3.9
1948–1949	− 0.4	+ 0.1	+ 2.1	− 8.8	+ 4.3	− 14.1	− 12.9	− 3.5	− 4.8		
Expansion											
1958–1959	+ 8.1	+ 6.4	− 1.3	− 0.1	+ 3.6	− 8.1	− 4.0	+ 1.7	+ 0.8	− 11.4	− 1.9
1945–1948	+ 21.5	+ 8.9	− 1.9	+ 37.5	+ 44.5	+ 29.9	+ 38.6	+ 36.8	+ 42.0	+ 43.2	+ 3.6
1954–1957	+ 21.7	+ 11.2	− 1.3	+ 1.0	+ 7.5	− 16.7	− 4.5	+ 3.2	+ 0.8	− 9.0	− 12.3
1949–1953	+ 42.1	+ 27.4	− 3.0	+ 10.6	+ 18.3	+ 0.3	+ 2.0	+ 10.4	+ 7.6	+ 17.3	− 11.0
1960–1968	+ 71.8	+ 45.1	− 1.9	+ 27.3	+ 81.0	+ 7.3	+ 9.2	+ 18.3	+ 10.2		

1 Excluding government payments.

contribute to, and coincide with, upturns in overall business activity. But like other businessmen, farmers curtail their investments in producer goods, in the downswing, hence, contribute to an intensification of the decline in business activity. This is made clear in Figure 15–4.

If we compare fluctuations, as reflected in the purchase of tractors, with the GNP in Figure 15–4, we see that the dips in tractor purchases coincide with the dips in the GNP. In the depression years 1930–32, during the tractor-short years of World War II, and in the recession year of 1954, farmers reduced their purchases of tractors. But in the periods of economic upswing, tractor purchases increase over the previous year. These increases coincide with the increases in GNP, as in 1947, 1955, and 1965. This tendency is very marked in the 1930s and 1940s but much less so during the 1950s and 1960s. This may be partly traced to the fact that the latter two decades covered a period of farm consolidation and a period that saw increasing size of tractors. These two factors tended to reduce the number of new tractors purchases annually from nearly half a million in 1950 to only 150,000 in 1968.

The Hathaway analysis with respect to farm production expenditures during the cycle is illuminating:

> ...it appears that variations in farmers' expenditures for current operating expenses have been partially obscured by the strong secular rise in such expenditures. However, it appears that in periods of very sharp reductions in farm income, such as those experienced in 1920–21 and 1929–32, farmers do reduce both expenditures and physical inputs of these items. As the upward trend in these expenditures tend to level off when their economic usage approaches the maximum point of profitability for most farms, it seems reasonable to expect the usage will become more sensitive to changes in farm income.[6]

The data on farm cash expenditures in Figure 15–4 show the relationship Hathaway discussed. The strong secular increase in farm cash expenditures is reflected in increases in those expenditures in nearly every year of the past fifteen. However, one can see little relationship between the size of the change in GNP and the change in farm cash expenditures during the post-World War II period.

Recessions and recoveries in the general economy have not played their earlier role in the farm economy in the 1950s and 1960s for several reasons. First and foremost, the farm economy has been plagued by overproduction and low prices and incomes throughout those years. Hence, farmers have responded in their investment decisions to the unique, but chronically adverse, conditions in agriculture that have not paralleled conditions in the general economy. Second, governmental price and income support have protected agriculture from drastic price and income declines.

[6]Hathaway, *op. cit.*, pp. 62–64.

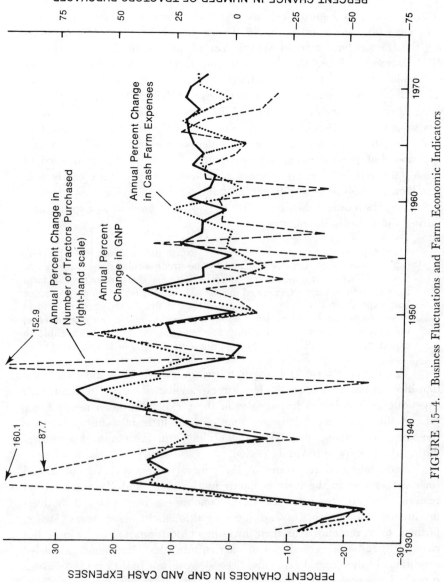

FIGURE 15–4. Business Fluctuations and Farm Economic Indicators

PERCENT CHANGE IN NUMBER OF TRACTORS PURCHASED

PERCENT CHANGES IN GNP AND CASH EXPENSES

Annual Percent Change in Number of Tractors Purchased (right-hand scale)

Annual Percent Change in GNP

Annual Percent Change in Cash Farm Expenses

272

Hence, farmers' investment decisions have been buoyed up to some degree by this supporting action. Thus, farm production expenditures and investments have tended to follow the depressed, but nonetheless stabilized, conditions of agriculture in the 1950s and 1960s rather than the historic response to changes in general business conditions.

Population in Agriculture

The pull of the city has been strong in the twentieth century. There has been a net movement of people out of agriculture in almost every year since 1920; and this net emigration has been great enough to more than compensate for the natural population increase in agriculture. Hence, the population in agriculture has declined persistently (see Table 15–2). But in concentrating on the net flow, we should not ignore the two-way movement. During the period 1950–59, when people literally poured out of agriculture on a *net basis* (at an average of 800,000 per year) the movement to farms averaged 540,000 persons per year and from farms 1,340,000 persons per year. A lot of people were moving to and from agriculture, as well as leaving on a net basis.

The net movement of people off farms, accelerates in each period of business revival or general prosperity (see Table 15–2). In periods of very great economic activity, such as 1939–44, when the economy was operating under a forced draft of war mobilization, farm people were literally sucked off farms. On the other hand, the only periods of net movement from city to farm over the years 1920–59 occurred in the depressions or recessions of 1932–33 and 1945–46.

The period 1950–70 is most interesting with respect to the migration of people off farms. In the first place, as already noted, it is a period of very heavy movement out of agriculture. In the second place, the influence of business fluctuations—of job opportunities in the nonfarm sector—on migration from the farm sector shows up most clearly. In the year 1956, over 1 million people moved out of agriculture, on a net basis.[7] But, as the national economy dipped into a recession in 1957, the net flow of people out of agriculture dropped sharply. In 1957, only 576,000 people left agriculture. In 1958, the new flow of people out of agriculture continued at a low level. It did not return to the 1956 level because recovery in 1958 was not complete. In 1959, 1960, and 1963 emigration from agriculture again reached the annual rate of 1 million.

These shifts in the direction of net movement make good sense. Young people leave the farms for the city in great numbers when job opportunities are more attractive in the city (when there are job openings in the city), and that is generally the case in periods of high-level eco-

[7]The year runs from April 1956 to April 1957.

TABLE 15-2

Farm Population and Migration, 1929-70

Farm Population (April 1)[1]

Period	Number (thousands)	As Percentage of Total Population[2]	Net Migration to and from Farms (thousands)[3]
1929	30,580	25.1	−477
1930	30,529	24.8	−61
1931	30,845	24.8	156
1932	31,388	25.1	607
1933	32,393	25.8	−463
1934	32,305	25.5	−527
1935	32,161	25.3	−799
1936	31,737	24.8	−834
1937	31,266	24.2	−661
1938	30,980	23.8	−545
1939	30,840	23.5	−703
1940	30,547	23.1	−633
1941	30,118	27.6	−1,424
1942	28,914	21.5	−2,975
1943	26,186	19.2	−1,563
1944	24,815	18.0	−564
1945	24,420	17.5	864
1946	25,403	18.0	151
1947	25,829	18.0	−1,686
1948	24,383	16.7	−371
1949	24,194	16.3	−1,314
1950	23,048	15.6	−1,302
1951	21,890	14.2	−271
1952	21,748	13.9	−1,996
1953	19,874	12.5	−962
1954	19,019	11.8	−25
1955	19,078	11.6	−435
1956	18,712	11.2	−1,134
1957	17,656	10.4	−576
1958	17,128	9.9	−548
1959	16,592	9.4	−740
1960	15,635	8.7	−1,142
1961	14,803	8.1	−1,000
1962	14,313	7.7	−646
1963	13,367	7.1	−1,086
1964	12,954	6.8	−533
1965	12,363	6.4	−703
1966	11,595	5.9	−856
1967	10,875	5.5	−793
1968	10,454	5.3	−481
1969	10,307	5.1	−198
1970	9,712	4.8	−642

1 *Farm population*, as defined by Department of Agriculture and Department of Commerce, is the civilian population living on farms, both urban and rural, regardless of occupation.
2 Total population as of July 1 including armed forces overseas.
3 Net change for year beginning in April, estimated by Department of Agriculture. For 1940 and subsequent years, includes inductions and enlistments into the armed forces, and persons returning from the armed forces. For all years, includes persons who have not moved but who are in and out of the farm population because agricultural operations have begun or have ceased on the place where they are living.

Sources: "Farm Population Estimates for 1910-1962," *Economic Research Service 130*, October 1963; *Economic Research Service 177, 233, 286, 344, 410.*

nomic activity. In periods of business depression, however, unemployment rises in urban areas and two things happen: (1) many young men and women, who would have migrated if business conditions were bright, remain on the farm; and (2) unemployed workers in urban areas return to the farm and live with the "old folks."

It would appear that this movement across the rural-urban line invalidates orthodox economic analysis, for what often happened in the past is the following: in periods of prosperity, farm prices rose relative to nonfarm prices and workers migrated on a net basis toward the area of lower product prices, to the city. In depressed periods, farm prices fell relative to nonfarm prices and the rate of off-farm migration slowed down or reversed itself. The movement of workers was inversely related to relative price changes.

These shifts in product prices, farm relative to nonfarm, do not dominate the net flow of people out of agriculture for at least one reason. Even when farm product prices rise relative to nonfarm prices, the resulting incomes in agriculture on the average remain low relative to nonfarm incomes. Thus, the income incentive to shift out of agriculture and into nonfarm employment remains strong whether farm prices are relatively high or low. Hence, the net flow has been in the direction of the city for many decades. What really governs this flow is the number of nonfarm employment opportunities together with information and access to them, not relative price movements.

The Farm Firm

It is often said that success or failure in farming depends on when a man is born. If he reaches maturity during a peak of prosperity and buys a farm during that period, the large and fixed payments for land in the following depressed period may force him into bankruptcy. But if a man is lucky enough to buy his farm in the trough of a depression, he can ride the crest of general business prosperity to success and perhaps riches. This view oversimplifies the problem of entrepreneurship. But it does symbolize an important problem in the business of farming: the problem of high overhead costs.

Many, if not most, of the resource inputs of the farm to which we attach a cost are in the nature of overhead costs. By this, we mean that the inputs cannot be varied in accordance with price, or with any other independent variable that we might select. Resource inputs such as land, buildings, labor, breeding stock, machinery, and equipment are tied to the farm and their costs go along whether they are employed or not. These resources, acquired in a previous period to be used over a long period of time, carry fixed charges that must be met periodically if the farm is to be operated on a commercial basis.

What, then, does the farm operator do when faced with a down-swing in business activity, which means lower prices to him? He perhaps reduces his applications of fertilizer, and he may skimp on his feeding rations. At least, the Hathaway analysis suggests that this is what happens. But our main point is this: the farmer continues to employ all his land, all the family labor, and the stock of machinery and equipment on hand. Further, the producer must undertake certain out-of-pocket costs, such as spraying and fumigating in the case of fruit and vegetables and irrigating if he lives in the arid West, if he is to harvest a crop at all. So, in the face of declining farm prices growing out of a downswing in business activity, the individual producer continues to turn out about the same total product. The total output of the farm may decline modestly, and the composition of the total may change modestly. But the change is not great, and often there is no noticeable change.

Constant total output on individual farms means constant aggregate output for the industry. In more precise language, the aggregate output curve is highly inelastic (we meet an old friend again). In this situation, the full force of a decline in aggregate demand, resulting from the contraction in overall business activity, shoots into a price decline. A significant reduction in total output does not come about to arrest or check the price decline. In sum, *the economics of overhead costs forces the individual producer, and producers in the aggregate, to employ their productive resources as fully as possible.*

The behavior of farm firms in the upswing of business activity does not follow the pattern just described. Producers can and, to some extent, do increase their inputs of such variables as fertilizer and feed. But for the most part, their actions are not limited to such a narrow field. Rising prices bring about rising incomes, which, in turn, create happy price and income expectations for the future. In this setting, farmers, as we have already noted, invest heavily in land, buildings, machinery, and equipment. But the area of innovation and investment is wider than construction and mechanization. Spurred into action by rising incomes and the expectation of even greater incomes, farmers adopt new methods and practices whenever possible. They are willing to incur the additional costs that are involved in trying out a new practice. This is the period in which technical practices on the farms undergo a great change for this is the time when farmers can afford to try and possibly fail.

But the net result of these periods of intense technological advance on farms is not failure. The average commercial farmer, in the present day, is too good a technician and too much research stands behind almost every technological development to permit wholesale failure. On the contrary, the acceptance and adoption of new technical methods, in combination with investments in heavy producer goods, almost always has the effect of expanding the total output of individual farms and of shifting the aggregate output curve to the right.

Do producers give up these new production techniques once prosperity gives way to depression? The answer is no. In most cases, the new practices are continued. In most cases, it would have been profitable for the farmer to have adopted the improved technologies in question at lower price levels. In most cases, they are cost reducing, not cost enhancing, when considered from the point of view of costs per unit of output.

One proof of this argument exists in the behavior of the aggregate supply curve (Figure 14–4). This curve did not drift to the left (contract) in the period 1929–33. Even taking into consideration the droughts of 1934 and 1936 and attempts at control during those years, the aggregate output of food did not contract. Farmers continued producing about the same amounts of the same kinds of products in the face of the worst depression in the history of the United States. And there has been no tendency for the aggregate output of agriculture to contract in any of the brief recessions experienced in the post-World War II period.

Some Conclusions

From his study of the effects of business fluctuations, Hathaway draws the conclusions listed above. They are valid and to the point, as with much of the discussion of the previous section dealing with the impact on the firm, *where the general business fluctuation breaks through and has an important impact on agriculture*. The devastating downturn in the early 1930s, the recession of 1937–38, and the spectacular upsurge of business activity in the period 1938–44 are cases in point. These business fluctuations had a direct and important impact on agriculture, and the consequences for, and the behavior of, agriculture were as Hathaway concludes, and as our discussion of the farm firm suggests.

But the 1950s and 1960s have been different. Since 1952, agriculture has experienced chronic overproduction and depressed prices and incomes. However, farm prices and incomes have not fallen disastrously in this context; they have not because they have been riding on a massive, price-supporting, loan-purchase, storage-disposal government program. Agriculture has been stabilized in a semidepressed state at the level of price and income support afforded by the government. In this context, agriculture has not felt to any important degree the impact of prosperity and depression in the general sector of the economy. Business fluctuations in the general economy have, so to speak, swept over the head of agriculture without touching it. Agriculture has responded to its semidepressed, but nonetheless stabilized, condition as well as to certain indigenous developments rather than the broad sweeps of general business conditions. Thus, for example, we have the curious phenomenon of agricultural incomes rising in 1958—a recession year for the general economy—and falling in 1959—a year of sharp recovery for the general economy. Price-supporting action, payments under the Soil-Bank program, a widespread crop-crippling winter freeze, and the build-up phase of the beef and hog cycles all met in a happy coincidence to push up farm prices and incomes in 1958, when past experience with business fluctuations would indicate that farm prices should have fallen.

In one respect, the response of agriculture to general business fluctuations in the past two decades has been traditional. The movement of people in and out of agriculture has followed the traditional pattern: in periods of business recovery and high-level employment, farm people have moved out of agriculture at a rapid rate, but in periods of business recession and heavy unemployment, the flow of people out of agriculture has slowed down and been reduced to a trickle. Even here, however, the pattern of response to business fluctuations differs from earlier peacetime periods. The migration response in agriculture to changes in general business conditions was much accentuated in the 1950s. In the 1960s, migration may have run its course, with so few people left on farms that agricultural migration can no longer pour people into the nonfarm economy.

But in other respects, agriculture in the 1950s and 1960s has reacted as if general business fluctuations did not exist. The aggregate output of agriculture has increased persistently without regard to changes in general business conditions and in spite of relatively low prices and incomes. It has achieved this through the widespread adoption of new and improved production techniques and the increased investments in such capital items as fertilizer, tractors, farm machinery, and electric power. The incentive of reducing unit costs and the expectation of continued price and income support have induced farmers generally to make these adoptions and investments. Commercial farmers have been able to do this because their asset positions, their financial positions, generally have not been seriously impaired—as long as they have had the land base and managerial ability to take advantage of advances in technology. Price and income support has kept commercial farmers solvent and in a position to finance the adoption of new and improved techniques, and investments in additional capital items.

In sum, the traditional response of agriculture to prosperity and depression has changed. Agriculture, by individual farms and in the aggregate, is adjusting and responding to a unique condition of chronic overproduction and depressed but stabilized incomes rather than to the ups and downs of general business conditions. So long as the above set of conditions continues to dominate agriculture, this type of unresponsiveness to prosperity and depression in the general economy will characterize agriculture.

POINTS FOR DISCUSSION

1. Describe the pattern of business fluctuations in the United States since 1920. What role did investment play in these fluctuations?
2. What do we mean by the income-expenditure approach to business fluctuations? What causes aggregate demand (aggregate expenditures) to expand and contract? How does the relation of saving to investment, in the circular flow of income, influence aggregate demand? What is the influence of consumption on aggregate demand?
3. Why does the total economy not stabilize automatically at full employment?
4. In what respect does the agricultural segment of the national economy behave differently from the nonagricultural segment in business fluctuations?
5. How is investment in agriculture associated with business fluctuations? How is investment in agriculture associated with expansion in output?
6. How do farmers' expenditures for production items vary over periods of business contraction and expansion?
7. In what periods do we find the rate of migration from farm to city accelerating and in what periods decelerating? What is the explanation for changes in the rate of farm-to-city migration?
8. What are the factors that operate to maintain farm output in periods of falling prices?
9. How has agriculture responded differently to business fluctuations in the 1950s and 1960s than it did in earlier times?

REFERENCES

HATHAWAY, DALE E., "Agriculture and the Business Cycle," *Policy for Commercial Agriculture,* Joint Committee Print, 85th Cong., 1st sess. (November 22, 1957).

KELLOGG, EARL D., "The Changing Relationships between Business Fluctuations and Agriculture," unpublished paper, Department of Agricultural Economics, University of Illinois at Urbana-Champaign (1971).

POLANYI, MICHAEL, *Full Employment and Free Trade,* pp. 1–64. London: Cambridge University Press, 1945.

SAMUELSON, PAUL A., *Economics,* 8th ed., Chaps. 10–13. New York: McGraw-Hill Book Company, Inc., 1970.

SCHULTZ, T. W., *Agriculture in an Unstable Economy,* Chap. 6. New York: McGraw-Hill Book Company, Inc., 1945.

TARSHIS, LORIE, "National Income and Employment," Part IV, *The Elements of Economics.* Boston: Houghton Mifflin Company, 1947.

Chapter 16

Agriculture in a Dynamic, Developed Economy[1]

In this chapter, we want to explore the growth problems of agriculture in the dynamic, developed economy of the United States. The rapidly growing and highly prosperous economy of the U.S. in the second half of the twentieth century has not produced an equally healthy and prosperous agriculture. Instead, during the 1950s and 1960s, farming has been characterized by an expanding sector of commercial-family and larger-than-family farms that have had to either grow or slip back to inadequate incomes, and a declining sector made up of small units that are nearly all characterized by inadequate incomes already. In general, agriculture has lagged in sharing the riches and affluence of the growing national economy of the United States. Because the reasons for this may be poorly understood, we inquire into them here.

THE LONG-RUN RACE BETWEEN AGGREGATE DEMAND AND AGGREGATE SUPPLY

As we already know, the farm price level fluctuates in response to a shift in aggregate demand relative to supply, or a shift in aggregate supply relative to demand. But it is not correct to visualize these aggregate relations shifting back and forth in a static, no-growth context. Over the long

[1]Adapted from Willard W. Cochrane, "The Agricultural Treadmill," in *Farm Prices—Myth and Reality* (Minneapolis, Minn.: University of Minnesota Press, 1958). Chap. 5.

run, both these aggregate relations have been expanding; what we have had is a race between aggregate demand and aggregate supply. And changes in the farm price level that have occurred, growing out of shifts in the *relative* positions of the aggregate demand and supply relations, have most often resulted from unequal rates of expansion in these aggregate relations. The race has rarely been equal, and at times it has been very unequal, with extreme income consequences.[2]

Demand Shifters

The important demand shifters for United States agriculture have been rising real incomes, population growth, and growing exports. Historically, exports have been an important supplementary market for U.S. agriculture and their importance is rapidly increasing. We will abstract from their impact in this chapter, although they will likely become even more important in the future. A full discussion of trade is included in Chapter 17.

During the nineteenth and early twentieth centuries, rising real incomes enabled the average American consumer to move away from a plain diet heavily weighted with potatoes and cereals to a varied and more expensive diet—varied in terms of more animal products, more fruits and vegetables in and out of season, and more delicacies (cheese, sea food, baked goods), and expensive in terms of greater dollar cost as well as more farm resources required to produce it. And population growth contributed more mouths to feed.

It is generally believed that the population elasticity for food approximates 1.0—meaning that a 1 percent increase in population results in a 1 percent increase in food consumption. This population elasticity estimate will vary as the means of population growth (from immigration and natural increase) varies, but it is probably a useful rule of thumb. Because the total population of the United States increased by about 2,000 percent between 1800 and 1920, it follows that the aggregate demand for food increased by roughly the same amount as the result of population growth. During this long period, the market for farm food products widened, first, because there were many more mouths to feed and, second, because each mouth demanded a more varied and expensive diet.

Now, let us take a more careful look at the causes of shifts in demand that have been at work in the first three-fourths of the twentieth century. Perhaps the most important demand shifter is change in income. Sometime in our national history, the income elasticity for food fell, and fell drastically —a development that probably occurred during the decades preceding and

---

[2]For a discussion of the relative rates of growth of aggregate demand and supply before World War II, see T. W. Schultz, *Agriculture in an Unstable Economy* (New York: McGraw-Hill Book Company, Inc., 1954), Chap. 3.

following 1900. In other words, it is posited here that real income increases for the average consumer were so great during this period (about 100 percent between 1880 and 1920), that the average consumer broke through, to an important degree, that real income range where rising incomes shoot into the purchases of more food and more expensive food, and moved into that income range where changes in income have little effect on total food consumption. In any event, the income elasticity for *farm food products* is now in the neighborhood of 0.2—meaning that the consumption of farm food products by the average consumer increases 2 percent with a 10 percent increase in his income. Consumers in the 1970s prefer to use additional income to purchase durable goods, sporting goods, vacations, and services of all kinds, including services built into food, rather than more food.

In this instance, we are *not* talking about the income elasticity of purchases by consumers in retail stores; the income elasticity of food items purchases by consumers at retail runs about 0.6 to 0.7, and it is this high because the income elasticity for nonfarm food services associated with or built into those food items (that is, storing, transporting, packaging, processing, and merchandising) is much higher—running between 1.0 and 1.3. In less technical language, consumers are ready and eager to buy more conveniences and services (TV dinners and restaurant meals) associated with food products as their incomes rise. But they are not so willing to buy more farm food products as their incomes rise.

The income elasticity of farm food products is not yet zero, but it is moving in that direction and may well approximate zero by the year 2000. Whether it reaches that point will depend on what happens to the incomes of the lowest-income groups in the U.S. because diets among these groups are still far from adequate. A citizens' group investigating hunger in the United States identified 280 counties in 1968 in which indications of serious hunger existed despite existing welfare and food distribution programs.[3] If the people living in those areas and the others across the nation who make up the millions living below the "poverty line" were to increase their real incomes, they would indeed demand more food. In fact, it is these families and others with incomes far below the national average who have kept the average income elasticity between 0.1 and 0.2 through 1970.

When we in the United States solve the poverty problem, the income elasticity of farm food products will fall to zero. This is the most critical impact of an affluent society on its agriculture. However, this is not to say that the income elasticity for *nonfarm* food services will have fallen to zero. On the contrary, this latter elasticity may remain above 1.0 as more and more wives escape from the kitchen and experience the joys of dining out.

---

[3]Citizens' Board of Inquiry into Hunger and Malnutrition in the United States, *Hunger, U.S.A.* (Boston: Beacon Press, 1968), p. 38.

Now, we turn to the second demand shifter, population growth. Fortunately, for the agricultural sector, developments with respect to population growth as a demand shifter have not paralleled those of rising real incomes. For awhile, it was feared that population growth as a shifter of demand was losing its power, too; in the 1930s, most predictions of population growth had the population of the United States leveling off and declining in the 1960s. But for some totally unexplainable reason, the people of the United States decided during and following World War II to wreck the prewar population projections of demographers by going on a child-producing spree. The rate of population increase in the United States in the 1950s was among the highest in the world. By the early 1970s, however, it appeared that because of the population explosion prophets or changing life-styles, Americans had again decided to wreck earlier population projections as the birth rate dropped to its lowest post-World War II level.

Total population increased about 9 percent in the decade ending in 1935, about 10 percent in the decade ending in 1945, almost 19 percent in the decade ending in 1955, 12 percent in the decade ending in 1965, and is projected to increase by 8 percent in the decade ending in 1975. Projections for 1985 show an 11 percent increase over 1975 due to a bulge in the age group forming families (the post-World War II "baby boom"), but even demographers hesitate to predict population with any degree of assurance.[4]

The picture that emerges with respect to further expansions in the demand for food looks like this: This United States is approaching that state of opulence where further increases in real personal incomes will not act to expand the demand for food. Expansions in the aggregate demand for food are becoming dependent upon population growth alone. If the rate of increase in population continues its downward trend, then population growth will not be a very important source of domestic demand increases. If the rate of population growth again changes, then the situation could reverse.

Supply Shifters

During the nineteenth century, total farm output in the United States increased as the result of two basic forces: (1) farm technological advance, and (2) an increase in the size of the total fixed plant—an increase in the number of acres incorporated into going farm units. The former was a minor cause and the latter the major cause. Regardless of the level of farm prices, or the pattern of commodity prices, settlers pushed

---

[4]Data from *Economic Report of the President, February 1971* (Washington: U.S. Government Printing Office, 1971), Table C-21.

back the frontier year after year and added land and farmsteads to the total fixed plant. Land settlement was part of the great westward movement in America over three centuries, and although it may have grown out of certain economic dislocation and adjustments in the Old World, it was in no way related to the pricing system, except insofar as hard times in the cities forced more people to the frontier.

With the turn of the century, this means of expanding total farm output began to disappear—the country was almost completely settled. By 1920, except for some irrigation developments in the arid West, the total agricultural plant stopped growing. *Total farm output did not, however.* Total farm output increased about 100 percent between 1920 and 1965. This great increase resulted almost exclusively from technological advance on existing farms—a process that gained momentum in the latter part of the nineteenth century, in the form of farm mechanization particularly, and became an all-inclusive, ever-present force by the end of World War I. The minor force behind output expansion in the 1800s became the major force in the 1900s.

The development and adoption of many new technologies have contributed to the expansion of the total marketable output of farm commodities since 1920, but none was so important as the tractor. The substitution of tractor power for animal power released some 70 million acres, or one-fifth of our crop land, for the production of marketable crops. The myriad of other mechanized innovations have released millions of workers into the nonfarm sector. Certainly, the gasoline engine in its many forms and uses dominated farm technological advance between 1920 and 1950. In a similar way, the spread of hybrid corn increased land productivity over a great part of the country in a relatively few years.

Now there are some who say, because they see evolving no single technology comparable in importance with the tractor, that farm technological advance is losing its steam as a shifter of the aggregate supply relation. We have seen, in earlier chapters, that the rate of technological change seems to have slowed between 1965 and 1971. Whether this is a temporary phenomenon or a permanent change is difficult to say with certainty, but we believe it to be temporary.

Granted, no single new technology such as tractors or hybrid corn dominates the imagination of innovators in the 1970s. But one dominant technology is not a requirement for rapid technological advance. Total farm output expanded in the 1950s and early 1960s as the result of technological development and adoption on many fronts: plant and animal breeding; plant and animal disease control; feeds and feeding practices; water control and usage; and soil, crop, and animal handling equipment. Advances on all these technological fronts, together with a more-skilled working force, contribute to a situation in which the typical farmer adopts one or several new practices each year, thereby becoming a more productive farmer.

In this connection, we should recognize, too, that the development of new technologies and their adoption on farms is no longer left to chance. The outpouring of new production practices and techniques that has occurred since 1920 did not result from a few lonesome inventors working in attics or old barns, rather, it resulted from organized and well-financed research at several levels: pure research on natural phenomena, applied research on agriculture problems, and commercial research on specific products and techniques.

The federal government alone currently spends up to $300 million, and private industry as much as $400 million each year on the development of new technologies for *farm production*.[5] All the efforts directed toward carrying these new technologies to farmers run into much larger sums. Consider all the agencies, private and public, involved: the federal-state extension service; the vocational agricultural teaching program in high schools; the soil conservation service; the service work of farm cooperatives; and, finally and probably now most important, the selling and service work of private seed firms, machinery and equipment firms, processing firms, and increasingly giant petro-chemical firms producing farm chemicals.

The adoption of new production techniques has become as much a part of farming as getting up in the morning; the farmer is "expected" to adopt new practices and technologies that reduce his costs and expand his output, in the same way that he is "expected" to care for his livestock, send his children to school, and honor his wife; the farmer is the last link in an endless chain of events called technological advance, which almost everyone considers good. In recent years, however, more and more people are becoming willing to question the "good" of technological advance. Especially among those concerned with the environment, questions are being raised about the long-run impact of agricultural chemicals that have helped increase agricultural output in recent years. As farmers come to understand the implications of continuous technological change, they, too, are beginning to question its value. However, these questions have not yet changed the basic forces operating on agricultural technology in the United States.

Those folks looking for (or trying to hide from) a second revolutionary development to follow the tractor may find it before the turn of the next century. If and when artificial photosynthesis breaks out of the laboratory, where it is now an established fact, that institution-shaking technology will have arrived. When we can produce carbohydrates directly

[5] T. J. Army and M. E. Smith, "Research and Development in Farm Related Firms," in *Structural Changes in Commercial Agriculture*, CAED #24, April 1965.

from the sun's rays, without the work of plants, then the production of foodstuffs can be transferred from farms to factories, and the greatest of all agricultural revolutions will rage across the land. And the process of artifical photosynthesis is certainly further advanced in the 1970s than was the unleashing of the atom in 1900.

So, we conclude that farm technological advance, development, and farm adoption gives every evidence of remaining a powerful force in agriculture, driving the aggregate supply relation before it in an expanding action. Truly revolutionary developments that could turn present-day agriculture upside down are in the offing.

The Picture to 2000

The long-run race between aggregate demand and aggregate supply, for all practical purposes, turns out to be a race between population growth and farm technological advance. Because nobody is omniscient, it is impossible to demonstrate that population growth will outrun technological advance between now and the year 2000, or the converse. If an observer is more impressed with capacity of Americans to reproduce themselves than with their ability to create new ways of producing goods and services, then he will probably conclude that population growth will win the race. But if, on the other hand, he is more impressed with their inventive genius and ability to adopt new technologies, then he will probably put his money on technological advance.

Which wins is terribly imporant to American farmers. If population growth out-races technological advance, other things being equal, aggregate demand will press against supply and push the level of farm prices upward, as occurred between 1895 and 1915. But if technological advance out-races population growth, other things being equal, aggregate supply will press against demand and drive farm prices downward, as has been the tendency since 1948.

If labor would flow out of agriculture at a faster rate than it has, and if some important blocks of land would drop out of production, these actions would offset the inflow of improved technologies and new capital, and hence act to slow down the rate of aggregate output expansion. But we are already aware that labor has been shifting out of agriculture at a furious pace—25 to 35 percent of the agricultural labor force in one decade—and it is difficult to speed up this already rapid rate of emigration without further aggravating grave social problems on the land, along Main Street, and in urban receiving areas. Further, sunk capital (for example, fences, specialized machinery) and farm land have few good economic alternatives; hence, they are slow to go out of agricultural production. In short, it is terribly difficult to shrink the agricultural plant: capital sub-stitutes readily for labor and land, and sunk capital items have a low opportunity cost. Land and labor resource adjustments have not been able, and give little evidence of being able, to offset the inflow of improved technologies over the next quarter century. If this offset does not occur, either the farm price level must fall, the aggregate demand for agricultural products must be expanded, or the aggregate supply of agricultural products must be restricted. In other words, the capacity to expand farm output beyond the needs of U.S. population growth exists, and *unless counteracted in some effective way*, will continue the downward pressure on farm prices that has existed over the past twenty years.

MARKET ORGANIZATION AND TECHNOLOGICAL ADVANCE

Why, in the face of falling farm prices and declining gross incomes, do farmers persist in adopting new technologies and thus expanding output? Why, since the 1950s, have farmers pushed aggregate output ahead of demand through widespread technological advance and thus driven down the prices of their own products? And why are they likely to keep right on behaving in this seemingly irrational manner? In the main, the answer is to be found in the market organization of agriculture. But given this market organization, some other factors need to be considered: the role of society acting through government and the financial position of farmers. So let us inquire into the manner in which farmers adopt new technologies to see how and why this results in declining incomes.

Market Organization and the Adoption Process

To this point, farm technological advance has been considered in terms of the total agricultural industry—in terms of its shifting effects on the aggregate supply relation, hence upon the farm price level. In this view, we see the effects on the industry of a particular technology or pro-duction practice after it has been *widely adopted throughout the industry*. If, however, we take as a unit of analysis not the industry but rather different firms in the dynamic process of adoption, the story changes. This is what we shall do now: consider the effects of farm technological advance on firms that adopt the technique early, then on the more typical followers, and finally on the laggards.

It should be recognized, first, that farmers typically operate in a special sort of market—one that satisfies the key conditions of a purely competitive market: namely, a market in which no one farmer can have, or does have, any perceptible influence on the price of his product (or his factors of production). The farmer is a price taker; he takes the price offered him because he is such a small part of the total market that he can have no perceptible influence on the market or on the market price.

Second, it will be recalled that a technological advance has the effect of lowering the *per unit costs of production* of the farm firm (typically, per unit costs of production are reduced as the total value product on the farm in question increases by more than the increase in total costs; it is extremely difficult to think of a new technology that does not increase output). This being the case, farm producers who adopt a new technology early in the game realize increased net returns from undertaking that enterprising act. The new technique reduces cost of production for the enterprising few, but they are such a small part of the market that total output is not increased noticeably and price does not come down. Net incomes of the few who adopt the new technology are increased, and a powerful incentive is created for other farmers to adopt the technique.

In this explanation, we find the basis of continuing and widespread farm technological advance. The operators who first adopt a new technology reap the income benefits (the difference between the old price and the new, lower unit costs). Then, other farmers in the community see the income advantage accruing to Mr. Early Bird; also, the extension service and other educational units spread the information around. Thereupon, Mr. Average Farmer decides he will adopt this cost-reducing technique, and this includes most farmers in the community. *But the widespread adoption of this new technology changes the entire situation. Total output is now increased, and this increase in the supply of the commodity lowers the price of that commodity.* And where the price elasticity of demand at the farm level is less than 1.0 (that is, demand is inelastic), as is commonly the case in agriculture, gross returns to all producers must fall.

As the dynamic process of technological adoption unfolds, we see two things happening: (1) in those cases in which the output of the commodity is increased, the price of the commodity falls relative to commodity substitutes; and (2) unit costs of production rise after their initial decline, as the gains from the new practice or technique are capitalized into the value of the fixed assets involved. So in the long run, by the time most farmers have adopted the technology the current income benefits that the first farmers realized have vanished. Mr. Average Farmer is right back where he started, as far as his income position is concerned. Once again, average unit costs of production are equal to price and no economic surplus remains.

If this is the typical result, why do farmers generally adopt new methods? It is easy to see why the first farmers undertake a new method or practice. They benefit directly. We can understand why neighbors of the enterprising first farmers adopt the technology; they see the income advantage and make up their minds to give it a try. But as more and more farmers adopt the new technology, output is affected and the price of the commodity declines. This price decline acts as a burr under the saddle of the followers, the average farmers; the price of their product is declining, but their units costs of production are unchanged. *To stay even with the world, these average farmers are forced to adopt the new technology.* The average farmer is on a treadmill with respect to technological advance.

The position of the laggard, who will not or cannot adopt the new technologies, is a tragic one. The farmer who belongs to a religious sect that does not permit technological advance, the aged or beginning farmer who cannot afford the initial cost of the technology or production practice, or the lazy fellow who prefers to go fishing, finds himself in an income squeeze. The relative price of the commodity falls as one technique after another is adopted throughout the industry, but his unit costs of production do not come down. Thus, the farmer who does not adopt new technologies and practices is squeezed and squeezed. Farm technological advance for him is a nightmare.

In the preceding analysis, we reached the conclusion that any economic surplus growing out of the introduction of a new technology is squeezed to the zero point or below in the long run. But this does not mean that the labor income to operators and hired labor *must* fall, even when the price level is falling. We have yet to take up another dynamic consideration: the substitution of machinery and equipment for labor. Increased farm mechanization most often takes the form of substituting a machine process for a hand process. If in these situations gross returns are unaffected and total costs of the units under consideration (the firm, or total agriculture) decline, then the labor income of those workers remaining *must* be increased.

In the more typical case for agriculture, in which demand is inelastic, as output expands, gross revenue declines. If the impact of the new technology is to reduce the number of workers required in the industry, as well as to reduce total costs of production, the average labor income of those remaining *may not* decrease; or if it does, it will not decrease as much as would otherwise be the case. In this situation, the average labor income of those remaining in agriculture develops into a three-sided struggle between declining total revenue, declining total costs, and declining number of workers. Experience in the past several decades suggests that workers do not, and probably cannot, move out of agriculture rapidly enough to hold up and increase their rates of return, given the present and prospective technological revolution in agriculture. The technological revolution in agriculture requires a rate of emigration (if labor incomes are to be maintained and enhanced) that is incompatible with the aspirations of farm people, nonfarm job opportunities, and a stable social structure. Hence, returns to farm workers continue to lag.

Social Action and Technological Advance

The typical small family farmer, of course, is not and has not been in a position to undertake the costly, time-consuming work of developing new technological practices for his farm operation. But the many small farmers who make up the agricultural industry have rarely organized to promote and finance research and development through their own private agencies. If the availability of new production practices and techniques for farm adoption were dependent upon farmers' initiative, such practices and techniques would have been in short supply for many years.

But new production practices and techniques for agriculture have not been in short supply; to the contrary, there has been a continuous out-pouring of these new technologies in the twentieth century. The most important reason why there has been this generous supply since the turn of the century is that the *total society* decided to take collective action to assure this ample supply of new technologies through the establishment of "agricultural and mechanical arts" colleges. Society, through the federal and state governments, has generously financed the research and development work in those colleges and in governmental research agencies ever since. This is not to say that every important technological development in agriculture has been the direct result of work in the land-grant colleges and governmental research agencies. Far from it: private agencies have contributed many new technologies for use in agriculture and appear to be providing an increasing proportion. But it is to say that *society has covered the overhead costs of training scientists and carrying on the basic research that lies behind every applied technique.*

If farm technological advance does not out-race United States population growth in the next quarter century, it will not be because of a lack of support for farm technological research. Through this support, society has made as certain as possible that an ample outpouring of new techniques will continue. The willingness of society to finance research and development in agricultural production is in many ways a strange phenomenon. Perhaps, in some collective and intuitive sense, society feels that a rapid rate of technological advance in agriculture is basic to rising levels of living for its members—as indeed it is. By underwriting a rapid rate of technological advance, society assures itself of a bountiful food supply at relatively low prices. But the strange aspect of all this is that this generous financing of research and development is done in the name of helping farmers, and it is so accepted by most farmers and their leaders.

Now in the short-run monopoly sense (that is the highwayman sense), nothing could be farther from the truth. The monopolist always seeks a position where his product is relatively scarce and the products of all other groups are plentiful; from this position of market power, the monopolist trades scarce, dear items for cheap, plentiful items. But a rapid rate of technological advance—a rate of technological advance that drives aggregate supply ahead of aggregate demand—places the farmer in just the opposite position: places him in the weak market position of producing bountiful supplies at low prices.

Farmer Asset Positions and the Adoption Process

In a free market at least, aggregate supply cannot outrace aggregate demand indefinitely. At some point in time, its pace must slow down and become equal to, or perhaps even lag behind, the rate of demand expansion. In other words, the expansion rates of these two relations are related; the connection is somewhat indirect, but it is there. The aggregate demand and the aggregate supply functions are related through the nexus of the *asset positions* of farmers.

Most new technologies adopted on farms are capital using—that is, their adoption requires an additional cash outlay, or some kind of additional financial commitment. But because the adoption of a new technology reduces unit costs, farmers are willing to make the additional investments as long as they can. And they can as long as their liquid and capital asset positions are strong and unimpaired.

But these asset positions deteriorate under a falling farm price level with the attendant declines in gross and net incomes. The liquid asset position typically goes first; but with the passage of time, capital assets become encumbered in order to cope with losses resulting from declining incomes. In a free market situation, then, farm technological advance sows the seeds of its own slowdown. If aggregate output outraces aggregate demand long enough and far enough, and the farm price level falls far enough and stays down long enough, the asset position of farmers generally will become weak, and the process of farm adoption of new technologies must be choked off. In this way, the rate of output expansion is slowed down and brought into equality with the rate of demand expansion.

This, of course, is a painful process, as farmers have discovered in a limited way in the 1960s. Furthermore, it is no simple process. The slowdown in farm technological advance will not be uniform. It will first strike the inefficient farmers and the beginners: the vulnerable asset positions of these farmers deteriorate rapidly when the farm price level declines.

The average farmer will hold out longer, and the very efficient farmer succumbs to the slowdown only in extreme situations. The efficient farmer, the early adopter of new techniques who reaps the income rewards accruing to him as such, and who successfully increases his labor income by substituting machinery and equipment for labor, can withstand and even thrive in a major decline *to a point.*

It should be emphasized here, however, that the rate of output expansion, powered by farm technological advance, does not slow down immediately when it encounters a price-level decline. Witness the rapid rate of output expansion in the 1950s in the face of a falling farm price level. Farmers generally came out of the World War II period with strong asset positions and for this reason generally were able to maintain a rapid rate of technological advance in the face of a falling price level. Farm expansion and emigration combined with government programs kept incomes to many farmers high enough so they could preserve their asset positions. Those whose land base or managerial skills did not allow them to take advantage of new technologies fell further behind with regard to income and hence asset positions. Price and income support programs help keep producers solvent but market forces eventually will make it impossible for producers to finance high-capital technologies. As the slowdown in the adoption of new technologies engulfs more and more farmers, the rate of aggregate output expansion must also slow.

THE CONSEQUENCES OF FARM TECHNOLOGICAL ADVANCE

The spotlight in this section will be on the period 1920–68, the period in which total inputs employed in agriculture remained constant, and when increases in total output must therefore have resulted from new configurations in the use of productive resources made possible by technological advance. It will be recalled that total farm output increased throughout the nineteenth century and during the first two decades of the twentieth as a the result of: (1) an expansion in the size of the fixed plant of agriculture and (2) technological advance, with the former decreasing in importance and the latter increasing over the long period. Hence, it is difficult, if not impossible, to know what part of the increase in total output is attributable to technological advance and what part to an increase in the size of the fixed plant during that long period. But from 1920 to 1962, all, or practically all, of the increase in total marketable output must be attributed to technological advance (in the inclusive sense discussed in Chapter 6). There is nothing else to which it can be attributed.[6] The important consequences of the rate of technological advance have been three: (1) a cheap, adequate food supply for United States consumers; (2) the release of a substantial supply of labor resources to the nonfarm sectors; and (3) an income treadmill for American farmers.

The technological developments that occurred during the period 1920–62 and that were adopted on commercial farms during that period enabled farmers to produce, with the same total volume of resources, a more-than-adequate food supply for the growing population. Thus, the first and most necessary goal of this and every society was achieved: an adequate food supply. Never before had it happened that an adequate food supply for an expanding population was provided without the employment of more total resources in agriculture.

First, through the beneficence of plentiful and fertile land resources, and second, because of technological advance, consumers in the United States enjoy a rich, varied, and, if they so choose, nutritious diet. And the fraction of their real income that American consumers spend on food is the lowest in the world—approximately 16 percent in 1970. This diet at this cost has never before been achieved and is enjoyed by relatively few people in the world today.

Farm technological advance not only assures Americans of an adequate food supply but over the years it has released millions of farm-reared people to work in manufacturing, in the distributive system, and in the arts, sciences, and professions. This, of course, is the mark of economic progress: first, the release of workers from agriculture to go into manufacturing, and then, the release of workers from both of these categories to enter the service trades (and to enjoy increased leisure time) *as the real incomes of all continue to rise.*

The process by which these people have been released from agriculture has not always been a kindly one, but it has taken place. It has happened as workers in agriculture have become increasingly productive —as one worker, armed with new production techniques, has been able to produce enough food and fiber to meet the wants of more and more nonfarm people. To illustrate: in 1820, one worker in agriculture could support 4.1 persons including himself, and by 1920 this had doubled to 8.3 persons. By 1950, it had again doubled, and by 1964 had again doubled!

[6]It is sometimes argued that increases in total output between 1920 and 1962 may be attributed to farm firms' becoming more efficient (that is, that farmers were successful in locating and moving toward the minimum point of their long-run planning curves) over this long period. But this argument flies in the face of facts and logic. The state of the arts was changing over the entire period, sometimes slowly, sometimes rapidly. Farmers were continuously adjusting to new levels and patterns of technology over the entire period. By what logic, then, can one argue that farmers were more nearly at the minimum point of their long-run static cost curves in 1962, than farmers were in 1920? None, except by assertion. The facts are that farmers were adjusting to new technologies over the entire period, not seeking minimum points on *static* planning curves.

The doubling process that took one century in the first instance, took just 13 years in the last, so that in 1964 one farm worker could support 33 people. By 1970, the figure was up to 47.

The proportion of the total labor force of the United States employed in agriculture has declined steadily over the long-run past: from 72 percent in 1820 to 18 percent in 1920 to 5 percent in 1970. This is common knowledge. But not so generally known is the fact that total employment in agriculture reached a peak of 13.6 million workers in 1910 and has been declining ever since. And as we saw in Table 15–2, the movement of labor out of agriculture has continued in recent years. Total farm employment has *fallen* by over 5 million persons in the last twenty years.

At the same time that farm technological advance has provided increasing quantities of nutritious food at decreasing real costs and has released large quantities of labor to the nonfarm sector, it has kept the American farmer on an income treadmill. The three trends are functionally related: if food is to decrease in price, total farm income will fall and will encourage individuals to leave farming for other vocations.

What has been the income trend for farmers in the U.S.? *Incentive income* is a concept developed by J. R. Bellerby to describe the return to human effort and enterprise.[7] In farming, this is the return to the farmer as a manager, laborer, and technician. It does not include any return to property or capital. The income incentive ratio relates the incentive income of farmers on a per-man unit basis to the incentive income of persons engaged in nonfarm enterprises on a per-man unit basis. The incentive income ratio, thus, compares the average or per unit return to human effort and enterprise on the two sides of the farm-nonfarm fence. By five-year intervals, the farm-nonfarm incentive income ratio since 1920 is as follows:[8]

1920	.46	1950	.44
1925	.38	1955	.31
1930	.32	1960	.27
1935	.43	1965	.34
1940	.32	1970	.26
1947	.50		

Thus, rapid technological change has not resulted in greatly altering the relative income-earning ability of farmers. In fact, their incentive incomes have declined to far less than half as large as incentive incomes in the nonfarm sectors. This is not to say that *personal disposable* incomes of

[7] J. R. Bellerby, *Agriculture and Industry Relative Income* (New York: The Macmillan Company, 1956), p. 16.

[8] *Ibid.*, p. 187 for the 1920–1940 data. The data for the other years have been calculated by the authors.

farmers are this much lower than those in the nonfarm sector. As we saw in Chapter 1, farmers on the average have incomes three-fourths as large as nonfarmers. It has been the increasing capital investment in farming that has kept incentive incomes so much below disposable incomes.

Truly, the American farmer is on a treadmill. On it, he is running faster and faster in the quest for higher incomes growing out of the adoption of new and more productive techniques, but he is not gaining in income. *He is losing.*

THE GENERAL THEORY OF AGRICULTURE IN A DYNAMIC, DEVELOPED ECONOMY

The capacity of American farmers to command good and stable prices and incomes in the market is weak; the power position of farmers in the market is weak. The farmer *takes* the prices that the market offers him, and very often these are low prices.

The farmer's weak position in the market (that is, his inability to reject the low prices that are offered to him and command higher ones) grows out of four related circumstances: first, the high value that American society generally places on technological development and application; second, the market organization within which farmers operate; third, the extreme inelasticity of the aggregate demand for food; and fourth, the inability of resources previously committed to agricultural production to be shifted readily and effortlessly out of agriculture. These are the essential components of the general theory of agriculture in a dynamic, developed economy such as the economy of the United States in the 1970s.

As we have noted, society has been generous in financing research and development in agriculture. It has expected a rapid rate of technological development and increasingly expects that technology be free of harmful environmental effects. If technological advancement continues to be a highly regarded value, farm output will continue to expand, although possibly at a slower rate than during the 1950s and 1960s.

The farmer operates in a sea of competitive behavior; each farmer is a tiny speck on this sea and the output of each farmer is a tiny drop in this sea. With rare exceptions, the single farmer operates in a market so large that he can have no perceptive influence on it. In this situation, the farmer must take as given to him the prices generated in the market.

Confronted with this situation, he reasons, "I can't influence price, but I can influence my own costs. I can get my costs down." So, the typical farmer is always searching for some way to get his costs down. By definition, a new technology is cost reducing; it increases output per unit of input. Thus, the farmer is always on the lookout for new, cost-reducing technologies that usually increase the total output of his farm. Built into the market organization of agriculture, then, is a powerful incentive for adopting new technologies and expanding output—the incentive of reducing costs on the individual farm.

If the demand for food were highly elastic, all would be sweetness and light in agriculture. If the aggregate demand for food were *elastic,* the bountiful and expanding supplies of food that farmers want to produce would sell in the market at only slightly reduced prices; gross incomes to farmers, in the aggregate and individually, would increase. But the aggregate demand for food is not elastic; it is inelastic and extremely so. For this reason, a little too much in the way of total output drives down the farm price level in a dramatic fashion and reduces the gross incomes of farmers in a similar fashion.

Finally, the persistent pressure on each farmer to adopt new technologies and thereby reduce unit costs has the effect of continuously putting a little too much in the way of supplies on the market where there is not an offsetting outflow of resources from agriculture. And it is not easy to achieve the necessary rate of resource movement out of agriculture where technological advance is rapid and widespread, and becoming more so. Land and sunk capital cannot be moved. Labor does not move into new jobs easily for many reasons: the value of agriculture as a way of life, monopolistic restrictions in nonfarm labor markets, insufficient financial base, lack of nonfarm skills, and so on. Resource adjustment, particularly human resource adjustment, takes time, but the technological revolution in agriculture sweeps forward. Hence, we find a general tendency, in peacetime, for aggregate supply to outrace aggregate demand and thus keep farm prices relatively low.

An integral part of the technological advance that has been such a pervasive force in American agriculture over the past thirty years has been an increasing reliance on man-made chemicals, monoculture crop systems, intensive land use, and heavy energy use. One of the nonproductive aspects of these practices is the environmental pollution they bring about.

National concern for the environment is becoming more and more important, and agriculture is squarely in the path of these concerns, although it may not have yet felt their full impact. Feet-lot runoff, nitrites in ground water, persistent chemicals in wildlife foodchains, livestock odors, silt in streams, and even such things as the effect of intensive agriculture on the amount of future wilderness available are all coming under attack from those concerned with preserving the environment.

One reason why environmental problems are becoming an active social concern in the United States is that real incomes for many members of society have reached the level at which people can afford and would prefer to spend additional income on a *better* environment than on *more* material goods and services. As one agricultural economist has put it:

> ...in relatively high-income economies the income elasticity of demand for commodities and services related to sustenance is low and declines as income continues to rise, while the income elasticity of demand for more effective disposal of residuals and for environmental amenities is high and continues to rise.[9]

This increasing demand for environmental amenities is reflected in a variety of ways. Certain farm chemicals have been banned. Environmental protection agencies have been established to monitor industries and enforce laws regarding pollution. Pollution fees or charges have been suggested as a means of discouraging pollution as well as a way of obtaining funds to offset the damage caused.

Recognition and action to curb agriculturally caused pollution is an important potential force that could radically affect the future of the food and agricultural situation in the United States. Restricting or banning the use of fertilizer and pesticides would tend to dampen the rate of increase in food production and hence act to raise food (and farm) prices. Other actions to improve the enviroment would have similar effects.[10] Thus, environmental concerns may tend to offset the output effects of farm technological advance that have been stressed in previous sections of this chapter. Depending on how strong and how rapidly actions are taken, farmers may well find themselves in a favorable price situation as the rate of expansion of supply slows relative to demand.

A general theory of agriculture in a dynamic, developed economy has been sketched. The high value that society places on technological advance guarantees a continuous outpouring of new technologies. The incentive to reduce costs on the many small farms across the country results in a rapid and widespread adoption of the new technologies. Rapid and widespread farm technological advance drives the aggregate supply relation ahead of the expanding aggregate demand relation in peacetime; and, given the highly inelastic demand for food together with the inability of resources previously committed to farm production to be shifted readily and effortlessly out of agriculture, farm prices fall to low levels and stay there for long periods. The extent to which new constraints growing out of environmental concerns will affect this theory is still to be determined, although their effect will be to offset earlier technological advances.

---

[9]Vernon W. Ruttan, "Technology and the Environment," *American Journal of Agricultural Economics*, Vol. 53, December 1971, p. 707.

[10]We discuss these problems in detail in Chapter 21.

POINTS FOR DISCUSSION

1. What have been the long-run shifters of the aggregate demand for food in the United States? Indicate their role and relative importance.
2. What have been the long-run shifters of aggregate supply in the United States? Indicate their role and relative importance.
3. What is the outlook in the race between aggregate demand and aggregate supply in the 1970s?
4. Who gets the benefits of farm technological advance—farmers or consumers? By what line of reasoning do you reach your conclusion?
5. Why do we have widespread and rapid farm technological advance in the United States?
6. What is the nexus between movements in long-run supply and long-run demand in a free market?
7. What have been the consequences of the rapid and widespread farm technological advance in the United States for food supplies, workers in agriculture, and workers' incomes?
8. What do we mean by *incentive income?* Is it a good measure for comparing farm incomes with nonfarm incomes?
9. What is the general theory of agriculture in an advanced economy such as the United States?

REFERENCES

COCHRANE, WILLARD W., "American Farm Policy in a Tumultuous World," *American Journal of Agricultural Economics* (December 1970), pp. 645–55.

———, *Farm Prices—Myth and Reality,* Chap. 5. Minneapolis, Minn.: University of Minnesota Press, 1958.

RUTTAN, VERNON W., "Technology and the Environment," *American Journal of Agricultural Economics* (December 1971), pp. 707–17.

SCHULTZ, T. W., *Agriculture in an Unstable Economy,* Chap. 3. New York: McGraw-Hill Book Company, Inc., 1945.

Chapter 17

Imports, Exports, and

American Agriculture

Since colonial times, farmers have been interested in the export market. This interest became particularly keen in the first half of the nineteenth century, with the settlement and development of the fertile Mississippi Valley. The tariff question commanded the principal attention of those giants of the United States Senate—Calhoun, Clay, and Webster —and their followers for four decades, but they could not evolve a satisfactory solution to it. The Civil War itself grew in large measure out of the struggle over trade policy: the agrarians versus the industrialists. The war split the agrarians into two camps and dissipated their demands for an expanded foreign market. Further, the tremendous growth in domestic population in the latter decades of the nineteenth century dulled the previous acute need for an expanding export market. The agrarians mellowed with the widening of the domestic market. The foreign market more and more came to be viewed as an overflow market for American farmers.

The importance of foreign sales to United States agriculture has varied considerably even during the present century. In 1910, exports accounted for 16 percent of total cash receipts from farm marketings; in 1919–21, they were up to 25 percent. Following 1921, world economic events contributed to the withering of trade until in 1940–41 exports accounted for only 6 percent of United States farm marketings. During and following World War II, exports increased to 13 percent, slumped briefly to 9 percent following the Korean fighting, and since then have stabilized at about 16 percent of total United States farm sales.

The interest of American agriculturalists in the foreign market today far exceeds its size, however. The foreign market has a very important characteristic that the domestic market does not have—the potential for rapid growth. We saw in the previous chapter that in the modern American economy the domestic demand for food will expand only as rapidly as population grows, but the potential rate of expansion of food supply is much greater. Meanwhile, the world is full of countries in which people live very close to the starvation level. There runs a feeling in the United States, a deep feeling, that in some way the needs of the world and the productive capacity of American farmers could and should be harnessed together. Thus, we must analyze the foreign trade problem and the farmer's position in it to complete the picture of the total market for farm products and its relation to supply.

AN OVERVIEW OF INTERNATIONAL TRADE

What is International Trade ?

Private commerical international trade is a two-way proposition. Any private trading transaction is, but this fact is sometimes overlooked in domestic transactions. We exchange money for goods at home, why not abroad? It happens, however, that American producers of wheat and cotton for export do not want to be paid in English sterling in London, French francs in Paris, or Dutch guilders in Amsterdam. They want to be paid in United States dollars in their home town. In order for this perfectly natural desire to be realized, commercial trade and "invisible" trade consisting of tourism and capital flows must come close to balancing. Imports into the United States earn dollars for traders in foreign countries that they may then use to buy wheat, cotton, trucks, and turbines produced in the United States. Imports provide the *dollars* with which exports are paid for; in reality, goods are traded for goods.

Imports and exports rarely balance exactly; the difference is made up by shipments of gold, dollars, or some other acceptable "hard currency" that can be used to make purchases in a third country, or by the extension of credit. A country whose exports exceed its imports must extend credit to the foreign buyers involved or accept gold shipments as payment from those buyers. But either of these means of balancing the payments between one country and others cannot go on indefinitely. Sooner or later, exports must fall to the level of imports. If trade is conducted on a commercial basis (rather than as foreign aid, in the form of grants, or by accepting payment in another country's currency), the exports of a country must be balanced by imports in the long run.

We should not get the impression, however, that the trade between any two countries must balance (that is, that the exports of country A to country B must, equal the exports of country B to country A). When such a bilateral condition is insisted upon, trade between the two countries is limited to the volume of the lesser country in the trading relationship.[1] For example, one pattern of world trade was as follows: the tropics exported more to the United States than they bought in return; the United States exported more to Britain and temperate Latin America than it bought; Britain and temperate Latin America exported more to continental Europe than they bought; continental Europe exported more to Britain than it bought. The circle of trade and payments was closed by Britain exporting more to the tropics than she bought from them. This is the multilateral system of trade sought after by countries interested in expanding free commercial world trade. Each of these trading areas had a deficit with one area, but each deficit was balanced by a surplus with another area. Thus, imports and exports for the system as a whole were in balance because imports and exports for each trading area were in balance, and payment balances between pairs of countries were effected through the purchase and sale of foreign exchange (another country's currency) in organized markets dealing in foreign exchange. *The key to the private commercial trade problem exists in each country importing as much as it seeks to export.*

Imbalances in International Trade

In a simpler age, the international trade of each country was of necessity kept in balance. At the end of each month or year, any imbalance was covered by shipping gold to cover the difference. In time, hard currencies, those that could be used to purchase almost any good in the issuing country, came to be accepted instead of gold because the governments of the issuing country guaranteed to exchange their currency for gold at a fixed rate. In 1933, the United States set its exchange rate for one ounce of gold at thirty-five dollars to any foreigners who wanted to make such an exchange. Most other countries set some rate of exchange between their own currency and gold, thereby fixing the rate of exchange between their currency and the dollar.

Following World War II, the total volume of international trade increased greatly. Most countries were willing to accept U.S. dollars instead of gold from other countries to cover deficits in trade. There came to be a demand for dollars to be used by other countries to cover their interna-

---

[1]The term *bilateral* refers to actions or decisions taken by two countries without consideration of the effects on other trading countries. *Unilateral* refers to action taken by one country, independent of their consequences on other nations. *Multilateral* refers to decisions taken in full consideration of the consequences to all other trading nations.

tional obligations. That is, the dollar became an international currency as other countries continued to hold dollars. As a result, the United States was able to have a deficit in its balance of payments year after year.

To the extent that foreign countries and individuals were willing to hold dollars to use as "international cash," they did not use those dollars to purchase goods made in the United States. Thus, the United States could buy more goods from overseas than she sold overseas, simply by giving foreigners dollars. As long as the dollars were not brought back to be exchanged for gold, the system was stable. When, in the late 1960s, foreigners began increasingly to demand gold for the dollars they held, the United States began to run low on gold. If unchecked, the supply of gold in the country would have been exhausted and the United States would have had to break its promise to exchange gold for dollars at the stated fixed rate. The obvious answer was to entice foreigners to buy goods with their dollars instead of demanding gold. However, during the 1960s European countries and Japan had become more efficient at producing many goods than the United States, so countries could buy small automobiles, electronic gadgets, and even steel more cheaply in those places than in the United States. It was impossible to expand United States exports fast enough to cover the deficits of the late 1960s. Foreign individuals and nations continued to turn in their dollars for gold.

In 1968, a two-tier gold market was set up that allowed countries to escape part of their promise to exchange their currencies for gold. They only had to honor such promises if the demander was another government. On the second tier, gold could be bought and sold at any price. By 1971, the United States deficit had reached crisis proportions. For a time, the United States suspended its buying and selling of gold at any rate and then took a series of steps that resulted in a depreciation of the dollar relative to Japanese, West German, and other currencies as well as a devaluation of the dollar. This devaluation brought the U.S. price of gold to thirty-eight dollars per ounce. The depreciation made Japanese and German imports more expensive in the United States and made her exports to those countries cheaper within those countries. It was expected that this step, along with a more moderate rate of inflation within the U.S., would result in a balance in the foreign obligations of the United States, but the deficit continued, and the dollar was devalued again in 1973.

What Does the Farmer Gain from International Trade?

To the cotton farmer of the South, the wheat farmer of the Great Plains, and the fruit grower on the Pacific Coast, international trade is advantageous because the export market provides an additional market for their products. The export market for these and other commodities supplements the domestic market; it increases demand and buoys up prices. Hence, the incomes of these farmers are directly affected by the volume of international trade in their commodities. Here, we find the first tangible gains from trade, as well as the source of the most vigorous arguments for expanding international trade.

But as was pointed out above, private trade is a two-way proposition: to export, we must import. If we are to export cotton, wheat, and dried fruit, we must import something. Therefore, we conclude that the market for *all goods and services* produced in the United States is not widened by international trade; we sell certain goods and services and in return buy others. It does not follow, however, that trade is not advantageous. On the contrary, all groups in the United States, including farmers, gain from international trade. The material level of living of the average American is enhanced by the production and export of commodities that we produce efficiently when they are exchanged for items that we cannot produce, or for the production of which we are not adapted. We all gain from the production and export of cotton, wheat, feedgrains, tractors, computers, and machine tools in exchange for bananas, sugar, coffee, tin, automobiles, color television sets, and travel.[2] What we have here is the old principle of comparative advantage, first encountered in Chapter 2, but now operating on a worldwide basis. The basic argument for international trade rests on the principle of comparative advantage. The real income of all people is increased by: (1) specializing in those lines in which they have the greatest advantage (or the least disadvantage); and (2) trading back and forth between specialized producing areas. It is what we do in the free-trade area of the United States, and that principle has worldwide application.

One more gain from international trade needs to be mentioned: if it is fairly developed and honestly conducted, world trade contributes to peace and economic development. Access to raw materials and markets through international trade tends to minimize frictions between nations. The less-developed nations of the world can obtain some of the capital equipment they require for development only by importing that equipment from the developed countries in which it is produced. In order for them to do so, they must have access to markets in the developed countries. The more highly developed a nation is, the more products of all types it buys on the world market. Thus, as nations increase their incomes through the development process, their imports of agricultural products may rise, thereby benefiting American farmers.

[2]Travel is an important invisible import. We cannot bring Buckingham Palace to the United States, but we can go to see it. And in so doing, we provide the British with dollars to buy dried fruit and steel plate in the United States.

What Trade Cannot Do

Private commercial international trade cannot provide an important market for farm products when the volume of imports is, for one reason or another, seriously restricted. As was pointed out above, the ability to export is limited by the willingness to import; when imports are restricted, exports are reduced. In such a situation, which has been typical in the United States, the export of farm products suffers doubly. First, a contraction in total exports has the obvious adverse effect on farm commodities. But second, and more important, the rest of the world has become increasingly dependent on the United States for heavy producer goods. Hence, if the total volume of trade between the United States and another country is restricted, the foreign customers will tend to use their dollars for the things they need most: machines, tools, and heavy equipment. They can purchase food products elsewhere, from the Argentine, Australia, and other surplus areas, which they do. The result, then, of a reduction in total exports, relative or absolute, is a disproportional contraction in farm exports. The export market for farm products cannot expand, and, in the past, has been hard hit by national policies aimed at restricting imports.

International trade cannot provide an important market for farm products when domestic prices for the commodities involved are held above the structure of world prices. Foreign buyers of wheat and cotton are not going to purchase those products from the United States if they can go elsewhere and obtain those supplies at lower prices, and domestic price policies have had the general effect of lifting prices of farm products at home above the structure of world prices.

A way out of this problem is sometimes suggested and sometimes acted upon; it calls for selling domestic supplies at the domestically supported price and selling the remainder in the world market for what it will bring. That part sold in the world market is excluded from resale in the higher home market by tariffs and import quotas. This trade tactic is called export dumping, and these are the kinds of trading actions that make competing countries angry. Competing nations argue, and not without good reason, that domestic policies aimed at supporting the prices of such commodities as cotton and wheat cause farmers to overexpand in those commodities. Then, if the "surplus" is "dumped" on the world market, it unfairly and unduly depresses the world price. Certainly, unilateral dumping is no way to win friends among trading nations.

Last, but not least, two-way trade does not and cannot contribute directly to the achievement of full employment. It can and will contribute to a more efficient use of resources, and it may contribute indirectly to a greater use of resources by influencing profit expectations. But of itself, two-way trade does not touch the employment problem. We say two-way trade because in the past some countries have found it expedient to "export" unemployment, that is, reduce unemployment at home by subsidizing the export of goods and services. In such instances, exports were maintained in excess of imports by the device of the national government extending credit to foreign purchasers. Needless to say, such actions by one national government, especially in a period of world depression when most governments are wrestling with unemployment and low prices, adds to the fear, uncertainty, and tension of such a period.

In the opposite direction, if the only purpose of economic policy were the creation of jobs, one way to achieve that purpose would be to withdraw entirely from international trade. Bananas and coffee could be grown in the United States in greenhouses. The various nonferrous metals that we import could perhaps be produced at home from low-grade ores, or from scrap. Of course, we would have smaller quantities of these products, probably of poorer quality, which would make them and associated products more expensive. But to build and operate the facilities involved would require more labor than it now takes to produce the things that are traded for these commodities. In this way, jobs would be created. But it is extremely doubtful that we would want to create employment by this method.

COMPOSITION AND TRENDS OF FOREIGN TRADE

The Long-run Past, 1866–1940

The composition of foreign trade has shifted steadily since the Civil War, as shown in the chart of exports in Figure 17–1. First, we see the decline in the relative importance of raw material exports. In the period 1866–70, those exports constituted two-thirds of the total, and the big item in this component was raw cotton. This proportion declined over the years, until in the period 1936–40, crude materials accounted for less than one-fifth of total exports. Second, we see that, as raw materials lost ground, finished manufactured goods replaced them in importance. The pattern of change in imports was roughly the opposite. Finished manufactured goods decreased in importance over this long period as crude raw materials increased from about one-fourth to about one-half of total imports. Of interest in this group of crude raw material imports are food imports, most of which are products that cannot be grown in the United States, except at prohibitive costs: coffee, tea, cocoa, and some tropical fruits and nuts. The more important imports of raw materials, in either a raw or partially

PERCENTAGE OF TOTAL EXPORTS AND IMPORTS REPRESENTED BY
FINISHED MANUFACTURED GOODS AND CRUDE MATERIALS (INCLUDING
FOOD STUFFS), UNITED STATES, FIVE YEAR PERIODS, 1866-1940

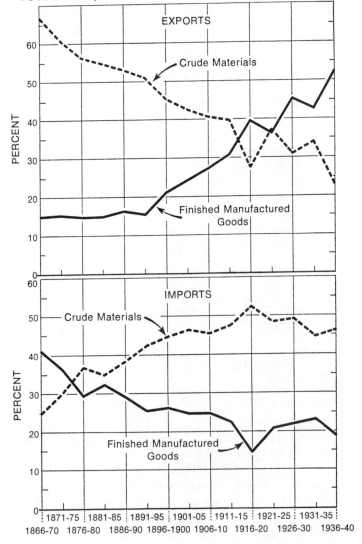

FIGURE 17–1.

processed state, include: rubber, wood pulp, hides, furs, wool, silk, vegetable
oils, jute, copper, tin, nickel, petroleum and a variety of steel alloys.

Between World Wars I and II, exports of agricultural commodities
declined more sharply, relative to our capacity to trade, than did total
exports. As might be expected, the United States' share of total world trade

was declining during this period. In sum, the world trade picture and the United States' part in it was bleak indeed in the period between the two world wars.

Post-World War II Trade Developments

The trend in agricultural exports from the United States did an about-face during and immediately following World War II, as is clear from Figure 17–2. Exports of agricultural products expanded beyond any reasonable expectation in the years immediately following World War II. A chronic food crisis in Europe and Asia, which continued into 1949, created a great need for the surplus food products of the United States. The federal government contributed importantly to a solution of the financing problem by making loans and gifts to needy nations. Thus, the dollar value of agricultural exports increased from $748 million for the period 1935–39 to $3.6 billion in 1947, although the percentage of agricultural exports in total United States exports increased from 26.4 percent in 1935–39 to only 27.6 percent in 1945–49. In short, we increased our exports in all lines.

Between 1946 and 1956, agricultural exports fluctuated around $3 billion, rising above that level in some years, then falling back. Beginning in 1956, the level of agricultural exports has increased rather steadily, surpassing the $7 billion mark in 1971. This steady growth in agricultural

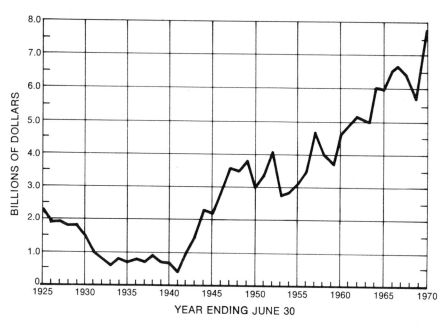

FIGURE 17–2. U.S. Agricultural Exports, 1925–1970

exports is one of the bright spots in the foreign trade situation of the United States during the past fifteen years.

Foreign trade developments in agriculture commodities of the United States cannot be fully understood and appreciated without an understanding of the important role of government in that trade. Special governmental export programs dominated the export trade in agricultural commodities from the United States after 1946. Prior to World War II, almost all agricultural exports were commercial in the sense that transactions were initiated and negotiated by private firms. But during and following World War II, substantial quantities of agricultural products have been exported by government, or with the aid of some kind of governmental program. Hence, agricultural exports are now regularly reported under two headings—"exports under government programs" and "commercial sales for dollars."

Table 17–1 shows that in some years between 1946 and 1957, government-aided exports made up 40 to 60 percent of total agricultural exports. Beginning in 1958, commercial sales for dollars grew substantially while

TABLE 17–1

Agricultural Exports, Total, Commercial, and Government Aided, 1946–71

Year	Total	Commercial Sales for Dollars	Exports Under Gov't. Programs	Percentage Under Gov't. Programs
1946	2857	875	1982	69
1947	3610	1540	2070	57
1948	3505	1606	1899	54
1949	3830	1486	2344	61
1950	2986	981	2005	67
1951	3441	2201	1210	35
1952	4053	3157	896	22
1953	2819	2273	546	19
1954	2936	2225	711	24
1955	3143	2213	930	30
1956	3496	2157	1339	38
1957	4728	2809	1919	41
1958	4003	2794	1209	30
1959	3719	2492	1227	33
1960	4628	3345	1283	28
1961	4946	3443	1503	30
1962	5142	3572	1570	31
1963	5078	3612	1466	29
1964	6068	4627	1441	24
1965	6097	4499	1598	26
1966	6676	5288	1388	21
1967	6771	5463	1308	19
1968	6311	5013	1298	21
1969	5741	4697	1044	18
1970	6748	5712	1036	15
1971	7759	6696	1063	14

government-aided exports continued to grow at a much slower rate. After 1965, changes in United States' policies resulted in a gradual reduction of exports under government programs. Thus, it appears that foreign commercial sales of agricultural products are a bright spot in the total demand picture for U. S. agriculture. In the balance of this chapter, we examine the structure of foreign trade in agricultural products and the potential for expanding such trade.[3]

THE STRUCTURE AND FUTURE OF COMMERCIAL AGRICULTURAL FOREIGN TRADE

Principal Export Markets and Products

Because both commercial trade and foreign food aid increased in the 1950s and 1960s, farm exports to two very different kinds of countries increased during this period. Private commercial exports to the prosperous, rapidly developing countries increased importantly. In 1971, Japan, West Germany, Canada, and the Netherlands were the top four markets for American farm products (Figure 17–3). All have increased their commercial farm imports significantly during the past twenty years. At the same time, countries in a new category became important markets for American farm products through their participation in government-assisted food aid programs. Figure 17–3 shows India, South Viet Nam, and Mexico among the primary importing countries, due to their participation in food aid programs.

The case of Japan is interesting not only because it is the largest single farm product importer but also because it shows what can happen to the pattern of a country's imports as it achieves a rapid rate of economic growth beginning from a relatively low base. The value of American farm exports to Japan between 1955 and 1959 was about $400 million (including $68 million under government programs), roughly 10 percent of our agricultural exports. By 1971, agricultural exports to Japan exceeded $1.2 billion (all commercial) and accounted for nearly 30 percent of all American agricultural exports. In that period, Japan's per capita income increased from about $635 to $1190.

The rapid economic development of Japan and the resulting per capita income increases were directly responsible for the purchases of more and better food commodities by the average Japanese consumer. American farm exports provided a share of that food. The projections by the Feed

[3]Some of the following material is adapted from Willard W. Cochrane, "The Foreign Market," in *The City Man's Guide to the Farm Problem* (Minneapolis, Minn.: University of Minnesota Press, 1965), Chap. 6.

FIGURE 17–3.

Grain Council of Japan, shown in Figure 17–4, indicate how the average Japanese consumer is expected to further increase his consumption of several important livestock commodities. Naturally, American farmers hope to sell much of the grain necessary to produce those livestock products.

Of course, we are not suggesting that very many of the world's less-developed countries will be able to grow as rapidly as Japan has, but even more slowly growing countries may gradually increase their purchases of agricultural products on the world market.

Figure 17–5 shows how important the export market is for certain U.S. farm commodities. Over 50 percent of the rice, soybeans, and wheat produced in the United States in 1972 was exported. Over one-quarter of the tobacco, cotton, tallow, and hides was exported. Another measure of the importance of exports for agriculture is in the fact that over one-quarter the total acres of crops harvested in 1970 was used to produce export commodities.

Figure 17–6 illustrates how important the export market is for these farm commodities. With the existing export situation, market price within the United States is determined by the intersection of the market supply curve (S) with the market demand curve (D_{d+x}). The latter is, of course, the sum of the domestic demand (D_d) plus the export demand. Equil-

PER CAPITA CONSUMPTION, JAPAN

Year	Number
1960	98
1964	180
1969	269

Year	Pounds
1960	0.88
1964	3.08
1975, forecast	8.14

(includes veal)

Year	Pounds
1960	4.0
1964	5.0
1975, forecast	5.4

Year	Pounds
1960	2.9
1964	5.7
1975, forecast	14.7

Year	Pounds
1960	48.4
1964	69.1
1975, forecast	90.2

FIGURE 17–4.

Source: *Foreign Agriculture*, Feb. 1, 1971, p. 5.

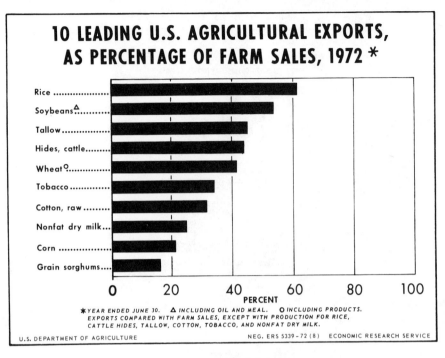

FIGURE 17–5.

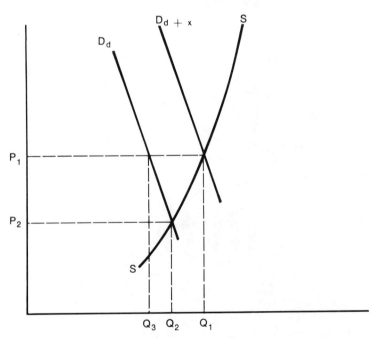

FIGURE 17–6. Effect of Exports on Domestic Market
Equilibrium

ibrium price and quantity are P_1 and Q_1. In the absence of trade, the equilibrium would settle at P_2, Q_2, resulting in a lesser quantity being sold at a lower price. Thus, the export market not only absorbs large volumes of the commodities shown in Figure 17–5 but also tends to keep their prices up.

Trade Restrictions

As already noted, commercial exports increased very importantly in the 1960s, reaching an all-time high of $6.7 billion in 1971. Part of this increase in commercial farm exports resulted from forces beyond the control of American farmers, businessmen, and government administrators. The rapid economic growth of Western Europe and Japan and the corresponding increase in the demand of their populations for a higher quality diet was an important factor that led to important increases in the exports of wheat, feedgrains, soybeans, and protein meal to these rapidly growing areas.

Another part of the increase in farm exports has resulted from efforts by many people throughout the economy—private export firms and trade development groups, the United States Departments of Agriculture and State, and the Congress through laws providing for the opportunity to reduce the degree of protection and thereby to expand trade. These groups had important roles to play because of the maze of trade restrictions that now typify international trade. Every important trading nation of the world has a barrage of control devices through which farm commodities must pass. These devices include tariffs, quantitative import restrictions, variable levies to bring the import price up to some minimum internal price, plant and animal sanitary and quarantine practices, state purchasing agencies, and state trading monopolies.

Because of their importance in the foreign trade situation, it may be well to review how certain trade restriction devices operate. The most common and longstanding device is a tariff. Tariffs are taxes placed upon imports by the government of the importing country on an *ad valorem* or percentage-of-value basis. For example, if there is a 10 percent tariff on wheat imported for $1.00 a bushel, the tariff is ten cents, and therefore the price within the importing country becomes $1.10. The total quantity imported at $1.10 will be reduced by the fact that consumers will buy less at $1.10 than at $1.00. Producers within the country will be able to sell wheat at $1.10 because that is the price of alternative sources of supply.

Quantitative restrictions or quotas operate somewhat differently. The importing country makes a determination of the quantity of a product that it will permit to be imported. Licenses are issued to importers within that country for quantities up to that amount. The importers then procure the quantities from whatever sellers they desire, but only up to the amount of the total import licenses.

The European Community uses a third device known as the variable levy. Under this system, a minimum import price, usually slightly above the internal price for the commodity, is determined. For example, say the minimum import price for wheat in a Common Market country is $3.00, whether the exporter sells the wheat for $3.00, $2.00, or $1.00. At the first price, the variable levy is zero; at the second, $1.00, at the third, $2.00. The importing country simply levies a fee equal to the difference between the sale price and the minimum import price. Under this system, the price to the buyers is independent of the price charged by the seller. Exporters gain no advantage through price competition because the buyer must pay the same price to all sources, with only the government of the importing country benefiting from a lower price through the correspondingly higher levy.

There have been moves within the United States to increase the restrictions we currently place upon imports. Among agricultural commodities, additional beef quotas and dairy product quotas have been most strongly supported. The economic effects of trade restrictions of any kind are well known—they assist the domestic producers of the protected commodity while resulting in higher prices and lower quantities for consumers. The analysis in Figure 17–7 shows this.

Free trade results in the P_1, Q_1 equilibrium situation, where the domestic market demand function (DD) intersects the total market supply function (domestic plus imports: S_{d+m}). Domestic suppliers provide Q_3 while importers supply Q_1-Q_3. Elimination of imports restricts the total quantity to Q_2 and increases the price to P_2. Domestic producers get a higher price and sell a greater amount (Q_2). Consumers pay a higher price for a smaller amount.

Taking Figures 17–6 and 17–7 together, we can see that free trade is favorable to producers of commodities that are exported and unfavorable to producers of commodities that are imported if one considers only the short-run market effects. On balance, more agricultural products have been exported from the United States than have been imported since 1960. What is more important is that about one-third of all agricultural imports have been noncompetitive with the products of American farmers. This includes cocoa, nuts, coffee, tea, bananas, and other tropical fruits. Thus, American farmers, as a group, have more to fear than to gain from trade restrictions.

It is not obvious from the diagrams, but the principle of comparative advantage shows that consumers will be able to buy their total needs more cheaply and can have more goods to consume in a free trade situation. Thus, the issue of freer trade versus more protection comes down to a question of benefiting producers of a protected commodity at the cost of the mass of consumers.

It must also be recognized that protection breeds retaliation by other

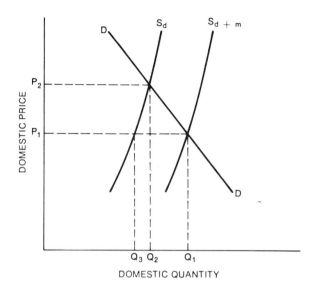

FIGURE 17–7. Effects of Imports on Domestic Market
Equilibrium

countries, which can result in reduction of one's own exports. Retaliation
can spread and result in a declining trend in all trade as it did in the
1930s. Then, it becomes more difficult to import those commodities that
cannot be produced internally under any circumstances.

With the tendency toward increases in all kinds of trade barriers in
the 1960s, the substantial increase in agricultural exports depended heavily
on the efforts of the groups mentioned earlier. Private traders have obtained
support and assistance from such organizations as Great Plains Wheat, the
Soybean Council, and the Feed Grain Council in seeking new users, inducing the foreign governments to interpret regulations favorably, and influencing the form of new regulations. In addition to these private efforts,
when laws and tariff restrictions are prohibitive, the leverage of government
must be brought to bear, and officials in the United States Departments
of Agriculture and State have negotiated long and hard to reduce the level
of restrictions on agricultural product exports.

Impact of Other Government Policies on International
Agricultural Trade

It is obvious that American farm products cannot be sold on the world
market if their prices are above the prices that other sellers are asking.
Due to internal price and income support policies, the prices of some farm
commodities, notably cotton and wheat, were above the world level in the
1960s. To move these commodities in the foreign market, Congress autho-

rized the use of government funds to subsidize their export. The subsidy, paid to United States exporters, permitted the sale of American farm products abroad at lower prices than paid in the domestic market. Of course, the subsidy was borne by the taxpayer and, because it encouraged greater U.S. exports, was an important stumbling block in relations between the United States and friendly competitors in world agricultural markets. These two reasons (among others) encouraged the change in the late 1960s from high support prices to direct payments as the principal domestic farm income support device. This in turn has permitted the prices of cotton and wheat to fall to the world level and allowed the government to remove the export subsidies on those commodities.

Another force at work with respect to commercial agricultural exports is the increasing tendency toward customs unions or common markets, which many governments have joined during the last twenty years. The main economic effect of a customs union is to increase the size of the market for countries within such unions. The larger market permits fuller exploitation of comparative advantage within such an area. One hoped-for result is faster growth, and the European Economic Community has been quite successful in this regard.

United States agricultural exports to the countries of the EEC have increased greatly since its formation. However, the EEC's desire for a common agricultural policy with uniform agricultural prices has resulted in a general rise in the internal level of agricultural prices within the European Community, and an increased level of agricultural production in certain European Community countries. This has meant an increasing trend toward self-sufficiency within the EEC and thus a potential reduction in total imports to the Community. That the potential has not yet been translated into reality is shown by the rising trend in Figure 17–8. However, if protectionist policies within the EEC are strengthened, the U.S. may lose part of this important market for agricultural products. As the EEC expands through the addition of new countries, the total potential of such a reduction is even more serious. This event would be the result of policies followed by the EEC rather than a natural consequence of a customs union but might encourage other customs unions to pursue similar policies.

The less-developed nations of the world, in their attempt to increase their levels of living, are trying to increase the exports of products that they can produce efficiently. In many cases, these are agricultural products that compete with American farm products on the world market, for example, cotton, tobacco, vegetable oils, protein meal, and rice. To the extent that they are successful in this undertaking, they will directly compete with American products in the world market. However, as pointed out at the beginning of this chapter, the only use they can make of foreign exchange is to purchase imports, and it is likely that some sector of the U.S. economy will supply part of those imports.

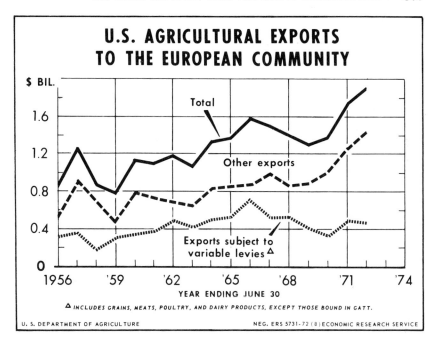

FIGURE 17–8.

In summary, the size and growth of commercial exports of farm products from the United States will depend in the future upon five major developments: (1) the rate of economic growth in Japan, Western Europe, and other high-income areas; (2) the skill and diligence of all Amercians engaged in foreign trade, both private firms and government; (3) the extent to which protectionist forces are resisted within the United States, which will influence (4) the extent to which protectionist policies come to dominate the European Economic Community; and (5) the extent to which less-developed countries increase their exportable surpluses of sugar, cotton, oilseeds, and tobacco and thereby become important suppliers of those commodities in world markets.

THE STRUCTURE AND FUTURE OF NONCOMMERCIAL AGRICULTURAL FOREIGN TRADE

Noncommercial or Government-assisted Agricultural Exports

Foreign assistance through food shipments has a long history. During and immediately following World War I, the United States operated programs of famine relief in Europe. In 1940, the United States had large stocks of wheat, cotton, and corn that had accumulated under the agricultural price support programs of the 1930s. These stocks were shipped to our allies during World War II, and to both victors and vanquished following the war. The United States became the principal supplier of food for relief during the "Bengal Famine" of India in 1943 and again to both India and Pakistan in 1952. The refugees created by the continuous war in the Middle East were also fed by emergency programs. In addition to these emergency situations, during the 1950s it seemed that many countries existed with barely enough food for subsistence while the United States had excess production capacity.

It became apparent that a permanent vehicle for food assistance would be desirable, and in 1954 the U.S. Congress passed the Agricultural Trade Development and Assistance Act, commonly known as Public Law 480. Amended in 1966 and 1968, and also known as the Food for Peace program, this law contains four titles.

Title I provides for the sale of U.S. agricultural commodities to friendly countries with payment in the currency of the recipient country.

Title II authorizes donation of farm products held in stock by the Commodity Credit Corporation for famine and disaster relief, community development, school lunches, and other economic development purposes.

Title III provides for the disposition of CCC-owned surplus commodities for domestic food donation programs administered by appropriate government or private agencies as well as for overseas donation through American volunteer or international agencies.

Title IV provides for sales of commodities on credit for dollars that are repayable over a long period of time at relatively low interest rates.

Some serious difficulties developed in the 1950s and early 1960s over the foreign surplus disposal programs of the United States. First, the promotional tactics in selling surplus agricultural commodities abroad at bargain rates created ill will among friendly competing nations. How much these concessional sales cut into the export market of Canada, New Zealand, and Denmark we will probably never know. Their losses may not have been as much as claimed; there is probably more fear expressed in the protests of these countries with respect to what we may do than with respect to what we have already done. Further, as experience has been gained with the various foreign disposal programs, responsible governmental agencies have acted to protect the foreign market interests of competing nations.

Second, although everyone likes a bargain, there were few lasting benefits to the recipient countries involved. Current consumption levels were raised, and this can be important to hungry people, but little else had been achieved. Thus, the critical question was fairly asked: What happens to the raised levels of living in these countries, if and when our disposal operations come to an end? In short, the agricultural disposal programs of the United States were expedient, temporary, disposal programs. Further, in some cases our disposal programs may have harmed the recipient countries, first by depressing prices for the domestic agricultural producers involved, and second by reducing the incentive to develop and thereby increase the productivity of the recipient countries' agriculture.

Third, and most important, our foreign surplus disposal programs created great uncertainty. Neither we ourselves, our competitors, nor the recipients knew how long we would place primary emphasis on this type of adjustment, what forms the programs would take, the extent of the price concessions and the nature of the conditions attached to such sales. In this context, rational action was impossible; plans involving economic development and adjustment in foreign nations, as they relate to agricultural exports from the United States, had to be made in a state of uncertainty, hence often were not made.

In recognition of these difficulties, the nature of P.L. 480 operations changed. Since 1968, there has been greater emphasis placed on the use of Title IV programs and much less on the use of Title I. In addition, there has been an increasing emphasis on self help and developmental uses of the commodities. That is, efforts are made to see that the food is used by the recipient countries along with other forms of assistance primarily to help those who help themselves, as for example, by using commodities as partial payment to laborers on a rural works project. Other elements in the current food aid strategy include an encouragement for recipient countries to carry out appropriate population programs, a closer integration of all U.S. assistance programs, increased encouragement for private investment within the recipient countries, and joining with other nations in undertaking relief to combat food deficits around the world.

The World Food Situation

Given the foregoing situation with respect to foreign concessionary sales in the past, what are the prospects for such sales in the future? The popular press has been full of news of a world "population explosion" and the accompanying implication that millions will die of starvation. But in the past twenty years, per capita agricultural production of both the less-developed and the developed countries of the world increased. And although it would be a mistake to say that most less-developed countries of the world are rapidly increasing their agricultural production, it would be equally wrong to think that they are slipping back significantly.

How short of food are the less-developed countries, and what is our best estimate of their needs in the near future? The Food and Agriculture Organization (FAO) of the United Nations has carried out a series of studies of world agricultural production and demand. The latest available examines trends over the 1959–69 period and projects these to 1980. Table 17–2 shows the rates of growth of gross agricultural production for the two periods for seven regions of the world.

TABLE 17–2

Annual Growth Rates of Gross Agricultural Production,
1959–69 and 1970–80, Major World Regions

| | ANNUAL COMPOUND RATES OF GROWTH | | | |
| | Total Production | | Per Capita Production | |
Region	1959–69 Actual	1970–80 Projected	1959–69 Actual	1970–80 Projected
Developed market-directed economies[a]	2.3	2.1	1.2	1.0
Africa	2.4	3.4	0.1	0.6
Asian centrally planned economies[b]	—[c]	2.5	—[c]	0.5
Near East	2.9	3.5	0.2	0.6
Asia and Far East	2.9	3.3	0.3	0.6
USSR and Eastern Europe	3.1	2.1	2.0	1.2
Latin America	3.3	3.3	0.4	0.4
World	2.7	2.5	0.5	0.4

a Includes North America, Western Europe, Oceania, and other developed countries.
b Includes Mainland China, North Korea, Mongolia, and North VietNam.
c Data inadequate to determine.

Source: *Agricultural Commodity Projections, 1970–1980,* Food and Agricultural Organization of the United Nations, Rome, Vol. 1, 1971.

Looking at the actual growth rates of agricultural production, the reader may be surprised to observe that it was the developed market-directed economies that had the *slowest* rate of growth of total output over the 1960s. This reflects the fact that many developed countries find themselves in a position similar to that of the United States, in which total demand for agricultural products is growing slowly and so total production has been restrained to prevent domestic prices from falling. The less-developed areas of the world experienced annual rates of growth from between 2.4 percent to 3.3 percent per year.

The projections to 1980 follow the actual rates of the 1960s fairly closely. This is, in part, a natural consequence of the methodology used in making the projections. Trends in the production of the major commodities of each country were projected to 1980, modified as necessary by the knowledge of commodity specialists. Thus, the developed market-directed economies are projected to have a slightly slower rate of growth of output and the less developed areas are projected to pick up their rates slightly.

Of course, population growth is occurring more rapidly in the less-developed countries, so it is important to examine the changes in per capita agricultural production. Table 17–2 shows that the USSR and Eastern Europe increased per capita production most rapidly, followed by the developed market-directed economies. The less-developed regions, beginning with inadequate absolute levels of availability, grew at modest rates of between 0.1 and 0.4 percent per year, and similar differences are projected to continue into the 1970–80 period. These projections reflect the assumed population growth rates of 2.7 for the developing countries, 1.0 for the developed, and 1.7 for the centrally planned countries.

TABLE 17–3

1965 Food Availability and 1980 Projected Food Availability
for Major Regions of the World, as a Percentage of Requirements

Region	Calories Available as % of Requirements		Protein Available as % of Requirements	
	Actual 1965	Projected 1980	Actual 1965	Projected 1980
Asian centrally planned economies	86	93	151	163
Asia and Far East	89	99	135	150
Africa	92	98	140	149
Near East	94	101	145	153
Latin America	104	110	169	179
Other developed countries	105	115	203	227
Western Europe	117	122	216	231
North America	120	125	237	249
Oceania	120	124	244	261
USSR and Eastern Europe	122	126	226	238
World	100	105	169	178

Source: *Agricultural Commodity Projections, 1970–1980*, FAO, p. 47, 57.

Table 17–3 shows the FAO estimates of food availability relative to food requirements for ten major regions in 1965 and the projected availability in 1980. These data are derived from "food balance sheets," on which the total available food from all sources is added and compared to the population. It should be recognized that many differences exist within the groupings, so that in an area with "adequate" food (that is, in which availability exceeds 100 percent of requirements), there may well be countries and certainly are individuals with inadequate diets. Recognizing this drawback, it is nonetheless useful to look at broad aggregates in order to discern the overall situation.

In 1965, four of the less-developed regions of the world had an overall inadequate availability of calories. Virtually all Asia and Africa, excluding the developed enclaves like Japan and South Africa, had fewer calories available than required to sustain health and normal activity. On the basis of the projections of production discussed above, all these regions, excepting the Near East, will continue to have inadequate supplies of calories through 1980. When one recognizes that the population of Africa and Asia was 2.4 billion, or two-thirds of the world's total in 1970, then the inadequacies in caloric availability become important, indeed.

Turning to the data for protein shown in the last two columns, one is surprised to note that in all regions availability exceeds requirements, even in 1965. The projections to 1980 show this excess over requirements increasing. This evidence contradicts the impression of widespread protein inadequacy that prevails in the discussions about the world food situation. FAO's comment on this is revealing:

> The apparent contradiction between the absence of protein deficits, as shown by the food balance sheets and the protein malnutrition revealed by clinical observations is because the food balance sheet is not an adequate statistical framework for revealing nutritional status in a country. Assessment of the protein deficit by a comparison of average intakes with requirements raises three types of difficulty. One is statistical and raises the problem of measuring the spread of protein intakes per family or per capita around the national average; the other two are physiological and relate to the interrelations between energy and protein intakes and the protein quality of food mixes.[4]

The psychological problem is that the measure of protein deficiency is not valid unless energy (calorie) requirements are fully met, and because energy requirements are not fulfilled in Asia and Africa, there is probably an overall deficit in protein as well as in calories. In addition, there clearly are groups within those regions whose diets are highly inadequate.[5]

The Future Role of Food Aid[6]

In light of this somewhat depressing view of the world food situation, should not the United States begin anew an effort to relieve hunger throughout Asia and Africa? If we went back to the same policies that we followed during the 1950s and early 1960s, the problems discussed earlier would again arise. In addition, we now recognize at least three situations in which food aid can be detrimental to the development process within the recipient country.

First, where food aid shipments depress farm prices within the recipient country and thereby reduce farmers' incentives to expand produc-

---

[4]*Agricultural Commodity Projections, 1970–1980*, Food and Agricultural Organization of the United Nations, Rome, Vol. 1, 1971, p. 48.

[5]It should be recognized that these findings and projections are consistent with those of other individuals and organizations that have carried out similar analyses. See for example, *The World Food Situation: Prospects for World Grain Production, Consumption and Trade*, Foreign Agricultural Economics Report 35, Economic Research Service, U.S.D.A., August 1967.

[6]This section is based on a discussion of food aid in Willard W. Cochrane, *The World Food Problem*, Chapter 7 (New York: Thomas Y. Crowell, 1969).

tion, they are clearly undesirable. If food shipments reduce farmers' incentives to such an extent that production falls so as to reduce the total availability of food within the country, they are highly counter-productive. Fortunately, such cases are rare; generally, the net effect is an increase in food availability. However, the disincentive effect of a price reduction has been demonstrated and it must be weighed against the benefits of additional food.

Second, if food aid substitutes for commercial food imports and the foreign exchange thereby released is used to import luxury consumer goods, there is no benefit to the recipient country beyond the few who can afford such luxuries.

Third, food aid that permits responsible government officials to postpone difficult decisions regarding modernization of their own agriculture is undesirable. Food shipments, when used for this purpose, can result in a false sense of security sometimes followed by economic disaster.

Thus, it may well be in the long-run interests of countries now receiving food aid to gradually reduce their dependence on that aid, even though it means that the present generation may suffer. It appears that governments are increasingly making this decision. As we saw in Table 17–1, the total volume of United States government-assisted food exports has been declining modestly since 1965. Part of this decline is due to our emphasis on sales for dollars rather than for foreign currencies. But changing attitudes of recipient governments also have payed a part. Food aid has been shifted from a *disposal* basis to an *assistance* basis so that emergency aid is available but dependency is avoided. It is unlikely to shift back, and so it is unlikely that disposal of large quantities of "surplus" commodities will again become as important an activity as it was during the 1950s and early 1960s.

POINTS FOR DISCUSSION

1. In what sense is international trade a two-way proposition? How does an international trading transaction differ from a domestic transaction?
2. What does the farmer stand to gain from an expansion in the foreign trade of farm products?
3. What do we mean by *dumping*? Why do countries sometimes engage in this practice? What are some of the consequences that stem from this practice?
4. Can employment in a given country be expanded through foreign trade? If so, how? And with what consequences?
5. What has been the trend in food and fiber exports from the United States over the past century? Can you give some reasons for this trend?
6. What is the probable development of private commercial agricultural exports from the United States during the 1970s and 1980s? Be able to defend your conclusion.
7. What means did the United States employ in the late 1950s to dispose of agricultural surplus abroad? Indicate strong and weak points of such programs

REFERENCES

COCHRANE, WILLARD· W., *The City Man's Guide to the Farm Problem,* Chap. 6. Minneapolis, Minn.: University of Minnesota Press, 1965.

———, *The World Food Problem: A Guardedly Optimistic View,* Chaps. 3 and 6. New York: Thomas Y. Crowell, 1969.

HOUCK, JAMES P., AND JAMES G. KENDRICK, "The Protectionist Mood and Midwest Agricultural Trade," *North Central Regional Extension Publication 24,* University of Minnesota, Agricultural Extension Bulletin 355, October 1968.

HOUTHAKKER, H. S., "Domestic Farm Policy and International Trade," *American Journal of Agricultural Economics* (December 1971), pp. 762–65.

JOHNSON, D. GALE, *Trade and Agriculture: A Study of Inconsistent Policies,* Chaps. 1–4. New York: John Wiley & Sons, Inc., 1950.

JOHNSTON, BRUCE F., "Farm Surpluses and Foreign Policy," *World Politics,* (October 1957).

PART FIVE

Human, Material, and Financial Resources of Agriculture

Chapter 18

Human Resources in
American Farming

People are the central concern of all social sciences. In economics, people are unique because they not only provide the specific economic inputs of labor and entrepreneurial skill but also are the owners of all other inputs and hence the receivers of the fruits of economic activities in the form of income. In the earlier parts of this book, we have been concerned largely with the production aspects of agriculture. We have considered the relationship between inputs and the outputs they produce. We now consider the distribution of returns among the owners of resources, the nature of the economic units receiving returns, and the factors affecting those economic units. We begin our examination of resources in agriculture with human resources.

We have already discussed two sectors of farming—the expanding sector with sales exceeding $20,000 per year and the declining sector with sales of less than $20,000. The farm families making up these groups are part of our concern with human resources. But we are also concerned with the hired laborers who work on farms, or those who have in the past worked on farms and no longer can find farm work. And last, we are concerned with the other people living in rural areas where, because agriculture is the primary economic activity, the changing economic structure of modern agriculture largely determines the economic environment.

We have also discussed many other aspects of modern agriculture. In 1970, one-fourth of the population of the United States lived in rural areas. Roughly 3 million farms employed less than 5 percent of the labor force. Productivity per man employed in farming doubled between 1960 and 1970. Over the past forty years, people have migrated out of agriculture rapidly when nonfarm economic opportunities were available. Nonfarm employment has become increasingly important as a source of income to farm people. Farming has continued to absorb a decreasing fraction of the labor force even in rural areas—in 1960, farm residents made up 30 percent of the rural population; in 1970, only 20 percent.

In our discussion of technological change, we described the economic treadmill that is modern agriculture in the United States. Have these economic changes caused a significant deterioration in the income position of rural Americans? What groups have suffered, what groups have gained? How have those groups reacted?

Incomes of Farm People

The disposable per capita income of the farm population has long been lower than that of the nonfarm population. Figure 18–1 clearly shows this for the 1960–72 period. It has been argued that farm families can attain a given real level of living with less disposable income than nonfarm families because of the farm products that they may consume

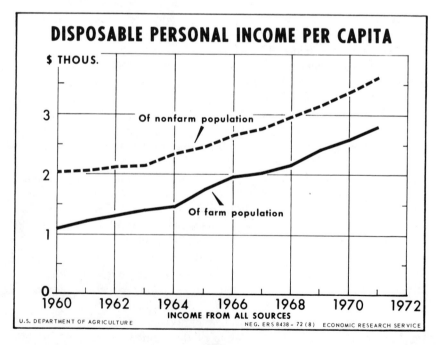

FIGURE 18–1.

directly, or because the homes in which they live are part of the farm rather than personal wealth. Adjustments reflecting these factors have been included in Figure 18–1. It has also been argued that farm families are willing to accept lower incomes because of the nonmaterial returns from farming—outdoor work, rural living, working with growing things, and being one's "own boss." Thus, farmers would accept somewhat lower disposable incomes than others, but they argue that they have been forced into sacrificing too much material income to obtain the nonmaterial benefits.

How much is too much? The answer, of course, depends on individual preferences. But we do know that over the past decade incomes of the farm population have been gaining relative to those of the nonfarm population. In 1960–63, disposable personal income per capita of the farm population average 60 percent of the nonfarm level; during 1967–70, it averaged 75 percent as much. Thus, despite the treadmill of prices and technology, the combination of fewer farms, direct government payments, and nonfarm earnings appear to have helped the average income position of American farmers over the past decade. However, many farm families still have inadequate levels of income, and in fact the rate of poverty among farm families is nearly twice as high as among nonfarm families.

The "poverty level" is a tenuous concept to use in analysis. Although one may be able to recognize poverty conditions when confronted with them, it is quite another thing to objectively measure poverty. The definition developed by the federal government provides for an income "threshold" level that varies depending on family size, number of children, and place of residence. The definition insures that families at and above the poverty threshold can afford the nutritionally adequate "economy" food plan designed by the U.S. Department of Agriculture (see Table 10–2). Annual adjustments for price changes keep the poverty threshold current. In 1970, a family with four members living on a farm needed an income exceeding $3385 to be out of the poverty class. The corresponding level for nonfarm families was $3968.[1]

In the early 1960s, when poverty again became a political issue, studies showed that about 40 million people lived in poverty in the United States. By 1969, the number had decreased to 24 million. Figure 18–2 shows the percentages of specific population groups in poverty. Of the 24 million in poverty in 1969, half lived in metropolitan areas and half lived in nonmetropolitan areas.[2] Two-thirds of the nonmetropolitan poverty

---

[1]U.S. Bureau of the Census, "Poverty Increases by 1.2 Million in 1970," *Current Population Reports,* Series P-60, No. 77, U.S. Department of Commerce, 1971.

[2]The precise definitions of *rural* and *nonmetropolitan* are somewhat different, but for our purposes we may consider them to refer to the same areas. Data from: U.S. Bureau of the Census, "24 Million Americans: Poverty in the United States, 1969," *Current Population Reports,* Series P-60, No. 76, U.S. Department of Commerce, 1970.

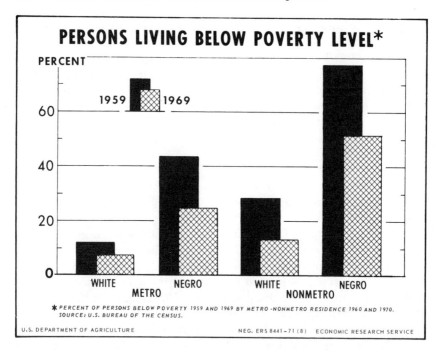

PERSONS LIVING BELOW POVERTY LEVEL*

PERCENT

1959   1969

PERCENT OF PERSONS BELOW POVERTY 1959 AND 1969 BY METRO-NONMETRO RESIDENCE 1960 AND 1970.
SOURCE: U.S. BUREAU OF THE CENSUS.

U.S. DEPARTMENT OF AGRICULTURE   NEG. ERS 8441-71 (8)   ECONOMIC RESEARCH SERVICE

FIGURE 18–2.

population lived in the South, one-third lived in the North and West. Two-thirds of the poor were white, one-third were nonwhite (blacks, Indians, and other racial groups). Fully 50 percent of the black, nonmetropolitan population was in poverty in 1969 (Figure 18–2). Progress in reducing the incidence of poverty is evident, but it has not been rapid enough to eliminate poverty, especially among nonwhites.

Rural Community Problems. The poverty problem in the United States is to a large extent a rural community and farm-related problem. Twenty percent of farm families are in the poverty class, compared to 12 percent of the nonfarm families. Poverty farm families, undoubtedly concentrated in the lower sales groups, probably had characteristics similar to nonfarm poverty families: relatively large families, relatively low educational attainment, and difficulty in finding employment on a full-time basis. These conditions are widespread in rural communities.[3]

The lack of community development not only means low income, it also means poor health, and this is true in both rural and urban areas. The proportion of individuals with one or more chronic activity-limiting health

[3]See: *The Economic and Social Condition of Rural America in 1970's*, prepared for the Committee on Government Operations, United States Senate, 92nd Cong., 1st Sess., 1971 (Washington, D.C.: Government Printing Office, 1971).

conditions is twice as high among those in the poverty class as among those with family incomes of $4000 to $7000. In rural areas, nearly 15 percent of the population have a chronic activity-limiting health condition as compared with less than 10 percent of those in large metropolitan areas. The number of physicians, hospitals, and hospital beds are all twice as large per 100,000 persons in metropolitan areas as compared to isolated rural areas.

Rural communities also have poor housing. Although the quality of rural housing has increased markedly since 1950 when 62 percent was substandard, in 1968, 20 percent was still substandard. That 20 percent either lacked one of the basic items of plumbing (usually a flush toilet) or was dilapidated. By comparison, 5.7 percent of the housing was substandard in the central cities, and 4.0 percent in the suburbs. The substandard rural housing is concentrated among minority groups, and even a large fraction of minority families with incomes exceeding $5000 lived in substandard housing.

A large number of federal programs to assist rural areas have been developed, but there is a general belief that these programs have not been as effective as they could be. Part of the ineffectiveness is due to a lack of knowledge by rural community leaders of the programs available. To offset this lack, the U.S. Senate has printed a *Guide to Federal Programs for Rural Development*.[4] That guide, over five hundred pages long, details programs of federal assistance for business, industry, agriculture, community facilities, community functions, community services, and community planning. However, it does not guarantee rural development. In fact, the large number of available programs indicates how unsure we are of the best way to achieve rural community development.

Proposals for long-run programs for the solution of this problem call for increased educational facilities in these communities, increased health and medical facilities, and vocational guidance services. Students of the rural poverty problem are in general agreement that although communication and transportation facilities have increased greatly in recent years, the migration of people out of these areas is not proceeding at a sufficiently high rate to raise the relatively low level of incomes. Also, although industrialization is spreading through many rural areas and the increase in nonfarm jobs in recent years is most encouraging, available evidence still indicates progress in improving poverty conditions in the areas outlined has been disappointing.

Based on an index reflecting the general level of family income, commercialization of agriculture, rate of population growth, and public welface case load, the counties with serious or substantial economic problems cluster in the South, Appalachia, northern New Mexico, the cut-over areas of

[4]Committee on Agriculture and Forestry, Senate Document No. 92–54, 92nd Cong., 1st Sess., 1971 (Washington, D.C.: Government Printing Office, 1971).

the Lake States, Maine, and northern Washington. These poorly developed areas all are outside the mainstream of modern economic activity. Figure 18–3 shows the location of urban employment centers, commuter counties and rural/small town noncommuter counties. These latter counties lie beyond effective commuting range of employment centers. Each of the regions that has been identified as having serious or substantial economic problems is largely made up of rural/small town counties. (In addition, much of the Great Plains and mountain regions fall in the same classification, but the economic base for modern farming is much stronger in those areas.) People in the rural/small town counties cannot benefit from employment generated in existing employment centers because they live too far from such centers. The answer is more complex and must be carefully searched out, beginning with an understanding of the origin of the low-income problem.

Low-income Farm Families in the South. The high incidence of poverty-class farm families in the South has been a continuing phenomenon. Seventy-one percent of all farm families with cash incomes (from all sources) of less than $1000 in 1949 were in the South. Fifty percent of all farm families with cash incomes of less than $3000 in 1959 were in the South. And in 1969, 59 percent of all poverty-class, non-metropolitan families were in the South.

Why has this heavy concentration of low-income farm families developed in the South?[5] Early settlement in the hillier areas of the upper South led to a pattern of pioneer, small subsistence farms. The favorable markets for their small offerings of crops and livestock products were soon lost in competition with the producers on the more productive lands of the Midwest. These early families failed to find alternative sources of income. Farms in the upper South became even smaller and the region soon became overpopulated and capital poor.

In the other parts of the South, the highly profitable combination of cotton and slavery in the early nineteenth century channeled most available capital into specialized cotton-producing, slave-holding plantations. The social organization of the rural communities was dominated by a planter class opposed to broadening the suffrage, establishing free universal education, and the taxing of property for community welfare programs. Prior to the Civil War, the importation of slaves created for the South a large, penniless class of people, the forebears of one of the region's most disadvantaged class of farm people. This slave labor helped reduce the earnings of all labor, free and slave alike, to the subsistence level.

Thus, even before the disastrous effects of the Civil War and Reconstruction were felt, the Cotton South had already developed social, political,

---

[5]The discussion in this section is based on an excellent report, *Rural Low-Income and Rural Development Programs in the South* (Washington, D.C.: National Planning Association, 1959).

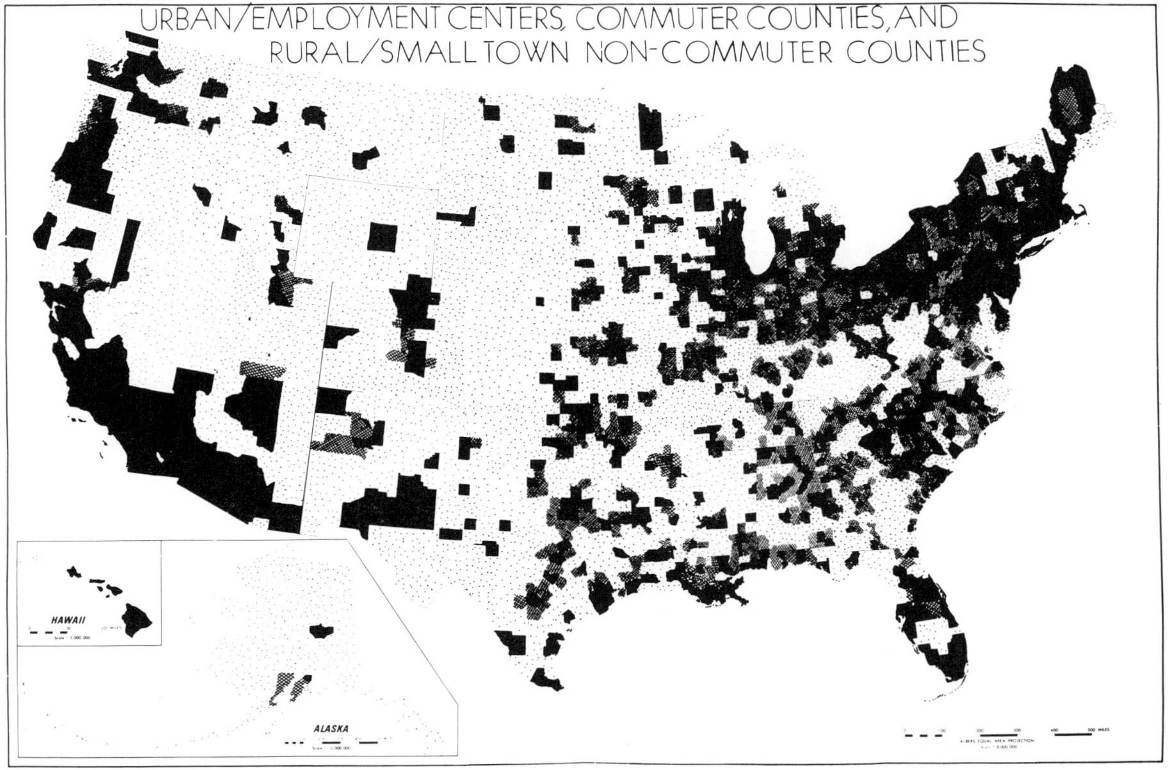

URBAN/EMPLOYMENT CENTERS, COMMUTER COUNTIES, AND
RURAL/SMALL TOWN NON-COMMUTER COUNTIES

FIGURE 18-3.

■ **Urban/Employment Centers.**—Counties with 25,000 or more urban population, or 10,000 or more nonagricultural wage and salary jobs, 1970. ▨ **Commuter Counties.**—Counties from which 10% or more of all workers commuted to jobs located in urban/employment centers, 1960. ▱ **Rural/Small Town non-Commuter Counties.**—Counties that are not urban/employment centers, 1970, and from which less than 10% of workers commuted to jobs in such centers in 1960. **Source:** 1970 Census of Population. County Business Patterns, 1970. Unpublished commuting data of 1960 census. Prepared by Economic Development Division, ERS, USDA.

333

and economic institutions that discouraged broadly based economic progress. War and reconstruction not only impoverished the South but also brought a system of crop-share wages for Negro labor and costly merchant credit for planters, saddling the region with a low-productivity organization of its agriculture.

The bitterness that Reconstruction aroused was slow to die. Cultural isolation and a backward-looking political and social system continued during the crucial years when the rest of the nation was undergoing one of its most rapid periods of economic development. Thus, poverty in the rural South tended to become community-wide and self-perpetuating as a consequence of its peculiar social and political history.

Poverty Areas Outside the South. Why have low-income rural areas developed and persisted outside the South, such as in northwest New Mexico, in the southern parts of Missouri, Illinois, Indiana, southeast Ohio, central Pennsylvania, and in the northern part of the Great Lake States? In a sense, these low-income areas can be explained only in terms of the failure of the economic system to function effectively in channeling labor resources into the more productive lines of employment. When farming was largely a matter of hand labor and ox power, differences between areas in levels of income per farm were not great. But as industry developed and farming outside the South became mechanized, differences between areas widened. The farms increased in size in the more level and more productive areas, and machinery was used to replace human labor wherever possible. The excess farm population migrated to industrial and other nonfarm employment.

But in the less-productive areas located some distance from expanding industries, where the land was too hilly for the use of power machinery, farm population continued to increase and hand-labor methods prevailed. However, when the less-productive areas, not adapted to power machinery, were located near expanding industries, as in the East and Northeast, farm people took up nonfarm employment, returning their farm lands to nonfarm uses. Northwest New Mexico is somewhat an exception to this general rule. The land in this section of New Mexico is little different from other parts of the Southwest, but the majority of the farm families are of Mexican or Indian origin. A majority speak Spanish, and many are illiterate. Families are large and health conditions poor in this area.

Community-wide poverty is the result of differential economic development. The key factors responsible for the lack of economic development in these areas, while the rest of the economy enjoyed unprecedented progress, are both cultural and economic. There is a saying that poverty breeds poverty. Lack of family income prevents parents from giving their children medical attention, education, and cultural advantages that fit them for a variety of job opportunities. Families living in poverty lack the reserves to cover the cost of moving to a new location in search of higher-paying jobs. This circle of poverty breeding poverty apparently explains the much higher man-land ratio and lower level of farm family income in poor rural areas, as compared with the Corn Belt, the Great Plains, and the dairy areas of the United States.

Incomes of the Hired Farm Labor Force[6]

Many hired farm workers depend on farming for their livelihood just as farmers do, but many depend on some other industry also. The hired farm labor force includes all individuals who work on farms for wages. Many of these people work just a few days, some work for part of the crop season, and others work virtually full time. In 1969–70, farm wage workers numbered 2.5 million, compared to 4 million in 1949–50. In 1950, two-thirds of those workers lived on farms; in 1970, three-fourths of them did not live on farms. Thus, the farm work force has not only shrunk but it has also changed from being largely farmers working for other farmers to being largely rural laborers working for farmers.

Of the 2.5 million farm workers in 1970, only about 625,000 had farm work as their chief activity. About 400,000 were chiefly engaged in nonfarm work, and the remainder either were unemployed, attended school, or were keeping house when not working on farms. About 200,000 were migratory farm workers who followed a regular pattern of travel through the year, working to harvest crops first in one area and then in another. Table 18–1 shows the employment and earnings of these four groups in 1970.

TABLE 18–1

Days Worked and Wages Earned at Farm and Nonfarm Work
by Hired Farm Workers, 1970

| | Farm Work | | Nonfarm Work | | Total Wages Earned per Year |
Type of Worker	Number of Days Worked	Wages Earned	Number of Days Worked	Wages Earned	
Chiefly farm workers	209	$2520	19	$ 261	$2781
Chiefly nonfarm workers	36	417	185	3729	4146
Chiefly not in labor force	38	318	20	156	475
Migratory workers	88	1202	45	727	1930

Source: *The Hired Farm Working Force of 1970*, Agricultural Economic Report No. 201, Economic Research Service. U.S.D.A., March 1971, pp. 15, 16.

All classes of agricultural workers have low earnings, and not only are they poorly paid but because of the nature of farming their work is highly seasonal. This suits some individuals well, for as is apparent from Figure 18–4 the greatest proportion of the seasonality is absorbed by people

[6]Data in this section taken from: *The Hired Farm Working Force of 1970*, Economic Research Service, U.S.D.A. Agricultural Economic Report No. 201, 1971.

whose chief activity is either school or homemaking. Many of those individuals work only a few days per year. However, those who are chiefly
farm workers or migratory workers suffer from the seasonality because they
are unable to find off-season employment to provide them with adequate
incomes.

Migratory farm workers have numbered between 200,000 and 250,000
in recent years, down considerably from 1 million in the 1950s. One-half
of these workers find employment in the South, one-fourth in the northern
states, and one-fourth in the western states. After World War II, foreign
nationals from Mexico, Canada, and the West Indies made up a substantial fraction of the seasonal farm labor force in Texas, California,
Florida, and Michigan. With the expiration of Public Law 78, this "bracero
program" was ended in 1964. Because the foreigners were willing to work
at lower wages than American farm workers, ending the bracero program
caused farm wages to rise somewhat. Along with that rise has come increasing pressure to mechanize fruit and vegetable harvesting, which are
the major sources of employment for migratory workers.

Wages of Hired Farm Workers. For many years, cash-farm wage
rates averaged less than $.25 an hour; they exceeded $.50 an hour for
the first time in 1946. Wages of hired farm workers have been relatively
low in past years because of the large number of farm boys seeking employment and their difficulty in finding nonfarm jobs. Each year, fully twice as

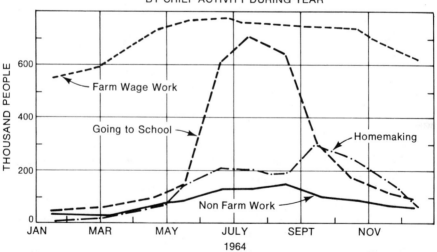

HIRED FARM WORKERS EMPLOYED MONTHLY IN 1964
BY CHIEF ACTIVITY DURING YEAR

Source: *Food and Fiber for the Future*, Report of the National Advisory Commission on
Food and Fiber, 1967, p. 220.

FIGURE 18–4.

many farm boys reach working age on the farms as there are farm jobs released by the retirement and death of older farm men. Typically, farm boys work for a short time on a farm in their home community and then either rent a farm of their own, take over the home farm, or find nonfarm employment and are replaced by the younger boys who are growing up. In this kind of labor market, wages are always depressed, as compared with markets in which laborers must be attracted in increasing numbers and in which the wages must be attractive to mature men throughout their lives.

During the Depression years, 1932 to 1936, average cash-farm wage rates dropped as low as $.11 to $.15 an hour, and even in 1940 the lack of nonfarm jobs kept average cash-farm wages down to $.17 an hour. As labor shortages developed during World War II, farm wage rates rose rapidly, reaching $.58 an hour in 1948. Since then, as nonfarm wages have increased, farm wages have been forced to rise also. As would be expected, in view of the nature of the farm labor market, farm wage rates have fluctuated much more than the hourly earnings of workers in manufacturing industries. From 1914 to date, years for which comparable data are available, the hourly earnings of workers in manufacturing industries have been a little more than double the average or composite cash-farm wage rates (Table 18–2).

TABLE 18–2

Composite Hourly Wages of Hired Farm Workers
and Manufacturing Workers, 1910–70

Period	Farm Workers	Manufacturing Workers
1910–14	.13	
1915–19	.20	
1920–24	.24	.53
1925–29	.24	.55
1930–34	.15	.49
1935–39	.16	.60
1940–44	.28	.84
1945–49	.53	1.22
1950–54	.63	1.66
1955–60	.73	2.05
1961	.99	2.32
1962	1.01	2.39
1963	1.05	2.46
1964	1.08	2.53
1965	1.14	2.61
1966	1.23	2.72
1967	1.33	2.83
1968	1.44	3.01
1969	1.55	3.19
1970	1.63	3.36
1971	1.73	3.56

Source: *Economic Report of the President, 1971*, Government Printing Office, 1971. *1971 Handbook of Agricultural Charts.* Agricultural Handbook No. 423, U.S.D.A., 1971.

A direct comparison of farm and nonfarm wage rates is not entirely valid because of differences in costs of living and in prerequisites furnished farm workers in addition to wages. Real wage differentials are not as great as is suggested by the cash wage differentials in Table 18–2. The difference in wage rates, nevertheless, plus the attraction of shorter hours of work and the social functions in the urban community, causes young people to leave farm employment rapidly when jobs are available in the city.

Hired Labor on the Family Farm. We have already noted that, in terms of numbers, about 10 percent of the hired farm working force has been made up of migrant workers in recent years. In general, these people are not employed on family farms. By far, the largest fraction of those employed on family farms are residents of the local community. What are the forces that determine the quantity of labor hired on the family farm? Most farms employing hired labor throughout the year are dairy or livestock farms. The size of the farm operated in such cases usually requires the labor of one hired man and the farm operator throughout the year, with some extra help provided by other members of the farm family during the cropping season. These are often called two-man farms, in contrast to the typical one-man farms, on which the operator has only the help of his family, none of whom are the equivalent of a full-time worker.

Table 18–3 shows the proportion of farms hiring labor by value of sales. Most farms hire some labor, but the operator and his family provide half or more of the labor used on all farms except those with sales exceeding $100,000. Arbitrarily, one might say that because most of the farms with sales of over $10,000 have hired laborers performing more than 25 percent of the work, they could be classed as two-man farms. Without question, in normal or prosperous years, the two-man farms are the most profitable. The operator

TABLE 18–3

Proportion of Farms Hiring Labor and Proportion of Labor Performed by Family and Hired Labor, 1964 and 1966[1]

| | | Percentage of Total Man-Hours Worked by[2] | |
Value of Sales	Percentage of Farms Hiring Labor	Operator and Family	Hired Workers
$5,000– 9,999	63	81	18
$10,000–19,999	66	78	23
$20,000–39,999	75	66	34
$40,000–99,999	86	47	53
Over $100,000	95	22	78

[1]Average of survey data for 1964 and 1966.
[2]The data are for farms that hired labor.

Source: *Labor Used on U.S. Farms, 1964 and 1966,* Statistical Bulletin No. 456, Economic Research Service, U.S.D.A., 1970, p. 6.

and his family on these larger farms usually have higher net incomes after paying the hired labor than the families on the smaller, one-man farms, for which only a small amount of seasonal labor is hired. While extremely high wage rates could influence farmers to cut back from a two-man to a one-man operation, usually a decision regarding the scale of operations and whether to employ one more hired worker turns on other factors fully as much as on the wage rates.

An important consideration limiting two-man farms is the difficulty many families have in acquiring sufficient land, either by rental or owner-ship, and sufficient operating equipment and livestock to utilize profitably the labor of two full-time men. Shortage of family capital and unwillingness to use credit, or the unwillingness of credit institutions to extend credit on satisfactory terms, is the key factor in many situations. As explained earlier, competition for small farms, for homes, and for self-sufficient farming activities often keeps rental rates and purchase prices of small farms at levels that make it unprofitable for one-man farms to expand their farming operations, particularly in the less-productive farming communities.

In recent years, an important consideration regarding hiring farm labor on a monthly basis has been the difficulty of obtaining steady workers. Rather than run the risks of being without hired help when they are needed, many farmers prefer to adjust the size of their businesses to the amount they can handle with their own labor and that of other members of the family.

Seasonal Hired Labor on Family Farms. Farming has peak labor requirements that grow out of the crop seasons. These requirements cannot be leveled out, either by the use of machinery or by adding supplementary enterprises. Crop farms, such as cotton, potato, wheat, and other cash grain farms, have sharp labor requirement peaks spaced between relatively long periods when little labor is needed. Livestock added to a crop farm provides profitable employment at times when labor would otherwise have no profitable use. Cattle fattening in the winter on Corn Belt farms is one of the best examples of a supplementary livestock enterprise that levels out labor requirements throughout the year. The cattle are often purchased in the fall after the crops have been harvested and are sold in the spring before field work starts.

Dairy farming has relatively uniform labor requirements throughout the year. For the dairy herd, these are highest in the winter months when cows must be housed and fed in the barns. In the spring, summer, and fall, when farm labor is needed in the fields, the cows spend most of their time in the pastures. Yet even in dairy farming, peak seasonal labor require-ments for the total farm operation occur in the spring and fall. In other types of farming, the seasonal peaks are even greater. These seasonal peaks in labor requirements are met by the operator working longer hours, by other members of the family helping, by employing workers for short seasons, and by using labor-saving machinery.

Figure 18–4 shows that most of the seasonal hired labor is made up of youths in school during the rest of the year. In addition, some labor is contributed by older men not otherwise employed, nonfarm workers taking on extra work or who may be temporarily laid off, and others. Seasonal labor is increasingly difficult to obtain, so greater use is being made of women and young people who normally are not part of the farm labor force. Labor-saving machinery also is being used to an increasing extent as a means of meeting the peak labor loads on the farm.

Machine harvesting of corn, small grains, cotton, and other field crops has done much to reduce the need for seasonal harvest labor compared to the 1940s and 1950s. In obtaining such machinery, the farmer has several alternatives to consider. He can buy the equipment outright, he can lease the equipment, or he can consider how much he can profitably change his farm enterprises to reduce peak load. Because the operator and family labor is available throughout the year, many farmers can profitably change their combination of crops and livestock to give themselves and their families fuller employment during the slack seasons of the year and to reduce the seasonal peak labor requirements.

Under practical farm-operating conditions, farmers often purchase labor-saving machinery, even though it raises their production costs in comparison with hiring seasonal labor or hiring a custom machine operator. They justify such purchases on the basis of reducing the uncertainty which is inherent in depending upon custom operations. Crop harvesting must be done within a short time after the crop has reached the harvest stage. If the custom machine operator fails to come on schedule, heavy losses are incurred. Much of the apparent overinvestment in machinery on family farms has occurred because of the operator's desire to remove this uncertainty associated with hiring labor or machines when needed.

Social Problems of the Farm Labor Force

Hired Farm Workers and Rural-urban Migration. Some writers view further mechanization of farming with apprehension, from the standpoint of the economic problems it will create for farm workers. This is particularly true in the South, where mechanization of cotton production and harvesting has been going on rapidly for a number of years.

The hired farm labor market has been a low wage market. Hired farm workers have had low annual incomes, as pointed out earlier, primarily because fully twice as many young men are born and reared on farms as are needed to replace the older men. Mechanization, which further reduces the number of jobs on farms, increases the number who must migrate to nonfarm jobs. There is considerable evidence to indicate that mechanization in recent years primarily replaced labor that had already left the rural community for nonfarm jobs, rather than taking jobs away from local workers. Whatever the cause, we know that off-farm migration has been one of the major social phenomena of the 1950s and 1960s.

Figure 18–5 shows the major streams of migration from rural to urban areas during the late 1950s. Much of the migration came from areas shown as having serious economic problems in Figure 18–3. The metropolitan areas of Chicago, St. Louis, Washington, and New York have attracted people from the rural areas of the Old South. Phoenix, Los Angeles, San Francisco, Dallas, Houston, and St. Petersburg, on the other hand, seem to have attracted their migrants either from rural areas in their own states or from other low-income areas throughout the nation.

Many observers believe that the rapid rate of off-farm migration contributed directly to the urban problems of the 1960s. They argue that unfulfilled employment expectations combined with deteriorating living conditions in the urban ghettos led to far worse conditions than would have existed had the rate of off-farm migration been slower. According to this view, farm technological advance, which created conditions making the replacement of labor possible, not only put the American farmer on a treadmill but pushed American farm workers into urban turmoil.

Social and Economic Problems of Hired Workers' Families. Many farm families accept lower incomes than they could earn as hired farm workers. Studies of farm family earnings in typical farming communities

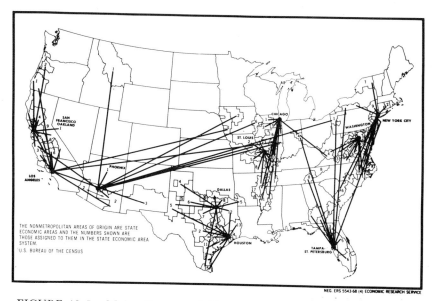

FIGURE 18–5. Major Streams of Nonmetro Migration to Selected Metro Areas, 1955–1960

in different sections of the United States indicate that families on the smaller and less-productive farms have lower incomes than the wages of year-round hired workers on the large, more productive farms in the community. A number of factors contribute to this situation. In some cases, they prefer the lower income to working as regularly as is required when employed by others. Other families keep no records and do not know that they could earn a higher income as hired farm workers.

Probably the most important reasons for renting or buying a small farm of low productivity rather than working as a hired man for another operator is the greater independence, the higher social status, and the greater security a family enjoys. Except in the South, nonmigratory, married, hired farm workers typically are young men who are just getting started. They seldom stay on the same farm or continue as hired farm workers more than a few years. Unless their parents were already well established in the community, these hired workers are relative strangers and have an inferior social position in the community. The housing provided for them by the farm owner is often inadequate and of inferior quality. The relations between farm operator and the hired man involve close, personal, day-to-day association and are subject to the usual difficulties of compatibility. Hired farm workers are often discharged or quit of their own volition as a result of personal disagreements with the farm operators. (A hired worker, however, can legally require the owner to furnish him employment for the duration of his contractual arrangements.) Legal protection and unionization of hired farm workers is just beginning, as we discuss below.

Special Social Problems of Migrant Labor. Most of the social and economic problems of hired farm workers' families outlined in the preceding paragraphs apply to migrant as well as to resident workers. In addition, migrant families have a number of other problems. Adequate housing is perhaps their most serious problem. Moving from community to community as they do, these families are almost wholly at the mercy of their employers and often live in congested camps with inadequate space and health facilities. Because the families will stay in the community for only a few weeks during the year, the employer and the community hardly feel justified in going to considerable expense for housing for migrant workers. As a result, the families move throughout the season, often living wretchedly, yet hoping for better accommodations in the next community.

Often, migrant workers find themselves in strange communities at times of the year when their children should be in school. The children may be kept at work to help increase the family earnings, thus breaking the local school regulations. But to attempt to send these children to school for a few weeks in a strange community places a great burden on the schools. No really satisfactory solution to the school training problem of children in migrant farm worker families has been developed.

Because many of the migrant farm worker families are other than native whites, they often encounter racial barriers in the communities where they go to work. They are looked upon as an inferior group and are segregated from the regular residents. Local residents sometimes object to having migrant workers' families brought into the community. Special problems are created if families become welfare cases because of the illness of workers.

Large fruit and vegetable growers and others who must depend on a large number of seasonal workers to cultivate and harvest their crops in a few weeks of the year want to assure themselves of a labor supply when needed, *but want to be free from any social or economic obligations to the workers* as soon as their short period of employment on the farm has been completed. In many areas, this has led to the development of the labor contractor or crew leader who organizes a crew of migrant workers and contracts with producers to do the work they need done. The contractor or crew leader may be able to arrange six months of employment for a group of workers, whereas any single producer may have only six weeks' work.

Often, the crew leaders make all arrangements for the workers in the community and act as arbitrators in disputes among the workers or between the workers and the farm employers; in short "wet nurse" the workers and their families. In some cases, the crew leader acts as a bonafide contractor, paying the workers hourly wages out of the fees charged the farmer. In other cases, the farmer pays the workers directly, giving the crew leader a commission for his services.

Migrant worker families are in the weakest bargaining position of any group of workers in our economy. They leave their home communities because of lack of employment possibilities. In strange communities without savings, they must accept the wages, working conditions, and housing offered them. Because of their position on the lowest rung of the social ladder, they have little political or economic recourse and have been largely ignored by the rest of society.

Legislation Affecting Farm Labor[7]

Farm workers were especially omitted from Social Security benefits in the early years, primarily because of the administrative difficulties in collecting payroll taxes and because of the large numbers of casual workers in agriculture who work only a short time during the peak seasons of the year.

Soon after the Farm Security Administration was created in 1937, it developed a program for migratory farm workers. An important part of its

---

[7]Data in this section are taken from: G. S. Goodpaster, "Scope of Public Regulation of Farm Labor Conditions," testimony before the House Subcommittee on Agricultural Labor of the Committee on Education and Labor, June 3, 1971.

farm labor program was the construction and operation of migratory farm labor camps. Migratory farm workers were housed in these government-owned camps under much better conditions of comfort and health than had been provided by the employers of migratory labor. During World War II, these camps continued to be operated by the government as a part of its labor supply program. When the wartime farm labor supply program was discontinued, however, the Farmers Home Administration, successor to the Farm Security Administration, was directed by Congress to sell these labor camps to public or semipublic nonprofit associations of farmers in the communities in which they were located. Later legislation permitted the government to maintain ownership of these camps.

More legislation affecting hired farm workers is contained in the Sugar Acts, dating from 1937. Basically, the Sugar Acts as amended provided for government participation in setting production quotas and prices for domestically produced sugar cane and sugar beets. One of the provisions of this legislation is that to be eligible for government benefits, the producers of sugar cane and sugar beets must meet certain minimum standards regarding working conditions and rates of pay for their hired workers.

Hired farm workers were not included in the provisions of Federal minimum wage regulations until 1966. Under that legislation, only employers who hire at least 500 man-days of agricultural labor in any quarter of the preceding calendar year and engaged in interstate commerce (defined as annual gross sales of not less than $250,000) are required to pay minimum wages to their employees.

Farm labor is excluded from compulsory coverage of workman's compensation laws in thirty states, and in two of these—Alabama and Texas—coverage by employers is prohibited. In seven states, farm workers are partially covered while using machinery. Only four states employing significant numbers of farm workers provide full workman's compensation coverage for farm workers. This, in spite of evidence that agriculture is the third most hazardous industry in the nation, following mining and construction. In all states except Hawaii, farm workers are excluded from unemployment compensation coverage.

Farm workers come under the Social Security Act if they receive cash wages of $150 or more from one employer or if they work for an employer for twenty days or more at a time rather than on a piece-rate basis. These limitations act mainly to disadvantage migrant workers, who typically work for very short periods for any one employer.

Those opposed to extending labor legislation to farm workers have argued that the additional bookkeeping would burden small family farmers and that the additional costs involved would reduce farmers' already narrow profits because they are unable to pass on the costs. The first objection might have been valid in the past, but today most farmers hiring labor must keep the same records as any other small business, so the additional amount of bookkeeping is minor. The second objection may be more valid if standards and rates are imposed piecemeal by individual states. However, uniform coverage throughout the country would insure that no specific group of farmers were put at a competitive disadvantage.

It appears that many of the labor abuses have been permitted to continue because the hired farm work force is largely composed of those in the lowest socioeconomic classes, often migrant workers.

Unionization of Farm Workers

Farm workers have been relatively unsuccessful in unionizing to improve their working and living conditions for several interrelated reasons.[8] First, there has always been a large reserve pool of unskilled labor that employers have used to offset potential strikes by unions. The immigration laws of the nineteenth and early twentieth centuries allowed employers to bring workers from other countries. This was the source of Chinese, Japanese, and Filipino workers in the early years, and Mexican and West Indian laborers until 1964.

Until recently, farm labor unions have had to go it alone with little or no support from others. Within the communities affected, sentiments were usually against farm labor unions. Organized labor has traditionally not supported farm labor unions, although in recent years secondary boycotts carried on by certain farm labor unions have been supported by organized labor.

The right of farm workers to organize into unions and engage in collective bargaining has never been recognized or guaranteed. Farm laborers have been excluded from the labor legislation that guarantees other workers the right to join a union and that insists that employers must bargain with unions certified by the National Labor Relations Board (NLRB) as representative. The law does not prohibit farm labor unions; it simply excludes them from the protection given to other groups.

Opposition to unionization of farm labor has focused around the argument that agriculture would be extremely vulnerable to strikes at harvest time—that small family farmers would be forced to give in or lose their entire crop. In addition, because they are price takers, it is argued that farmers would be forced to absorb labor cost increases. It is also argued that any increased labor costs will result in faster mechanization and hence less farm employment.

The last argument is conceded by proponents of unionization. How-

---

[8] D. Pollitt, "History of the Farm Labor Movement in the 20th Century," *Hearings* on HR 5010 before the House Subcommittee on Agricultural Labor of the Committee on Education and Labor, June 3, 1971, p. 71.

ever, they argue that the others are bogus issues. They point out that if in extending labor bargaining legislation to farm workers the NLRB retained its jurisdictional standard of $50,000 in interstate commerce, only 3.5 percent of all farms, hiring 45 percent of the farm labor force, would be covered. They argue that by increasing the labor costs of the largest farms, the small farmer would regain some comparative advantage lost due to scale economies. It is also pointed out that a no-strike clause can be written into contracts and that experience has not revealed any union inclination or desire to strike at harvest time.

Those supporting farm labor unionization are not uniformly in favor of extending current NLRB legislation, however, because it would prohibit secondary boycotts. These actions, by which a union convinces other unions not to handle, process, or sell a product, were extremely useful to the unions in concluding agreements with California grape producers in the late 1960s. In fact, some producers are actively campaigning to extend labor legislation to farm workers in order to obtain protection from such actions.

National Economic Policies Required

Low-income farm families without physical handicaps tend to be underemployed because they have far too little land and capital to employ their labor effectively. Improvement of opportunities within agriculture is limited by the relatively inelastic demand for farm products and by the limited supply of land in the low-income areas. Where opportunities do exist, local credit institutions and the Farmers Home Administratration may provide supervised credit for farm improvement and farm enlargement.

When all is done that can be done within agriculture, however, a large part of the solution to the underemployment of labor in these areas will have to be found in nonfarm employment. Few low-income farm areas have the resource bases needed to attract industries that can appreciably raise their levels of employment and income.

Thus, the poverty problem in agriculture is not one that individual low-income farm families or local areas can solve by themselves. The poverty problem in rural areas, in terms of both causes and possibilities for solution, is part of the nation's general employment and income problem as well as a part of the income problem of agriculture.

Since the end of World War II, the nation's economy has grown at an unprecedented peacetime rate. But the effect of this rate of growth on labor demand in rural areas has little more than kept pace with the growth in the working-age population. *The growth has been far from sufficient to create new jobs for those released by technological progress in industry and on the farms and to permit absorption of the underemployment in the low-income rural areas.*

In view of this inadequate growth trend, it is evident that the poverty problem is not one that can be solved by individual rural families or local areas through their own efforts. Nor is it primarily a farm problem.

It is true that individual families and single communities can do some of the things needed to solve their poverty problem. But some of the very important things needed for the problem's solution can only be done through appropriate national policies. In a modern exchange economy there is no family, no community, and no region whose income and well-being are not affected by what is done or not done in other parts of the economy.

Yet, in spite of the need for a solution to the poverty problem in rural areas, the nonfarm labor markets appear to have become less competitive in recent years. Wages in some industries are increased by collective bargaining even though there is substantial unemployment in the industry or in other closely related parts of the economy. Wage rates in industries are often maintained and the hiring of additional workers limited even though there is a surplus of labor in relation to employment opportunities in the community. Wage rates have tended to become institutionalized in this way, limiting the ability of nonfarm labor markets to absorb the underemployment from rural areas. Is it not possible that even with fairly rapid economic growth in the nation as a whole, with declining competition in the nonfarm labor market, that underemployment will continue to grow in agriculture?

Given less than full-employment conditions in the nation's economy, agriculture in general, and its lower income areas in particular, will continue to bear an unduly large part of the nation's underemployment. Given full employment, in view of developments to date, if the community-wide rural poverty problem is to be solved, there will be required a four-pronged attack: (1) improvement of educational and health facilities in these areas; (2) encouragement of industrial development in these areas; (3) policies to facilitate migration; and (4) policies to encourage farm improvement and enlargement for those families continuing in agriculture.

Poverty Problem a Dilemma for Farm Leaders

Underlying the lack of progress and the absence of widespread concern about the rural poverty problem are two sets of conditions. First, the low-income areas in Figure 18–3, and especially the lower-income families living in these areas, have few spokesmen in group meetings and in the legislative halls. The low-income rural people have little political power. Second, there is a widespread belief that our educational facilities and private enterprise system give all people, including all rural families, equal opportunities in the economy. There is a widespread belief that the Coxes and the Johnsons have no one but themselves to blame if they continue to live on small, run-down farms and get little reward for long hours of work.

Farm leaders are faced with a dilemma in this regard. Because low-income farm families are in a minority in general farm organizations and in most organized rural groups, how much time and effort should be devoted to a solution of their problems? The dilemma is even greater than this. An ample number of small tenants, sharecroppers, and small farm owners in a community assures the larger landowners in the community that they will have an ample supply of local labor for seasonal hire at "reasonable" rates. Programs and policies that drain off the underemployed workers in these rural communities increase the larger farmers' problems.

There also is the consideration that solutions to problems that are peculiar to low-income families and poverty areas, that is, increased school facilities and improved and expanded educational programs, usually require financial assistance from the rest society. These conflicts of interest create a serious dilemma for farm leadership in seeking solutions to the poverty problem in agriculture. Is it surprising that farm leaders have devoted most of their time and energy to finding solutions for the problems of commercial farmers? Is it also not likely that the rural poverty problem will continue to be of our most serious economic and social problems for *at least* the next decade?

POINTS FOR DISCUSSION

1. How many families in rural and urban areas were below the poverty threshold last year?
2. To what extent is the poverty problem in the United States located in rural areas?
3. What historic and cultural factors tended to create community-wide poverty in the South?
4. What factors tended to create farm areas of low income in other parts of the United States?
5. In what way is the rural poverty problem a part of the nation's general employment and income problem?
6. Why are so few of the workers in agriculture hired (as compared with other industries)?
7. To what extent do farmers use economic analysis in determining the amount of labor hired?
8. Why have farm workers been excluded from most social welfare legislation for urban workers?
9. Do the farmers in your state employ migratory workers? If so, what, if any, state legislation do you have for the protection of their health and welfare?

REFERENCES

Development of Agriculture's Human Resources, a Report by the Secretary of Agriculture, U.S.D.A. (April 1955).

The Economic and Social Conditions of Rural America in the 1970's. Prepared by the Economic Development Division, Economic Research Service, U.S.D.A., for the Committee on Government Operations, United States Senate, 92nd Cong., 1st Sess., May 1971.

"THE HIRED FARM WORKING FORCE." *Annual Reports,* Economic Research Service, U.S.D.A.

"LABOR USED ON U.S. FARMS, 1964 AND 1966," *Statistical Bulletin No. 456.* Economic Research Service, U.S.D.A. (1970).

"POVERTY IN RURAL AREAS OF THE UNITED STATES," *Agricultural Economic Report No. 63,* Economic Research Service, U.S.D.A. (November 1964).

"THE RURAL DEVELOPMENT PROGRAM," *Farm Policy Forum.* Summer 1958.

Seminar on Farm Labor Problems. Hearings before the Subcommittee on Agricultural Labor of the Committee on Education and Labor, House of Representatives, 92nd Cong., 1st Sess., Government Printing Office, June 1971.

WILCOX, WALTER W. *Social Responsibility in Farm Leadership,* Chap. 6. New York: Harper & Row, 1956.

Chapter 19

Agriculture's Use of Land

and Water Resources

Land Ownership and Control[1]

Although, as we discussed in the previous chapter, people are the central concern of economic analysis of agriculture, land is the resource that gives agriculture its distinctive nature. It is the factor that distinguishes farming, on however large and mechanized a scale, from other industrial activities. And regardless of how rapidly technology advances, it is difficult to conceive of producing the bulk of the food requirements of the nation without having farms spread over the land.

Of the 2.3 billion acres of land in the 50 states, 80 percent is either used in the production of crops and livestock or devoted to forests (Figure 19–1). Three percent is in urban and transportation uses. The other is made up of 5 percent in recreational uses, parks, refuges, and other public installations including military uses, with the balance of 12 percent unusable desert or tundra. Fifty-nine percent of the land is privately owned, 2 percent is owned by Indian tribes, and the remaining 39 percent is owned by federal, state, or local governments.

The distribution of private land ownership is important for our examination of the economics of American agriculture because the owners of agricultural land are the receivers of agricultural income. Water resources are often attached to certain land, and thus are naturally studied

[1]The data for the following review of farm land ownership is from the excellent review, "Land Tenure in the United States: Development and Status," *Agricultural Information Bulletin No. 538*, U.S. Department of Agriculture, Economic Research Service, June 1969.

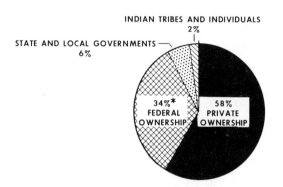

LAND OWNERSHIP IN THE 50 STATES, 1969

INDIAN TRIBES AND INDIVIDUALS
2%

STATE AND LOCAL GOVERNMENTS
6%

34%*
FEDERAL
OWNERSHIP

58%
PRIVATE
OWNERSHIP

TOTAL AREA 2.3 BIL. ACRES

*94 PERCENT IS IN THE ELEVEN WESTERN-MOST STATES AND ALASKA.
ABOUT 50 PERCENT IS IN ALASKA.

U.S. DEPARTMENT OF AGRICULTURE   NEG. ERS 8433-72 (8)   ECONOMIC RESEARCH SERVICE

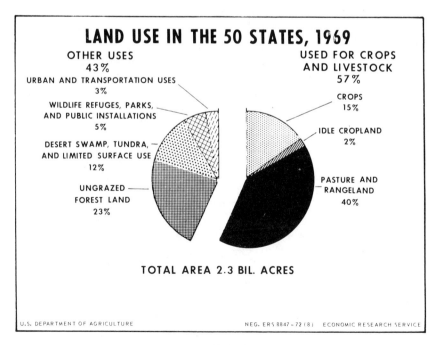

LAND USE IN THE 50 STATES, 1969

OTHER USES
43%

URBAN AND TRANSPORTATION USES
3%

WILDLIFE REFUGES, PARKS,
AND PUBLIC INSTALLATIONS
5%

DESERT SWAMP, TUNDRA,
AND LIMITED SURFACE USE
12%

UNGRAZED
FOREST LAND
23%

USED FOR CROPS
AND LIVESTOCK
57%

CROPS
15%

IDLE CROPLAND
2%

PASTURE AND
RANGELAND
40%

TOTAL AREA 2.3 BIL. ACRES

U.S. DEPARTMENT OF AGRICULTURE   NEG. ERS 8847-72 (8)   ECONOMIC RESEARCH SERVICE

FIGURE 19–1.

in conjunction with land. Adjustments in the relationships among people controlling and using land mean adjustment in the allocation of agricultural income among those people. Because many farmers continue to have inadequate incomes, it is of interest to examine the ownership of land. Over time, land prices affect ownership. Land prices have undergone a long period of upward movement in the United States, and because technology now permits one man to farm more land, thus creating pressures for larger farms, individual farmers are finding it increasingly difficult to purchase enough land to provide adequate incomes. One result is an increasing importance of part owners who rent a portion of the land they farm. These and other trends are examined in this chapter.

Ownership of land by the farmer operating it is highly valued in the United States. As early as the days of Thomas Jefferson, small farm owners were considered the most precious part of a state. This has resulted in a high value being placed on the "family farm." All political parties have shared this support of family farming, and in 1972 family farming was given explicit support in the rural development act passed that year. This explicit support reflects the long-held view that ownership of family farms is essential to the preservation of the democratic way of life in rural America, and is therefore to be encouraged.[2]

The wide acceptance of this point of view throughout the past 250 years has resulted in the passage of a number of acts designed to promote family farm ownership. Among these are the Homestead Act of 1862, the Reclamation Act of 1902, the Federal Farm Loan Act of 1916, and the Bankhead-Jones Farm Tenant Act of 1937. Early national leaders in the United States, holding the favorable views toward family farm ownership stated above, insisted on easy terms. Later, outright gifts in 160-acre units were provided under the homestead laws. In view of these land sale and settlement policies, it was a shock to learn that, in 1880 when the question was first asked by census takers, 26 percent of the farms in the United States were operated by tenants. At that time, as now, farm tenancy was highest in the southern states.

There have been several notable shifts in the distribution of land among various types of operators as indicated by the data in Table 19–1. In this table and the following discussion, *full owners* are individuals who operate only land in which they have an equity interest—that is, they operate no rented land. (Note that full owner status does not necessarily imply that the farm is free of a mortgage.) *Part owners* are individuals

TABLE 19–1

Percentage Distribution of Farms and Land in Farms,
by Tenure of Operator, United States, 1900–1964

Item	Total	Full Owners	Part Owners	Managers	Tenants
	Percent	Percent	Percent	Percent	Percent
1969: Farms......	100.0	62.5	24.6	a	12.9
Land	100.0	35.3	51.8	a	12.9
1964: Farms......	100.0	57.6	24.8	0.6	17.1
Land	100.0	28.7	48.0	10.2	13.1
1959: Farms......	100.0	57.1	22.5	0.6	19.8
Land	100.0	30.9	44.9	9.6	14.5
1954: Farms......	100.0	57.4	18.2	0.4	24.0
Land	100.0	34.2	40.7	8.6	16.4
1950: Farms......	100.0	57.4	15.3	0.4	26.8
Land	100.0	36.2	36.5	9.1	18.3
1945: Farms......	100.0	56.3	11.3	0.7	31.7
Land	100.0	36.1	32.5	9.3	22.0
1940: Farms......	100.0	50.6	10.1	0.6	38.7
Land	100.0	36.0	28.3	6.3	29.4
1935: Farms......	100.0	47.1	10.1	0.7	42.1
Land	100.0	37.1	25.2	5.8	31.9
1930: Farms......	100.0	46.3	10.4	0.9	42.4
Land	100.0	37.7	24.9	6.3	31.1
1920: Farms......	100.0	52.2	8.7	1.1	38.1
Land	100.0	48.3	18.4	5.7	27.7
1910: Farms......	100.0	52.7	9.3	0.9	37.0
Land	100.0	52.9	15.2	6.1	25.8
1900: Farms......	100.0	55.8	7.9	1.0	35.3
Land	100.0	51.4	14.9	10.4	23.3

aFarms operated by managers appear as full-owner farms in the 1969 Census.

Source: *1964 Census of Agriculture*, Census Bureau, U.S. Dept. of Commerce, Vol. 2, Chap. 8, tables 5 and 6, and data provided by U.S.D.A. from 1969 Census of Agriculture.

who operate a farm unit that is made up of partly owned and partly rented land. *Managers* operate land for someone else in exchange for wages, and *tenants* rent all the land they farm.

Historically, the rate of tenancy has been high in the West-North-central States as well as in the South. In contrast, tenancy was low in New England in 1880 and has declined still further since then. Obviously, differences in the land resources, the kind of farming followed, and the ratio of people to the land affects the percentage of tenancy in each area. Tenancy tends to be highest in the areas of highest land values and in commercial agricultural areas where the ratio of population to the land is high. In contrast, farm ownership is highest in the self-sufficing farming areas and in the less-productive parts of the commercial farming areas. An overall trend toward more rented farms was in process from 1880 to 1935. Since 1935, the trend has been downward again. In 1964, tenants made up 17 percent of the farmers and operated 13 percent of the farm land.

Part-owner status has been increasing in importance over the entire period. In 1900, only 8 percent of the farms were operated by owners who added land by renting from others. This proportion remained rather constant until about 1935. Since then, it has grown until by 1969, 25 percent was operated by part owners. Those part owners operated almost 50 percent of the total U.S. farm land and thus had farms of considerably above-average size.

Full owners operated more than half of our farms until the 1930s when the proportion of owners dropped to 46 percent. The high prices brought about by World War II reversed this trend and by 1945 full owners had increased to 56 percent and have retained that percentage ever since. The proportion of total farm land operated by full owners has declined however. In 1964, the 57.6 percent of farmers who were full owners operated 28.7 percent of the farm land. Full owners operate a less-than-proportional number of the farms in gross income Classes I, II, and III and a more-than-proportional number of noncommercial farms.

Manager-operated farms have always represented a small fraction of the total number of farms. They include institutionally owned units operated as commercial farms as well as units operated for special, noncommercial purposes. The average size of manager-operated units is very large. They have recorded a threefold increase in average value of land and buildings, from $128,221 in 1950 to $564,998 in 1964. A similar increase in value of farm products sold was recorded. Table 19–2 shows how the manager-operated farms compared to the other types in 1964. In examining these data, one should remember that different types of farms may produce different products and may be concentrated in dif-

TABLE 19–2

Characteristics of Commercial Farms by Tenure of Operator,
United States, 1964

Item	Unit	Full Owners	Part Owners	Tenants	Managers
Number	1000	1020	676	455	15
Average size	acre	246	761	302	4146
Average value	$1000	41.3	92.2	61.5	565.0
Value of sales per farm	$	11,243	20,590	14,338	163,117
Percent with tractors	%	83.7	95.6	77.2	92.3
Percent with combines	%	26.0	48.9	37.7	28.5
Percent with telephone	%	78.4	85.5	65.0	89.0
Percent with motortruck	%	70.1	87.9	65.5	89.8

Source: "Land Tenure in the United States: Development and Status," *Agricultural Information Bulletin No. 338*, U.S. Department of Agriculture, ERS, June 1969, pp. 367.

ferent areas of the country so that direct comparisons can be somewhat misleading. However, the differences are interesting simply to define the units.

The average manager-operated farms had nearly six times as many acres as the average part-owner farms, which in turn averaged more than twice the acreage of the average tenant farms. Tenants had slightly larger farms than full owners. This ranking holds for the other two measures of size as well—average value of the farm and value of sales per farm. Thus in 1964, full owners had fewer acres, less sales, and lower-valued farms than even tenants. And this tabulation includes only the commercial farms— those whose operators worked less than 100 days at off-farm jobs or who sold more than $2500 worth of farm products.

Tractors are owned by 95 percent of the part owners, 92 percent of the manager-operated farms, 84 percent of the full owners, and 77 percent of the tenants. The related proportions of the four types of farms with combines, trucks, and telephones is similar, with the part owners and the managers in better resource positions than either full owners or tenants. These data indicate that as a group full owners are clearly behind part owners and tenants with respect to capital resources. Tenants are behind the other classes, but their economic positions have improved as written leases, longer-term occupancy, and other reforms have taken hold.

Land Rental

Functions of Land Rental. Tenancy and land rental perform a very useful role in a capitalistic society in which individuals purchase and sell land on almost the same terms as other commodities. The advantages of being able to rent land to expand the size of an existing farm unit lies largely in the smaller debt for a given size of operating unit. Often, this additional land is rented from an older neighbor who wishes to discontinue his active farm work, but to contnue living on the farm. In 1964, there were 800,000 part owners, or about 25 percent of all farms enumerated in the United States. This part-owner group is classified with the full owners when computing the percentage of farms operated by owners and tenants. Tenancy, the practice of renting farm real estate, permits families with limited assets to obtain the use of productive farms that they would be unable to acquire by purchase. Conversely, it permits the land owner to obtain an income from the farm without working the farm himself, or without hiring the necessary labor to do the farm work. *Without tenancy, a larger proportion of our farm population would be hired workers and a large proportion of our farm owners would be heavily in debt.* Farm owners might let their farms remain idle or operate them at only part capacity in the later years of their life if they could not rent them to others.

Undesirable Aspects of Tenancy. The undesirable aspects of farm tenancy largely grow out of the peculiar conditions under which tenancy has been practiced in the United States. In all sections, farming practices have been of an exploitive character as a result of our virgin soil resources. In the South, they have been greatly influenced by the high ratio of people to the farm land and the low level of education generally achieved. The high mobility of the American people is another influence giving American tenancy some undesirable features.

Keeping in mind these underlying influences, we may examine the undesirable aspects of tenancy from the standpoint of the landlord's relations to the land, the tenant's farming practices, and the effect of tenancy on community development. The landlord is usually a retired farmer, a widow, or a business or professional man. These individuals may live in the community in which the farm is located, or they may live long distances away. If they do not see their farms frequently, they often lack interest in making the capital investments needed to permit tenants to develop efficient farming programs. Regardless of where they are living, they may not have as much interest in maintaining the land and in making improvements as owner-operators who live on their farms.

Tenants' farming practices are greatly influenced by their rental arrangements and by their expectations as to the length of time they will remain on the farm. Farm account records in the better farming areas of the Corn Belt show that tenants usually operate larger farms than owners in these areas; often, the rented farms are the better, more highly productive farms in the community. After adjusting for differences in personal capital invested, tenants often earn higher incomes than owners in the same community, largely because they are farming the larger, more productive farms.

But if one takes into account the poorer farms that are rented and the poorer tenants, as well as the better tenants, in the typical farming community of the United States, one concludes that tenants' farming practices are not as efficient as those of owner-operators. There are many individual exceptions to this generalization. Good tenant farmers, renting from up-to-date landlords who have a commercial farm management company managing the property for them, may excel most of the owner-operators in the community in both their cropping practices and their livestock program.

Yet, there are two basic reasons why, on the average, we may expect inferior farming practices on most rented farms. Most important is the tenant's expectation as to occupancy. He may stay on the same farm twenty years, but if he expects that each year may be his last one, he fails to seed legumes, cut the weeds, and do many other jobs that he would do if he were sure of staying on the farm long enough to get the full benefits. His livestock program is also under a cloud of uncertainty. He may have to move any year and the buildings on the next farm may be inadequate for a good herd of livestock. Tenants do not have the same incentives as owners for building up highly productive livestock herds.

A second reason for the poorer farming practices of tenants, taken as a group, as compared with owners, is the superior management qualifications of the owners. Tenancy is but a step toward ownership for many farm families. Tenant families are typically either young and relatively inexperienced or, if older, they are often below average in ability.

Community institutions suffer in areas where there is a high percentage of tenancy primarily because the tenant families move so frequently that they have little interest in building up local community services. Farm owners who do not live in the community often have more interests in keeping their taxes low than in improving such community services as the schools.

Part ownership does not suffer from these undesirable aspects of tenancy. Farmers who own a portion of the land they operate have the same incentive to keep up their land as do full owners. They also have a strong incentive to operate rented land on a continuously productive basis for several reasons. First, the availability of rental land within a convenient distance to the home farm is likely to be limited. Long-distance travel is impractical unless the rented unit is large enough to be operated as a separate farm, which is seldom the case. Part owners have permanent ties and interests equal to those of full owners in community facilities, so they take an interest in all aspects of rural life. Because of these factors, part owners are likely to want to continue renting a given piece of land and hence are likely to be more concerned with sustained productivity than are tenants.

The part owner is in a considerably stronger economic position in renting land than is a tenant. He is normally a better manager, has some equity interest that makes him a better credit risk, and is known in the community. His superior managerial ability and capital resources allow him to produce more than a tenant and thus he can afford to pay higher rent.

Need for More Landlord Management. Many, but not all, of the present evils of tenancy in the United States could be eliminated by good management on the part of the landlords. Tenants cannot be expected to take a long-run interest in the farms when they operate them under relatively short leases. But the landlords, in their own economic interests, should place restrictions in the leases requiring tenants to follow good rotations and approved soil conservation practices. Similarly, it is in the landowners' long-run economic interest to keep buildings in a good state of repair and to make additions to the buildings as necessary to house the livestock and machinery required for profitable farming.

An increasing number of such landowners are hiring managers on a fee basis to supervise their farms, especially in the Midwest. A large number of individuals and firms in that section specialize in managing farm properties for absentee owners. The services provided by these management companies include selection of tenants, drawing up a desirable lease, planning the farming program, advising on repairs and the improvements on the property, and collecting the rent.

Management companies specializing in this field keep up to date on the newer farm practices and advise the tenants on improving theirs. (Most of the farm properties managed by commercial farm managers are rented on the crop- or livestock-share basis.) Commercial farm managers charge fees based on the services they render. A rather standard practice is to charge 10 percent of the gross rental income for managing a farm leased to a tenant on a share rental basis, with extra fees charged for supervising the construction of new buildings or for other extra responsibilities. The landowner finds it profitable to hire a farm management company because it usually is able to find superior tenants and, by working with the tenants, it gets a superior job of farming done. The farm itself gets more attention from a company than the landowner has time to give it. Many of the evils of tenancy that are due to the landlord are corrected under the supervision of a good farm management company.

Need for Improvements in Leases. Many renters still lease their farms on a verbal basis, without benefit of a written contract. If misunderstandings arise and the issues are taken to court, they are settled on the basis of the existing state laws, or, if there are no state laws covering the issue, on the basis of common law. Verbal leases often do give rise to misunderstandings. But even more important, they result in a minimum of interest on the parts of tenant and landlord in the long-term productivity of the farm.

Landlords and tenants, to an increasing extent, are adopting the practice of signing a written rental agreement. The written lease is a memorandum of agreement in which the landlord agrees to perform certain functions and agrees that the tenant shall have certain rights in the use of the farm for a specified length of time. Among the requirements on the part of the tenant, the following are the most common:

1. That he will not sublet any portion of the farm without the landlord's permission.
2. That he will not damage the farm nor commit waste.
3. That he will yield possession of the farm at the end of the tenancy.
4. That he will operate the farm in a good workmanlike manner.
5. That he will cut noxious weeds as required by state law.
6. That he will use the buildings in conformity with specifications of fire insurance companies (for example, not keep gasoline or a tractor in a hay barn).

A short-term lease is preferred by many landlords and tenants because of the greater flexibility it gives them as compared with longer-term leases. An excellent compromise, one finding increasing favor, is the use of an automatic renewal clause in the one-year lease. Under a lease including such provision, the agreement remains in effect from year to year, unless notice of termination is given four to six months before the end of the lease year. This provision assures the tenant that he can continue leasing the farm as long as both parties are satisfied and that, unless notice is given before the specified time, he is expected to and can legally stay for the following year.

Fair Land Rental Rates. There are, from time to time, attempts to determine "fair rental rates" for land. It is often assumed that the rental is fair if the landlord gets a return equal to what he could obtain from some other investment, plus depreciation on the buildings, and the tenant gets interest and depreciation on his machinery and equipment, plus going wages for the unpaid labor. But this approach fails to recognize the essential nature of the rental rate.

The rent paid for the use of real estate is a price comparable in most respects to prices paid for other resources. If we ask the fair price of a dairy cow or a used tractor, we are told immediately that it depends on supply and demand. In the case of farms for rent, the supply of farms for rent varies with the economic advantage of owning farms for rental. Thus, if rental rates are high, relative to real estate prices, landowners rent their farms rather than sell them, and vice versa. Demand varies both with the profitability of farming and with the number of tenants wanting to rent farms. When farm prices are high and many families are in the market to rent farms, rents are bid up. However, if farm prices are high, but non-farm job opportunities are attracting many of the rural people into the cities, rental rates may not rise in the same proportion as the prices of farm products. Similarly, even though farm prices and farm incomes are relatively low, if there is unemployment in industrial centers the competition for farms to rent may cause prospective tenants to pay disproportionately high rents in order to get farms to operate until other job opportunities become available.

Share rental rates change far more slowly than cash rental rates. Within any community, the rental share of the crops or livestock products tends to be the same, regardless of the productivity of the farm. This share continues on the same basis from year to year, with very little change due to changes in the demand for farms to rent. Under these circumstances, how does a tenant bargain for a farm, or a landlord for a renter?

What we find in the share rental market is competition among tenants for the best farm at the established share rental rate Conversely, landlords compete with each other for tenants at the going rental rates.

The owner of a better-than-average farm can attract a better-than-average tenant. He is a poor businessman if he is satisfied with less. The tenant with good equipment and a reputation as a good farmer can have his pick of several of the best farms available for rent. In addition to this competition of tenants and landlords, each attempting to get the best farm or the best tenant available at prevailing share rental rates, there may be some bargaining on the cash rental charges for pasture, hay land, and buildings and the sharing of expenses for fertilizer, combining, and so forth. This is especially true when farms are rented for a share of the main crops, such as corn, small grain, and soybeans and when a cash rental charge is made for the hay land, pasture, and buildings. Competition takes the form of bidding higher or lower on the cash rentals associated with the fixed share of the crops.

It is only when demand gets badly out of adjustment with the supply that changes are made in prevailing rental shares. As pointed out earlier, there is a tendency for rental rates to lag on both the upswing and the downturn of economic activity. But if one views rental rates as the competitive price for the use of these resources, he will avoid the futility of trying to determine "fair rates" in an ever-changing market.

Elements of the Family Farm Transfer Problem

In recent years, more and more attention is being directed toward facilitating the transfer of the family farm to one of the children. Families run into difficulties from several sources. In the first place, the young people are ready to go into farming for themselves before their parents are ready to retire. A farm couple with children born when they are between the ages of 22 and 36 will have children ready to start farming for themselves when the parents are 44 to 58 years of age. Assuming that the son or son-in-law is married at 23 and is willing to work with the father on a partnership basis for five years, the young couple will be ready for a farm of their own when the father is 50 to 54. Yet, it is estimated that only 12 percent of the farm owners retire before the age of 55. Although there has been some tendency toward earlier retirement in industry, a trend toward later retirement has been observed among farmers.

Among the reasons for the later retirement of farm owners in recent years are the rising living standards that require more cash expenditures, the longer life span of individuals, and use of modern machinery that lightens the hard physical labor of farming and permits farmers to operate their farms at older ages. Older farm operators now often rent out a part of their land or hire field work done on a custom basis without actually retiring and turning the farm over to another operator. Older families often are forced to do this because of the loss of income they would suffer should they fully retire. Most farms are not large enough to furnish a living at modern standards for both the retired family and the young family that would like to acquire the farm. By the time the older family is ready or is forced to retire, the children are established on some other farm or in some other business and prefer not to move.

The declining number of full-time, commercial family farms further complicates the problem. Not only do the young people in the family desire a farm of their own before their parents are ready to give up theirs, but many of the farms are not large enough for an economic family unit if modern machinery is used. For every three farms vacated by older people in many communities, only one or two young families can obtain economic farming units.

Adequate Size of Farm Essential. Many of the conditions that have led to the relatively small number of farm transfers within the family are conditions associated with economic progress. We can expect these same dynamic conditions to continue to limit the number of farm transfers within families in the years ahead. Yet, the improvements in living and working conditions on farms, relative to the improvements in urban centers in the last twenty years, have greatly increased the incentive for the children reared on the larger, more productive farms to continue in farming. On these farms, plans can be adopted, without hardship to either family, that would permit an early transfer of farming operations and of a part interest in the farm itself to the younger family. Unless a farm is large enough to furnish productive employment for approximately two men, income difficulties would be serious.

The family cycle and its relation to the size of farm needed for economic utilization of labor is of interest. We can assume a son is ready to work full time at home at the age of 20, when the father is 45. During the next ten years, the father-son partnership can operate approximately a full two-man farm. As the father gets older and his labor contribution declines, the son's children reach working age and take over a part of their grandfather's duties. It may be necessary to hire extra labor for a few years if the family cycle does not fully match the labor needs of the farm. There is more likelihood, however, of an excess of family labor on this two-man farm at certain stages in the family cycle than of the need for hired labor. A normal farm family, with one to three sons, has a peak labor supply when the operator is 35 to 45 years of age and his boys are 13 to 23 years of age.

If family plans for keeping the farm in the family are successful, they must include provision for other children, as well as for the one that will take over the farm. From the standpoint of age, unless the children were born after the parents were past 35, the youngest rather than the oldest son is more likely to be ready to take over the farm when parents are ready to retire. Thus, parents might well make plans for their older children to take over other farms or go into other occupations.

Written Contracts for Farm Transfer Desirable. As pointed out earlier, the really difficult economic problems in transferring the farm within the family involve making a modest income from an average farm cover the needs of both a young, growing family and the older, retiring family. If the farm is sufficiently large and productive to give the son's family a good income (with opportunities for savings) on a full rental basis, and if the rental income is sufficient for the living needs of the parents, early contractual arrangements for transfer of the farm are necessary. No sacrifice of current income is involved for the son's family and, at the time of the parents' death, they may buy out the other heirs if they wish. It is indeed a happy family situation when these conditions exist, but even under these conditions it is usually preferable that the parents arrange in their will for the farm to go to the son (or son-in-law) who has been operating it. The other children can be provided for in the will by having the one who inherits the farm pay them some share of its fair appraised value. If the son or son-in-law on the farm has increased the farm's value during the time it was under his management, this should be recognized appropriately in the will.

The son or son-in-law who expects favored treatment by the parents in the disposal of their property is often disappointed. Parents often change their minds regarding verbal promises, or merely forget to put them in their will. Other members of the family do not recognize the special services that the family on the home farm have rendered to their parents or to the farm. They insist on an equal division of the inheritance under the prevailing laws of the state. If the members of a family on the home farm had expected compensation for past services out of the estate, without a written contract they are likely to be disappointed.

The Rising Value of Land. An important factor influencing land transfers is the rising value of land. As the value of farm land increases, if the earning power of the land does not keep up with its value it becomes increasingly difficult to transfer the farm. That is, if the prospective buyer cannot earn enough farm income to buy up the shares belonging to the other heirs, a satisfactory transfer of the farm cannot take place. There is much controversy about the causes of changes in farm land values, with some arguing that nonfarm demands for land exert the primary influence on land values and others arguing that the demand for farm uses of land combined with agricultural prices and income-support programs is the major cause of the increase.[3]

---

[3]Two of the authors analyzed this issue several years ago, with some interesting results, but the nature of the available data made it impossible to disentangle the relative weights of urbanization and farm-related causes. See: R. W. Herdt and W. W. Cochrane, "Farm Land Prices and Farm Technological Advance," *Journal of Farm Economics*, Vol. 48, May 1966.

Between 1959 and 1969, approximately 2 million acres of rural land per year moved into nonagricultural uses. Figure 19–2 shows that half of this went into extensive uses, largely for recreation and refuge areas. Urbanization took one-fourth, with highways and airports using less than 10 percent. During that period, the average value of farmland increased by about 25 percent. In fact, as shown by the data in Table 19–3, the

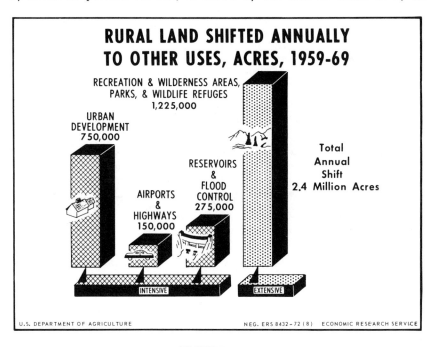

FIGURE 19–2.

TABLE 19–3

Average Farm Land Value, Farm Income per Acre

Time Period	Value of Land and Buildings per Acre	Net Farm Income per Acre	Ratio of Value per Acre to Income per Acre
1910–20	50	8.76	5.7
1921–25	55	8.23	6.6
1926–30	48	4.50	10.7
1931–35	32	3.05	10.5
1936–40	32	4.44	7.2
1941–45	43	9.12	4.7
1946–50	66	12.86	5.1
1951–55	85	11.76	7.2
1956–60	109	10.68	10.2
1961–65	131	12.05	10.8
1966–70	174	14.42	12.1

Source: *Farm Income Situation*, Economic Research Service, U.S.D.A., July 1971.

average value of farmland relative to the net income earned per acre of farmland has increased steadily since the 1941–45 period. In 1910–20, the value of land was 5.7 times its earning power. As land values increased in the 1920s, the ratio increased slightly. In the Great Depression, land values fell, but farm income fell even more rapidly, pushing the ratio over 10. As net farm income per acre increased during and after World War II, the earning power of land increased relative to its value, but beginning about 1950 land prices have increased more rapidly than income per acre. This steady increase has compounded the farm transfer problem.

Adequacy of Land Resource for Farm Production

Regardless of its impact on land prices, the urbanization process does not seem to pose any immediate threat to the availability of adequate land for agricultural production. A 1965 study of the nonurban, nonfederal land in the United States found 638 million acres of land suitable for regular cultivation.[4] Another 169 million acres were found to be suitable for intermittent ·cultivation. Because only about 300 million acres are presently being cropped, it is apparent that no absolute shortage of good agricultural land will occur in the near future. Of the 338 million suitable but uncultivated acres, about 75 million could be converted to crop production with relatively little investment.

Many of the acres potentially suitable for cultivation, but now in either grassland (113 million a.) or trees (125 million a.), would require substantial investment in clearing, draining, or other improvements in order to make them suitable for cultivation. Most of the uncultivated but suitable land is located in the Southeast, Mississippi Delta, and Appalachian regions, distant from markets and transportation facilities. At present farm commodity prices, it is simply not economic to convert very much of this land to agricultural production, but it provides a national resource reserve for the future.

Water Resource Use by Agriculture

Irrigation of agricultural land has nearly doubled since 1939, so that agriculture is the nation's biggest user of water. As is apparent from Figure 19–3, the bulk of the irrigated land is in the seventeen western states. Contrary to much popular opinion, as recently as 1957, 90 percent of the irrigated land in those states was the result of private enterprise. Yet, public irrigation projects have been increasing in importance at an accelerated rate in recent years.

[4]*Food and Fiber for the Future*, Report of the National Commission on Food and Fiber, July 1967, p. 245.

The federal government's active participation in irrigation development began with the passage of the Reclamation Act of 1902. It was intended that these projects be self-liquidating and that they give first preference to settlers who had abandoned dry land farms and to other families in need. A maximum limit of 160 acres was placed on the size of farm one settler could purchase in a federal irrigation district. During the 1930s, emphasis was placed on accomodating as many families as possible on irrigation projects, yet giving them an opportunity to earn a satisfactory minimum income. Administrative procedures effectively restricted the size of farms on many reclamation projects below the limit set by Congress. On the other hand, in a few cases, Congress has set aside the 160 acre limitation. With the general trend toward larger farms and the increase in reclamation projects, there has been increasing pressure in recent years to remove the 160 acre limitation adopted in 1902. Thus far, however, the demand for smaller units has been so great that the advocates of removing the size limitation have been unsuccessful.

Issues in New Reclamation Projects. Proposals for rapidly increasing the acreage of irrigated land in the West by government reclamation projects (especially the projects involving interbasin transfer of water) should receive careful review because they add to total production and

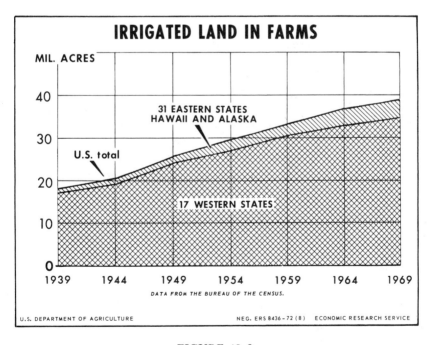

FIGURE 19–3.

lower farm prices and because the projects are seldom self-liquidating, thus increasing government taxes. Though much of the present irrigated acreage in the West is devoted to vegetables, fruits, and cash crops such as sugar beets, dry beans and potatoes, most of the additional acreages proposed to be brought under irrigation will be used primarily to produce feed crops for livestock, in direct competition with feed and livestock production in other sections of the country. The question has been raised: "Should the government invest large sums to bring additional lands under irrigation when farmers, under government programs, are attempting to limit the production of the basic crops?"

The inherent inconsistency of the government on the one hand trying to reduce farm production to obtain higher farm prices and on the other engaging in land reclamation and irrigation to increase farm production has been recognized by many. One analysis of costs and benefits of reclamation projects that takes into account the subsidized prices received by farmers concludes that the direct costs involved in the proposed new interbasin water transfer projects are far higher than the direct benefits. The value of water under hypothetical free market prices ranged from $6 to $18 per acre foot, while its cost was over $50 per acre foot. Even considering additional indirect benefits of up to $10 per acre foot, the cost was far in excess of possible benefits.[5]

Such projects, if built, not only impose a burden on the general taxpayer but also serve to change the location of production over the long run. By subsidizing producers located on irrigated land more than producers outside reclamation areas, the projects put the "outside" producers at a competitive disadvantage. The disadvantage may eventually encourage them to switch to production of another crop. The area served by reclamation projects increased by 3 million acres between 1944 and 1964, at the same time that the nation's total cropland decreased some 66 million acres. It would seem that some of the 66 million acres could have been substituted for the 3 million irrigated acres with far less cost and dislocation.

Property Rights in Water. In the dry Western states, water is the limiting resource and is more valuable than land. As a result, a new body of "water law" has been developed and continues to be modified as new conflicts of interest in water rights develop and are adjudicated.

The legal basis for the use of water was developed under state laws, with priority of appropriation the primary basis of legal rights to the water in flowing streams. More recently, underground water supplies have been depleted by pumping operations of industrial and irrigation users. A body of law dealing with these newer claims is being developed. Purchasers of

[5]R. A. Young, "Irrigation Development and Agricultural Abundance: Conflicting Elements in Public Policy Toward Agriculture," *Looking Ahead*, National Planning Association Newsletter, October 1971.

land who expect to irrigate their crops should carefully investigate the adequacy and legal rights to irrigation water.

Irrigated farming requires economy in the use of water. The annual allotment of water must be allocated among the various crops in such a manner as to maximize the value of the total output of the farm. Because the allotment of water for the year or for certain seasons in the year is often fixed, the managerial decision is concerned with the most economic use of a fixed supply, rather than with the determination of the most profitable total amount to use.

Farmers, with fixed allotments of irrigation water at specific times during the year, plan their rotations and plant their crops at certain times, with a view to maximizing the value of crops produced with this fixed supply of water. In contrast to the situation in the humid sections of the United States, where farming operations are planned around a relatively fixed supply of land and family labor, irrigated farming operations are planned almost entirely in reference to a fixed supply of water.

Issues in the Future Use of Water.[6] Water use is classified into three categories: (1) "withdrawal" uses, in which water is taken out of the source and used in a process—irrigation, industry, and household uses fall into this class; (2) "on site" uses of water, including swamps, wetlands, and water used in soil conservation programs; and (3) "flow" uses of water, includeing navigation, hydroelectric power, sport fishing facilities, and waste dilution. In recent years, agriculture has accounted for 55 percent of the withdrawal use of water, with other major industries using the

TABLE 19-4

Proportion of Water Used by Five Major Sectors, 1960,
and Projections to 2000 (Percent of Total by Industry)

	Agriculture	Mining	Manufacturing	Steam-Electric	Municipal
Withdrawal Uses[a]					
1960	55	1	9	26	8
1980	33	2	10	44	10
2000	22	3	11	51	11
Losses from Withdrawal Uses[a]					
1960	76	2	3	2	17
1980	65	2	6	3	24
2000	55	2	6	5	29

[a]Medium projections.

Source: Nathaniel Wollman and Gilbert W. Bonem, *The Outlook for Water* (Baltimore: Johns Hopkins Press, 1971), pp. 58, 61.

[6]*The Outlook for Water*, by Nathaniel Wollman and Gilbert W. Bonem, provides a comprehensive examination of water use, quality, and distribution between now and the year 2020. Published for Resources for the Future, Inc., by Johns Hopkins Press, Baltimore, 1971.

proportions shown in Table 19–4. Agriculture's share of total withdrawal use is projected to decrease sharply by 1980 for two reasons. First, irrigated land is projected to increase at a much slower rate than in the past as the land and water resources most suitable for irrigation have been largely exploited. Second, the demands for nonagricultural uses of water are projected to increase much more rapidly than agricultural uses.

The data on water losses from withdrawal show a different picture. *Water losses* refer to water that is withdrawn from its source and "used up" or lost, largely through evaporation and, in agriculture, through transpiration. Agriculture will continue to be the biggest contributor to losses simply because the purpose of irrigation is to permit transpiration in order to encourage plant growth. Obviously, water once lost cannot be recycled as can other water used by industry. Thus, irrigation use precludes use for other purposes, setting an absolute limit on total availability, but industrial use has the effect of changing the quality of the water.

It is this changing of the quality of water that is the most serious problem associated with the future water resources situation. Pollution of the nation's water resources is associated with the level of economic activity, the level of population and its concentration, and the investment made in facilities to control pollution. All studies show that acceptable water quality can be obtained only by making substantial capital investments in treatment facilities and flow control structures. To some extent, treatment and flow are substitutes for preserving water quality, but in some areas the potential for flow control is much lower than in other areas.

Both the water quality and the total water availability must be viewed as regional issues because of the great regional variability in the United States. Irrigated agriculture is concentrated in the Western states, population and industry are concentrated in several scattered belts, and water resources are much more abundant in the east than in the west. The recent Resources for the Future study that projects water requirements and the cost of treatment and flow control structures to meet those requirements indicates that at the present time three of twenty-two United States water resource regions lack the water to cover their losses, let alone their required dilution flows. Those three are all in the arid Southwest. By the year 2000, according to the study's medium projections, three more regions will reach deficit status.[7]

Projections for the other regions (at the lowest cost strategy) of the required investments to meet quality and availability and to come as close as possible in the deficit regions, show that 90 to 95 percent of total water costs can be attributed to quality maintenance with the remaining 5 to 10 percent attributed to quantity. The summary measure of the "cost of water" includes the annual costs of investments for flow regulation, treatment,

[7]*Op. cit.*, p. 119.

and recirculation (a major requirement to eliminate thermal pollution in steam electric generation). Geographically, "about half of the total projected costs of storage treatment, and recirculation are found in the regions that contain the three future megalopolises of 'Boswash' (New England, Delaware and Hudson, Cheseapeake Bay); 'Chippits' (Ohio, Eastern Great Lakes, Western Great Lakes); and 'Sansan' (Central Pacific)."[8] Allocation of the cost of water by industry shows 47 percent attributable to manufacturing, 35 percent to steam electric power, 13 percent to municipal uses, and 5 percent to agriculture.

It would appear that agriculture will play a decreasing role in water resource problems both as to utilization and to degradation. However, it should be noted that the study cited above did not account for the polluting effects of agricultural production through nitrate contamination, feedlot runoff, and possible pesticide contamination of water supplies. As yet, insufficient information is available to include these in cost estimates. As we will see in a later chapter, however, the farming industry will probably have to bear some cost for water treatment to prevent future pollution.

POINTS FOR DISCUSSION

1. Why has farm ownership been the goal of most farm families?
2. What is needed to cure the "evils" of tenancy in your community?
3. Do tenants have lower incomes and lower living standards than farm owners in your community?
4. Why are so few farms kept within the family over a period of two or three generations?
5. Outline a desirable procedure for parents to use in transferring their farm to a son or son-in-law.
6. How have reclamation and irrigation projects contributed to farmers' welfare? How have they detracted from farmers' welfare?
7. What are the important forces that will influence the management of U.S. water resources over the next thirty years?

REFERENCES

"Land Tenure in the United States: Development and Status," *Agricultural Information Bulletin No. 538,* Economic Research Service, U.S.D.A. (June 1969).

Renne, R. R., *Land Economics.* New York: Harper & Row, 1958.

Wollman, Nathaniel, and Gilbert W. Bonem, *The Outlook for Water.* Baltimore: The Johns Hopkins Press, 1971.

Young, R. A., "Irrigation Development and Agricultural Abundance: Conflicting Elements in Public Policy Toward Agriculture," *Looking Ahead,* National Planning Association Newsletter (October 1971).

[8] *Ibid.,* p. 24.

Chapter 20

Farm Inputs, Credit,

and Finance

INPUTS USED IN FARMING

An examination of the aggregate income statement for the United States farming sector shows that in recent years farmers have retained only 30 percent of their gross sales receipts as net income. The other 70 percent has been used to pay hired labor, pay property taxes and mortgage interest, and to pay for current inputs. The percentage of gross receipts going to each of these inputs since 1910 is shown in Table 20–1.

In the early part of the century, farmers retained over half their gross receipts as net farm income—the return for their family labor, the resources they own (land, buildings, and livestock), and their managerial input. The fraction retained as net income dropped to nearly one-third during the 1930s, increased to nearly one-half during World War II, but then dropped back to one-third, remaining at about 30 percent since the late 1950s. About 20 percent of gross farm receipts are used for intrafarm transfers to pay for livestock, seeds, and feed. Industrially produced inputs claim about 20 percent of gross farm income, with depreciation, land taxes, interest, and hired labor accounting for the balance. In this chapter, we will examine the inputs that are produced outside the farming sector and the methods farmers use to finance their businesses.[1]

---

[1]Unless otherwise indicated, specific figures in this discussion were obtained from the excellent review of agricultural inputs: *Six Farm Input Industries*, ERS-357, U.S.D.A., (January 1968).

TABLE 20–1

Percentage of Gross Farm Receipts Returned to Selected Inputs

Year	Hired Labor[a]	Interest and Property Taxes	Feed Livestock Seed	Industrially Produced Inputs[b]	Depreciation and all other Expenses	Net Farm Income[c]
1910–14	10.0	10.5	8.8	12.5	6.8	51.2
1915–19	8.6	10.9	9.4	11.3	6.4	53.1
1920–24	10.6	13.3	10.9	15.1	8.9	41.0
1925–29	9.5	12.4	11.2	14.5	7.4	44.7
1930–34	9.8	14.7	10.2	18.1	10.1	36.7
1935–39	8.5	10.7	11.1	15.5	8.3	45.5
1940–44	8.7	8.3	14.6	13.5	7.0	47.6
1945–49	8.6	7.1	16.6	13.9	6.2	47.3
1950–54	7.8	7.3	17.7	17.6	9.8	39.6
1955–59	7.7	7.8	19.1	20.1	11.8	33.2
1960	7.6	8.1	20.6	20.3	11.7	31.4
1961	7.4	8.4	20.8	19.6	11.1	32.3
1962	7.0	8.5	22.1	19.8	10.8	31.5
1963	6.9	8.8	22.3	19.9	10.9	30.8
1964	6.9	9.6	20.8	21.3	11.8	29.3
1965	6.2	9.4	20.2	20.0	11.3	32.6
1966	5.8	9.5	21.0	19.6	11.1	32.7
1967	7.8	9.9	21.2	20.9	10.1	29.9
1968	5.9	10.3	20.0	21.4	13.0	29.0
1969	5.7	10.2	20.4	20.4	12.7	30.3
1970	5.9	10.6	21.2	21.4	12.6	28.0

[a]Cash wages plus prerequisites.
[b]All inputs listed in Table 20–2.
[c]Return to family labor and resources owned by farmers.

Source: Calculated from data in *Farm Income Situation*, Economic Research Service, U.S.D.A., June 1971.

In simpler days, the farm was considered the origin of food and fiber for the nation, but today the farm is simply a way station, one stop in a system that begins with an iron mine, an oil field, or a research laboratory and ends at a supermarket, a fast food drive-in, a restaurant, or a clothing store. The farmer is only a small part of the industrial system providing the food and fiber for consumers. One reflection of the farmer's changing position in the food-fiber system is that he now retains only 30 percent of gross receipts, but in 1910 he retained 50 percent. Data in Table 20–1 show that the proportion of gross farm income used for industrially produced inputs (and their financing) increased from 12.5 percent in 1910 to 21.4 percent in 1970. Feed, livestock, and seed expenses more than doubled from 8.8 percent to 21.2 percent, and depreciation (largely on purchased capital equipment) has also nearly doubled from 6.8 to 12.6 percent of gross receipts. These figures attest to the growing financial importance of purchased inputs as contrasted with the labor and land owned by farm families.

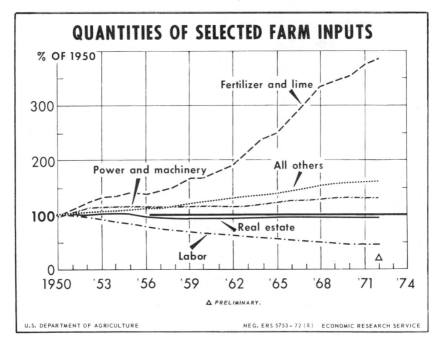

QUANTITIES OF SELECTED FARM INPUTS

FIGURE 20–1.

Figure 20–1 provides a comprehensive picture of the *quantities* of selected inputs used by farmers since 1950. The dramatic increase in fertilizer is familiar to all. It may seem surprising that the quantity of power and machinery has increased so little; but the main change in tractors and machinery since 1952 has been in size, while the total quantity has remained approximately fixed. The period of most rapid mechanization was between 1910 and 1940, which does not show in this figure. The prices of the inputs shown in Figure 20–2 helps to explain their utilization. Real estate prices have increased the fastest, followed by wage rates. As a result, real estate use has remained roughly constant and labor has declined. The gradual rise in farm machinery prices may have contributed to the nearly constant use of power and machinery. The stable price of fertilizer is a major factor contributing to its rapidly increasing use. Of course, price alone does not explain the changing use of inputs. Technology and product demand also are important, as has been discussed in earlier chapters.

The Livestock Feed Industry

The feed industry is somewhat different from the other farm input supplying industries because much of its raw material is farm produced. Feed is an important purchased input for many users because grain pro-

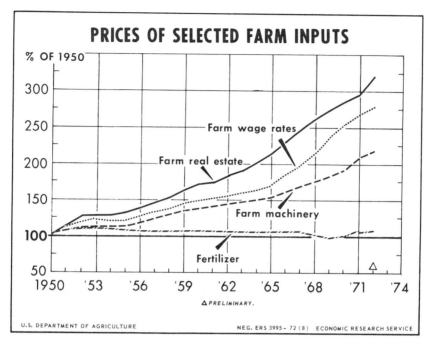

FIGURE 20–2.

ducers and feed buyers are tending toward greater specialization and are often located in different parts of the country. The trend toward increasingly complex feeds with large numbers of ingredients and the trend toward vertically integrated farming initiated by feed producers are two additional changes in the industry.

The total concentrates consumed by livestock and poultry in the United States increased from about 100 million tons in 1940 to over 170 million tons in 1966. In the same period, the proportion consumed by poultry increased from 9 to 12 percent, and the proportion consumed by beef cattle doubled from 22 percent in 1940 to 44 percent in 1966. As a result of the growing importance of poultry and beef, the fraction consumed by all other kinds of livestock decreased.

Changes in the demand patterns of consumers, in the technology of production, and in the institutional arrangements for production have caused substantial changes to occur in the feed industry. The demand for more livestock products is a continuing result of affluence in America. Beef consumption per capita doubled from 60 pounds in 1950 to nearly 120 pounds in 1970, poultry meat consumption went from less than 35 pounds per capita in 1960 to about 50 pounds per capita in 1971. The development of large-volume production units for eggs, broilers, turkeys, beef cattle, and hogs has transformed these enterprises from supplemental activities to primary year-round endeavors, often resembling factories more than farms.

The evolution of institutional devices such as contract farming and vertical integration has also changed the livestock feed industry. Vertical integration from the feed manufacturer is most complete in the poultry industry. At least 90 percent of the broilers are currently produced under these arrangements with contractors who have either feed manufacturing or broiler processing facilities or both.[2] National feed companies are involved to a substantial degree in contract egg production and perhaps 90 percent of the turkeys produced in the United States are fed under some form of extended credit program sponsored and backed by a feed or processing company. The rapid vertical integration of the poultry industry during the 1950s and 1960s is heralded by some as the precursor of things to come in the rest of the livestock industry. However, movements in that direction have been limited up to the present time.

Vertical integration via direct ownership or contract in the beef business is limited to the largest commercial feed lots. A recent survey of the feeding business identified nine cattle feeding firms having more than one feed lot. Together, they had a total one–time capacity of 744,000 head —or 4 percent of the 1970 commercial slaughter. Vertical integration probably does not involve more than 2 percent of the total production of hogs. Thus, beef and hogs have not yet become as fully integrated as the poultry business.

Contracting and vertical integration mean that the individual farmer loses his decision-making power, but it also results in some real advantages to the farmer. He gains technical assistance, access to better strains of livestock, financing, and access to markets. In many cases, it provides a small farmer with the external inputs necessary to permit him to continue farming. It has also resulted in substantial decreases in the real price of poultry products to the consumer. Whether these effects will spread to include substantial proportions of beef and hog production depends in part on whether there are technological factors that might prevent as high a degree of integration with these enterprises as has occurred with poultry.

The number of firms producing prepared animal feeds doubled between 1940 and 1966, and the value of feed shipments increased from $288 million in 1935 to over $3.6 billion in 1963. At the same time, the degree of market concentration decreased slightly. The largest four firms had 17 percent of total sales in 1964 compared to 21 percent in the mid-1950s and

---

[2] J. Phil Campbell, Under Secretary, U.S.D.A., in an unpublished statement on proposed legislation (HR 11654) before the Antitrust Subcommittee of the Committee on the Judiciary, U.S. House of Representatives, March 1972.

25 percent in the mid-1930s. Growth has been concentrated in the Mountain States (beef fattening), and the South Atlantic region (poultry).

INDUSTRIALLY PRODUCED INPUTS

Table 20–2 shows how the dollar expenditures of farmers on six classes of industrially produced inputs has changed from 1910 through 1970. Expenditures on all classes of purchased inputs have increased substantially. Interest on non-real-estate debt makes up the largest item. Petroleum, fuel and oil products make up the second largest single component. Expenditures on machinery (operation and repairs) and expenditures on fertilizer are next most important. The increase in expenditures on pesticides (which are not regularly separated and therefore are not shown for all years) is very noticeable throughout the 1960s. Repairs on structures contributed the least to the itemized expenses in 1970. The residual category of "all other" is the largest and illustrates how the reality of production conditions have outrun the mechanism set up to keep account of those conditions. "All other" includes expenditures on pesticides (except for the years where such are shown separately), electricity, veterinary services, net insurance premiums, marketing charges, and other similar costs. It is obvious that a more detailed breakdown of this group would be useful, but it is not regularly published.

Although it is clear that purchases of petroleum products are an important input into farming, it is completely impossible to determine what, aggregate role electricity has in farm production. Since 1960, "all other" expenses have increased about 50 percent while, except for fertilizer, the other categories have increased much less. However, even without precise data on certain inputs, we can gain some insight into the changing role of industrially produced inputs.

Petrochemical Inputs in Agriculture

The farm market accounts for only 5 percent of total petroleum sales, and it is likely that this proportion will continue to decrease as farmers become more efficient and nonfarm utilization increases. However, the production of chemical fertilizer and pesticides are also carried out largely by the petroleum industry or by firms supplied their raw materials by the petroleum industry. Thus, the petrochemical industry views farming as one of its growth areas. Farmers do not always recognize this, but industry spokesmen are not hesitant to express it.

> We look at the progressive farmer of today and the farmer of tomorrow as an associated businessman in the chemical industry. After all, these men are

TABLE 20-2

Expenditures on Industrially Produced Inputs in United States Farming, 1910–70 (million dollars)

Year(s)	Petroleum, Fuel, and Oil	Pesticides	Fertilizer and Lime	Motor Vehicle Operation other than Fuel and Oil	Repairs on Machinery	Repairs of Farm Business Structures	Interest on Non-Real-Estate Debt	All Other[b]
1910–14	18	—	170	12	42	127	225	382
1915–19	74	—	252	74	42	127	319	558
1920–24	160	—	280	135	64	160	463	617
1925–29	256	—	296	196	53	167	365	643
1930–34	251	—	182	159	45	96	241	521
1935–39	307	—	252	192	60	168	149	536
1940–44	436	—	428	320	151	238	197	741
1945–49	831	—	763	639	325	354	224	1,170
1950–54	1,286	179[a]	1,122	935	429	464	407	1,623
1955–59	1,443	—	1,203	1,185	490	453	526	1,891
1960	1,468	287	1,315	1,252	525	432	725	1,817
1961	1,476	345	1,373	1,191	498	428	757	1,834
1962	1,475	395	1,474	1,259	523	424	837	1,903
1963	1,470	435	1,570	1,283	519	414	945	1,935
1964	1,508	484	1,701	1,263	512	407	1,017	2,014
1965	1,538	564	1,754	1,345	535	405	1,099	1,965
1966	1,570	619	1,952	1,454	538	411	1,244	1,991
1967	1,621	679	2,124	1,594	580	432	1,429	1,960
1968	1,645	787	2,130	1,666	640	427	1,562	2,102
1969	1,713	853	2,023	1,722	661	447	1,776	2,134
1970	1,747	899	2,097	1,820	854	457	2,055	2,233

aRefers to 1950 only.
bIncludes interest on veterinary services, electricity, insurance, etc.

Source: Compiled from *Farm Income Situation*, FIS-218, Economic Research Service, U.S.D.A., July 1971. Pesticide data from *Six Farm Input Industries*, ERS-357, Economic Research Service, U.S.D.A., January 1968.

producing proteins, fats, celluloses, carbohydrates—all of which are processed chemicals. . . . The goal of this chemical plant operator, the farmer is not to grow a crop of lettuce, a herd of steers, etc., but to maximize his return on investment.[3]

Oil and chemical companies sell their chemical inputs through dealers, their own distribution system, or through farmer-owned cooperatives. They have been among the leaders in developing retail farm service centers that are designed to provide a "one-stop" purchasing center for farmers. Most of the centers thus far developed fall short of the one-stop concept, but efforts are being made to include outlets for more and more of the inputs farmers need.

Farm Machinery and Equipment

The development of efficient, relatively inexpensive farm machinery has multiplied the production power of the average American farmer and, as we have seen in earlier chapters, has permitted a rapid reduction in the labor force on farms. The industry producing and marketing this equipment is quite interesting.

Manufacturers of farm equipment are classed as "full line," "long line," and "short line" producers. Only seven firms are full-line producers, making tractors and a complete line of tractor-powered equipment, self-propelled equipment, attachments, and other agricultural machines. Of those seven, only three depend on farm machinery for more than one-third of their total sales. The other four are diversified into the production of automobiles, trucks, industrial equipment, and other machinery. Several of the full-line companies are multinational corporations with stockholders, manufacturing plants, and managerial personnel located in a number of nations.

The long-line machinery companies are smaller than the full-line companies and tend to be specialized in machinery rather than tractor production. The short-line companies produce specialized mechanical and automatic equipment such as that used in the feeding and care of livestock and poultry. Thus, farming is dependent on a rather small number of firms for its mechanical inputs.

Farmer Cooperatives as Suppliers of Inputs

Farmer cooperatives have important intermediaries in the supply of certain farm inputs. Cooperatives sold petroleum products amounting to one-fourth the total petroleum expenditure by farmers in 1964. Outlets in

[3]T. J. Army and M. E. Smith, "Research and Development in Farm Related Firms—Its Impact on Agriculture," in *Structural Changes in Commercial Agriculture*, Center for Agricultural and Economic Development Report 24, (Ames, Iowa: Iowa State University, April 1965), p. 133.

the three states in which cooperatives sell the most petroleum products (Iowa, Minnesota, and Illinois) accounted for 27 percent of the total cooperative petroleum volume in 1964, and cooperatives were important distributors in many other states as well.

Farmer cooperatives own a substantial fraction of the fertilizer production capacity in the United States. In 1964, the eleven cooperatively owned ammonia plants included 14 percent of domestic capacity. At the retail level, cooperatives have registered a steady increase in their market share of fertilizer sales—from 9 percent in 1943 to 15 percent in 1951 and up to 30 percent in 1965. This upswing has been partially due to the rapid increases in fertilizer use in the Midwest where cooperatives are strong. Their organization has been geared to serve farmers' needs, emphasizing high-analysis fertilizer, bulk blending based on soil tests, and bulk spreading for farmers.

Cooperatives have an important role in the distribution of pesticides, although they have not entered the business of production. They own approximately 30 formulating plants throughout the country, and their retail outlets supplied about 15 percent of the total farm use of pesticides in 1965.

Farm-owned cooperatives have supplied about 20 percent of the commercial formula feeds used by farmers in recent years. Farm machinery is the one major input area that cooperatives have not entered in any substantial way. It is difficult to generalize about the effect of farmer cooperatives on the farm input industries. In some areas, they have led the way in innovating, in some regions they have become the primary supplier of one or more inputs. Perhaps their main contribution has been to provide that added degree of competition necessary to encourage lower cost, more efficient production.

The Future for Farm Input Industries

As long as United States agriculture continues its present direction, the quantities of industrially supplied inputs required for farming will continue to grow, and as farms become larger, the purchasing, delivery, storage, and use of such inputs will constitute a larger fraction of the farm management problem. Some input suppliers see this as an area for the development of conglomerate firms selling seed, fertilizer, pesticides, petroleum and fuel, insurance, feed, tractors, custom operations, and even management and credit. Although such a firm would be under central control, its sales or delivery locations might be quite diffuse. One individual's description of such a series is as follows.

> ...although the proposed conglomerate joint venture would handle the distribution of a complete line of farm inputs, it could not have one set of locations all distributing the same mix of items. To serve optimally, the logistical and sales requirements of such a diverse group of products and

services would require a stratified system of physical handling points and sales and service offices. The concept here is similar to that used by department store chains that have regional, community, and neighborhood stores, each of which carries a different product mix according to product characteristics, inventory costs, and shopping habits.

The optimum logistics of a distribution system for all material and service inputs is obviously a complex, intricate job for the computer. But on the sales side, farmer motivation studies show that large farmers, who buy a larger portion of total farm inputs, want a consistently reliable supplier from whom they can purchase more in less time and with less effort. This circumstance will mean less frequent purchase confrontations between the farmer and a sales representative, with more items purchased under contract and with the supplier responsible for the timing of delivery to maintain the needed supply inventory. LP gas and petroleum tanks are now kept full by the supplier and, on some large farms, even bins of frequently needed repair parts, such as oil filters, spark plugs and fan belts.[4]

This view of the farm input industry fits with the earlier view of the farmer as one link in the food and fiber system. Such a view seems consistent with the trend toward fewer, larger farms. All these factors point to an increased role for institutions financing the purchase of inputs. As a result of similar forces over the past thirty years, the role of finance has grown to the point where interest on non-real-estate debt is one of the largest of the input payments among those shown in Table 20–2.

FARM FINANCE AND CREDIT

The Financial Position of Farming

The most comprehensive view of the economic health of a firm or sector of the economy is provided by its balance sheet. A balance sheet lists all the assets—"everything the firm owns"—and all the liabilities—"everything the firm owes." By accounting definition, assets must equal liabilities plus owner's equity. The listing of assets shows the income-earning capital items, land, and other income-producing items owned by the firm, whether free of debt or not. The liabilities include all the debts of the firm. That portion of the business that is owned free of debt is known as the proprietor's equity. Changes in the balance sheet over time are taken by some analysts to be the best indication of the economic health of the business or sector.

Table 20–3 shows the balance sheet of the farming sector along with certain other data at ten-year intervals between 1940 and 1970. Assets more than doubled between 1940 and 1950 and again between 1950 and 1970. The most rapidly growing asset item was land, with financial assets growing

[4]R. O. Aines, "Rationale for Conglomerate Growth in the Farm Input Sector," in *Economics of Conglomerate Growth*, Leon Garoian, ed., (Corvallis, Oregon: Department of Agricultural Economics, Oregon State University, November 1969), p. 67.

TABLE 20–3

Balance Sheet and Other Selected Data for U.S. Farming

	1940	1950	1960	1970
Assets ($ billion)	52.9	132.5	203.1	311.4
Real estate	33.6	75.3	130.2	208.9
Livestock, machinery, crops, etc.	15.1	41.3	54.7	78.7
Financial assets	4.2	15.9	18.2	23.8
Liabilities ($ billion)	10.0	12.4	24.8	58.1
Real estate debt	6.6	5.6	12.1	28.4
Debt to reporting institutions	1.9	4.5	7.9	18.5
Dept to nonreporting creditors	1.5	2.3	4.8	11.2
Liabilities as a proportion of assets (%)	19.2	9.4	12.2	18.8
Proprietors' equities ($ billion)	42.9	120.1	178.3	253.3
Number of farms	5,800,000	5,200,000	4,000,000	2,900,000
Average equity per farm	7,396	23,096	44,550	87,345
Averaged operators realized net income per farm (return to labor and equity)	662	2,277	2,962	5,374
Income as percent of equity	9.0	10.0	6.6	6.2

Source: *Agricultural Finance Review,* Vol. 31, Supplement December 1970, Economic Research Service, U.S.D.A.; and *Farm Income Situation,* FIS-218, Economic Research Service, U.S.D.A., July 1970.

somewhat more slowly than the average. Liabilities have also grown rapidly but have always formed a small fraction of total assets.

In 1940, liabilities amounted to 19 percent of total assets, but the prosperity brought on by World War II permitted farmers to reduce their debts and increase their equity so that liabilities were reduced below 10 percent of assets by 1950. Since then, liabilities have grown, nearly reaching the 19 percent level again in 1970. Equity per farm has increased more than tenfold as a result of increasing asset values and decreasing numbers of farms. Thus, it appears that the farming sector is in healthy financial shape. However, the return obtained by farm operators as a percentage of their equity has declined substantially since the 1940s and 1950s to approximately 6 percent in 1970. It appears that along with the gains in asset values (particularly in real estate) have come reduced current returns and hence relatively low incomes. One problem that can arise from this situation is a limitation on the capacity of farmers to purchase inputs from current returns and hence the need to depend more on credit than in the past.

The availability and use of credit in farming permits individuals to acquire ownership of physical assets for use in production before saving the necessary funds to make a purchase. In a sense, credit permits the transfer of one person's savings to another person or firm who in turn uses it in a production process. It is only one, but is a very important method by which a farmer can expand his business more rapidly than he accumulates savings.

In a sense, credit performs the role of catalyst, permitting farmers to acquire and utilize resources in production on the basis of their ability to realize profits, rather than making them entirely dependent upon their own capital (equity) accumulated out of savings or inheritance.

Production versus Consumption Credit

At this point, we should distinguish between production and consumption credit. In our increasingly credit-based economy, personal financial difficulties and even personal bankruptcy have become common as individuals overextend themselves. Thus, care in using consumption credit is warranted. Yet, credit used for productive purposes and debts assumed in the organization of a profitable business has an entirely different standing than credit used and debts acquired for consumption purposes.

Credit is said to be used for production purposes when the loan is used to purchase assets, land, livestock, machinery, fertilizer, seeds, and so forth, which are employed with the expectation of increasing net income sufficiently to repay the loan and interest. Credit of this type, or debts incurred in such transactions, if the business investments are profitable, will increase the family's income in the future, rather than decrease it. The successful business venture based on credit produces a surplus over and above the funds necessary to repay the loan with interest.

In contrast, consumption credit (which has increased greatly in recent decades) consists of loans that permit individuals and families to purchase durable or nondurable consumer goods in larger quantities than they have cash to pay for at any particular time. Much of the consumption credit outstanding today is used for residential housing loans and installment credit on automobiles, household equipment, and furniture. The spreading popularity of credit cards has extended the list to the point at which today anything can be purchased on credit. Some families find it necessary to borrow from their local banks, local credit unions, or personal finance companies to meet doctor bills, extra expenses associated with weddings or deaths in the family, and for other purposes. Considerable credit is extended by merchants, doctors, and undertakers who sell the family merchandise or perform services for them. Merchants who make a practice of extending credit or who accept credit cards must charge higher prices than those who do business on a cash basis, but the competitive pressure to extend consumption credit is intense.

Consumption credit, consistently used over a period of years, reduces rather than increases the size of the income stream that can go for personal goods and services. At the time the credit is extended, the family obtains the use of more consumer goods than could be purchased out of current income. But the future purchases of consumer goods must be reduced sufficiently to repay both the loan and the interest charges.

It is only in the case of credit for residential housing and similar investments that families find the criteria governing the economic use of consumption credit similar to those governing the use of production credit. Thus, under certain circumstances, a family may be able to obtain the use of a given amount of housing cheaper by purchase through the use of credit than on a rental basis. Under such circumstances, the appropriate consideration is the cost of hiring or renting the comparable consumer goods as against purchase through the use of credit.

Criteria for Use of Production Credit

From the standpoint of efficiency, credit should play a neutral role in entrepreneurs' decisions. Plans for business expansion or contraction should be based upon the expected returns over costs from the particular activity. The entrepreneur should earn a return on his own funds comparable with the interest he pays for borrowed funds. Whether or not he has to borrow funds for the venture should be a matter of indifference. Actually, of course, it is never a matter of indifference. Many business decisions turn on whether or not credit must be used. *And in many cases, entrepreneurs are prevented from making and carrying out plans because lending institutions will not grant them the credit requested.*

One way of looking at the use of credit is to think of it as the hiring of liquid capital. When a farmer borrows $1,000 at the bank for a year, he has hired the use of that capital for twelve months for a wage of $80 if the interest rate is 8 percent. From this point of view, employing credit is similar to renting land, hiring labor, or hiring machine work done at fixed rates. The farmer uses marginal analysis to determine how much of any factor of production to hire in each production operation. Thus, a farmer may find it highly profitable to borrow $800 to buy two cows to fill his dairy barn and utilize extra feed available, but without the two empty stalls in his barn he could not house more cows and hence could not use more credit for such a purpose.

Figure 20–3 shows how farmers' use of credit has grown since 1954. In the technologically dynamic context of modern farming, credit is necessary to insure growth. One study showed that a family-run commercial hog-beef fattening operation with capital of $55,000 in 1950 had capital of $99,000 in 1963 and would likely use capital of $157,000 by 1980. The comparable figures for a Kansas winter wheat farm were $58,000, $110,000, and $179,000; for a cattle ranch in the intermountain region $70,000, $96,000, and $129,000.[5] Credit would likely play an important role in permitting farms to grow by such amounts.

Figure 20–4 shows the flow of credit among the most important farm credit institutions in the United States. These institutions provide invest-

---

[5]C. B. Baker and L. G. Tweeten, "Financial Requirements of the Farm Firm," in *Structural Changes in Commercial Agriculture*, CAED Report 24, April 1965, pp. 31–2.

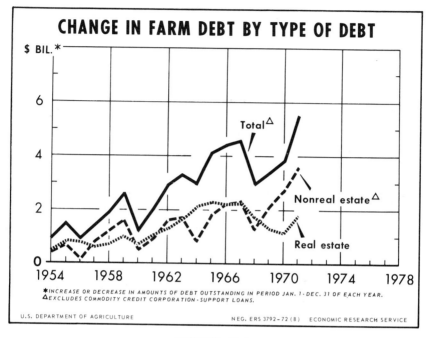

FIGURE 20–3.

ment opportunities to some individuals while providing credit to farmers. They bring together lenders and borrowers. For example, holders of life insurance policies may not consider themselves to be lending money to farmers, but life insurance companies are a major source of farm real estate mortgage credit. Investors who buy debentures and bonds issued by federal farm credit agencies also provide credit to farmers. The federal government provides a small amount of subsidized credit, but the major contribution of the federal government is insuring and supervising lending agencies. The details of the farm credit system are of some interest.

Farm Real Estate Mortgage Credit Agencies

As early as 1913, dissatisfaction with existing farm mortgage credit facilities led Congress to appoint a special commission to study European experience and development in the farm real estate mortgage field. Following the report of this commission, the Federal Farm Loan Act was passed in 1916. This act provided for the establishment of twelve Federal Land Banks.[6] Although the banks were set up by this act subject to supervision by a Federal Farm Loan Board, they were planned as cooperatives. Farmers

---

[6]This act also provided for the establishment of a national system of Joint Stock Land Banks, which were later liquidated.

PRINCIPAL FARM CREDIT FLOWS

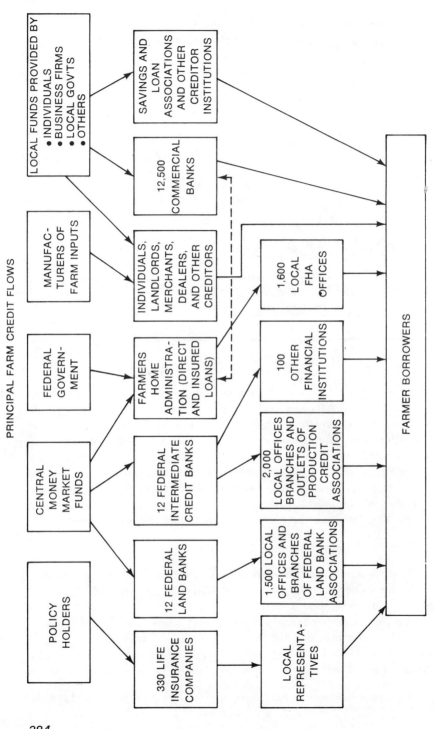

FIGURE 20-4.

interested in borrowing funds organized into local National Farm Loan Associations. Five percent of each loan was used to buy stock in the Federal Land Bank. Thus, the borrowing members of the local associations gradually acquired ownership of the capital stock of the Federal Land Banks, which was first subscribed by the United States Treasury. Funds for the loans to individual borrowers were obtained by pooling the mortgages as security for Federal Land Bank Bonds, which were sold in the investment fund market to financial institutions and individuals.

Before the passage of the Federal Farm Loan Act, the two chief complaints of farmers were the high interest rates charged for farm loans and the unavailability of longer-term loans, especially in the higher-risk areas of the United States. Most insurance company loans on real estate mortgages at moderate interest rates were located in the Corn Belt. The availability of funds through the Federal Land Banks caused a sharp drop in interest rates in the high interest sections of the country. The land banks met the demand for longer-term loans by introducing the thirty-three-year amortized loan for farm borrowers. Under the terms of these loans, a borrower liquidated his debt in thirty-three years by making annual or semiannual payments on the principal, when paying the interest. This longer amortized loan was an important innovation that has now been adopted, in modified form, by many private lending agencies.

In addition to the loans available through the Federal Land Banks, which are now fully owned and operated by farmers, a few farm families may obtain long-term real estate mortgage loans from the Farmers Home Administration, or similar loans from private agencies insured by the FHA. This government agency is authorized to loan a few million dollars each year to outstanding tenants for 100 percent of the purchase price of family-type farms, and to owners of inadequate, unimproved, low-production farms for farm improvement and enlargement purposes.

Table 20–4 shows the distribution of farm real estate debt among the principal holders. The most important extenders of farm real estate credit have long been individuals and other nonreporting lenders, although this

TABLE 20–4

Proportion of Farm Mortgage Debt Outstanding to Major Lenders

Year	Federal Land Banks	Farmers Home Administration	Life Insurance Companies	All Operating Banks	Individuals and Other Nonreporting Lenders
1940	30.5	.4	14.9	8.1	45.9
1950	16.2	3.4	21.0	16.7	42.4
1960	19.3	3.6	23.3	13.4	40.2
1970	23.4	1.5	20.1	14.4	40.2

Source: "The Balance Sheet of the Farming Sector," *Agricultural Information Bulletin No. 356*, Economic Research Service, U.S.D.A., December 1971.

source of credit has decreased somewhat in importance since 1940. The Federal Land Banks and life insurance companies each supply about 20 percent of the farm real estate credit, with some tendency for the Federal Land Banks to increase in importance in recent years. Operating banks, which supplied a small fraction of real estate loans in 1940, have since increased their share to nearly 15 percent.

Non-real-estate Credit Agencies

As was pointed out earlier, merchants and dealers with a financial interest in selling supplies furnish a large part of the short term, non-mortgage credit to farmers. Machinery and equipment companies have organized affiliated finance companies, which arrange for installment credit to cover the purchase of their products. Commercial banks have long been a primary source of short-term loans. Farmers have found their local bank a relatively satisfactory source of short-term credit, except during depression periods. The amount of funds available for loans by banks depends on their volume of demand deposits. As demand deposits grow, the bank may expand its loans. But the reverse is also true; banks must reduce their loans as demand deposits shrink.

If a farmer does not wish to use installment or bank credit, in most communities in the United States he can go to a local Production Credit Association and borrow funds for the purchase of livestock, equipment, and supplies used in farm production. These local cooperative associations of borrowers are backed by the Farm Credit Administration, under legislation passed in 1933. As with the Federal Land Banks, the government provided the original capital required in setting them up, but the system now obtains no funds from the federal government. Production Credit Associations obtain loan funds by discounting notes of farmers with the government-owned Federal Intermediate Credit Banks (set up in 1923). These Federal Intermediate Credit Banks get their funds by selling debenture bonds to banks and other investors in the money market.

Although the Production Credit Associations furnished only 15 percent of the total short-term credit used by farmers in recent years, government-sponsored cooperative credit is an essential part of the short-term credit system. It was brought into existence in the depression years when banks were unable and unwilling to meet the short-term credit needs of farmers. Because their loan funds are not dependent on bank deposits, Production Credit Associations are believed to be a much more stable source of funds than commercial banks.

Farm families without sufficient assets to borrow from these commercial lending agencies in some cases may borrow directly from a government agency, the Farmers Home Administration. In 1935, a program of granting supervised rural rehabilitation loans for periods of five years was undertaken by the Farm Security Administration as an alternative to continued relief payments to destitute rural families. Legislation in 1946 established the Farmers Home Administration as a successor to the Farm Security Administration. The FHA was granted authority to continue making operating loans as well as real estate loans under certain conditions.

Since 1935, loans totaling several billion dollars have been made by the FHA. To be eligible for such loans farm families must: (1) be unable to get the loan from regular agencies; (2) develop a farm and home plan indicating that they can maintain their family and repay the loan out of increased income; and (3) accept the supervision of the local officer of the Farmers Home Administration, who will advise the family on improved farm management practices.

TABLE 20–5

Proportion of Non-real-estate Farm Debt Owed to Principal Lenders

Year	All Operating Banks	Production Credit Ass'ns	Federal Intermediate Credit Banks	Farmers Home Admin'n	Nonreporting Creditors	Commodity Credit Corporation
1940	26.1	4.4	0.9	12.1	43.5	12.9
1950	29.8	5.6	0.7	5.0	33.7	25.0
1960	37.9	10.7	0.7	3.1	38.3	9.1
1970	34.7	15.1	0.7	2.6	37.7	9.0

Source: "The Balance Sheet of the Farming Sector," *Agricultural Information Bulletin No. 356,* Economic Research Service, U.S.D.A., December 1971.

Table 20–5 shows the distribution of non-real-estate debt among principal holders. Commercial banks and the merchants and dealers making up the "nonreporting" creditors have each provided roughly equal proportions of the non-real-estate credit in recent years. The major activity of Federal Intermediate Credit Banks is in backing up Production Credit Associations (see Figure 20–4) so that they lend very little directly to farmers. The Commodity Credit Corporation, through its nonrecourse loans, which support commodity prices, is a substantial creditor of farmers, but because these loans are treated as sales if not repaid, there is some question whether they should be considered credit at all.

Economic Instability, Economic Progress, and Farm Credit

Business fluctuations, which lead to fluctuations in demand deposits, affect commercial banks' ability to make loans. Fluctuations in the value of farm assets that are used as collateral in obtaining loans also have forced lending agencies to adopt a relatively conservative policy with respect to the size of the loan in relation to the value of the assets of the farmer. On the borrower's side, uncertainty with respect to production but especially with respect to prices, forces him to limit his borrowing in the interest of security, regardless of his technical competence to manage a larger business.

Economic fluctuations are an inherent part of a growing, expanding economy. We must expect them to continue, but there is general agreement that they have been unnecessarily severe in some past years. One of the substantial gains resulting from a reduction in economic fluctuations would be increased effectiveness of credit in permitting and assisting resources to combine more efficiently in farm production.

Between 1940 and 1970, farmers' investment in machinery, equipment, livestock, crops, and inventories of supplies increased five times over (Table 20–3). On a per farm basis, the increase is even larger because the number of farms declined during the period. Although somewhat over one-half of this increase is the result of rising prices, it is clear that technological advance in farming is increasing capital investment requirements at a rapid rate and is giving rise to problems in obtaining adequate intermediate credit on terms adapted to farmers' needs. The land banks and other mortgage-lending institutions provide an adequate source of long-term real estate credit needed by farmers. The local banks and the production credit associations supply the short-term or seasonal credit needed.

An increasing number of farmers, however, find themselves in need of three- to seven-year loans to finance capital investments required for technological advance, yet most commercial banks are unable to grant credit for periods in excess of twelve months. In recent years, Production Credit Associations and a limited number of other financial agencies have begun to make intermediate term loans. Great expansion will be required in this field as technological advance requires larger and larger capital investment in both real estate and equipment for an optimum operating unit.

If farm prices and income continue to fluctuate sharply, as they have in the past 50 years, it may be impossible for the typical farm operator in the early part of his productive life to borrow sufficient funds on a loan basis to achieve an economic producing unit involving an investment of $100,000 to $200,000 or more.

Alternatives to Credit

The need for access to larger quantities of resources and the difficulty that existing institutions face in providing such access have led to the development of alternatives to credit. In Chapter 19, we saw how increasing the size of a farm through land rental has become a growing practice. The possibility of leasing machinery and capital items has attracted considerable interest. Any comparison of the economics of leasing and buying must consider the opportunity cost of the funds freed by leasing, the costs of borrowing, terms of the lease, availability of investment tax credit, and other factors. There is no simple answer to the question of whether leasing is better than buying, but its growth attests to the fact that some individuals find it useful.

Vertical coordination through integration or contracting usually carries with it the availability of credit. It is possible that in the future processors or suppliers may provide large-scale equipment that farmers find difficult to finance. The funds drawn into the farm production system through vertical coordination often originate outside the agricultural sector entirely, and hence expand the availability of credit to farming as a whole.

Incorporation is sometimes suggested as an alternative to borrowing. One problem with incorporation is that most farmers are somewhat reluctant to sell ownership outside the family. However, incorporation can help solve the problem of farm ownership transfers, as shares can be transferred to heirs or sold by one heir to another. Incorporation has permitted acquisition of large amounts of capital outside agriculture through sale of stock, but as yet there is practically no organized market for farm stock. Because farm businesses are generally small, it is difficult to see that this situation will change in the near future.

Merger of several farm units is a more drastic step than incorporation. However, it may be advantageous under certain circumstances. Suppose there are several farmers who are neighbors: one is ready to retire, one is seeking to expand, and another has decided to leave farming. A merger with managerial responsibility vested in the second individual might create a unit large enough to take advantage of all scale economies and with the financial characteristics to generate greater credit than before.

POINTS FOR DISCUSSION

1. What are some of the reasons that industrially produced inputs have increased in importance to U.S. agriculture?
2. On the basis of past trends, which of the industrially produced farm inputs would you expect to grow in importance most rapidly during the next 10 years?
3. What factors are likely to change the structure of the farm input industry in the near future?
4. Evaluate the contention: the average farmer has always had access to commercial credit so the establishment of a Federal farm credit system was uncessary.
5. How does production credit differ from consumption credit?
6. Do farmers use too much or too little credit?

REFERENCES

Agricultural Finance Review, Economic Research Service, U.S.D.A., annual publication.

BAKER, C. B., AND L. G. TWEETEN, "Financial Requirements of the Farm Firm," *Structural Changes in Commercial Agriculture,* Center for Agricultural and

Economic Development Report 24, Ames, Iowa: Iowa State University, April 1965.

"The Balance Sheet of the Farming Sector," *Agricultural Information Bulletin 356,* Economic Research Service, U.S.D.A., annual publication.

"The Farm Income Situation," *FIS-218,* Economic Research Service, U.S.D.A. (July 1971). (Quarterly publication.)

"Six Farm Input Industries," *ERS-357,* Economic Research Service, U.S.D.A. (January 1968).

Chapter 21

Agriculture and the

Environment

Problems of environmental pollution have come to occupy a central position of concern in our society. Agriculture, because it controls much of the land and water in the United States and is based on natural resources to a somewhat greater extent than other industries, has a very great potential impact on the environment. Any steps taken to limit agriculture's impact on the environment may have a great impact on agriculture, and through it on the rest of the economy as well.

Related to the environmental problems of our time is the rapid increase in population and the change from a largely rural to a largely urban life style. Also related is the rapid increase in the real level of income and rapid technological change. Of course, it is too simple to blame all environmental problems on the rate of population growth or on the rate and level of real income growth or any other single cause. These factors are interrelated and only through an understanding of the total problem will we be able to understand how each affects environmental quality.

The environment has been changed by man ever since he appeared on earth. The hunters and food gatherers affected the environment. The great cities and civilizations of the Romans, the Mayans, and the early Chinese all changed the environment. The agricultural practices of the settlers who spread across the North American continent changed the environment. Why then is such intense concern about the quality of the environment just now becoming apparent? One answer to this question is that we are really just becoming aware of the consequences of certain processes. Another answer is that because many socially aware individuals in our country have achieved all that might be desired in terms of material possessions, they now want to improve the quality of life rather than consume more things.[1] Another answer is that the nature of the compound growth process is such that problems can continue to grow for a long period at a steady rate and remain below the crisis level and then suddenly reach the crisis point.[2] A fourth answer holds that it is only in recent decades that mankind has been able to produce large quantities of "synthetic" commodities that require, as inputs, chemicals that are not rendered harmless by natural biological processes, and the resulting buildup of these substances is at the root of the environmental problem.[3]

We cannot attempt to discuss all the problems commonly associated with environmental problems in this chapter. We do discuss a few economic aspects of controlling environmental pollution by agriculture. We also recognize that the environmental problem is much broader than simply pollution because economic growth, population growth, food production, industrialization, land use patterns, and exhaustion of nonrenewable resources all are interrelated. A recent attempt to combine these interrelated problems in a formal model provides some interesting insight into a possible path of future events.

Using a computer simulation model, a team of MIT scientists has constructed a simplified "world model" from which they conclude:

1. If the present growth trends in world population, industrialization, pollution, food production, and resource depletion continue unchanged, the limits to growth on this planet will be reached sometime within the next one hundred years. The most probable result will be a rather sudden and uncontrollable decline in both population and industrial capacity.
2. It is possible to alter these growth trends and to establish a condition of ecological and economic stability that is sustainable far into the future. The state of global equilibrium could be designed so that the basic material needs of each person on earth are satisfied and each person has an equal opportunity to realize his individual human potential.
3. If the world's people decide to strive for this second outcome rather than the first, the sooner they begin working to attain it, the greater will be their chances of success.

   These conclusions are so far-reaching and raise so many questions for further study that we are quite frankly overwhelmed by the enormity of the job that must be done. We hope that this book will serve to interest other people in many fields of study and in many countries of the world to raise the space and time horizons of their concerns and to join us in understanding and preparing for a period of great transition—the transition from growth to global equilibrium.[4]

---

[1]V. W. Ruttan, "Technology and the Environment," *American Journal of Agricultural Economics*, Vol. 53, December 1971, p. 709.

[2]D. H. Meadows *et al.*, *The Limits to Growth* (New York: Universe Books, 1972), Chap. 2.

[3]Barry Commoner, "Biology and the Human Condition," the Martin E. Rehfuss Lecture, November 19, 1970.

[4]Reported in Meadows *et al.*, *op. cit.*, p. 23.

The model specifically includes technological advance to determine whether a continuation of the "technological revolution" would change the rather gloomy outlook. The team's conclusion with respect to technological advance is that:

> When we introduce technological developments that successfully lift some restraint to growth or avoid some collapse, the system simply grows to another limit, temporarily surpasses it, and falls back.[5]

They find that as long as population and capital growth are left to seek their own levels, growth ends with an extremely rapid fall of income and population at some future time as natural resource constraints are reached. Their system is stabilized at acceptable real income levels over a two-hundred-year horizon only when the average family size is two children and the economic system maintains average industrial output per capita at about the 1975 level.

We do not suggest that the results of the MIT team's efforts are conclusive, nor indeed do they. However, such a model is a beginning toward understanding the complex natural and technological system that man has created. Management of that system to achieve successful future human existence is an extremely complex problem. Whatever ultimately occurs, it is undeniable that society is now and will increasingly become concerned with human activities that make the environment in which we live less safe, less pleasant, less varied, and less able to sustain a high quality of life, for all people, indefinitely.

Economists are convinced that one cause of environmental problems is the disregard for *economic externalities—consequences of economic activities that do not enter the calculations of the economic unit engaged in the activity.* Economic units not only produce useful products to be sold in the market but also produce nonuseful products (waste products) for which no market exists. Because the institutions of our market economy have not, until recently, hindered it, the most economic means of disposing of the wastes has been to release them into the environment. Thus, the environment has provided an economic service to many firms at a very low or zero cost to them. We say those firms have enjoyed external benefits. On the other side of the picture, the effect of releasing wastes into the environment has been to create external costs to other firms and individuals—the air or water or space they use is of a lower quality than it would be in the absence of the activities of the first set of firms.

If externalities are concentrated on only a few individuals or firms outside the economic unit causing them, they can be rather easily internalized. For example, an onlooker injured by falling debris at a construction site can obtain compensation directly. Externalities become a social problem

[5]Meadows *et al., op. cit.*, p. 143.

when their effects are so diffuse that no single individual is very greatly affected by a particular activity. For example, air pollution is an annoyance to the general population, but even (in the unlikely case) when the cause of such pollution can be identified as a single firm, there is no market mechanism by which the general population can be compensated by the firm for the service of accepting its waste products in the form of air pollution. The effect on each individual in the general population is so small as to make seeking compensation, as in the case of falling debris, unfeasible.

Some additional examples may make the general concept of externalities somewhat clearer.[6] A number of wells that all tap a common source of water involve external diseconomies because the more water pumped from any single well, the less that remains for the others. In this case, the external effects are reciprocal—each economic unit (well) has the same effect on every other unit. River pollution by the discharge of industrial effluent has an obvious external benefit to the discharging firm because it disposes of its wastes at zero cost. This case is unidirectional because those who bear the costs do not also inflict similar costs on the firm in question.

Externalities alone are not responsible for the environmental problems we face. The increasing concentration of wastes is a second significant cause. The natural environment has the ability to assimilate and render harmless a large quantity of wastes. As long as population density is sufficiently low, little health hazard is posed by dependence on wells for drinking water and septic tanks for waste disposal. As long as the number of industrial operations emitting smoke and chemical substances in a region is rather low, the wind and rain keep the air acceptably clean. "But as the regional densities of industry and human population increase, a point is ultimately reached (as is now the case) where the flow rates of wastes exceed the capacity of the natural environment to dilute and assimilate them."[7] This strengthens the need to internalize the environmental costs so that the units causing environmental damage have the incentive to change their actions.

Direct Environmental Effects of Agricultural Production

Eight important types of environmental pollutants largely related to agriculture have been identified and discussed in a special study by the United States Department of Agriculture.[8] Soil sediment, animal wastes,

---

[6]These are mentioned in the enlightening discussion of this issue by Ralph Turvey, "Side Effects of Resource Use," in *Environmental Quality in a Growing Economy*, Henry Jarrett, ed. (Baltimore: Johns Hopkins Press for Resources for the Future, 1966).

[7]H. E. Koenig, W. E. Cooper, and J. M. Falvey, "Industrialized Ecosystem Design and Management," Unpublished paper, Department of Electrical Engineering and System Science, Michigan State University, 1971, p. 14.

[8]*Control of Agriculture-related Pollution*, a report to the President of the United States, submitted by the Secretary of Agriculture and the Director of the Office of Science and Technology, Washington, D. C., 1969.

wastes from industrial processing of raw agricultural products, plant nutrients, forest and crop residues, inorganic salts and minerals, pesticides, and certain kinds of air pollution all are sources of environmental problems directly traceable to agriculture.

In terms of quantity, soil sediment from eroding farm land is the biggest single source of agricultural pollution. Much of this is in the form of invisible sheet erosion rather than the more dramatic gully erosion. The direct effect of sediment is physical impairment of the quality of the water receiving the sediment, but the indirect effect of chemical and biological agents carried by the sediment are substantial. Storage capacity of artifical reservoirs is being reduced at an annual rate of about 1 million acre-feet each year through the deposition of sediment. Other physical damage includes wearing or abrasion of power turbines, pumping equipment, and other structures, the degradation of fishing or swimming, and destruction of shellfish and game fish habitat. Sediment from nonagricultural land uses such as rural road construction, strip mining, unstable stream banks, and extension of subdivisions adds to the problem.

It is estimated that approximately 1.7 billion tons of animal wastes are produced annually, with up to 50 percent coming from concentrated production systems. Continuation of past trends toward increased concentration of animals will add to the problem. As urban and suburban developments reach into formerly rural areas, the odor, dust, and insect problems associated with intensive livestock production become a source of friction between producers and the community. Runoff of wastes from feedlots increases the rates of eutrophication of water sources, concentrates nitrates in ground water, and generally degrades the quality of receiving water. As the density of animals increases, the investment necessary for effective waste management increases rapidly, offsetting some of the apparent economies of large-scale production. Effective resolution of this problem is a challenge facing agriculture in the next decade.

The wastes from the industrial processing of raw agricultural products have been estimated to have the same biochemical oxygen demand as 168 million people. The biggest contributors to this problem are paper mills, textile mills, fruit and vegetable processing plants, leather tanning and finishing plants, meat processing plants, and dairies. These processing plants produce pulp wastes, organic waste materials, and acid whey that are generally disposed of in the most convenient stream. Methods of control and reusing waste products are being intensively investigated, and may be expected to generate demands for some modifications in the characteristics of raw product demand by processors.

The escape of fertilizer plant nutrients from the soil into lakes, streams, and groundwater is cause for serious concern. Nutrients in surface waters contribute to excessive growth of aquatic plants, which in turn adversely affects the value of water for fish, recreation, or human consumption.

Excessive nitrates in drinking water can lead to nitrite poisoning of children and ruminant livestock.

Rising rates of fertilization may be related to nutrient pollution from a number of chemicals, but nitrogen and phosphorous are the two most important. Nitrogen gets into water as dissolved nitrogen, so abatement involves reducing the excessive available nitrogen. Phosphorous, on the other hand, is carried into water attached to soil particles, so its control requires control of the sediment referred to earlier.

Lumbering, land clearing, and forest cultural work result in considerable quantities of forest residues. These residues present fire hazards, reservoirs for diseases, and pest insects. Improper harvesting methods can lead to excessive soil erosion and stream degradation. Burning of forest residues, now the most economical means of reducing insect and disease problems and lowering the probability of forest fires, is a source of air pollution. Burning of crop residues, also practiced to some extent, creates the same problem.

The use of chemical pesticides has increased rapidly in the last two decades. These chemicals, if they remain in the environment after their intended purpose is accomplished, or if they damage some species other than the intended target, become pollutants. Accidents with these materials add to hazards that arise from regular use. The environmental issues involved in pesticide use are very complex and numerous. Some relate to long-term, low-level exposure to humans, some relate to their effect on wildlife, some to residual effects on soil or water, others to immediate toxic effects. Intensive investigation of many of these long- and short-term effects of pesticides are underway. Improved control over manufacture, distribution, and use of the materials and better methods for disposal of containers is one means of reducing pollution from pesticides. Alternative means of pest control are being actively pursued, but relatively few practical methods have yet been developed. Some pesticides have been banned and the use of others has been much more tightly controlled.

Environmental Quality Controls on Variable Inputs

In the discussion of agriculture's effect on the environment, those involved seem to have lined up in two opposing groups: the supporters of the environment versus the supporters of farmers. This development is not only uncomfortable for most but is also unlikely to lead to the best resolution of the problem, and is doubly unfortunate because both groups of scientists are equally dedicated to the welfare of society. This book is not the appropriate place to try to discuss the evidence regarding the ecological and environmental effects of agricultural practices. That evidence is so incomplete and fragmentary that even the experts disagree over its interpretation. It is enough to recognize that it is likely that some of the agriculturally related environmental problems mentioned above will be counteracted by legislation, regulation, or other means of social control. The issue we wish to deal with here is—what will be the economic effects of such control measures?

The direct and indirect effects of such measures will be distributed over time, and the long-run effects may well differ from the short-run effects. Control measures will have direct effects on agricultural producers by changing their methods of production, direct effects on producers of certain affected inputs, and indirect effects on society through the market as well as through the environment.

The direct short-run effects on farmers of controlling or restricting the application of particular variable inputs are relatively easy to conceptualize. Such inputs presently have a function in the production process. Elimination of an input from the production process means that either some other input will be used or the level of production will be reduced. The cost of using an alternative input will be higher in the short run, because otherwise producers would have been using that input already. Thus, the shift to a higher-cost input is equivalent to "reverse" technological change as that concept was discussed in Chapters 4 and 6. Our analysis here is similar to, but the reverse of, the analysis there. Higher unit costs, if they affect all firms, will be reflected in a leftward shift in the supply curve of the industry. That reduction in supply will result in a higher market price. Because the demand for most agricultural products is inelastic, the upward movement along the demand curve brought about by a reduction in supply will increase total revenue to producers. Net income may either increase or decrease depending on whether costs or revenue rise more. If, instead of shifting to a higher-cost input, producers simply eliminate an input from the production process, the level of production is reduced and again the result is an increase in unit costs. The reduction in supply again leads to an increase in total revenue, but now because total costs are lower, net revenue to producers will increase.

In the long run, several events may occur as a result of input restriction. Those crops for which net income is increased may well attract producers, shifting the supply curve to the right and thereby increasing output over time as a result of input restrictions. If net income of one crop is reduced more by restrictions than net income of some other crop, then the comparative advantage of the first will suffer and it may be replaced in a cropping system.

For example, the practice of burning off sugar cane prior to harvest in order to eliminate excess foliage and make harvesting easier has come under attack because of the air pollution it creates. Prohibition of burning would mean that harvesting costs would be higher. It might well be that the costs could increase to such an extent that producers would find it more profitable to produce something other than sugar cane. Suppose the next best alternative to sugar cane harvested using the burning technique is the production of cotton. Cotton production would increase, and because its demand is inelastic, the total revenue to cotton producers would fall (assuming no government policy action to prevent such an event). On the other hand, the supply of sugar cane would be reduced, its price would tend to increase, and if demand is inelastic, total revenue to the remaining domestic sugar cane producers would increase. (This might result instead in increased quotas for imports, in which case prices might go up, go down, or remain constant.)

Changes in the comparative advantages of crops that result from environmentally dictated restrictions are likely to be fairly widespread, but they are not likely to completely eliminate important crops in an area; rather the relative acreages of particular crops would be changed.

The direct short-run effects of restricting the utilization of certain inputs on input producers are also easy to visualize. Their sales are reduced, and hence the firms suffer a reduction in business. It is significant that pesticide producers rather than farmers have challenged the action of the Environmental Protection Agency in banning the use of particular pesticides. One long-run effect of input control is to stimulate the development of new and better means of control. Research on biological pest control, nonpersistent chemicals, and resistant plant and animal varieties has been greatly increased in light of the prospect of controls on certain inputs.

Environmental Controls Involving Capital Investments

Another issue is encountered if one considers situations involving large capital investments. One example is restricting the allowable runoff of organic material from livestock production units. The average size of such units has increased substantially in recent years, and with that increase have come almost critical problems of waste management. These problems are affected by the proximity to densely populated areas, the high cost of labor, the relatively low cost of commercial fertilizer, and the limited availability of land on some farms for waste disposal.

Livestock production managed as a confinement operation requires a great deal more capital investment in specialized buildings, feeding equipment, and waste handling facilities than with other management systems. Strict limits on runoff may force producers to make additional large capital investments. These intensify the financial problems discussed in Chapter 20. Because such investments add to the fixed costs of production, and change the proportion of fixed and variable costs, the analysis of their effects on individual farms is somewhat different than the analysis of restricting a variable input.

Producers have two possible reactions to pollution control regulations. They may comply by making the required investment, or they may shift their resources to produce some other enterprise. The first alternative will result in increased costs. Initially, this cost will be borne by producers because they have no control over price. To the extent that total supply is reduced, because some producers drop the enterprise, prices will rise. The amount of the price rise may be enough to cover the increased costs, but this is by no means an assured result. In the long run, production may expand as the remaining producers attempt to exploit the economies of scale inherent in capital-intensive waste management systems.

The decision of whether to make the investment necessary for abatement will be analyzed by the farmer as follows. The system is a variable cost until it is installed. The decision of whether to add the abatement system and continue production or shift resources to another enterprise depends on whether the incremental average unit costs of the abatement system plus existing average variable costs exceed the price received. If they do, the producer will not install the system, but if those unit costs are less than price, it will be economically rational to go ahead.

The cost of a pollution abatement system depends on soil, water, and rainfall conditions and on the type of livestock production unit. Van Arsdall and Johnson identified four different types of hog production units.[9] On a 50-hog pasture based unit, annual added costs of pollution abatement might be $.30 per hog. On a 500-hog summer pasture operation with open-front shed housing and a paved lot for winter use, pollution abatement might cost $5.75 per hog. A 1500-hog total confinement system might only have to incur an added cost of $.16 per hog because it probably would have a nearly complete waste handling system. It appears that the middle sized unit, typically a moderately successful family operation, will have the largest adjustment, and the very big and very small units will be much less affected. This might result in the middle unit dropping hogs and shifting resources to intensive crop production. The eventual effect on consumer prices is difficult to predict because it depends on what proportion of farmers make what decision.

Effects on Consumers

The effects on consumers are perhaps the most often overlooked and oversimplified. The basic mechanics of supply and demand mean that a leftward shift in the supply function will result in a higher price. Consumers will ultimately bear that higher price, just as they have been the major beneficiary of the reduction in real food prices that occurred with the introduction of mechanization, new varieties, and fertilizer. A careful analy-

[9]R. N. Van Arsdall and J. B. Johnson, *Economic Implications of Water Pollution Abatement in Family Farm Livestock Production*, ERS-508, U.S.D.A., (December 1972).

sis carried out by Iowa State University showed the effect of limiting or banning the application of chemical fertilizer.[10] Limiting the application of nitrogen fertilizer to 50 pounds per acre would result in 13 percent higher consumer food costs in 1975 and 23 percent higher food costs in 1980 than with no limitations. Although the study included only six major crops and entailed a large number of assumptions, its findings are consistent with the theoretical analysis discussed above. A similar study by the U.S. Department of Agriculture showed that the annual costs of banning the use of the growth stimulant diethylstilbestrol (DES) in cattle feeding might amount to $300 to $460 million. Translated into prices, it might mean an increase of 3.5 cents per pound.[11]

The economic impact of controlling the level of an input used will depend on the contribution of that input to the production process. Fertilizer makes a large contribution to production, so restricting fertilizer application would have a considerable effect on production and consumer prices. The same is true for pesticides. A total ban would have a very sharp economic impact, and restriction of any individual pesticide would have a relatively small impact except where that material is very important in the production of a particular crop. Marginally productive inputs would have a much smaller overall economic effect.

The aspects of increased consumer costs that have been often overlooked are the distributional welfare aspects. An increase in food prices is a disproportionate burden to low-income people because they spend a relatively high fraction of their incomes on food. This income distribution effect must be kept in mind when discussing controls that would reduce the level of farm output.

Individuals with very low incomes might well experience a very rapid reduction in the quantity of goods available to them as a consequence of higher food prices resulting from actions to improve the agricultural environment. We know that low-income individuals spend a large fraction of their income on food. As its price increases, they continue to purchase about the same amount (at least at the levels of income of the poor in the U.S.). As a consequence, the quantity of other real goods they can purchase declines. Because they already are poor, the reduction in their total welfare may be substantial. From their viewpoint, the optimum action to protect the environment may be considerably less than for the society as a whole. This analysis of the distributional effects is only partial because it is likely that actions to improve the environment will be taken in a number of,

[10]L. B. Mayer and S. H. Hargrove, *Food Costs, Farm Incomes and Crop Yields with Restrictions on Fertilizer Use,* Center for Agricultural and Economic Development Report 38, Iowa State University, March 1971.

[11]*Economic Consequences of Banning the Use of Diethylstilbestrol (DES) in Cattle Feeding,* prepared for the Intergovernmental Relations Subcommittee, Committee on Government Operations, U.S. House of Representatives, by Economic Research Service, U.S.D.A., June 1971.

sectors of the economy simultaneously. Because the poor probably suffer the most from air pollution, urban crowding, and certain other environmental problems, efforts to solve those problems may benefit the poor more than the rest of society. Any evaluation of the distribution or welfare impact of steps to improve the environment would have to include these aspects as well.

Soil Conservation and Land Use Economics

One environmental area in which the agricultural sector has a long-term interest is in the land. Historically, farmers viewed the land and soil resources of North America as inexhaustible, but by the twentieth century that view had clearly been proved wrong. Yet the growth and development of our country, our schools, hospitals, churches, and our educational system has been made possible by the transfer of assets from virgin soil fertility into these other forms. It is clear, however, that man cannot continue to take without seriously depleting the future productive capacity of the land.

The economic problems associated with use and maintenance of soil resources involve problems of externalities. Individual producers have the incentive to carry out certain high-return conservation practices. Many other practices involve high costs to private land owners and substantial public benefits but few private benefits. In certain low-productive areas, public land ownership appears to be desirable in the interests of conservation.

Influence of Available New Land. Without question, the availability of additional new land had a great influence on the land use and soil management practices followed by the early farmers. But probably even more important, the large store of fertility in the virgin soils permitted farmers to continue exploitive cropping practices for many years before important declines in yields took place. Improvements in seed strains and cultural implements permitted the farmers to maintain, or even increase, crop yields, without employing good soil management practices. When the cropland, after years of use, failed to respond to the usual cultural practices, farmers were at a loss to know what changes were needed. They had developed practices suitable to the exploitation of a new continent and had forgotten the farming practices of the older, stabilized farming areas. For example, during the first fifty to seventy-five years of farming on the prairie and hardwood timbered soils of the humid sections of the United States, there was sufficient calcium in the topsoil to obtain good stands of legumes. Later, when clover seedings failed year after year, farmers did not know what measures were needed to correct the difficulties. It is only in the last fifty years that the general need of agricultural limestone was recognized.

Influence of Private Ownership. One of the important advantages attributed to private property is the ownership interest that results in better care than public property would receive. It was partly with this interest in mind that the decision was made to vest all the ownership rights in land in individuals. Our government not only followed the policy of selling the publicly owned land to individuals at low prices as rapidly as possible, it failed to reserve to the government any control concerning its use. One hundred years later, when the public became concerned about excessive soil erosion losses, the farm land was in private ownership and the federal government had no authority to restrict even the worst abuses of the land.

Comparisons between public and private ownership indicate many advantages for private ownership in line with our American ideals. Yet, the fact that the farm land of the United States is owned by nearly 3 million different families adds to the difficulty in making rapid progress with public soil conservation programs. Under our constitution, the power to regulate land uses remains with the states rather than the federal government. The federal government may encourage soil conservation by making payments for specific conserving practices. It may furnish technical assistance to help farmers make soil and water conservation plans, and it may carry on educational programs. Yet any particular farmer or group of farmers may ignore all these programs if they wish.

Conservation versus Production. Soil conservation, in the minds of many people, is the prevention of soil erosion losses. When we go beyond this very general statement to a more precise definition, we have difficulty. There are four major ways of preventing excessive soil erosion on farm land. The most spectacular one, engineering practices, involves terracing sloping fields, planting crops on the contour, strip cropping (alternating strips of sod and intertilled crops planted on the contour), planting of wide grassed waterways, and diversion check dams to slow down the water runoff.

A second method of reducing soil erosion losses involves the use of crop rotations with more years of sod-forming grass and legume crops and fewer years of intertilled crops. Soil losses are at a minimum when the soil is held together by heavily rooted, sod-forming grass and legumes and are at a maximum when the land is planted to an intertilled crop, such as corn or cotton. The third method of reducing soil losses is to build up the organic matter in the soil. Organic matter in the soil absorbs and holds the moisture while acting as a stabilizer of the mineral particles. Soils high in organic matter permit a greater infiltration and reduce the runoff as compared with soils of the same slope and texture but low in organic matter. Reduced runoff means reduced soil losses. The fourth method is to change the use of land from cultivation to permanent grass or trees.

Conservation has been defined as the use and treatment of land to maintain its capacity to produce on a sustained basis. Other definitions differ in detail, but agree that the central objective of conservation is the saving of a resource for future production in contrast to present use or waste. Thus, we think of conservation activities as those directed toward maintaining resources for future use, in contrast to production activities that are directed toward the transformation of resources into products wanted by consumers.

When one attempts to classify activities relating to land use and treatment into these two categories, conservation and current production, he finds that often they are not competing objectives. Terraces, contour strip cropping, and contour cultivation not only retard and reduce water runoff and soil erosion, saving more of our soil for future generations, but at the same time increase production. Terracing, where practiced in the southern states in the early history of this country, was primarily a practice to increase crop yields currently, rather than a means of saving soil resources for future generations.

Other practices, such as rotations including more grass and legumes, not only reduce soil losses but also increase total production as compared with prevailing crop rotations in most of the northern, humid sections of the United States.

The use of agricultural limestone, phosphates, and potash increases legume growth, improves the organic matter content of the soil, and thus reduces erosion losses. But here again, soils high in organic matter and in plant nutrients (resulting from the legumes) produce much higher crop yields than similar soils low in organic matter and nutrients. Farmers usually do not decide whether to include more grass and legumes in their rotations or to use soil amendments and fertilizers entirely on the basis of their interest in conservation. They adopt these practices to increase or maintain production as well as to conserve the soil. Additional inputs of materials and labor, or rotations including more grass and legumes that reduce soil erosion losses, usually increase crop yields immediately, or in the near future. (Grassed waterways may be an exception.) In most agricultural areas, the conflict between soil conservation objectives and current production objectives is not serious when farmers are following accepted good farm management practices. In almost any community of the United States where soil erosion losses are large enough to be considered serious, most changes in cropping and fertilizer practices that conserve the soil also increase current crop production. Thus, we conclude, much of the problem of soil conservation is solved by better farm management, including land use, crop rotations, and fertilization practices that are profitable production practices.

Economic Formulation of the Conservation Problem. Obviously, to the extent that increased soil conservation results from the adoption of improved (more economic) land use and production practices, there is no conflict between conservation and production objectives. There is no economic problem in the adoption of these soil conservation practices. Farmers who fail to adopt them are failing to take full advantage of their economic opportunities.

But there are conservation practices that reduce current production and income. A farmer in the northern Corn Belt, with a rotation that keeps one-third of his cropland in intertilled crops, one-third in small grains, and one-third in sod crops, might increase his total production and reduce his soil erosion losses by increasing his grass and legume acreage to 50 percent of his cropland and reducing his intertilled crops and small grain to 25 percent. He could reduce erosion losses further by keeping even more of his cropland in grasses and legumes. But if he does, his feed production and income is lower than when only 50 percent of the cropland is in sod crops. Here, we find the conservation objective in conflict with the current use objective. This conflict is common on wheat farms where rotations are virtually impossible and the land must either be continually cropped to wheat or reseeded to range grasses. Under these conditions, what level of conservation is economic for the individual farmer?

In production, marginal costs are balanced against the marginal value of the output. *In conservation, marginal costs are balanced against the marginal losses prevented or marginal value added to the resource conserved.* The primary difference is that conservation costs include the value of current production given up in the interests of conserving the soil as well as direct labor and capital investments in conservation practices. These are related to the value of the soil saved for future use.

Alternative Means of Ensuring Environmental Quality

We have focused on regulation as a solution to the environmental problems because it is the simplest to conceive of and the method most commonly used or proposed. It is by no means the only method. Education is being used to make people aware of the problem and what they might do to combat it. Public investments to overcome existing problems are often the only practical means of dealing with certain situations. The provision of economic incentives to encourage firms to correct environmental problems for which they are responsible is a fourth means that many economists believe to be the best long-run solution. Changing prices or providing subsidies or taxes then give each individual the incentive to operate in the interest of society. This may be looked upon as internalizing an externality.

As we have already pointed out, farm producers, as rational decision makers, consider the effect of conservation practices on the profitability of their operations. At present, there is no economic incentive to consider the external impact of possible erosion on streams and reservoirs, which may include destruction of the natural environment for fish and other aquatic life, reduced efficiency of waterways and reservoirs, increased dredging, and increased cost of municipal water treatment. One way of internalizing these costs, if that method of control is desired, is discussed below.[12]

Public programs for supporting farm incomes generally involve a payment to farmers who comply with certain requirements to reduce planted acreage. It is suggested that income objectives and environmental protection objectives could be jointly achieved if such programs required added conservation practices for participation. It is likely that payment levels would have to be increased and that to be effective such a program would require long-run commitments by the government. It is also recognized that producers not participating in the income programs would have no incentive to carry out added conservation practices.

The further step of implementing a sediment effluent charge would provide an incentive for participation by all farmers, in proportion to the degree of sedimentation from their farm. Using known relationships between rainfall, slope, slope length, soil type, crop and management practices, and conservation practices, the gross soil loss from a field can be calculated. With this information, the quantity of sediment eroded and entering a stream or river can be estimated. A charge based on this quantity could then be assessed.

The producer then would have the alternative of paying the charge or changing his production practices to reduce the quantity of sediment discharged. If the charge were high enough, it would be cheaper to change production practices rather than pay it. Of course, costs to producers will depend on their soil type, slope, and other characteristics entering the formula. The implementation of a sediment charge would thus have the effect of increasing the economic advantage already enjoyed by level, permeable land as compared to sloping, impermeable land. That is an inevitable effect of shifting land toward less-intensive uses.

Economic incentives resulting in the production of less output, as in the case of regulation, will result in a reduction of output relatively smaller than the increase in price, so total revenue to remaining producers will increase. Those producers on poor land who shift to less-intensive production will bear the burden of economic adjustment. This may suggest that some added policy to assist in making the necessary adjustment is required. It does not, however, suggest that the sediment charge is poorly designed. In fact, if the objective of the charge is to allocate the external costs of

---

[12]The conceptualization of this problem owes much to a paper by W. D. Seitz and R. G. F. Spitze, "Environmentalizing Agricultural Production Policies," *Journal of Soil and Water Conservation*, March-April, 1973.

sedimentation among the units responsible, then those farms contributing the most should bear the highest costs.

POINTS FOR DISCUSSION

1. What are some of the reasons that environmental problems are currently so important in the United States?
2. Explain the concept of external costs, using the example of runoff from a livestock production unit.
3. Briefly identify the major environmental protection standards that affect farmers in your local community.
4. Explain why reducing the use of an input by one farmer would hurt that farmer and not help other farmers, but reducing the use of the same input by all farmers would help the farming sector.
5. Why might consumers oppose environmentally directed changes in U.S. farming?

REFERENCES

"Agriculture in the Environment," *ERS-481,* Economic Research Service, U.S.D.A. (July 1971).

BREWER, M. F., "Agrisystems and Ecocultures, or: Can Economics Internalize Agriculture's Environmental Externalities?" *American Journal of Agricultural Economics,* Vol. 53, (December 1971), pp. 848–57.

COALE, A. J., "Man and His Environment," *Science,* Vol. 9 (October 1970).

Economic Research on Pesticides for Policy Decisionmaking. Proceedings of a Symposium, Washington, D.C., April 27–29, 1970. Economic Research Service, U.S.D.A. (April 1971).

JARRETT, H., ed., *Environmental Quality in a Growing Economy.* Baltimore: The Johns Hopkins Press, 1966.

MEADOWS, D. H., D. L. MEADOWS, J. RANDERS, AND W. W. BEHRENS III, *The Limits to Growth.* New York: Universe Books, 1972.

RUTTAN, V. W., "Technology and the Environment," *American Journal of Agricultural Economics,* Vol. 53 (December 1971).

Chapter 22

Taxation and Social Control

of Land Use

Taxes are of concern to every citizen because they support the services provided by and for society in general, but also are a direct cost to the individuals paying them. Like everyone else, farmers pay property, sales, income, and excise taxes (sales taxes levied on specific goods, for example gasoline or cigarettes). Because they own considerable real estate and personal property, taxes on this property are of particular concern to them. In recent years, the level of real estate taxes have climbed at a rapid, and to some, an alarming rate. Table 22–1 shows how these taxes have changed over the past fifty years.

Real estate taxes and personal property taxes are largely paid to the same units of government. If one increases, it means that relatively less revenue needs to be raised from the other. Real estate taxes have been increasing very rapidly, and Table 22–1 shows that farm personal property taxes have been increasing more slowly. In fact, personal property taxes are losing favor as an increasing number of states exempt all classes of personal property from taxation. Because tangible personal property is easily located and assessed, farmers, with mostly tangible personal property, may pay a higher rate than others who have considerable financial wealth. The move away from personal property taxes relieves the tax burden of farmers to a somewhat greater extent than most other groups because farmers have a disproportionately large share of their wealth in tangible personal property.

Real estate taxes have increased very rapidly in absolute terms, but

TABLE 22–1

Property Taxes Paid by Farmers, 1925–70

Year(s)	Farm Real Estate	Farm Personal Property	Real Estate Taxes per $100 of Value	Real Estate Tax per $100 of Net Farm Income
	——(million dollars)——			
1925	516.8	71.7	1.07	8.47
1930	566.8	81.3	1.31	13.30
1935	392.3	42.0	1.14	7.43
1940–45	405.3	66.0	.98	4.58
1945–49	590.2	126.7	.84	4.03
1950–54	811.0	210.3	.92	5.77
1955–59	1034.6	238.5	.95	8.74
1960–65	1371.3	307.8	1.00	10.75
1966	1715.2	368.3	1.00	10.55
1967	1857.9	382.5	1.02	12.48
1968	2066.0	415.0	1.06	13.94
1969	2263.0	416.6	1.12	13.39
1970	2493.9	445.8		15.64

Source: Derived from data in *Agricultural Finance Review*, Volume 32, Supplement, Economic Research Service, U.S.D.A., January 1972; "Revised Estimates of Taxes Levied on Farm Real Property, 1950-1967," *Statistical Bulletin No. 441*, Economic Research Service, U.S.D.A., July 1969; *Farm Income Situation FIS-218*, Economic Research Service, U.S.D.A., July 1971.

in relation to the value of land they have not registered much change, as shown by the third column in Table 22–1. This simply reflects the fact that property taxes are based on the value of land, and as we have seen earlier the value of land in the U.S. has been increasing very rapidly. On the other hand, real estate taxes have increased rapidly relative to net farm income—a measure of the ability to pay. Thus, farm land owners are assessed on the basis of growing land values that only have operational significance when the land is sold or used as debt collateral, but their ability to bear the taxes is constrained by constant income levels. This dilemma adds to the farm financial problems discussed earlier.

Shifting and Incidence of Taxes in Relation to Agriculture

Farmers have a special interest in taxes because of the effects of particular kinds of taxes on the demand and supply of farm products, land use, and land tenure. We will first review the general principles governing the shifting and incidence of taxes and then examine the general property tax in some detail, as it affects farmers.

Taxes levied on products or services do not fall wholly on either the consumers or the producers of those products. As an illustration, suppose a special excise tax is levied on rail and air transportation (such a tax has been in effect since World War II in our country). The effect of a general sales tax is similar, but it is clearer to trace the impact of such taxes through a specific commodity. The tax is not borne entirely by the transportation companies. It may be added directly to the regular transportation charges or, if paid in the first instance by the transportation companies, it may cause companies to raise their rates. But a rise in transportation rates growing out of the new taxes is not fully passed on to the consumers. If consumer prices of lumber, for example, are raised by the higher transportation charges, home builders who had been considering local brick or masonry construction rather than lumber are likely to use more of these local building materials and less of the shipped-in lumber. Lumber companies, faced with higher transportation charges, find they must either lower their prices at the sawmill or accept a smaller volume of sales.

Under the pressure of these economic forces, consumers probably pay somewhat higher prices for lumber and use a somewhat smaller quantity of shipped-in lumber, thus reducing the profits of both the lumber companies and the transportation companies (because less lumber is transported). This tendency of taxes to be distributed among consumers, producers, and other business groups transporting, processing, or distributing the product is referred to as the shifting of taxes. The incidence of the tax refers to its final resting place. The extent to which a tax will be shifted and the location of its final incidence depend primarily on the elasticity of the supply and demand for the particular products the prices or costs of which are affected by the new tax levy.

The tax burden is shifted by changing the amount of a particular product produced and consumed. We put special taxes on luxuries during war times as this is one way of both raising revenue and discouraging the production of these unnecessary products. A tax system that interferes as little as possible with normal business operations is preferred by most people. Taxes on special products or services are undesirable, unless there are reasons for discouraging their production and use. It is on this basis that high taxes on liquor and tobacco products are justified.

The great merit of personal and corporate income taxes is that they cannot be shifted. The tax falls directly on the individuals or corporations from whom the tax is collected and, under ordinary circumstances, does not affect their business decisions or practices. Congress, in specifying the tax rates for individuals and corporations in different income groups, decides how much of the relative burden to place on each. Farmers are subject to the personal income taxes as are other citizens, but this tax creates no special problem for them. They are affected as are all producing and consuming groups by most other special taxes on products and services mentioned at the beginning of the chapter. But farmers have a special interest in the general property tax because it is a major fixed cost. Real estate taxes measured as a percentage of net farm income more than doubled between 1950 and 1970. In the last five years of the 1960s, real estate taxes varied from over 20 percent of net farm income in Oregon, California, and Alaska to less than 3 percent in Mississippi and Louisiana. Variation within states was nearly as great.

Characteristics of General Property Tax

The property tax is one of the oldest forms of taxation. In the early days of its use, the ownership of property was roughly indicative of a man's income and ability to contribute to the expenses of government. When farming was the primary source of income in a community, as in colonial times, taxes based on the amount and value of property were roughly equivalent to taxes based on the incomes of the individuals in the community. As compared with income, sales, and excise taxes (taxes on products), property taxes have the advantage of being a stable source of income year after year, and evasion of property taxes on land is minimal.

General Weakness of the Property Tax. In the early days, land taxes were largely at a uniform rate per acre, with little or no adjustments for differences in value or income-producing ability.[1] Today, however, farm lands are periodically "appraised" by the tax assessor and are taxed at a uniform rate on their appraised value. The assessor, in most states, is instructed to appraise farm lands on the basis of their sale value, or on some percentage of sale value. Under this appraisal procedure, different farms should be taxed in relation to their income-producing ability. Actually, however, great inequities exist. The primary difficulty is that a large number of different assessors are required in each county and state. In spite of appraisal review procedures, substantial differences exist between values placed on equally productive lands in different parts of a county or state that are subject to uniform tax rates. Studies also have shown repeatedly that tax assessors tend to value all farm lands in their administrative unit close to an average figure. The best farm lands are systematically undervalued and the poorest farm lands overvalued relative to their income-producing ability.

Most states provide that their property taxes shall apply to personal, as well as real or landed, property. Experience with the property taxes on intangibles, such as money in bank accounts, stocks, bonds, mortgages, and jewelry, indicates they are especially difficult to administer because of the ease of concealment. For this reason, a number of states have specifically exempted intangible property from taxation. Administration of personal

---

[1]For a history of the property tax, especially in relation to land, see R. R. Renne, *Land Economics*, rev. ed. (New York: Harper & Row, 1958), Chap. 14.

property taxes is probably even more inequitable than the administration of real estate taxes because of the failure of different assessors to be equally successful in placing all taxable personal property on the tax rolls and because of differences in appraisal values assigned to similar property by different assessors.

A further weakness in the general property tax is its rigidity from year to year, regardless of the income earned by the farm family. While their stable yield to governmental units is one of the outstanding advantages of property taxes, they often cause severe hardship to farm families during extended periods of drought or low prices.

Trend in Property Taxes on Farm Real Estate. Records of tax levies on farm real estate exist dating from 1890. At that time, they averaged $.13 an acre in the United States. After 1900, there was a gradual rise in tax rates that continued more or less regularly until rates hit a peak of $.58 an acre in 1928 and 1929. Following this peak, there was a general decline with property tax levies on farm real estate, reaching a low of $.37 in 1943. Since that time, they have increased to surpass $2.00 per acre.

As the cost of local and state governments continued to rise through the years, increasing pressure was exerted on legislatures to find other sources of income that were not reached by the property tax, except to a minor extent. With the increase in numbers of automobiles, a new source of revenue was imperative to provide the necessary road-building funds. This led to the general adoption of state excise taxes on gasoline. Some states segregate all their income from gasoline taxes for road building. Others use a part of it for other purposes.

During the 1930s when farm incomes were extremely low, there was a strong demand from property owners in most states for shifting a part of their tax burden to other forms of taxation that corresponded more nearly to ability to pay. In some states, this resulted in the passage of state income taxes; others added a few excise taxes, such as those on liquor and cigarettes, to supplement their property taxes. To an increasing extent, states have been adopting aid programs that allocate a part of these state funds, derived from other than property taxes, to local units of government. This has permitted the lowering of local property tax levies, or the improvement of government services, without a corresponding increase in local tax rates.

In the last decade, the number of states levying general sales taxes and the rates of such taxes have increased. The move toward a national sales tax in the form of a value added tax (VAT) was initiated in the early 1970s. A VAT is assessed at each stage in the production process. If applied to farm production, it might work as follows in the case of feeder cattle. The producer would keep account of all the purchased inputs used in production—initial purchase price, food, hired labor, and so on. When the animals where sold, the difference between sale revenue and the cost of all inputs would be the "value added," or that contribution made by the resources provided by the producer. The VAT would be computed on this value added. The incidence of a VAT depends on the elasticity of the supply and demand for products, just as is true for any excise tax.

Influence of Property Tax on Land Use. Taxes on land affect its use under several different conditions. In the northern counties of the Lake States and, to a lesser extent, in other natural forested areas, lands that are marginal or almost marginal for crop production have been cleared and farmed. Local government services have been developed to meet the needs of the population, resulting in tax rates that are high relative to the income-producing ability of the land. Farmers who might reforest substantial acreages of these marginal lands, cannot continue to pay the taxes year after year while waiting for an income from their forest crop. Faced with the necessity of paying taxes on the land annually and with the need for income for family living, they continue to grow poor crops, always hoping that next year will be better. Absentee owners of woodlands, which are marginal for crop production, find it more economical to cut off all salable timber and let the land become tax delinquent, rather than maintain sustained yield timber-cutting programs when annual taxes are relatively high.

In the Great Plains states, under the incentive of high prices during both World War I and World War II, thousands of acres of range land that were marginal for crop production were plowed up for wheat production. Although the long time income-producing ability of these lands is greater in grass than in wheat, reseeding takes place very slowly. When property taxes represent a substantial annual charge, the landowner either keeps the land in wheat or allows it to become tax delinquent. He cannot afford the reseeding costs, the annual taxes, and the other costs that must be incurred while waiting for income from grass lands again.

Heavy property taxes on land, especially during periods of low prices, may cause farmers to crop their land excessively, in an effort to meet their overhead costs. Taxes may be only one of a number of overhead costs, including interest payments on the mortgage and minimum family living expenses, but they are an important part of this group of overhead expenses that cause a farmer to fully maintain, or even expand, his cropping operations when prices fall.

During the 1930s when farm incomes were at extremely low levels because of both unfavorable weather and unfavorable prices, property tax delinquency and tax foreclosure were widespread. This was most serious from the standpoint of effective utilization of the land and from the standpoint of the government services dependent upon property taxes as a source of revenue in the Great Plains states. A high percentage of the farm real estate taxes became delinquent in these states in 1932 and 1933.

Exemption of Homesteads. Probably one-fourth the states now have homestead exemption provisions in their tax statutes. The purpose of these exemptions is to encourage home ownership. Although provisions of the different state laws vary, owner-occupied residences on the farm or in the town or city are granted special tax discounts. These discounts are continued each year as long as the owner continues to occupy the residence. Although the practice of granting homestead exemptions has not been adopted by many additional states in recent years, it continues to be popular in the states in which it is in force. Although the lower taxes increase the inducement for home ownership, in the sense of lowering the cost, they may hinder, rather than assist, tenants who are attempting to accumulate sufficient capital to buy their own farm or home. Tax funds not contributed by the current home owners must be raised by those who do not own their homes.

Special Taxation of Forest Lands. Because of the adverse effect of existing property taxes on the development of sound forestry practices on private lands, a number of states have special exemption privileges for lands used only for forestry purposes. Wisconsin passed a special forest-crop law in the 1930s that provided for a low annual tax on the land for fifty years, plus 10 percent of the value of the timber cut, at the time of cutting.[2] The object of this law was both to prevent tax delinquency and to avoid the adverse effects of a heavy annual tax on the landowners' forestry management plans. An important part of this legislation is the provision for state reimbursement of counties for revenues lost by shifting to this plan of taxation. Revenues from the cutting-yield tax are prorated to the counties according to a formula.

Incidence of the Property Tax. The property tax on land, like the income tax, is believed to be superior to other taxes because it cannot be shifted. A landowner cannot pass on a higher tax levied on his farm land. Because the tax does not affect the supply of land and affects the use of land only under marginal farming conditions, a farm owner's production plans are seldom affected by an increase in the tax levied on his land.

Because taxes on land are a first charge against any income that may be derived from it, they are taken into consideration in determining its value. Two farms with equal income-producing ability may have different values because of differences in prevailing tax rates.

Using the capitalization formula: $\text{Value} = \dfrac{\text{Annual income}}{\text{Capitalization rate}}$

if the capitalization rate is 5 percent, a $.50 increase in taxes per acre,

[2] See *The Wisconsin Forest Crop and Woodland Tax Laws* (Madison, Wisconsin: Wisconsin Conservation Department, 1938).

expected to continue indefinitely, lowers the market value of a farm by $10 an acre:

$$V = \frac{\$.50}{.05} = \$10$$

Increases in land values, associated with the growth of population or general increases in price levels, are "unearned," in the sense that they accrue to the owner merely because he is an owner. They are not the result of any capital investments. Hence, the owner is still as well off as other members of society, even though these increases in value are absorbed by rising property taxes. Australia and New Zealand, in particular, have tax systems incorporating this principle. In the United States, however, difficulties in applying the principle have prevented more than a modest use of it. To the extent that property taxes are based on the appraised value of land, rather than at a flat rate per acre, land that has increased most in value over a period of years pays the highest taxes. But a forthright attempt to follow the principle of taxing away unearned increases in land values would result in such an adjustment in tax rates that no increases in value would occur, except those added by capital investment.

In principle, a prospective buyer of a farm should take into account the prevailing tax levies and adjust his price offer accordingly. In this sense, the buyer of land, after a tax has been levied, buys it tax free. On the other hand, if taxes are increased after the farm has been purchased, they are an unexpected burden. Because only 3 to 4 percent of the farms change hands each year, it would take twenty-five to thirty-five years for changes in tax rates to be capitalized into the land values: approximately the productive life of a farmer.

Another disadvantage of relatively heavy taxes on farm land is the financial distress caused in depressions. Even though the purchaser of a farm took into account the prevailing taxes when he bought the farm, heavy property taxes may contribute to his insolvency during a period of low farm prices. It is for these reasons that most students of public finance believe that, in a modern industrial society, property taxes should play a decreasing role in raising the necessary public revenues. With this brief consideration of the tax problems of most concern to farmers, we will turn to the second topic to be considered in this chapter, the social control of land use.

SOCIAL CONTROL OF LAND USE

Our national government has limited powers and does not have the constitutional authority to enforce land use legislation. If there is to be legislation at all, it must be legislation by the several state governments.

State land use legislation may provide for at least three types of governmental activity by the State and local governments:

(1)   Direct administration of lands by a government agency. Instances
—State or community forests and parks.

(2)   Public regulation of private land use. Instances—rural zoning
ordinances; conservation ordinances adopted by soil conservation districts;
statutory requirements applicable to farm leases.

(3)   Payment of subsidies by a governmental agency on the condition
that particular land use adjustments are made. . . .[3]

Even though states have engaged in the first two activities for some
time, they seldom have used subsidies to achieve land use adjustments on
privately owned land. In contrast, the federal government uses subsidies
extensively to influence the use of privately owned land. Because use of the
police power is reserved to the states, the activities of the Federal government in controlling land use on privately owned land are limited to education, provision of free technical services in connection with soil conservation
and forestry management problems, and payments for the performance of
soil conservation practices. In addition to these activities relating to the
use of privately owned land, the federal government has repurchased limited
acreages of low-productivity lands in order to control their use more effectively.

Federal and State Ownership

Some 765 million acres of land were in Federal ownership in 1970.
Most of this land is public domain that has never been in private ownership.
In the "lower" 48 states, most public land is either too arid, or is otherwise
unsuited to farming. Nearly half of all public land is located in Alaska,
which is 98 percent publicly owned.

In 1934 with the passage of the Taylor Grazing Act, the federal
government assumed active management of publicly owned lands used for
grazing purposes. Prior to that time, grazing had been allowed on these
public lands with no consideration for their conservation or for good range
management practices. Under this legislation, grazing districts supervised
by the Bureau of Land Management, Department of Interior, have been
organized. The bureau administers more land than any other public agency,
nearly 65 percent of all federally owned land. The objectives of the grazing
districts include: (1) stabilization of the use rights on the federal range,
thus increasing the efficiency and security of the livestock industry using it,
and (2) controlling the total amount and seasonal distribution of grazing,
thus conserving the range itself.

The United States Forest Service has the second largest amount of

---

[3]"State Legislation for Better Land Use," *Interbureau Committee Report*, U.S.D.A., April 1941,
pp. XII–XV.

land to administer. In 1966, it was responsible for 186 million acres. This amounts to over 30 percent of all forested lands in the U.S., including 19 percent of the commercial forest area.

The reasons for public ownership and administration of these forest lands were well stated in the following quotation from a government report on government land ownership.

> Even before the country was fully settled it was recognized that the forests were not inexhaustible but were, in fact, being liquidated rapidly. Depleted forest communities found here and there over large areas were in distress. This brought attention to some of the problems and difficulties of private owners in the practice of forestry and forest land management. The desirability of sustained timber management and the insuring of a future supply large enough for the needs of the Nation led to a general acceptance of the necessity of public action and cooperation.
>
> ... public acquisition is aimed toward lands that are unsuitable for private ownership or where private owners are not able to develop sustained-yield forestry. Such land would include that unsuitable for private ownership for reasons of inaccessibility, inherent low productivity, liquidated timber values, need for reforestation or because of inherent public values for watershed protection. . . .[4]

Other federal agencies that own land primarily to control its use in the public interest, with the total acreage acquired by each agency, are as follows:[5]

National Park Service	22,930,000
Fish and Wildlife Service	27,114,000
Department of Defense	30,472,000
Bureau of Reclamation	9,017,000
Bureau of Indian Affairs[6]	4,935,000
Atomic Energy Commission	2,152,000

During the period of agricultural distress in the 1930s, considerable acreage was acquired by the federal agencies as a part of an aggressive policy of improving land use. During that period, around 10 million acres of land, believed to be submarginal for general farming purposes, were acquired from private owners. Some of this land was added to the wildlife areas, some to the national forests, and a million acres were transferred for administration to state agencies under agreements with the Department of

---

[4]*Federal Rural Lands* unpublished paper of the Bureau of Agricultural Economics, U.S.D.A., June 1947, p. 20.

[5]Data on federal land ownership are taken from *Agricultural Information Bulletin 338*, Economic Research Service, U.S.D.A., June 1969.

[6]Does not include Indian trust properties.

Agriculture. The bulk of these submarginal lands, however, is now administered by the Soil Conservation Service, with grazing as its primary use.

Since 1943, very small acreages of submarginal land have been acquired by the government. Little public support now exists for a submarginal land purchase program. Further additions to the land in federal ownership are limited to donations and strategic purchases for parks, wildlife areas and national forests. Interest of nonrural people in these uses of land is increasing as leisure time activities in parks and wilderness areas become more popular

In addition to these federal lands, the states have acquired about 20 million acres of state forests, parks, and wildlife areas to control the use of these lands in the public interest. Although most of the forested lands not in private ownership are either state or national forests, county units of government have established forestry units on lands that have been taken over for tax delinquency in several states.

Rural Zoning

Rural zoning is the division of the community, by means of local laws called zoning ordinances, into suitable kinds of districts or zones for agriculture, residences, business, forestry, and so on. Local laws are then applied in each kind of district to regulate: (1) the use of land, buildings, and structures; (2) the size and coverage of building lots or tracts; (3) the height and size of buildings and structures; and (4) the density of population.

Zoning ordinances are an excercise by local units of government of the police powers granted by the State—that is, the power to safeguard and promote public health, safety, morals, or the general welfare. The general constitutional requirements to which each zoning regulation must conform if it is to be valid are:

1. The objectives of the regulation must promote general welfare.
2. The methods used must have a substantial relation to the ends or objectives sought.
3. The regulation must not be arbitrary, unreasonable, nor oppressive.[7]

One of the important objectives of rural zoning has been the promotion of local governmental efficiency through the prevention of scattered settlement in nonagricultural areas. Further, by guiding the location of residences and industry as they expand into rural areas, zoning can help avoid land use conflicts that might arise when these uses adjoin one another. Zoning can also insure that nonfarm land use does not occur on the best

[7]"State Legislation for Better Land Use," *op. cit.*

farm land. Zoning ordinances adopted by local government units describe the districts zoned, the regulations applied to each, and the means of enforcing them. These districts are usually located on maps. Under most zoning ordinances, existing forbidden or "nonconforming uses," such as year-round residence and farming in an area zoned against such use, may be continued. But if and when such use has been voluntarily discontinued for a specified period, it cannot be started again.

Zoning, as a method of social control of land use, was first tried in rural areas of Wisconsin in 1929. Almost all states now have adopted legislation, enabling local government units to zone rural areas. The success of zoning regulations in controlling land use in the counties having land that is marginal for agriculture led to the adoption of zoning ordinances in some agricultural-industrial counties. These ordinances are designed to prevent the construction of undesirable buildings, of undesirable suburban developments, and so on, especially near the lakes and streams in the country. Rural zoning ordinances have been tested in the courts, and it seems probable that this method of restricting a limited number of undesirable uses of privately owned land will be extended.

Land Use Regulations

Through legislation establishing their soil conservation districts, most states authorize the supervisors of these districts to establish and enforce land use regulations. The procedures require a favorable majority vote by all landowners or users, or a majority of both groups before land use regulations may be imposed. Except in a few isolated instances, the local soil conservation districts have preferred to rely on education and technical assistance, rather than to adopt land use regulations and attempt to use the police power in enforcing desirable land use in the interest of soil and water conservation. Although rural communities are aware of the need for adopting soil conservation measures and will support educational programs for this purpose, it seems unlikely that in the near future they will favor land use regulations.

Use of Economic Incentives

The use of economic incentives to control land use was undertaken on a grand scale in 1933 with the adoption of the agricultural adjustment program. In the early years, the government entered into contracts with farmers to reduce the acreage of specified crops on the basis of an announced scale of payments. These early contracts were designed to reduce the production of these crops; other effects were secondary. When the Supreme Court declared these individual contracts and the purpose for which they were made unconstitutional in 1936, the program was changed somewhat.

The new program adopted in 1936 provided for payments at announced levels if the farmer kept certain crop acreages within specified limits and for small additional payments if he performed certain soil conservation practices. Payments for these conservation practices have been continued, even though acreage adjustment programs have changed. The effectiveness of the use of these funds in increasing conservation practices is limited by the political desirability of making the conditions for earning payment sufficiently general to permit most farms to qualify. As a result, a substantial proportion of the funds are used to pay farmers for practices that are recognized by most as good farming practices and that would be followed even though no payments were made.

Continuing Problems of Taxation and Land Use Control

Improvement in the administration of the property tax is a continuing problem. Serious inequities exist in the appraisal of farm property for taxation purposes in every state and county. The appraisal and tax assessment problem is particularly acute on the marginal and low-productivity lands, where excessive taxes force the land out of private ownership or encourage destructive land use.

Counties with sparse populations and large areas of low-productivity lands often have governmental costs that are excessive in relation to the income produced in the county. When this situation prevails, improvement in property appraisal helps but little. The only effective action is the consolidation of counties and the reduction of local government expenses to a minimum.

Rural zoning has been adopted in relatively few of the states and counties where it would be useful to limit the major uses of rural land by local governmental action. Studies are needed of both the effectiveness of existing rural zoning ordinances in meeting current needs and of the conditions in counties where zoning ordinances are believed to have a useful role to perform.

Educational programs to promote better land use can be improved as additional studies are made to indicate more clearly the best land use practices for the different areas and communities. Economic incentives may have a larger role to play in supplementing educational programs to improve land use, especially if the government continues economic aid programs for farmers. One of the most important areas for study is the ways and means by which improved land use practices might be made a requirement for obtaining benefits from the price support or other economic aid programs.

SPECIAL PROBLEMS OF THE
WESTERN STATES

Over half the land in the eleven western states is in federal and state ownership.[8] These eleven states contain 85 percent of the irrigated land in the United States, which, in turn, accounts for 70 to 75 percent of the cash farm income from crops sold. Thirty to 35 percent of the income from livestock products also comes from irrigated lands in these states. The Great Plains states, just to the east of these eleven western states, have a climate neither consistently humid nor consistently arid. Uncertainty of the climate from year to year is the dominant factor in farming in the Plains states. These three facts—large acreages of public land, large acreages of irrigated land, and an uncertain climate—provide the setting for most of the western land use problems. This section examines the conservation, land management, and other land use problems that grow out of the setting described above in the western states.

As one writer puts it:

> In the arid western part of the United States we face a test of wisdom and leadership—a test which is going to prove decisive during the coming...years. This test will determine whether we can learn to use the resources of arid lands without destroying them, or whether we shall fall victim to the errors that have overtaken the peoples of arid lands, without exception, in the older countries of the world....
>
> To a degree seldom fully realized, the western parts of the United States are yet a frontier in many aspects of land and water use. We have yet to find the key to best uses and stability for much of the land and water resources of the arid West.[9]

Problems Growing out of Public Ownership

We saw that most of the land remaining in public ownership in these western states has been withdrawn from private entry and small amounts have been repurchased from private owners to control its use in the public's interest.

Most of these public lands are grazed by privately owned cattle and sheep, but they have other uses. Many of these lands have strategic watershed protection values. The high-elevation mountain lands of the West, comprising only 20 percent of the watershed area, yield 80 percent

[8]The eleven western states are California, Oregon, Washington, Arizona, New Mexico, Utah, Idaho, Montana, Wyoming, Colorado, and Nevada. Data on importance of irrigated land from H. E. Selby, "The Importance of Irrigation in the Economy of the West," *Journal of Farm Economics*, Vol. 31, pp. 955–64, 1949.

[9]Mont H. Saunderson, *Western Land and Water Use* (Norman, Oklahoma: University of Oklahoma Press, 1950), pp. 43, 202.

of the water.[10] When properly managed, these lands, largely in national forests, perform a vital function in stabilizing the flow of water for irrigation and urban uses on the lower lands.

Many of the lands in the national forests are open range, others are used for grazing interspersed with timber production. Obviously, forestry is the primary use of much of the national forest lands, with grazing and watershed protection as other important uses. In any particular area, however, any one of these uses may be most important, with the other two uses of secondary importance. But there is still a fourth use of much of this land in public ownership. Americans place a high value on recreation, on camping, hunting, and fishing. Land grazed too closely by cattle and sheep may cause deer and other wild animals to starve. The recreational and wildlife use of many of these lands must be integrated with the other three uses mentioned.

The administrative agency (the U.S. Forest Service in the case of national forest lands, and the Bureau of Land Management in the case of most other public lands) makes the decisions when conflicts of interests among these various uses occur. People concerned with each of these uses organize into interest groups to present the claims that are often set forth in the public press and before Congressional committees. Administrative agencies and committees of Congress are responsible to these interest groups, yet government officials attempt to adjudicate the various uses in the public interest on the basis of the best scientific information available. Thus, land use on over half the land in the western states is determined not by the pricing process, which directs land use on privately owned land, but by bureaucratic decisions based on scientific information, as modified by political pressures.

Government as a Landlord

In the early days, these western public lands were grazed by ranchers free of change. With the organization of the national forests and later with the organization of grazing districts under the Taylor Grazing Act, the government began to charge fees for the use of this grazing land. At first, Forest Service grazing fees averaged about $.15 a month per head for cattle, and $.05 per head for sheep. Public lands in the grazing districts were grazed for a fee of $.05 a month per head for cattle, and $.01 per head for sheep in the early years of their organization.

Because these lands had been grazed free of charge, low fees such as these seemed high to the stockmen. Although there have been some increases, stockmen have successfully resisted their increase to more than perhaps one-half the market value of the grazing, as compared with forage

[10]*Ibid.*, p. 57.

on adjacent privately owned ranches.[11] These relatively low fees result in adjacent ranches (with grazing rights) being bid up in price until much of the advantage of the cheap grazing has been capitalized into the land values of such ranches. Current proposals for increasing grazing fees are resisted, with considerable justification, on the grounds that an increase in fees would be a severe economic burden for ranchers who had recently purchased their properties on the basis of the current grazing fees on the public lands.

The continued low fees have another normal economic consequence. The demand for grazing permits is always in excess of the supply. The Forest Service has reduced the number of stock allowed to graze on the national forest lands in the past twenty years, in the interest of conservation of the native grasses. Range specialists recognize the necessity of these reductions, but livestock men object to them on the grounds that they reduce operations and income. If grazing fees were more nearly in line with the value of the forage grazed, there would be less resistance to a reduction in grazing permits.

Livestock men, dependent upon grazing on the public lands, have tenure problems distinctly different from those of farm owners in other sections of the United States. Many of the ranges furnish only seasonal grazing and a livestock ranch cannot operate without a balance of the different seasonal ranges. Because of the need for continued adjustments in grazing on public lands, the government agencies have not entered into long-term rental contracts with adjacent livestock raisers. When conditions are well stabilized, they grant permits on a ten-year basis. Yet, these ranchers must have some assurance with respect to continuity of grazing permits when ranches are bought and sold.

As a means of meeting the need for stability from year to year, the Forest Service has developed a set of rules and regulations guiding its range management practices that are published in *The Use Book*. The Bureau of Land Management has developed a "Federal Range Code" that covers its rules and regulations worked out in consultation with its advisory boards.

The Problems of the Plains States

During the drought years of the 1930s, a high proportion of the farmers in the Great Plains states were forced to go on public relief programs. Thousands with relatives in the more humid sections of the country also moved in with them. During the period from 1933 to 1938, drought conditions were rather general in most of the Great Plains states each year, and the people in the area can be said to have existed on the public and

[11]*Ibid.*, pp. 132–35.

private philanthropy of those sections of the United States enjoying more favorable weather.

Fortunately, during the years of World War II, the weather was highly favorable. Large wheat and small grain crops were obtained each year from 1941 through 1950. High levels of wheat, feed grain, and livestock production attained during World War II and in the years immediately following were, in large measure, due to the series of years of favorable weather in the Plains states. Farmers who survived the drought and low prices of the 1930s became moderately wealthy in the 1940s.

Drought conditions were serious and special drought programs again were organized in most of the Great Plains states from 1951 through 1956. Although in some areas the drought was even more severe than in the 1930s, the effects on farm families and local institutions were not as serious as twenty years earlier.

Farmers have developed a low-cost stubble mulch that reduces wind erosion, increases the absorption of water into the soil, and reduces the labor and power requirements in summer fallowing land. Water, rather than grass, is the factor limiting the survival of cattle in some areas. A program of building stock ponds has been completed, which makes water facilities available within 1.5 miles of practically all grazing. The reserve water supply is expected to last as long as the supply of grass under drought conditions. An aggressive program of reseeding the less-productive lands most subject to wind erosion resulted in some 10 million acres of plowed land being returned to permanent cover in the 1930s and 1940s. Small, individual farm irrigation systems, using both surface and well water, have added to the stability of crop production on thousands of farms. The size of farms has been increased sharply to permit economic use of modern, large-scale machinery. As the population in these states shrank during the drought and war years, local people came to realize that their entire system of public and private services must be adapted to a less-dense population than had been originally planned for.

Many of these gains were offset by widespread plowing of marginal wheat lands during the period of urgent world food needs following World War II. The acreage of land seeded to wheat increased over 50 percent, or almost 30 million acres, between 1943 and 1949. Much of this increased acreage came from summer fallow lands and from plowing range lands in the Plains states. Farmers who seeded these new range lands to wheat were fortunate with respect both to weather and prices received. Probably, the wheat grown on these marginal lands had produced sufficient income to cover the cost of reseeding them when they were no longer needed for wheat production. But the shift from range land to wheat is a simple, low cost adjustment as compared with shifting wheat land to permanent grass. It can be done, as it was on 10 million acres before the war, but it is doubtful if the individuals who received the income from growing the wheat on these lands would bear the cost of returning them to grass cover. In 1950, the Great Plains Council recommended that 12 million acres of wheat land be reseeded to grass. After several years of discussion, a fifteen-year Great Plains Conservation Program (GPCP), Public Law 86-1021, was adopted in 1956. This legislation authorizes three- to ten-year conservation practice, cost-sharing contracts with farmers and ranchers in the ten Great Plains States.

An evaluation of the Great Plains Conservation Program was not encouraging on the progress made in returning the projected 12 million acres to permanent vegetative cover.[12] Under price relationships prevailing between 1956 and 1970, income per acre has been higher from land in crops than from livestock even on low-grade cropland. The long-term contracts, which were an innovation of the GPCP, were not proved to have any substantial advantage in encouraging soil conservation practices. Of the total federal expenditures under cost-sharing arrangements, less than 15 percent had gone to assist in converting low-grade cropland to permanent vegetative cover. The rest was used for some 23 other approved practices in the program.

Continuing Problems

In some ways, mistakes made in the use of land resources in the West are more serious than in other sections. If the range conservationists are correct in their expectations of continued decline in the productivity of the ranges under present use patterns and if the public does not become aware of this until the decline has taken place, it may be too late to reverse the trend. The same situation holds for dry land crop farming. Although the issues in conserving the land and grazing resources in the West are similar to those in other sections of the United States, they take on a special importance in the arid and semiarid climate. There is probably less understanding of the many problems involving our most economic use of land resources in the West than in any other major section of the country. This, in part, arises out of the relative youth of western agriculture, including grazing. Thus, we find that increased attention must be given to technical studies and educational activities concerned with resource conservation in this relatively new, dry country.

Our experience in public management of land for private use is even more limited than our agricultural use of these lands. The Forest Service experience covers somewhat more than fifty years, and only in the last forty has scientific management been attempted. The management of grazing on

---

[12] J. Kasal and W. B. Back, "An Economic Evaluation of the Great Plains Conservation Program," *ERS-440*, Economic Research Service, U.S.D.A., July 1970.

the public domain is even newer. The central problem is one of perfecting means whereby the public's interest in the various uses of these lands can be made known to the administering agency. A corollary of this is the development of administration policies that give a maximum of security and stability to the livestock industry, yet permit necessary changes to be made in an evolving pattern of multiple land uses.

POINTS FOR DISCUSSION

1. Review the major advantages and disadvantages of the property tax.
2. Are farmers favored or discriminated against under our current system of real and personal property taxes?
3. How and to what extent is the use of land controlled in the public interest in your community?
4. What land use problems could be solved by rural zoning? What land use problems could be solved by land use regulations of local soil conservation districts?
5. Under what conditions does government ownership of land appear to be more desirable than private ownership?
6. In what ways do the problems associated with land in the western states differ from those found in other sections of the United States?
7. What are the more important problems facing farmers in the Plains states?

REFERENCES

CLAWSON, M., AND B. HELD, *The Federal Lands.* Baltimore: Johns Hopkins Press, 1957.

Journal of Farm Economics, Vol. 31, No. 4, Nov. 1949, and Vol. 32, No. 3, Aug. 1950 have a series of special articles on Western land use problems.

KASAL, J., AND W. B. BACK, "An Economic Evaluation of the Great Plains Conservation Program," *ERS-440,* Economic Research Service, U.S.D.A. (July 1970).

KRAUSZ, N. G. P., *Land Use Controls.* University of Illinois, College of Agriculture Special Publications No. 7, 1964.

"Our American Land," *Agricultural Information Bulletin 321.* Soil Conservation Service, U.S.D.A. (July 1968).

RENNE, R. R., *Land Economics,* rev. ed. New York: Harper & Row, 1958.

SAUNDERSON, M. H., *Western Land and Water Use.* Norman, Oklahoma: University of Oklahoma Press, 1950.

SOLBERG, ERLING D., "Comprehensive Plans for Improving Rural Communities," *Agricultural Information Bulletin 316,* Economic Research Service, U.S.D.A. (March 1967).

PART SIX

Price-Income Policy

Problems

Chapter 23

The Growth of Government

in Agriculture

EARLY BEGINNINGS

Government price supports and production controls for crops undertaken in 1933 were not as new and novel as most of us believed. Government assistance in marketing staple crops began in early colonial days. Everett Edwards, relating the history of American agriculture in the first three hundred years, tells of the tobacco farmers' price difficulties and government help as early as 1619.

Tobacco became the chief exchange medium for Virginia in the early years. The Virginia Colonial Assembly in 1631 set a minimum price on tobacco of sixpence per pound; exchanges at prices lower than sixpence were punishable by imprisonment. By 1639, it became necessary to adopt a crop curtailment program to supplement the price-fixing measures. The colonial government limited the crops of 1639 through 1641 to 1,200,000 pounds of good quality tobacco. Viewers (local colonial officials) were authorized to destroy inferior tobacco and excess crops. The merchants cooperated in this program and agreed to pay not less than threepence per pound.[1]

Tobacco production became so popular in the early colonial years that the government found it necessary, or at least desirable, to require producers to plant minimum acreages to corn and other feed and food

---

[1]Everett E. Edwards, "American Agriculture—The First 300 Years," *Yearbook of Agriculture,* U.S.D.A., 1940, 184–85.

crops, rather than to plant tobacco alone. Here again, there is great similarity between the activity of the early colonial government and the extension programs to increase the production of home feed and food crops on the cotton and tobacco farms.

Agriculture depended less on export crops in the northern colonies than in the southern, hence, there was less emphasis on crop controls in the North. But the northern colonies had their problems, too. In New England, the agricultural problem took the forms of scarcity of labor and "oppressive" wage rates. Thus, continuous attempts were made through the courts and legislatures to regulate (place ceilings over) wage rates of "mechanics and day laborers." Taken as a whole, however, price fixing and governmental controls, which were important for some crops and in certain areas, were the exception, rather than the rule. Although tariffs and subsidies were employed from time to time, they usually were a part of the mercantilistic policies of the mother countries, instead of being regulations originating in the colonies.

Colonial Times to 1862

Land ownership policies were a primary concern of our early national government. The colonists who came to this country were revolutionists. They believed in the right of every man to hold title to real property without restrictions. They also believed in an equal distribution of estates, in contrast to the traditional hereditary rights of the eldest son in the family, or similar semifeudal customs. These two ideals dominated our land disposal and ownership policies from early colonial days.

In the first years of our national government, another issue arose regarding land disposal. Should the public domain be held and disposed of in a manner that would bring in the greatest revenue possible to the national government, or should it be sold rapidly at nominal prices to settlers? Alexander Hamilton and the eastern businessmen favored getting the maximum revenue from these lands. But Thomas Jefferson and those who believed that widespread ownership of family farms was the "backbone of democracy" favored selling the lands at low prices on easy terms. As the nation became older, these latter views came more and more to prevail.

The legislation for disposing of land passed in 1796 provided for sales in units of 640 acres at $2.00 an acre. Four years later, the minimum size of unit was reduced to 320 acres, and in 1804 a family could buy 160 acres from the government at $2.00 an acre. Fifteen years later, the price was reduced to $1.25 an acre and the minimum size of unit was reduced to 80 acres. In 1841, the government again took action to allow settlers to obtain property rights in land on still easier terms. The Pre-emption Act, passed in that year, gave squatters, who had tenanted public lands without purchasing them, legal rights to the land they had occupied.[2]

This broad, public demand for the rapid disposal of public lands to settlers on easy terms reached its climax in 1862 after the southern states had seceded from the Union. The passage of the Homestead Act in that year represented the culmination of the efforts of the frontiersmen and the western politicians to give every family that wanted it enough free land to make a living. This act provided that any family could obtain title to 160 acres of public land by living on it and cultivating it five years. Unfortunatley, it came too late. Most of the public lands available for sale or settlement after 1862 were semiarid and arid lands located in what we now know as the Great Plains. Hundreds of thousands of families took up homesteads in these areas only to be forced to return to the more humid areas after several seasons of toil and heartbreaking crop failures because of drought.[3]

Disposal of public lands was not the only activity of the early national government relating to agriculture. Chew reports that Thomas Jefferson, while he was the first Secretary of State, took a great interest in the introduction of new plants and animals.[4] The Patent Office, located in the Department of State, received and distributed foreign seeds and plant cuttings. As agricultural societies sprang up, they requested government help in promoting their activities of farm improvement. Thus, we find the Berkshire (Massachusetts) Association for the Promotion of Agriculture and Manufacturing petitioning Congress in 1817 to set up a national board to help agriculture and manufacturing.[5]

By 1839, demands of this sort resulted in the first specific appropriation for agriculture. In that year, Congress appropriated $1,000 to be spent by the Patent Office for the collection and distribution of seeds, carrying on agricultural investigations, and collecting agricultural statistics. This was the formal beginning of two governmental functions for agriculture, research and service, which have been of incalculable value to farmers and to the public generally over the last century.

Studies of tea and silk were undertaken. Peas and clover were recommended for worn-out lands. Collection and dissemination of statistics on crop production and marketing, forerunning our present outstanding government Crop and Livestock Reporting Service, were recognized as proper service functions of the government. This initial appropriation of $1,000 in 1839 was gradually increased and the range of investigations widened until in 1854 Congress appropriated $35,000 for seed collection, investigations

---

[2]This development is briefly summarized in Gaus and Wolcott, *Public Administration and the United States Department of Agriculture* (Chicago: Public Administration Service, 1940), pp. 116–17.
[3]B. H. Hibbard, *A History of the Public Land Policies* (New York: Peter Smith, 1939).
[4]Arthur P. Chew, *The Response of Government to Agriculture* (U.S.D.A., 1937), pp. 7–8.
[5]*Op. cit.*, p. 10.

(research), and the collection of statistics. The growing importance of these services to agriculture was recognized by the members of Congress and, in 1862, they created a Department of Agriculture under direction of a Commissioner. The work and influence of the United States Agricultural Society, the forerunner of our present national farm organizations, is given credit for obtaining this legislation for agriculture.[6] The Commissioner of Agriculture and the newly created "Department" continued as a part of the Patent Office for twenty-five years, but this legislation of 1862 is generally recognized as the "organic act" of the present Department of Agriculture.

RESEARCH, EDUCATION, SERVICE, AND REGULATION, 1862–1916

The period from 1862 to 1916 was characterized by a great expansion in the scientific work of the Department of Agriculture. Adult education activities were begun, government services were increased, and the first regulations needed to prevent the spread of insects and diseases were adopted. The first marketing regulations also were adopted during this period.

The year 1862 is a memorable one for agriculture. The passage of the Homestead Act and the legislation creating the Department of Agriculture have already been noted. The Morrill Act, also passed in 1862, provided for public land grants to the several states to assist in the establishment of state colleges and universities that included teaching agriculture and mechanic arts: the land-grant colleges and universities. Of the three laws, the Morrill Act was probably of greatest significance for it started a program of state and federal support for an institution of higher learning in each state, devoted to the education of young people regarding the "practical problems" of agriculture and the mechanic arts.

This federal assistance to state educational institutions was followed in 1887 with legislation authorizing continuing federal assistance to state agricultural experiment stations, usually located at the state colleges, for carrying on research in the sciences relating to agriculture. It was twenty-seven years later, in 1914, before Congress authorized federal aid to the states to carry on adult educational work, the present Federal-State Extension Service. The research and educational activities relating to agriculture were firmly established during this period.

Early Regulatory Work

In 1884, Congress was suddenly confronted with a problem that threatened the economic welfare of the nation's livestock producers. Arthur Chew relates the circumstances as follows:

[6]Gaus and Wolcott, *Public Administration and the United States Department of Agriculture* (Chicago: Public Administration Service, 1940), p. 5.

Another infection [of pleuropneumonia] broke out in 1859 in Massachusetts; it had been brought there by four cows from the Netherlands. Port inspectors saw that the animals were sick, but the infection escaped, and within four years it had appeared in 20 towns in Massachusetts. Soon it developed in Connecticut, Delaware, Pennsylvania, Virginia and the District of Columbia. Alarmed cattlemen demanded joint action by the states, but the states could not get together. It was necessary to invoke federal action. Congress had to pass laws to provide funds and to create an administrative organization, for it was a new type of emergency.[7]

This disease outbreak resulted in the creation of the Bureau of Animal Industry. Similar crop diseases and pest infestations led to federal legislation covering the interstate movement of insect pests and disease-infected plants and seeds. Federal regulations forbidding the interstate movement of diseased plants and animals have been supplemented by similar legislation in many states designed to prevent or slow down the spread of diseases and pests within their borders.

Early Conservation Activities

Dwindling forest resources, as early as 1876, caused enough concern to result in a special study encouraging timber growing and forest protection. A few years after this study was completed, a forestry research and educational unit was formed in the Department of Agriculture. These early studies awakened political leaders and Congress to the need for conservation of our natural forest resources. In 1891, Congress responded by authorizing the President to set aside forest reserves from the public domain to be held by the national government. These reserves were the beginning of our present national forests.

Land Policies, 1862–1916

The Homestead Act of 1862 was far from the last legislation dealing with the disposal of public lands. When the 160-acre homestead proved to be too small a unit in the dry land areas, Congress passed other legislation granting title to larger units when the settlers met certain requirements. Some of these requirements included the development of small irrigation works. In 1894, an act was passed granting lands to the western states on condition that they develop irrigation on them.[8] Then in 1902, as related earlier, the federal government itself undertook the building of irrigation projects. The cost of these projects was to be liquidated over a ten-year period by the farmers' payments for the land and irrigation water. We have already pointed out that all too often the farmers were unable to pay the irrigation costs in the time period set.

---

[7]Chew, *op. cit.*, p. 31.
[8]R. R. Renne, *Land Economics* (New York: Harper & Row, 1958), p. 498.

THE PERIOD OF ECONOMIC
ASSISTANCE–1916 TO DATE

Farm Credit for Agriculture

Great mechanical improvements were made in farming tools in the late 1800s and early 1900s. In spite of financial panics at irregular intervals, farmers came to depend more and more on markets and market prices in selling farm products and buying supplies. Industrial developments were moving ahead at an unprecedented pace. Farm leaders believed that urban and industrial progress was outstripping improvements in farming and farm life.

President Theodore Roosevelt, in 1908, was persuaded to appoint a "Country Life Commission." The commission's report covered a wide range of topics in the area of improving rural living. In the field of business, the commission reached the conclusion that farmers did not have credit facilities that served them as adequately as industry was served by the city banks. They believed that more adequate credit would help farmers attain their farm ownership goal more rapidly.

Following the report of the commission, a group was sent to Europe to study the cooperative land mortgage credit banks, especially those in Germany. The group was favorably impressed and recommended that the government sponsor a national farm-credit cooperative to make land mortgage loans to farmers. It was 1916 before these recommendations were embodied in legislation setting up twelve regional land banks with government capital. Seven years later, in 1923, a system of twelve federal intermediate credit banks was established.

Funds were obtained from the sale of mortgage-secured bonds in the private bond market, and loans were made at uniformly low interest rates in all sections of the country. The first effect of this new act was to lower real estate mortgage credit interest rates in the high-interest-rate areas of the West and elsewhere. It was not until the Great Depression of the 1930s, however, that the government-sponsored farm-credit system proved of greatest value to farmers.

At that time, commercial banks, insurance companies, and other commercial lending agencies, finding many of their borrowers delinquent, started thousands of foreclosure proceedings. Special legislation was rushed through Congress in 1933 to supplement the Farm Loan Act and to permit the land banks to refinance delinquent notes held by commercial agencies. At the same time, the farm-credit system was expanded to include production (short term) credit facilities and credit for cooperatives. Thus, we find that when the need developed, the original farm-credit legislation was amended and broadened to deal with the new situation. This legislation in 1916 marked the beginning of the federal government's direct assistance in the business aspects of farming and opened a new chapter in the relations of the farmers to their government.

The Growth of Cooperatives

Farmers and farm leaders were dismayed by the sharp fall in prices after World War I. Many proposals were put forward for dealing with the situation. Farm leaders had had little experience with direct price controls since colonial times and found it difficult to agree on a plan for governmental help. Local cooperatives had been rendering effective service in the marketing of several farm products, however, and there was general agreement that more cooperative marketing should be encouraged.

The legal position of large cooperatives was not clear. As late as 1921, courts held that cooperative associations were in violation of existing antitrust legislation. Congressional leaders decided to strengthen the cooperative movement and give cooperatives a clear charter to expand their activities. The result was the Capper-Volstead Act of 1922 defining a cooperative association and exempting their usual business activities from antitrust legislation. This legislation gave impetus to a great expansion in cooperative activity. Certain cooperative leaders got the idea that, if a cooperative could sign up all the producers of a crop, they could control the supply of it and, hence, dictate prices. But they found it difficult to sign up all producers; some always wanted to remain outside the cooperative. Further, they discovered that controlling the crop after it is produced is one thing, and controlling production is another. They could control the former, but not the latter. Thus, their dreams of monopoly control and price dictation failed to materialize, and cooperatives failed to obtain satisfactory prices for farm products in the 1920s.

The Need for Governmental Controls

Farm leaders, aware of the sharp drop in farm prices after World War I, as compared with the modest drop in nonfarm prices, believed that legislation should be adopted that would "make the tariff effective" for farmers. The central ideas of the leaders, who drafted a number of bills sponsored by Senator McNary in the Senate and Congressman Haugen in the House of Representatives, were: "(1) that the centralizing power of the Federal Governments should be used to assist farmers to dispose of the surplus abroad and raise prices to the desired level in the domestic market, and (2) that the loss on the segregated exports was to be paid by the farmers themselves by means of an equalization fee."[9]

[9]Chester C. David, "The Development of Agricultural Policy Since the End of the World War," *Yearbook of Agriculture*, U.S.D.A., 1940, p. 307.

Bills embodying these principles passed both houses of Congress twice in the late 1920s, only to be vetoed both times by President Coolidge. John D. Black, writing on this topic in 1928, said the significance of the so-called McNary-Haugen movement was far more political than economic.

> The issue involved is more fundamental than McNary-Haugenism itself. It is agriculture's stand against the domination of its affairs and the affairs of the country by the commercial and industrial interests. Labor has never contested this supremacy successfully in the political field; and in its present condition of relative prosperity, it is even less inclined than before to contest. The agricultural interests of the country for a long time have felt the need of protecting themselves politically against the business interests. The formation of the "agricultural bloc" [in Congress] in May, 1921, was a visible expression of that feeling. But the bloc needed some vigorous measure around which to rally the forces of agriculture. The McNary-Haugen plan proved to be that measure.[10]

Although the agricultural forces were unable to pass these McNary-Haugen bills over the President's veto, they did force both political parties to include measures "to give equality to agriculture" in their 1928 political platforms in the presidential election. Hoover and his associates in the Republican party proposed to set up a Federal Farm Board that would: (1) assist in organizing the producers of each commodity into large national cooperatives, and (2) stabilize market prices through loans or direct purchases out of a $500 million revolving fund. President Hoover persuaded Congress to pass such a bill soon after he was elected; it was known as the Agricultural Marketing Act of 1929. The passage of this legislation marked a new departure in government relative to agriculture.

The 1929 Agricultural Marketing Act committed the government to help farmers obtain better prices for their products. Financed by government stabilization loans, national cooperatives were to purchase and hold supplies from the market when individual commodities' prices were "temporarily" depressed. The experience of the Federal Farm Board, set up to administer this legislation, was most disappointing. The Great Depression of the 1930s caused the $500 million revolving fund to disappear like a snowball on a kitchen stove. Many loans advanced to the large cooperatives to purchase and hold distressed stocks were never repaid because market prices kept right on falling.

Early Beginnings of Production Controls

It was unfortunate that the depression of the 1930s began about the same time that the Federal Farm Board started its operations. Economic conditions deteriorated rapidly and the Farm Board soon found all its

---

[10]John D. Black, "The McNary-Haugen Movement," *American Economic Review*, Vol. 18, No. 3, June 1928, p. 405.

stabilization funds committed, yet farm prices continued to fall. Alexander Legge, Chairman of the Federal Farm Board, drawing on his experience as former president of the International Harvester Company, soon became convinced that farmers should restrict the production of wheat and other major crops in view of the sharp decline in farm prices.

Legge addressed farm audiences in many parts of the United States, advising them that the Federal Farm Board could not improve farm prices and incomes unless there was a reduction in supplies offered for sale in the markets.[11] He was not alone in his belief in the necessity of production controls if farmers were to realize better prices. Most farm leaders, acquainted with the inability of the Federal Farm Board to improve economic conditions for farmers, were of the opinion that an adjustment (restriction) in the production of the major farm crops was needed at that time. When the Democrats took office as a result of the elections in 1932, they promptly sponsored passage of an Agricultural Adjustment Act. This act authorized production adjustment programs, a direct outgrowth of the experience of the Federal Farm Board. The Agricultural Adjustment Act of 1933 also authorized the use of marketing agreements and marketing orders that had been used successfully on a small scale by California producers to promote orderly marketing of perishable fruits and vegetables.

The first acreage adjustment programs for cotton, tobacco, wheat, corn, and hogs were financed by special funds made available by new taxes levied on the sale of these products to processors. These new taxes often were referred to as processing taxes. Generally speaking, each processing tax was set at a level that would create the funds needed to make attractive rental-benefit payments to producers for limiting their production to two-thirds or three-quarters of their recent level of output.

Production adjustment or control in the first Agricultural Adjustment Program was conceived of as entirely voluntary. It was planned to make the rental-benefit payments so attractive for holding the production of the selected crops and hogs at levels about one-third lower than in the previous three years that almost all producers would gladly enter into production adjustment agreements with the government. The crop acreage history was assembled for every farm in the United States where the products listed above were produced on a commercial basis. Each producer was offered a rental-benefit payment for limiting his acreage or limiting his marketings, in the case of hogs, to about two-thirds that of recent years.

It was believed that an adjustment in the market supplies of these more important farm products brought about in this voluntary manner would result in substantial improvement in the prices of these products. Farm

---

[11]Forrest Crissey, *Legge, Alexander, 1866–1933* (privately printed, 1936), p. 201. In his letter of resignation to President Hoover, he said, "While there are still a few of the agricultural leaders who lower their voices when they speak of production control yet practically all of them have accepted the principle as essential." (p. 206).

leaders believed that an adjustment program for the major products, by reducing aggregate farm output, would indirectly result in an improvement in the prices of the less-important farm products. Within the first year of its operation, however, the Agricultural Adjustment Program departed from its voluntary character with respect to tobacco and cotton. In order to achieve the desired results more promptly, the administration also shifted from complete reliance on production restrictions to achieve price and income improvement to the use of price supporting loans in conjunction with the adjustment program.

In the case of tobacco and cotton, producers showed such unanimity in desiring production adjustments to improve market prices that they secured the passage of additional legislation assessing high taxes on any tobacco or cotton produced on acreages not included in the acreage allotments announced under the voluntary adjustment programs for those crops. Also, in the fall of 1933 market prices of corn and cotton at harvest time had not yet responded to the adjustment program to the extent that could be expected if a similar program were continued for another year or two. In order to assure farmers' prices for their 1933 crops in line with prices that might be expected if the adjustment program were continued, the Secretary of Agriculture made available loans on cotton and corn at levels in excess of the current market prices. These loans made available by the Secretary of Agriculture in the fall of 1933 mark the beginning of our current government price-support loan operations. The government loans were made to producers on the basis that if the market price did not rise to the level of the loan rate before the date for repayment, the producer might deliver his crop to the government in full repayment of the loan. Because these loans could be repaid in full by delivery of the crop regardless of its current market price, they were called nonrecourse loans—no other property of the producer was obligated for repayment of the loans.

Objectives of Agricultural Programs in the 1930s

Throughout the 1930s, the Agricultural Adjustment Program attempted to adjust annual supplies of the major crops and marketings of the perishable crops in line with available market outlets at satisfactory prices. Marketing agreements and orders, which were authorized in the 1933 Act and strengthened by additional legislation in 1937, were utilized effectively by the producers of perishable fruits and vegetables and producers of milk for fluid use in city milksheds.

Marketing agreements and orders required a two-thirds majority vote on the part of producers before the Secretary of Agriculture could issue a marketing order that was binding on all producers and all handlers of the product. The more common provisions of marketing orders for fruits and vegetables have been regulations with respect to the minimum grade and size of the product that may be sold in commercial markets. Such marketing regulations tend to reduce quantities moving to market when production is greater than can be sold at satisfactory prices. Such regulations usually have been accompanied by a diversion program for the unacceptable grades and sizes of the product. Often the diversion program has been financed by government purchases utilizing funds from custom receipts that were earmarked for surplus removal activities for perishable products by Congress in 1935.

Marketing agreements and orders for fluid milk differed somewhat from the typical market orders for perishable fruits and vegetables. They had as their main objective the establishment of uniform producer prices and uniform market prices of the milk sold to the distributors on the basis of its use. Sugar producers always have been in a special category. Because the United States imports much of its sugar, special legislation was passed in the 1930s allocating the domestic market between domestic producers and foreign producers and providing for supplementary payments to domestic producers from a special tax on all sugar.

A Supreme Court decision in 1936 declared that the collection of processing taxes to finance government production adjustment contracts with individual producers was in violation of the Federal Constitution, with the individual states having the right to legislate in this area. The entire production adjustment program was discontinued temporarily and the special tobacco and cotton production control programs were repealed. Before the 1936 crop was planted, however, production adjustment was made an integral part of the popular, relatively new nationwide soil conservation program.

Where the earlier program had been made possible by the collection of processing taxes and use of the funds to pay farmers for reducing their acreages of specific crops, the substitute program adopted after the court decision was financed from general treasury receipts. Farmers were promised payments after harvesting if they reduced the acreage of soil-depleting, intertilled, and small grain crops. Performance and payments were based on the amount of shift in acreages found on the farm at harvest time as compared with previous cropping practices.

Two years of experience with this type of program convinced farm leaders that a more effective program was needed to stabilize supplies and prices of the major crops. After much discussion, new legislation was passed in 1938 authorizing comprehensive supply adjustment programs for each of the major crops. This new legislation was based on the interstate commerce clause of the Constitution and has never been successfully challenged in the courts. The Secretary of Agriculture was directed to make nonrecourse loans available to producers of the major storable crops within a range of 52 to 75 percent of parity. The support level for several of the crops was specified by a formula that related the loan level to the size of the supply in relation to normal marketings.

This new legislation also authorized the Secretary of Agriculture to invoke marketing quotas upon the approval of two-thirds of the producers if supplies reached certain levels in relation to normal marketings. When marketing quotas were invoked by the Secretary of Agriculture, penalty taxes were imposed on any products grown on acreages in excess of those allotted by the Agricultural Adjustment Administration.

It will be noted that it was 1938 before revisions in the basic agricultural adjustment legislation made it mandatory for the Secretary of Agriculture to offer price-supporting loans on the major storable crops. By that time, however, government price-supporting loans had become one of the most popular features of the farm program. During the 1930s, it is fair to say that the general philosophy of the farm program was that of assisting producers to adjust their production and marketings to improve and stabilize farm prices and income in a period of continued unemployment. Officially, the overall objective was the attainment of farm prices that gave farmers a "parity" in purchasing power with nonfarm groups—a purchasing power equivalent to that enjoyed by farm products in the period between 1910 and 1914.

1933 Definition of Parity

The parity idea, which is essentially an equity concept, was developed by farm leaders in the 1920s. Price indexes compiled by government agencies indicated that farm prices had fallen much more than nonfarm prices following World War I. As public discussions of "farm relief" measures continued in the late 1920s, more and more attention was centered on the disparity between the levels of the farm and nonfarm price indexes.

In view of the widespread acceptance of the idea that the postwar disparity in these indexes should be corrected by appropriate government action, it is not surprising that the achievement of a parity in farmers' purchasing power was made the goal of the Agricultural Adjustment Act of 1933. The parity goal is stated in the opening paragraph of the Agricultural Adjustment Act of 1933 as follows:

> It is hereby declared to be the policy of Congress—(1) To establish and maintain such balance between the production and consumption of agricultural commodities, and such marketing conditions therefore, as will re-establish prices to farmers at a level that will give agricultural commodities a purchasing power with respect to articles farmers buy, equivalent to purchasing power of agricultural commodities in the base period. The base period in the case of all agricultural commodities except tobacco shall be the pre-war period, August 1909–July 1914. In the case of tobacco, the base period shall be the post-war period, August 1919–July 1929.

The computation of parity under this act of 1933 was simple. Let us take, as an example, the computation of the parity price for wheat in June 1933. The average price of wheat on farms in the United States from August 1909 to July 1914 was $.884 per bushel. Prices paid by farmers were 3 percent higher in June 1933 than in the base period; thus, the index of prices paid stood at 103. The parity price for wheat in June 1933 was $.884 times 1.03 or $.91 per bushel. The actual United States farm price in that month was $.59 per bushel, or 64 percent of parity.

Wartime Modified Farm Program Objectives

Demands for food and fiber and for manpower in World War II furnished a temporary solution for two of agriculture's basic problems. One of these problems is the fundamental tendency for agricultural production to expand more rapidly than domestic and foreign markets can absorb the supplies at prevailing prices. The other is the long-run excess of manpower in farming.

When general price-control legislation was adopted soon after the United States was drawn into World War II, in view of the continued low farm prices at that time, the Secretary of Agriculture was given the veto power over price ceilings on farm products. The most important single farm price action taken during the war period, however, was the so-called Steagall Amendment requiring government support of many farm prices for two years following the close of the war (Public Law 792, October 2, 1942). In a sense, the precedent for the Steagall Amendment grew out of the commodity loans started in the fall of 1933 and made available to farmers each year since that time. In another sense, it was considered an equitable method of compensating farmers for submitting to price ceilings during World War II after experiencing many prewar years of low prices.

Early Postwar Objectives

The wartime price supports adopted under the Steagall Amendment expired at the close of 1948. Congress, anticipating their expiration in the Agricultural Act of 1948, extended price supports to 1950 on a substantial list of farm products at 90 percent of parity and provided a range of price supports from 60 to 90 percent of parity after that. The 1938 legislation providing for the innovation of marketing quotas on the basic crops—cotton, corn, wheat, rice, tobacco, and peanuts—when supplies became excessive came back into use.

During the war and early postwar years, a shift in policy emphasis had occurred. In the prewar years, the central purpose of the government farm program was adjustment in supplies. Price-supporting loans were a supplement to the adjustment programs. In the 1948 and subsequent postwar legislation, major interest centered on the mandatory price-support levels. Little thought was given to the problem of keeping production in line with available market outlets at the support price levels. Acreage allotments and marketing quotas as provided for in the 1938 legislation were believed to be adequate.

Shift to Modernized Parity Formula

During the war years, there was increasing criticism of the 1933 parity formula, which had been modified only in the case of a few commodities by giving them more favorable base periods than the common 1910 and 1914 base period. As a result of this criticism, statisticians developed an alternative method of computing parity prices that was incorporated in the Agricultural Act of 1948, generally known as the formula for "modernized" parity. This formula makes the pattern of parity prices dependent upon the market price relationships of the most recent ten-year period. At the same time, the average level of prices is determined by the level of the prices-paid index, computed on a 1910–1914 basis. In respect to the prices-paid index, the wages of farm labor were included in the index for the first time. The formula that accomplishes all this involves the following steps:

1. Compute the average United States farm price of the product in the ten most recent calendar or crop years.
2. Compute the average of the index of prices received by farmers on a January 1910 to December 1914 base during the same ten-year period.
3. Compute an "adjusted base price" for the product by dividing (1) by (2) and multiplying by 100.
4. Compute the parity price by multiplying the adjusted base price by the current index of prices paid by farmers (the parity index), on the 1910 to 1914 base, and dividing by 100.

Let us take, as an example, the computation of the parity price for corn for January 1972. The ten-year (January 1962 to December 1971) average price of corn was $1.24. The ten-year average of the index of prices received by farmers was 269. Dividing $1.24 by 269 and multiplying by 100 gives $.46, the adjusted base price. Multiplying this adjusted base price by 420, the parity index for January 1972, gives a parity price for corn, using the modernized formula, of $1.94 per bushel. The average of prices received by farmers for corn in January 1972 was $1.09 per bushel or 56 percent of parity.

The use of the modernized parity formula results in each farm product having a parity price that bears the same relation to the parity prices of other farm products as their market price relationships bore to each other in the most recent ten-year period. At the same time, the period from 1910 to 1914 is maintained as the base period for the index of all farm parity prices.

Thus, there is no change in the base period with respect to all farm prices under the modernized parity formula and a farm price parity ratio of 80 indicates that farm products as a group have 80 percent as much purchasing power per unit as they did from 1910 to 1914 in terms of supplies and services purchased by farm families for use in production and for family living.

Adoption of Flexible Price Supports

At the close of World War II, the sharp controversy that developed with respect to the appropriate level of price supports for the major storable crops overshadowed all other developments. Dissatisfaction with the low levels of support provided in the 1948 act led to an upward revision in the minimum levels for normal crops in 1949. Increased domestic and foreign demand as a result of the hositilies in Korea temporarily reversed the build-up in Commodity Credit Corporation stocks that took place in 1948 and 1949, and led to a renewal of legislation making price supports on basic commodities through 1954 mandatory at a minimum level of 90 percent of parity.

Nineteen fifty-four stands out in the postwar period as the year when the new Republican administration made its first fully considered recommendations to Congress with respect to desirable changes in the farm program. In that year, the temporary legislation requiring price supports for basic commodities at 90 percent of parity expired. Whether or not to allow the earlier permanent legislation of 1949 to become operative, providing flexible supports within the range of 75 to 90 percent of parity for the basic crops, was a sharply debated issue. The administration and the largest farm organization took the position that flexible price supports in the long run would be most effective in stabilizing farm prices and incomes in a favorable relation to other sectors of the economy. They believed that price supports at 90 percent of parity were pricing the products, cotton and corn especially, so high that they were stimulating increased production and utilization of competitive products. Supporters of flexible price supports also advanced the argument that with the lower price supports in effect, fewer government controls would be necessary.

Opponents of flexible price supports insisted that within the range of flexibility proposed, 75 to 90 percent of parity, any reduction in price supports would have little effect on either production or sales. They urged the continuation of price supports on the basic crops at 90 percent of parity on the grounds that lowering price supports would merely lower producers' incomes without either reducing production and the need for government controls or having any important stimulating effect on commercial marketings. The Agricultural Act of 1954, as it was finally approved, provided for a range of price supports from 82.5 to 90 percent of parity for the 1955 crops of basic commodities and for price supports within the range of 75 to 90 percent after 1955.

Objectives of Related Legislation

Congress, in the same session in which more flexible price supports were approved, passed the Agricultural Trade Development and Assistance Act (Public Law 480), which permits sales of surplus stocks of farm products in foreign countries for local currencies and donations of surplus stocks to needy people, both at home and abroad. This act and related legislative actions authorizing special foreign and domestic distribution programs were put forward as temporary measures. Many of those sponsoring the legislation believed that temporary foreign and domestic supplemental distribution programs were needed only to liquidate the surplus accumulated in the last years of stable price supports.

Bountiful harvests and sagging livestock prices in the fall of 1955, however, caused some farmer leaders to propose additional emergency action aimed at bringing supplies into balance with available market outlets at reasonably stable prices. The emergency action agreed upon in 1956 took the form of a Soil Bank program made up of two parts. One part was an acreage reserve program for the three years 1956, 1957, and 1958. Under the acreage reserve program, farmers were paid for renting a part of their allotted acreage of the basic price-supported crops to the government. Under this program, any producer who had an allotment to produce corn (in the commercial corn-producing area), cotton, wheat, peanuts, rice, or most types of tobacco if in compliance with all other acreage allotments, might elect to put up to one-half or more of his allotted acreage in the Soil Bank. Acreages placed in the Soil Bank could be devoted to soil conserving uses, but no crop could be harvested or pastured (except in drought areas).

The second part of the Soil Bank was designed to assist producers to reduce production of crops through shifting acreages of cropland to long-range conservation uses, by sharing the cost of the establishment of conservation practices and by making an annual payment for keeping such acreages in the conservation reserve. Producers wishing to place any or all of their cropland in the conservation reserve were required to sign a contract retiring the land from crop production for a minimum of three years, and it might be placed in the Soil Bank for a maximum of fifteen years if the land were planted with trees.

After 1957, the conservation reserve program featured the rental and retirement of entire farms in the belief that in those instances in which whole farms were rented, the operator and his buildings and equipment also would be retired from agricultural production. Local tradesmen in the less-productive areas soon became alarmed about the adverse effects that would result for their community if a substantial number of farm operators placed their entire farms in the Soil Bank for a period of years. Objections of this type and lack of evidence that production was appreciably reduced by this program costing in excess of $300 million a year, led farm leaders to look for other more effective supply control measures.

Temporary Measures and Lower Support Levels Ineffective

Beginning in 1955, price supports were lowered, and intensive efforts were made to expand commercial markets both at home and abroad, to develop extensive domestic and foreign surplus disposal programs, and to establish a Soil Bank program to hold 15 to 30 million acres of cropland out of production in 1956, 1957, and 1958. Yet, these efforts to bring supplies into balance with market outlets available at stable prices were not notably successful. In the four and one-half years of surplus disposal operations ending December 31, 1958, the government bartered, sold for local currencies, and gave away at home and abroad $8 billion of farm products. In the same period, total loans and inventories of farm products held by the Commodity Credit Corporation increased from $6.0 to $8.7 billion, making a total of $10.7 billion of farm products removed from commercial markets by government programs. In spite of all the temporary or emergency measures that had been employed, surplus stocks reached new record levels in 1959 and 1960.

Price and Income Program Changes in the 1960s

Early in 1961, under the leadership of a new administration, a voluntary feed grains adjustment program was adopted that was successful in reducing feed grain stocks in the next few years. A voluntary adjustment program was also added to the mandatory marketing quota program for wheat that, together with favorable export developments, resulted in a substantial reduction in government-held wheat stocks. The magnitude of this reduction between 1960 and 1966 is apparent from Figure 23–1.

The administration proposed several mandatory production adjustment and marketing order programs, all of which were turned down either by the Congress or by the producers of the commodity.

Finding resistance to mandatory controls, the Congress, with administration support, continued the voluntary adjustment program for feed grains and enacted new price-support legislation for cotton and wheat for 1964 and 1965.

By 1965, it was evident that the earlier programs of the 1950s were inadequate, yet producers were unwilling to return to the earlier mandatory

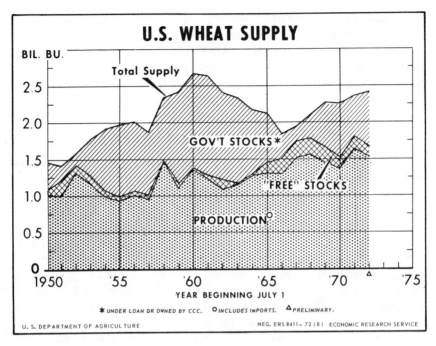

FIGURE 23–1.

production controls. It also was evident that domestic price support levels should be related more closely to prices prevailing in the export markets.

In that year, the administration obtained congressional approval of a four-year Food and Agriculture Act that authorized government price-supporting loans at or near world price levels, rather than at the higher levels of earlier years. Government payments to voluntary cooperators were conditioned on planting within acreage allotments for cotton and wheat and for diversion of a part of the farm's base acreages of feed grains to conservation or nonfarm use.

This act recognized excess capacity as a continuing problem and gave the Secretary of Agriculture authority to deal with it on a flexible basis for a four-year period, later extended an additional year. The Secretary was directed to reduce stocks, where excessive, to desirable reserve levels. Government expenditures were authorized primarily for payments to farmers to divert base acreages, maintain income, or for the purchase and distribution of products outside commercial market channels.

As a result of these changes, the level of price support was lowered dramatically, as illustrated for wheat in Figure 23–2, while "returns" to participants continued to insure that their incomes were supported. Participants collected an average of $.75 per bushel of wheat marketed with

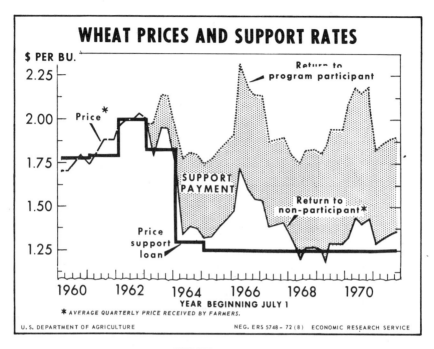

FIGURE 23–2.

certificates in 1970 to bring the return per bushel near $2.25. Other commodities included in the act behaved similarly.

Authorization for a moderate long-term cropland retirement program was included in the 1965 Act, but Congress refused to appropriate funds for this purpose after the first year or two. Voluntary adjustment programs combined with aggressive export activities and continued food aid distribution programs reduced government-owned stocks to desirable levels in the 1960s and contributed to an improvement in national net farm income from $11.7 billion in 1960 to $15.7 in 1970.

During this period, direct government payments to cooperators increased from $702 million in 1960 to $3,717 million in 1970. The average size of farms receiving payments, especially in cotton production, also increased greatly. By 1970, several large-scale cotton producers were receiving over $1 million a year for cooperating in the voluntary cotton and similar adjustment programs.

Public criticism of large payments to individual producers became extensive in the late 1960s and attempts were made to impose congressional restrictions on the size of the annual payments made to an individual producer.

Also, as a result of a series of unfavorable growing seasons beginning in 1966, cotton yields dropped from a record high of 527 pounds an acre in 1965 to 434 and 441 pounds an acre in 1969 and 1970, respectively. Increased losses from insects, especially on the irrigated acreages in the Western states, also contributed to the lower yields.

With cotton price-support loans lowered to world levels and cotton yields disappointingly low, the cotton adjustment problem in the late 1960s shifted from one of holding excessive production in check to one of encouraging an adequate production to maintain domestic supplies and exports at reasonable levels.

Cotton production dropped from 15 million bales in 1964 and 1965 to as low as 7.5 million bales in 1967 and remained near 10 million bales in 1969 and 1970. Many producers in the sections of the cotton belt where acre yields were relatively low planted only the minimum acreage required to qualify for their government payments.

Price and Income Program Changes in the 1970s

One goal of the administration elected in 1968 was to give farmers increased freedom in their cropping plans rather than requiring them to comply with annual commodity adjustment programs under the Food and Agriculture Act of 1965, as amended. When the 1965 Act expired in 1970, it proposed a set-aside program with government payments and price-support loans for each of the major crops, cotton, wheat, and feed grains, continued at approximately former levels. Producers would be free to plant any crop they wished on the cropland not set aside. Mandatory production controls for tobacco, rice, and peanuts provided for in continuing legislation prevented increased plantings of these crops. Otherwise, there were no limits on the use of the cropland not set aside.

The new set-aside program, approved for a three-year period with a $55,000 limitation per crop on individual producer payments, was essentially an annual general cropland retirement program. Government payments were designated as income support and adjustment payments. Acreages required to be set aside in order to qualify for the payments were related to the acreages of the price-supported crops grown on the farm in earlier years. The cotton set-aside payments were based on the previous cotton acreage allotment on the farm, and so on.

The results of the first two years of the set-aside programs, 1971 and 1972, were somewhat disappointing. Although farmers liked the additional freedom given them and cooperation in the voluntary programs increased, government payments to farmers in 1972 set a new record, yet acreage adjustments obtained in feed grains and wheat were smaller than desired.

In view of the rapid increase in farm size, the limited adjustment effect of the set-aside program on grain acreages, and increasingly widespread public opposition to large government payments to individual farmers and corporations, it appeared probable that further substantial changes would occur in the farm price and income programs in the 1970s.

Although opinion is divided, a majority of analysts expect farm technology to continue to advance at such a rate that no increase will be needed in the harvested acreage of crops for many years. Since 1961, the acreage of crops harvested each year has varied from 294 to 310 million with 38 to 65 million acres of cropland withheld from production by annual and long-term adjustment programs.

Unless effective adjustment programs are continued for the grains for a number of years, it is probable that United States farmers would oversupply domestic and export markets at current price levels.

POINTS FOR DISCUSSION

1. What were the basic economic factors in the 1920s that led to agitation for selling farm products abroad at prices lower than domestic market prices?
2. How was the experience of the Federal Farm Board utilized in creating the Agricultural Adjustment Administration in 1933?
3. Outline the major changes that have taken place in government price-supporting programs for farm products, 1933 to date.
4. Explain how marketing agreements and orders may be utilized to increase the returns to the producers of a perishable fruit or vegetable. What, if any, farm products from your community are marketed under federal market order?
5. From U.S. Department of Agriculture Statistics, determine the amount of government payments to farmers in each of the last five years as a percentage of realized net farm income. What are the reasons for the trend, if any, shown by these percentages?
6. What changes do you expect in the next few years in price and income programs for farmers? What are the reasons for expecting these changes?

REFERENCES

BENEDICT, MURRY R., *Can We Solve the Farm Problem?* Chaps. 7 and 11. New York: The Twentieth Century Fund, 1955.

HUNTER, DONALD J., ed., *Food Goals, Future Structural Changes, and Agricultural Policy: A National Basebook,* Chap. 3. Ames, Iowa: Iowa State University Press, 1969.

NOURSE, E. G., J. S. DAVIS, AND J. D. BLACK, *Three Years of the Agricultural Adjustment Administration,* Chaps. 1 and 15. Washington, D.C.: The Brookings Institution, 1937.

SOTH, LAUREN, *Farm Trouble,* Chaps. 5 and 10. Princeton, N. J.: Princeton University Press, 1957.

WILCOX, WALTER W., *The Farmer in the Second World War,* Chaps. 1–3 and 23. Ames, Iowa: Iowa State College Press, 1947.

Chapter 24

Price and Income Policies

for Agriculture

American agriculture is affected by a number of deep-seated problems. Low incomes for a large proportion of farmers and price instability for many farm products have attracted the most attention and have been characterized as the commercial "farm problem." Early government policies were aimed at reducing risk and uncertainty. It was believed that a set of policies that could offset the price fluctuation brought about by natural phenomena and the response of farmers to expected prices (see Chapter 14) would solve the farm problem. However, rapid technological change tended to depress farm prices over time so that pressures for policies to raise prices and incomes became irresistible. As we have seen in the previous chapter, between 1920 and 1970 the purpose of farm programs changed from primarily stabilizing prices to primarily supporting incomes, although aspects of both have always been present in programs actually implemented.

Before discussing the types of policies that are possible, it is useful to consider some broader issues. We are concerned here with *public policies* for agriculture, a phrase that implies that the society in general undertakes actions to achieve certain purposes. The purposes are generally recognized as the *goals* of policy and more broadly as the goals of society. The goals of any society are developed from that society's cultural beliefs and values. Therefore, before stating the goals of policy for commercial agriculture, it is useful to examine the beliefs and values underlying those goals.

Our society is undergoing such rapid changes in beliefs and values that one feels most apprehensive in enumerating any specific set. However,

cultural beliefs and values transmitted from earlier, less-industrialized societies and widely-held considerations of justice and equity, the desire that each
one deserves what he gets and gets what he deserves, have largely shaped
the rules that govern our economic life today. Economic life today is far
different, however, from economic life at the time these beliefs, values and
governing rules were formulated. This is especially true in rural America.
The technological revolution sweeping rural America is uprooting widely
held personal beliefs and values just as ruthlessly as it is uprooting long-
established production and marketing practices.

Some of the more important beliefs and values that we have inherited
from our cultural forefathers living in a less interdependent society may be
listed as follows:[1]

1. The work ethic that gives high personal esteem to excellence in useful
    employment and low esteem to the "easy ways," and that expresses the
    judgment that society owes to each (a) the equivalent of his contribution,
    and (b) an equal opportunity to the means necessary for developing his
    creative potential to the fullest extent possible.
    In its American environment, the work ethic reserves for highest esteem
    those who achieved success "the hard way" and includes the optimistic
    judgment that men (and nations) in their workmanlike capacities possess
    ample means for closing the gap between present circumstance and aspira-
    tion.
2. The democratic creed, with its two central value judgments that (a) all
    men are of equal worth and dignity, and (b) none, however wise or good,
    is wise enough to have dictatorial power over any other.
3. The enterprise creed, with its three judgments that (a) proprietors, or
    their legal representatives, deserve the exclusive right (power) to prescribe
    the working rules for their production units; (b) the individual (or
    family) is and ought to be wholly responsible for his (or its) own eco-
    nomic well-being throughout life; (c) therefore, government's prime func-
    tions are to prevent anyone, including government itself, from invading
    the unfettered freedom of proprietors or their legal agents, of running
    their business as they wish, and to prevent the improvident from pressuring
    either government or business into assuming responsibility for their well-
    being.

Although all three creeds are deeply rooted in American character,
there is no causal connection between them. A people may feel deeply committed to the work ethic and yet totally reject the enterprise creed. Again,
men possess no specific meritorious capacity in equal degree; hence, there is
a sharp clash between the democratic imperative that we accord all men a
status of equal dignity and worth and the work-ethic imperative that we
accord them differential status in line with the results of their productive
effort.

[1]The following statements on the role of beliefs and values draw heavily on the writings
of John M. Brewster, especially, "The Impact of Technical Advance and Migration on Agricultural
Society and Policy," *Journal of Farm Economics*, December 1959.

In American life, however, these disconnected creeds became interlocked in one of the most unified belief systems in history. This came about through a three-hundred-year development and use of what is often called the Lockean model of social organization. This model takes its name from John Locke who, in his seventeenth-century *Treatise on Civil Government,* first held that the good world lies in a sharp division of society into a big economic sphere and a tiny political sphere of popularly controlled government. The government's role would be limited to that of protecting the "natural" rights of proprietors and the "State of Nature" later interpreted as the free market.

Farm people and rural communities today are experiencing many of the social conflicts that were common in the urban communities in the early years of the industrial revolution. Widely held personal value judgments and beliefs play a greater role in slowing economic change in the rural community than in the urban community, however, for in the urban community the management of technological change is largely in the control of the boards of directors of the corporations. In the rural communities, if there is to be any organized management of technological change, it must be placed in the hands of democratic government, subject as it is to the prevailing structure of political power. These beliefs and values underline the goals of rural people and are reflected in the policies they support.

But farm people are not the only group concerned with setting goals for the nation's agriculture. The rest of the population, far more numerous and far more politically powerful than farmers in 1970, have a strong hand in determining goals for agriculture. Thus, any list of goals for United States agriculture will reflect goals of both farmers and nonfarmers. One such list follows.[2]

1. The provision of abundant food supplies for the domestic population at reasonable cost.
2. The creation of a situation in which resources employed in farming receive a return equal to that earned by comparable resources employed in nonfarm pursuits.
3. The establishment of a set of family and social institutions in rural areas consistent with the aspirations of the people and equal in quality to those in urban areas.
4. The establishment of a foreign policy with respect to food and agriculture that increases commercial exports, meets foreign food aid commitments, and expands markets for the developing nations.
5. The establishment of an agricultural production system consistent with an environment capable of sustaining healthful life indefinitely.

These are the major goals that farm policy must achieve if it is to be a success. The first two have received the most attention by agricultural

[2]The following discussion of goals is adapted from Chapter 10 of W. W. Cochrane, *The City Man's Guide to the Farm Problem*, (Minneapolis: University of Minnesota Press, 1965).

economists. Goal three is difficult to implement with a single policy because it is pluralistic and necessarily must reflect the goals and aspirations of many individuals. Policies for goals four and five have been discussed in previous chapters. The remainder of this chapter will focus on policies to achieve the first two, and discuss them under two headings: reducing risk and raising incomes.

POLICIES TO REDUCE RISK AND UNCERTAINTY

Entrepreneurship involves assuming the risks and uncertainties that accompany production. The farmer as an entrepreneur makes decisions regarding crop and livestock production practices, financial management, purchasing, buying, and personnel decisions. All involve some risks and uncertainties, some of which are technical, others, economic. Some risks and uncertainties can be offset, others cannot.

All-risk Crop Insurance

The farmer can insure against fire or windstorm damage to his buildings, equipment, and supplies; theft of his automobile and equipment; and personal injury or property damage to other parties that might be caused by his automobile, equipment or livestock. In addition, farmers in some areas may be able to insure certain of their crops against damage by hailstorms, but in the past, other weather risks have been of such a nature as to prevent their successful transference to insurance companies.

In the 1930s, farm leaders believed that with government research and experience it would be possible to develop an all-risk crop insurance that would result in a substantial reduction in the risk and uncertainties inherent in crop production. Accordingly, legislation was passed authorizing the creation of a wholly government-owned crop insurance corporation. It offered agricultural producers crop insurance providing protection from losses caused by such natural hazards as insects and wildlife, plant diseases, fire, drought, flood, wind and other weather conditions.

After experiencing heavy losses in its early years, the Federal Crop Insurance program was reorganized in 1947 and authorized to continue on a limited experimental basis. As a result, since 1948 premiums collected have equaled losses incurred. Much progress also has been made in developing a standard policy to cover all important crops. Under this standard policy, the production of all crops on the farm is used to determine whether or not a loss has occurred. Unless a general loss occurs, no insurance payment is made.

Premiums charged for Federal Crop Insurance are determined in large part by the history of losses in each individual county in which the Federal

Crop Insurance program operates. In this way, the premium rates for insurance are much higher in the western parts of such states as Nebraska and the Dakotas, where the crop production hazards are greater, than in the eastern parts of these states.

In 1970, Federal Crop Insurance was available in more than 1400 counties with insurance coverage available on wheat, cotton, flax, corn, tobacco, beans, citrus, soybeans, barley, peaches, oranges, and grain sorghum. Although this insurance was available in about half the counties in the United States, the percentage of eligible acreage insured was relatively low in all states. In 1968, 31 percent of the area planted to wheat in Montana, 28 percent of the wheat in Colorado, and 25 percent of the wheat in North Dakota was protected. Twenty-three percent of the land planted to corn and soybeans in Minnesota was protected, but Federal Crop Insurance was used relatively little in the cornbelt. About 16 percent of cotton acreage was insured and over 25 percent of tobacco acreage. One could not conclude from these figures that farmers found Federal Crop Insurance very attractive, despite its wide availability.

Diversification and Outlook Information

The time-honored method of adjusting farming operations to minimize the adverse effects of both unfavorable weather and price changes is to produce a diversity of products for the market. Diversified farming not only reduces technological and price uncertainties, but, as was pointed out in earlier chapters, it also may make possible more complete utilization of the land, labor, and machinery on the farm. Outlook information on prospective economic conditions is useful. By analyzing, interpreting, and relating the mass of information on supplies, consumer demand, and prices for various agricultural products, professional economists from the land-grant colleges and U.S. Department of Agriculture provide farmers with a valuable economic service. Diversified farmers who have the opportunity to shift resources among several alternative enterprises find this service especially helpful. Despite the fact that all statements about the future are only estimates, for the most part outlook reports have correctly forecast coming economic changes.

The United States Department of Agriculture issues outlook, or what are more appropriately called "situation" reports, one to twelve times a year on twenty to twenty-five different subjects of interest to farmers. Situation reports are issued from four to six times a year for such commodities as cotton, dairy products, livestock and meat, poultry and eggs, and wheat. A demand and price situation report is issued monthly, and the farm cost situation and the fertilizer situation reports are issued annually. Many land-grant colleges also issue outlook reports on a monthly or periodic basis throughout the year. These outlook analyses, when properly applied, somewhat reduce the economic uncertainty farmers face when planning their breeding, seeding, and marketing operations.

Technological advance in agriculture in recent years, requiring high capital investments in specialized equipment, has resulted in greater specilization, less diversification, and less opportunity to make short-term adjustments in farming plans based on outlook information. Larger amounts of credit also are required to finance the increased investment in specialized equipment and to permit operators to achieve the scale of operations necessary for the realization of minimum production costs. The increased vulnerability of specialized producers to fluctuations in prices and a more complete realization of the costs of these fluctuations in recent years has led to the development of several proposals for further reducing the risk of uncertainty associated with fluctuating market prices.

Forward Prices

One of the original proposals called for the establishment of a forward pricing system to announce a series of assured government prices or their equivalent in advance of the planting or breeding season.[3] The basic aspects of a forward pricing system as outlined by Johnson and others who advocated its adoption were as follows:

1. The prices should be announced sufficiently far in advance to enable farmers to adjust their production programs to the prices.
2. The announced and guaranteed prices should cover a sufficient period of time to permit farmers to complete their production and marketing plans with considerable certainty.
3. The price announcements should be sufficiently clear and precise so that each farmer could readily interpret their implications for him.
4. The prices adopted should be those that would keep farm production in line with demand commodity by commodity.

A system of forward prices as outlined above would not be a system of stable prices. Rather, it would be a system of prices approximating free market prices except that the prices would be determined and announced before the planting and breeding seasons rather than at the time the products were marketed. Prices for individual products would vary as necessary from one production period to the next to encourage increased production of some products and decreased production of others. The important advantage of a system of forward prices for producers is that the element of price uncertainty largely would be removed. Farmers could undertake their production plans using credit as needed with the assurance that when the product was

[3] For a comprehensive and analytical treatment of this proposal, see D. Gale Johnson, *Forward Prices for Agriculture* (Chicago: University of Chicago Press, 1947).

ready for market the expected prices would be realized. This would result in increased efficiency in the use of resources in food and fiber production.

Modified Forward Prices

Gray, Sorenson, and Cochrane, reviewing the price and production responses in potato production, have suggested a modified forward price system for potatoes regardless of whether or not forward prices are adopted for other commodities.[4] They found that both prices and the production of potatoes vary greatly from year to year with a tendency for producers to over-adjust to price changes. (See Figure 24–1.)

Their suggestion for reducing these annual fluctuations involves announcing an assured price for a supply of potatoes equal to but no greater than estimated requirements. At the same time, the government would announce lower guaranteed total crop values for quantities in excess of estimated requirements. The total crop values for supplies in excess of estimated requirements would be determined with reference to the demand curve for potatoes with an elasticity demand of perhaps −0.5. Although a schedule of prices and total crop values assuming a demand elasticity of −0.5 would discourage excessive production, it would be less inelastic than the demand in the market. Hence, the assured crop values would decline

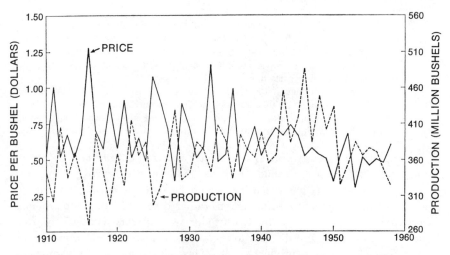

FIGURE 24–1.   Deflated Seasonal Average Price and Production of Potatoes in the U.S., 1910–1958

[4]Roger W. Gray, Vernon L. Sorenson, and Willard W. Cochrane, "An Economic Analysis of the Impact of Government Programs on the Potato Industry of the United States," *Technical Bulletin 211* (Minnesota Agricultural Experiment Station, 1954), pp. 178–84.

less for large crops than in a free market, and the annual incomes of potato producers would be more stable than in a completely free market.

Under this plan, no individual farmer would receive either a price or a value guarantee. After the crop had been marketed, so that the quantities and values were known, any deficiency in crop value for a given quantity would be made up in direct government payments to farmers, apportioned to the total value of each farmer's crop. For example, if the assured total value for a crop of the quantity produced were $460 million and the crop actually sold for $400 million, each farmer, upon producing evidence of the total value of potatoes marketed by him, would receive a government check equal to 15 percent of his market receipts from the sale of potatoes. This price and income stabilization proposal for potatoes maintains the incentives for orderly marketing throughout the crop season and for the production of high-quality potatoes, because the payment is based on the percentage difference between the total guaranteed crop value and the actual market value of the crop. Thus, the guaranteed cash receipts of the producer are increased by a flat percentage applied to his market receipts. This plan also avoids the many problems that are associated with direct price supports, such as administrative determination of relative prices for different locations, different grades and qualities, and for different periods in the marketing season.

Weakness of Forward Prices

In spite of the apparent advantages that systems of forward prices have in reducing price uncertainty, these plans have never won widespread political support. Instead, relatively stable price supports on important storable crops have been continued from year to year.

Soon after the advantages of a system of forward prices were outlined, a modified version of this idea was incorporated in existing farm price-support legislation. The government was required to announce price-support levels in advance of the planting season, rather than at the beginning of the harvest as had often been done in earlier years. But farm people have been unwilling to accept the level of prices implicit in a system of forward prices as outlined. They have insisted on the maintenance of relatively stable support price levels regardless of the prices needed "to keep production in line with demand commodity by commodity."

The political problems involved in administering a system of forward prices in line with the requirements outlined appear to be almost insuperable. Price levels largely determine farm family income levels over short periods of time. For this reason, because both the demand for and supply of farm products are highly inelastic, it seems unlikely that any legislative body would delegate sufficient authority to an administrative agency to permit it to publish prices that would keep production in line with demand. This is especially true under conditions of rapid technological advance where supplies increase more rapidly than market outlets.

An Expanded System of Futures Markets

Some economists have suggested that an expanded futures market rather than a system of forward prices might be developed for farm products as a means of reducing the uncertainties that arise out of month-to-month and year-to-year price variations. Commodities such as corn, wheat, and cotton, which can be stored and which can be bought and sold on the basis of federal grade specifications, for many years have been bought and sold for delivery some months in the future. In these futures markets, buyers and sellers enter into contracts to deliver and to accept delivery within specified future time periods. Trading rules require that the product tendered for settlement of the contract must meet certain minimum grade specifications.

At the present time, few producers sell their products in the futures market at planting time. Rather, futures markets are used largely by the marketing agencies and processors as a means of protecting themselves against unexpected price changes while conducting their commercial processing operations.

No doubt there are many reasons why so few producers use futures markets. One of the most important reasons, however, is that price uncertainty is a risk that must be borne by someone or some group in the economic system and future prices that processors and speculators are willing to offer at planting time usually are unattractive to producers. Most producers prefer to assume the risk of still lower prices at harvest time than those offered in the futures market at planting time in the hope that when the crop is harvested market prices will be higher. Although the price risks and uncertainties in farming are high, it appears that no other group in society is willing to assume them at a cost that farmers are willing to pay. As in the case of government all-risk crop insurance, most farmers prefer to carry the risk themselves than accept future prices that prevail at the breeding or planting time.

If futures markets were developed to the point that producers at planting or breeding time could sell their products for delivery at harvest time or when they were ready for market, much of the uncertainty associated with future price variations would be eliminated. This is not an entirely new idea. For many years, vegetable-canning companies, in advance of planting time, have entered into firm contracts with growers with respect to prices to be paid for the canning crops at harvest. A few other processors and handlers of special products such as pure strains of seeds enter into contracts with producers before planting time, agreeing upon prices to be paid for the product when it is ready for sale.

Usually, products are produced on the basis of contract prices when the product is so specialized that there are only one or two possible purchasers. The local canning or sugar beet company is the only sales outlet for producers of sugar beets or of crops for canning. Under these conditions, the processing company enters into contracts before planting time in order to assure itself of a supply that can be processed profitably, and producers do not plant the crop unless they are assured of a market outlet by entering into a contract with the processor. In recent years, a great deal of interest has developed in using organized bargaining procedures to arrive at acceptable prices for groups of producers. Bargaining would stabilize prices if it came to be a routine procedure, in the same way that expanded use of contracts would.

Direct Payments

Over the years agricultural economists have investigated a number of alternative policies for stabilizing farm prices and income against business cycle fluctuations, especially against a decline in demand for food and fiber resulting from substantial unemployment such as occurred in the 1930s. A number of these investigations resulted in recommendations that market prices be allowed to perform their function of guiding production and consumption but that a system of direct (compensatory) payments to farmers should be used to reduce the instability of farm income. Ideally such a system would make the payments:

1. In a manner and at a time that would give a counter-cyclical effect.
2. In such a way as to minimize their effect on agricultural production and trade.
3. In an amount and at such a time as to substantially stabilize farm income.[5]

Direct payments were first suggested as a substitute for individual commodity price supports; they would be used to make up the difference between the seasonal market average and, say, 85 percent of the predepression prices of the more important farm products. A compensatory plan of this type might be illustrated as follows: If, during a depression, the seasonal market average prices of corn, wheat, and potatoes dropped below an announced support level by, say $.10 a bushel on corn, $.25 a bushel on

---

[5]For a comprehensive analysis of several types of compensatory payment plans, see Geoffrey S. Shepherd, *Farm Policy: New Directions* (Ames, Iowa: Iowa State College Press, 1967), Chap. 11.

wheat, and $.25 a bushel on potatoes, a farmer who produced these crops would get a payment from the government equal to the amount of the seasonal price deficiency multiplied by the number of bushels of each crop sold during the season.

A payment program of this type stabilizes the effective price of individual commodities at some level, yet individual producers continue to receive premiums for quality. Producers also continue to have an incentive to follow orderly marketing procedures throughout the season because the payment is related to the difference between the seasonal market average and the announced support price level rather than between the actual price received by the producer and the support price level.

Several agricultural economists have proposed that the payments be based on total farm income rather than on the seasonal price disparities of individual products. The essential features of an income payment plan may be illustrated as follows: The government might agree to support all farm prices as an aggregate at, say, 85 percent of some predetermined level. It might do this by offering to increase each farmer's income from the sale of farm products by a percentage equal to the increase required to bring the annual index of all farm prices up to the announced support level. If the government agreed to make up the difference between the annual average and an index level equal to 85 percent of the predetermined price level, the computations would be relatively simple. If market prices fell to 77 percent of the base, an increase of approximately 10 percent would be required to bring them up to the 85 percent level. Each farmer could then submit evidence of his total sales, and the appropriate payment would be equal to 10 percent of his sales. In this way, farmers in the aggregate would receive income from crop and livestock sales plus payments equal to the income they would have received from crop and livestock sales if prices had averaged 85 percent of the predepression base period. (Some adjustments would have to be made for interfarm sales, however.)

In principle, either of these systems of direct payments is an improvement over the practice of allowing farm income to decline sharply when prices fall. Direct payments tend to stabilize farm income, yet permit production of farm products to be maintained and the price of food to decline as necessary to clear the market.

With the 1965 Agricultural Act, farm programs began to take on more of the characteristics of the first type of direct payment plan. Price supports were not eliminated, but they were allowed to fall to approximately the world level to encourage exports. Direct compensatory payments to farmers were made conditional upon their reducing acreage planted. The amount of the payment was based on the difference between season average price and a predetermined level for each crop.

POLICIES TO RAISE FARM PRICES
AND INCOME

Solving the price instability problem, although an important step toward achieving improved resource allocation in agriculture, would not necessarily raise incomes or prices. A series of possible alternatives have been proposed to achieve the goal of higher incomes. They range from complete absence of government action to complete government control. We will discuss several programs that have been seriously proposed.

A Return to the Free Market

A significant body of opinion has held that a return to the free market would be the best policy to follow for U.S. agriculture. Steps in that direction, in the form of less-restrained production have also been proposed. Throughout most of the 1950s, a large number of agricultural economists and farm leaders, including the Secretary of Agriculture and his policy-making staff, in the years between 1952 and 1960 believed that a policy of less-restrained production and marketing would improve the income and welfare position of farm people. They held that the price and income stabilization programs developed in earlier years maintained the prices of a number of farm products at too high a level, thus "pricing them out of the market."

Even though farm income continued to be depressed in spite of temporary surplus disposal programs and the accumulation of $9 billion in farm products by the Commodity Credit Corporation, the Secretary of Agriculture and some other influential leaders in agriculture continued to advise farmers that the most appropriate policy for improving their incomes was progressively to remove planting restrictions and to lower price-support levels on price-supported crops. The ultimate objective of a return to the free market was not achieved, and in 1960 with a change of administration that objective was abandoned.

Analysis of the economic characteristics of U.S. agriculture, including that presented earlier in this book, indicates that such a policy would have undesirable income and price results. All the available evidence shows that the demand and supply of agricultural products in the United States are highly inelastic and that supply expands more rapidly over time than demand. As long as this basic situation holds, less-restrained production and marketing will result in greater output, lower prices, and lower farm income.

The most efficient producers could weather a return to the free market most easily because by definition their costs are the lowest. Inefficient producers would suffer the most, and would bear a large share of the cost of such a policy. Even so, it is not at all clear that the inefficient producers would leave farming in sufficiently large numbers to have any effect on total production and prices. The small, inefficient producers are large in number but contribute little to output. Farmers from this group have been moving out of farming at a very rapid rate. It is difficult to see that a faster rate would be practical or desirable from the social point of view. And, we have seen very little historical evidence that low prices will slow the rate of increase in aggregate output.

Government Assistance in Shifting to Nonfarm Jobs

As mentioned earlier, a number of students of the economic problems of agriculture have observed that continued new investments in cost-reducing technology have caused too many resources to be utilized in agricultural production. Because land and farm capital investments cannot be transferred to other activities, some interest has centered on accelerating the shift of farm workers to other lines of activity as a means of offsetting the over-rapid rate of technical advance. Proposals for programs to achieve this objective were similar to the proposals outlined for improving the widespread underemployment and low-income problem in agriculture (Chapter 18).

Those who advocated these lines of activity as a means of improving the income and equity position of farm people usually have not proposed them as the only programs to be utilized in achieving a balance between aggregate output output expansion and aggregate demand expansion. They would place major reliance, however, on programs for accelerating the shift of farm workers to nonfarm jobs. Again, personal value judgments—in part acquired with their professional training—may influence their recommendations. The authors find much merit in these proposals. But to seriously propose these activities as the major programs for achieving an important improvement in the income position of commercial farmers appears to involve a mistaken appraisal of the economics of technological advance. We believe it also involves a substantial overestimate of the effectiveness of such programs in view of the fact that nearly 25 percent of the farm laboring force moved out of agriculture in the 1950s, and another 25 percent in the 1960s, but excess productive capacity still remains, and in fact was greater in 1970 than it was twenty years earlier.

Retirement of Land (Soil Bank)

The retirement of large acreages of land from agriculture as a major program for improving farm income has been advocated by a number of farm leaders and agricultural economists. The advocates of land retirement as a major program for achieving a balance between agricultural output and available markets usually proposed that emphasis be placed on securing the retirement of whole farms.

Most often, the proposal is that the land be rented. In the 1950s, the Soil Bank program was initiated, under which the government rented land from farm owners for periods of five to fifteen years and allowed it to be devoted to conservation uses. Some 28 million acres of cropland were rented to the government under this program in 1960. The rental rates offered under this program by the government were high enough in most cases to equal the value of the land in a ten-year period. With this in mind, a small minority of farm leaders proposed that the desired acreages be retired from farm production by government purchase on an offer basis rather than by the relatively expensive rental agreements.

There is little doubt that a large-scale rental or purchase program retiring 50 to 70 million acres of land from crop production would temporarily bring aggregate farm output into balance with available markets. Assuming that the less-productive cropland and the less-productive farm workers and equipment would be removed from farm production by a conservation reserve program that emphasized the rental of whole farms, a total of 50 to 70 million acres would probably have to be retired to effect an 8 to 10 percent reduction in crop output and a 6 to 10 percent reduction in aggregate farm output.

Those who advocate this method of bringing total farm output into balance with available market outlets believe that a well-designed rental or purchase program that removed the less-productive lands and the farms operated by the older and otherwise less-productive farm operators would be the most efficient means of adjusting agregate output downward to a level that would move through commercial markets at reasonably stable prices. Such a program would require a minimum of government activity. With this much land and a large number of farm operators taken out of agriculture on a completely voluntary basis, they believe that the remaining land and the remaining operators could be freed from production and marketing restrictions, returning relative prices and costs to their appropriate role of directing the use of resources within agriculture. Such a program would leave the remaining operators free from production restrictions while shrinking the total land base to a point at which aggregate output would not be excessive in relation to market outlets. The strongest advocates of this approach would retire additional land each year as necessary to offset potential aggregate output expansion in excess of aggregate demand expansion resulting from continued technical advance.

The weakness of whole farm land retirement appears to be its differential effect on rural communities and established trade centers. Small-town tradesmen, especially those in the rural areas of the Southeast and those in other less-productive rural areas, vigorously and effectively opposed further expansion of government land rental or purchase programs after their first years of operation. The most widespread support for this approach came from the more-productive farming areas of the Midwest. People in these areas thought largely in terms of removal of small acreages including the less-productive farms in their home communities and the removal of large acreages of less-productive land "elsewhere."

The Soil Bank shares a major weakness with other production control programs that depend on land restrictions for bringing aggregate output expansion into balance with aggregate demand expansion. They can affect total output by reducing the supply of only one of the input factors without measures for preventing the substitution of other factors for land. Recent technical studies indicate that land contributes about 15 percent of the total annual inputs in agricultural production. Labor contributes about 30 percent and capital contributes about 55 percent of the total annual inputs. Technical advance is resulting in continued increase in the importance of capital as an input while the relative importance of inputs from labor and land in agricultural production are decreasing. Increased use of fertilizers and supplemental irrigation on the remaining farm land would offset much of the land retirement. From this point of view, it appears unreasonable to expect that aggregate output can be kept in balance with available market outlets by a moderate reduction in cropland utilized, although placing a part of the cropland in a conservation reserve may be an important supplement when used in conjunction with other measures.

Supply Control or Marketing Quotas

In professional papers and in a book entitled *Farm Prices—Myth and Reality,* one of the authors has outlined another approach for dealing with the price-income problems of agriculture.[6] This approach would have Congress assume the responsibility for determining the fair price for each commodity coming under control, after which a national sales quota would be established, taking into consideration market and special demands. Sales quotas would be the estimated amount of the commodity that would move through the market at the defined fair price, hence, they would be determined by the Congress with the interests of both consumers and producers in mind.

Each farmer would receive a pro rata share of the national sales quota for each commodity, based largely on his historical record of production or sales. Under this plan, it would be illegal for a farmer to market any commodity having a national quota unless he had a marketing quota covering

---

[6]W. W. Cochrane, *Farm Prices—Myth and Reality* (Minneapolis, Minn.: University of Minnesota Press, 1958), Chap. 8.

the quantities marketed. One of the important features of this proposal is that the marketing quotas of individual farmers might be bought and sold under a minimum of restrictions—quotas would become negotiable. The total farm marketing quota might be represented by marketing certificates having a face value equal to a part of the total marketing quota. A farmer could sell any part or all of these marketing quota certificates if he so desired. In this way, the individual farm operator would be free to expand production, or contract it, in the light of his production and marketing costs, including the cost of additional marketing certificates if he wished to expand output beyond the marketing quota allotted to him.

Control programs making use of quotas, where those quotas are tied to the land or to a farm, have long been criticized on the grounds that the short-term gains of the control program are capitalized into the land and in the long run average unit cost rises to meet price per unit. In this way, the short-term gains of the program are imputed into costs, and nothing remains in the long run except the nuisance of the controls. The supply control approach is criticized on similar grounds; namely, in the long run the short-term gains arising out of supply control would become capitalized into the negotiable marketing certificates.

This constitutes a valid criticism. The capital value of the fixed factor, or factors, in farming is based on the residual share of the cash receipts from the sale of products that can be attributed to them after paying market prices for the variable factors used in the production process. All increases in net returns from farming tend to become capitalized into the fixed factors, whether this increase originates out of population growth or out of successful sales promotion, a change in tastes, output restriction, or war. This criticism of all programs designed to increase farm income by restricting marketings to quantities that can be sold at stable, reasonable, or good prices applies equally to programs for expanding the utilization and demand for farm products.

Where wage rates and the returns to labor are below average for the various reasons outlined in Chapter 18, the asset value of fixed factors such as land or marketing quotas are greater in relation to product prices than they would be if wage rates were competitive with those in nonfarm activities. The extent to which increased income resulting from supply controls is capitalized into the value of the marketing quotas depends to a great extent on alternative employment opportunities for the rural people.

Tobacco-marketing quotas have attained substantial capitalized values in many communities even though the returns to labor in tobacco production were low relative to industrial wage rates in other communities. In a few communities, however, tobacco allotments have been unused and had no value because alternative employment opportunities offered higher returns.

Land prices in the irrigated valleys of California were influenced to a substantial extent by the past availability of low-cost foreign labor made possible by special labor legislation.

Regardless of the other employment opportunities of rural labor, however, supply controls would have certain economic advantages for farmers. These advantages are: (1) they make possible short-term gains in income to farm operators who have not shared in the national prosperity of the 1950s and 1960s; (2) they provide protection against major farm price level declines in the future that might destroy asset positions; and (3) they assure increased certainty in resource planning and use.

A storage program designed to stabilize year-to-year market supplies and diversion programs for perishable commodities in years of above-average yields would be needed to complement annual sales quotas. Where commodities such as wheat have both a food use and a feed use, the marketing quota might be limited to the product marketed for use as food. All products moving through commercial market channels would have to be accompanied by marketing certificates indicating that they were being marketed within the legal market quotas of the originating producers.

A plan of this kind, if properly administered, would be reasonably successful in coordinating aggregate output expansion with aggregate demand expansion. Such a plan, however, would be subject to the same technical and political difficulties in determining fair price levels as those involved in setting forward prices at levels that would keep supply and demand in equilibrium. Also, the administrative problems involved with its 1 million commercial producers and hundreds of thousands of processing and marketing agencies are believed by many to make such an approach extremely difficult to administer.

The Marketing Order Approach

In the late 1950s, the National Grange and a substantial number of farm leaders in commodity organizations turned to what was loosely called a commodity-by-commodity approach for an alternative to the then-outmoded and excessively costly existing price support programs. In a leaflet published in 1959, the National Grange used the term *domestic parity concept* to refer to a whole array of programs—on a commodity-by-commodity basis—to raise farm income and put an end to Government's progressive destruction of private trade in farm products and Government's increasing control of production patterns in farming. Each program would call for the use of that combination of economic devices, marketing certificates, import duties, processing taxes, marketing orders, and direct assessments against products sold that would be best suited to the particular commodity involved.

Those who advocate this approach to the solution of the problems of over-rapid output expansion recognize that technological advance contributes to increased specialization and increased integration and that these trends are likely to continue at an accelerated rate for the foreseeable future. Increased specialization, in turn, is accompanied by the organization of new commodity groups and by increased staffing and expanded activities on the part of the older commodity organizations.

Given a highly inelastic demand for the aggregate output of foods and fibers and a relatively inelastic demand for most groups of foods, such as dairy products, meats, turkeys, broilers, eggs, cereals, and potatoes, commodity groups can increase the income of their members by appropriate orderly marketing programs. Advocates of this approach note that marketing orders issued by the Secretary of Agriculture have facilitated orderly marketing of perishable fruits and vegetables and of fluid milk in urban markets. The marketing order approach, they believe, might be utilized by other commodity groups and it might be expanded to include the allotment of marketing goals or quotas among producers, as well as the collection of marketing fees by a check-off system.

Based on experience and the analysis of economic forces at work, a number of conditions have been identified that increase the probability of success with a marketing order. The commodity involved should meet these conditions:

1. The demand should be price inelastic.
2. The elasticity of supply and cross elasticities of supply should not be too high.
3. A geographically concentrated production area where growers feel a community of interest and where a commodity promotion group can operate help in getting approval for the order.
4. The marketing channels for the product should be clearly identifiable and relatively few in number.

This approach has the merit of being very flexible. It allows producers a maximum of producer freedom in organizing productive resources. The marketing goals could be made negotiable, thus permitting regional specialization in production in line with relative costs. One of the outstanding difficulties in this approach is the conflicts of interests between producers within a single producer group. Although the group as a whole may benefit from some specific proposal, a substantial part of the group may be inadequately informed regarding the group benefits and a minority may be adversely affected. These factions may block effective action on any group proposal. Also, there is a general tendency for commodity groups to overestimate the inelasticity of demand for their particular product and to underestimate its elasticity of supply with the result that the membership may become committed to a self-defeating program.

The Farm Bargaining Approach

In recent years, the national farm organizations have embraced bargaining as the solution to the problems of farmers. It is similar to the marketing order approach in that marketing agreements play a prominent role. The growth of the bargaining view is fueled by the recognition that farmers are price takers in the market place because they are numerous and each sells a very small fraction of total output. Collective action through bargaining is seen as a way to offset this.

Bargaining is viewed by some simply as group action to force buyers to pay higher prices for production. The instruments of power are strikes or holding actions. But the higher prices gained through such actions cannot be sustained unless total production is consistent with those higher prices. In other words, if the price that would be established by the existing demand and supply conditions were lower than the agreed-upon price, not all output would be purchased at the agreed-upon price. Leakages would develop that tended to lower price. Thus, bargaining to raise prices requires the ability to control supply. This is possible in a number of ways.

A secondary market, such as for manufactured products in the milk industry, provides one means to control supply. Production in excess of that required for fluid consumption is diverted to the manufactured products market and sold for a lower price. The average of the high-price fluid milk and the low-price manufactured milk will be higher than if all milk were sold for fluid consumption. Unfortunately, few commodities other than milk have an effective secondary market.

Control over production is the most effective means of insuring that the agreed-upon price will hold. This might be achieved by quotas or by marketing goals. Regardless of what they are called, if they are not compulsory and enforceable, the program will be ineffective. It is on this point that bargaining efforts have been stymied. Farmers have not been willing to give up their freedom to produce in exchange for a higher price.

A Redirected Allocation of Research and Development Resources

The impact of modern technology on farm production has been stressed so often that by now the student of this book may be impervious to the phrase. It should be clear that "improved" technology does not always result in a better situation in the long run. It is likely that the long-run solution to low farm prices and income will result from a slower rate of technological advance resulting from a redirection of research and development expenditures that provide the new technology. New technology (in the form of capital) substitutes for land and labor, increasing output more rapidly than demand, thereby making land and labor surplus. The dynamic situation is thus a substitution of technology for land and labor.

As a result of this dynamic situation, less land is subjected to more intensive use with the consequent environmental problems discussed in Chapter 21. At the same time, more land is made "surplus" and more farmers are unable to compete in the face of technological progress. It would seem that a redirection of research resources away from immediate production-increasing developments toward understanding the environmental problems and the development of environmentally neutral or beneficial means of increasing production (which will be needed as we enter the next century) would help solve both types of problems.

In fact, this redirection of research resources is occurring, but it is not generally viewed as a policy to help improve farm prices and incomes. If one sees the agricultural sector in the dynamic terms discussed above, then environmental improvement and price policy can be directed toward consistent ends. A *conscious* consideration of the allocation of resources to output-increasing research would help. The generally accepted view is that the research and development resources that have been applied in agriculture have worked wonders, therefore, a greater application would be good. But good for what? More production-augmenting research will speed the rate of potential output increase. But do we need a faster rate of output increase in the next ten years than we had in the last ten? The answer would appear to be no. We need a slightly slower rate, and then perhaps the pressure on "surplus" resources and the pressure on the environment will both be lessened.

This does not argue for less resources for agricultural research, but for a redirection of some of those resources. We need to attack the longer-range problems of how to increase food production at the *required* rate (not faster) without overloading the environment with chemicals, effluents, and other residuals. We need to develop institutions to accomplish this without continuing to overload society with surplus individuals created by technological "progress" that leaves them with inadequate incomes. These difficult problems will not solve themselves—adequate research, directed at the right problems, is required.

POINTS FOR DISCUSSION

1. Summarize the economic outlook for one commodity of your choosing, based on the current U.S.D.A. situation report.
2. What practical steps can be taken by farmers to reduce the risk and uncertainty involved in their production operations?
3. Why cannot a price and income policy in food and agriculture be laid down with scientific objectivity?
4. Make an outline of the principal schools of thought regarding a desirable price and income policy for agriculture. Set forth the main conceptual points of each of these schools.
5. What basic similarities and differences emerge from your outline?

6. With which school of thought do you find yourself most in agreement? Or do you prefer some combination of ideas not presented in this survey? If so, set forth your suggested price and income policy for agriculture.
7. What would be the effect on land values if the present land-based system of farm income support were replaced with the "supply control" approach?

REFERENCES

Bargaining Power for Farmers. Proceedings of the 1968 National Farm Institute. Ames: Iowa State University Press, 1968.

COCHRANE, W. W., *The City Man's Guide to the Farm Problem*, Chaps. 8–10. Minneapolis, Minn.: University of Minnesota Press, 1965.

HATHAWAY, D. E., *Government and Agriculture: Public Policy in a Democratic Society*, Chaps. 10–15. New York: The Macmillan Company, 1963.

SHEPHERD, G. S., *Farm Policy: New Directions*, Chaps. 7–11. Ames: Iowa State University Press, 1964.

BAILEY, W. R., AND L. A. JONES, *Economic Considerations in Crop Insurance*, ERS-447, Economic Research Service, U.S.D.A. (August 1970).

Chapter 25

The Future of American

Farm Policy[1]

Commercial farmers entered the 1970s as they did the 1950s and the 1960s—with excess production capacity, with the capacity to produce more farm products than the commercial market will take at the current level of prices. As we have seen in earlier chapters, this problem grows out of the interaction of a slowly growing demand based largely on the domestic market for food and fiber products and a rapidly growing supply propelled by a technological revolution in the production of farm products. In spite of the exodus of millions of workers from agriculture in the 1950s and 1960s, and an array of governmental control programs, the inflow of new and improved technologies has caused total farm output to increase more rapidly than the domestic demand and hence has created a condition of chronic excess production capacity. A rapidly growing export market comprised, first, of commercial exports to Western Europe and Japan and second, of foreign aid to the developing nations, saved American agriculture from more massive resource and social adjustments than it has experienced. But the growth in foreign markets was not sufficiently rapid to enable the growth in total demand to keep up with the increase in production. Hence, we have had a continued pressure of supplies on demand and a continued downward pressure on farm prices.

What the changing elements of the world situation and the U.S. economy will do to the American farm economy in the 1970s no one can state

[1]Adapted from the Fellows Lecture entitled "American Farm Policy in a Tumultuous World" by Willard W. Cochrane, *American Journal of Agricultural Economics*, Vol. 52, No. 5, December 1970.

with certainty. But we will briefly review and appraise some of the basic forces that will be involved in an effort to understand better possible developments in agriculture in the years to come. We then consider the outlook for the next decade and discuss possible changes in farm policy.

Key Economic and Social Forces

The farm population of the United States has declined steadily for two decades, reaching a low of 9.7 million lonely, frustrated souls living on just about 3 million farms in 1970. They constituted slightly less than 5 percent of the total population. The commercial farms (that is, those grossing over $10,000 per year, which produce 90 percent of the products sold) numbered approximately 1 million.

With these dwindling numbers, of course, has come diminished political power. The term *farm bloc* has been forgotten, and although farm people and rural areas still maintain a respectable degree of power in the Senate, the political strength of farm people in the House of Representatives has declined to an extremely low level. In 1969, for example, only 31 Congressional districts contained 25 percent or more farm population.[2] With the 1970 census results, a good number of Senators who have thought of themselves as coming from a farm state will recognize that they really represent an urban state with a largely industrial economy. The redistricting resulting from the census will further reduce the handful of House members whose interest it is to represent the farmer. The House of Representatives, which is now overwhelmingly urban in its outlook, will become even more so as time passes. In this kind of situation, farm people are going to find it exceedingly difficult to pass legislation that is designed to protect their economic interests, or needs, at any substantial cost to the nonfarm sector. On the other hand, farmers are learning the art of interest-group politics. As they do, we can expect to see farm interest groups operating on the Washington scene much like other small special interest groups—that is, avoiding major legislative battles and seeking favorable decisions from administrators and Congressmen in the daily operation of the government.

The urban interests will press their needs, and those needs are undeniably great. The cities are in trouble. We do not dispose of human wastes in a satisfactory manner; we do not dispose of garbage; we do not eliminate the smoke and the smog; and we do not control crime and violence. Urban areas need new and improved educational services, airport services, police services, rapid transit services, park and recreation services, and all kinds of housing; to get these, we need to discipline ourselves to pay for them. We have largely spent our rising incomes of the 1950s and 1960s on automobiles, durables, roads, and single-unit houses, and let the service systems that hold

[2]*Congressional Quarterly*, June 27, 1969, p. 1137.

cities together go begging. We have not been willing to pay the price to build and maintain the service systems—police, welfare, education, sewage, public transportation—required by a complex, opulent, modern urban society.

Only the federal government has the power and the prestige to raise the funds required to do this job of rebuilding and repairing our cities. This in turn means higher taxes for everyone (a reduced level of gadget living) and a new set of priorities in the use of existing federal revenues. It seems probable that any serious effort to reestablish national priorities by an urban society, through an urban Congress, will have some negative effects on federal spending for agriculture.

The American farm sector produced abundantly during the 1960s but not at the rate of the 1950s. Total farm output increased by some 2 percent per year in the 1950s but at only 1.5 percent per year in the 1960s. The index reflecting technological change stopped rising about 1962 and has held essentially constant since that year. Farm technological advance with its cost-reducing, output-increasing effects was not a very important force in American agriculture after 1962. Total farm output continued to increase through the 1960s, but after 1962 total farm output increased as farmers applied more production inputs—usually nonfarm-produced inputs such as fertilizer, pesticides, and machines.

One would be foolish to predict the end of the technological revolution on American farms, especially when so great a potential for increasing the efficiency of production would seem to exist in the livestock area. But if the situation existing during 1963–71 should continue, some important new implications follow for farm policy. With a decline in the level of farm product prices, one might expect the total input of productive resources in farming to decline, and hence total output to be reduced. In this situation, farmers and their policy leaders are freed of the curse of a perfectly inelastic aggregate response curve and might logically expect some corrective action to a general surplus condition from falling farm prices—namely, a contraction in aggregate output. It is just possible that *farm price level* changes in the future might begin to affect aggregate output in agriculture, unlike the situation during the 1950s and 1960s.

The index of prices received by farmers declined about 25 percent between February 1951 and June 1961; between 1961 and 1971, prices received by farmers increased modestly, regaining about one-half the loss experienced in the 1950s. During the same twenty-year period, the index of prices paid by farmers increased by just about 50 percent. Thus, while prices received by farmers declined overall from 1951 to 1971, the prices farmers paid increased by some 50 percent, most rapidly in recent years, especially since 1964.

No businessman likes to see his costs rising while the prices of the products he is selling are falling. Nevertheless, this is a somewhat tolerable situation when unit costs of production are declining through technological advance. In the 1950s, this was the situation for the more alert, aggressive farmers who were able to adopt new and improved production techniques. But with the slowdown of farm technological advance following 1962, the representative farmer has not been able to reduce his unit costs of production. On the other hand, the prices of the producer goods that he buys rose dramatically during this same period. Thus, the representative farmer was caught in a price-cost squeeze in the middle and late 1960s. On a national basis, net income from farming trended downward between 1966 and 1971. Net income per farm from farming held almost constant because the number of farms declined substantially—by over 300,000 between 1966 and 1970.

While these events were dominating American agriculture, some exciting developments were taking place around the world with respect to grain production. In the hot regions of the world, stretching from Morocco to the Philippines, a revolution in the production of grains is taking place. Between 1964 and 1968, production in the developing countries increased by 52 million tons. The most spectacular developments have occurred in wheat, but there have been noteworthy gains in rice production and progress is being made in the production of other grains and legumes.[3] This revolution—the Green Revolution—has lifted the spectre of starvation from these countries and replaced it with the expectation, and a not unreasonable expectation, of improved levels of food consumption. At the same time, grain production during 1964–68 in the developed countries—principally Australia, Canada, the European Community, and the United States—quietly, almost secretly, increased by 123 million tons, or by 25 percent.

Thus, in the second half of the 1960s, a great increase in world grain production has occurred, with more than two-thirds of the increase provided by the developed world. The result has been rising wheat stocks and declining wheat and rice prices in the late 1960s. The increase in world wheat stocks was moderated by a sharp reduction in wheat production in 1970 in Canada, Argentina, Australia, and the United States—partly through deliberate production control and partly as a result of bad weather. But Europe had a bumper crop of wheat in 1971; grain production increased in Canada, the United States, and India. Thus, grain production soared again in 1971 after a temporary setback in 1970.

World grain production will certain continue to fluctuate, but the trend will be to increase importantly in the decade of the 1970s. That increase will be shared in some unknown proportions between the developed and developing worlds, but the sharing roles may well be reversed from that

---

[3]For a summary of this production revolution in grains, as well as its export implications, see Ralph W. Cummings, Jr., "U.S. Export Potentials and the Green Revolution," *Farm Program Choices*, CAED Report 35, (Ames, Iowa: Iowa State University of Science and Technology, 1970). For a good popular treatment see Lester R. Brown, *Seeds of Change* (New York: Praeger Publishers, 1970).

of the 1960s. Given this situation, we can expect: (1) average diets in the developing countries to improve slowly; (2) the United States to lose much of its P.L. 480 market and that part of the P.L. 480 market that remains to become increasingly unstable; (3) pockets of surpluses to accumulate intermittently in the developing countries and to come gushing onto the world market as distressed grain; (4) wheat, rice, and possibly other grain stocks to increase further, unless they are held in check by production control measures in the developed, surplus-producing countries; and (5) world grain prices to continue to sag, unless supported by control measures in the developed, surplus-producing countries.

Another unknown for the next decade is the effect of environmental concerns. If we learn that many of the chemicals regularly used in fertilizers and pesticides constitute a serious threat to man and his environment, and society takes action to restrict or eliminate their use, such action would have important implications for agriculture and the production of food. Restricting or banning the use of low-priced fertilizers and pesticides now regularly used in farm production would dampen down food production increases and raise food prices as either (1) those output-increasing inputs were banned from use; or (2) more expensive, but environmentally safe, substitutes were developed for use in food production. Either way, the goal of a safe, clean environment would have the effect of increasing the cost of producing food, reducing food supplies, and increasing food prices.

If this is the case, we may be entering a new era in agriculture: one that continues to rely heavily on science and technology, but one in which the adverse consequences of new technologies to man and his environment are largely neutralized. In this kind of situation, we should expect technological advances in agriculture to come more slowly, at greater cost to society, and hence result in a slower rate of agricultural output expansion and possibly a slowly rising level of food prices.

The Outlook for the 1970s

We began this chapter with the argument that commercial agriculture in the United States was entering the 1970s with excess production capacity —that it had the capacity to produce more than the commercial market could take at the current level of prices. Hence, it carried within itself the capacity to overproduce, to press market prices downward, to create surplus stocks, and to force more farmers off the land. Yet, two of the key forces reviewed in the previous section act to offset this chronic excess capacity problem *in the long run*. If some new technological developments do not come along with the capacity to importantly increase production efficiency in farming, the rate of output expansion will certainly be reduced below that realized in the 1960s. And the "clean environment" forces will certainly render the development of new production technologies more time consuming and more costly, hence their adoption on farms will take place more slowly. These two forces, then, acting and interacting, could in the long run slow the rate of output expansion to the rate of demand expansion and give rise to a buoyant situation for farm prices and incomes.

But such a development is both "iffy" and far down the road. Farmers are confronted in the early 1970s with a price-cost squeeze in which the prices of the products they sell are rising slowly, if at all, and the prices of the products they buy are rising rapidly. The price inflation of the late 1960s and early 1970s is squeezing farmers badly because the excess productive capacity of their industry keeps farm product prices in general from rising. Compounding this domestic farm problem is the strong tendency for the world production of grains to increase relative to world demand (economic demand, that is). In other words, grain production developments in both the developed and the less-developed world could easily lead to increased grain exports in the 1970s, which on a thin international market would in turn lead to low and chaotic world grain prices. This development is by no means a certainty; many things can happen, but the propensity to increase world grain production and expand exports is there. In such a situation, world grain prices would exert a strong downward pressure on grain prices in the United States, and through the process of substitution, falling grain prices would result in a general lowering of farm prices in the United States, an increased accumulation of commodity stocks, and increased program costs. This is the way that world grains surplus in the 1970s could come home to further complicate the domestic farm problem.

A dwindling farm population, reduced representation in the Congress, and mounting pressures in urban areas to cope with their formidable problems could contribute to a weakening of commodity programs in agriculture at the very time that farm prices and incomes are falling. This is not to suggest that farm programs of price and income support will be dismantled in the early 1970s, but it is to suggest that it is not unrealistic to expect political support for commodity programs in agriculture to be reduced in the 1970s with a concomitant reduction in financial support—perhaps only a little, perhaps a great deal. And this could have disastrous price and income consequences for commercial farmers in the United States as they and other farmers around the world struggle against a growing grain surplus.

Of course, a great drought in a densely populated Asian country, or a big war in the Middle East (or anywhere, for that matter), could drastically change the potential developments sketched above. But, barring such contingencies, the middle 1970s could well look like the farm price trough of the mid–1890s and for somewhat the same reasons—a world surplus of grain created by the farmers of the new world, plus those in the now developing world. But those American farmers who ride out this crisis-still-to-be may discover a new set of forces emerging to control their destiny. This new set of forces would operate to protect and improve man's environment, to render technological developments more sophisticated and more costly, to increase the cost of producing food, to slow the rate of output expansion, and to drive farm prices upward. This, indeed, would be a new era for farmers of the developed world.

Some Specific Policy Suggestions

Given this long-run perspective, what can be done now to improve on present agricultural policy provisions? In this section, we explore specific changes in existing farm policy, beginning from the Agricultural Acts of 1965 and 1970. The discussion builds on economic analyses of the effects of the acts, pointing out the implications of various provisions and indicating possible changes that may be made.

The Agricultural Act of 1965 serves as our point of departure. It provided price and income stability and support for the grain-livestock sector without forcing farmers to accept compulsory supply management; it provided supplementary income to a large number of small- to medium-sized farmers who participated in the voluntary programs; it moved commodity price support levels close to world market price levels and thus facilitated the export of American farm products without the use of subsidy; and it assured American consumers an adequate supply of food, including food reserves, at reasonable prices.

The Agricultural Act of 1970 introduced the set-aside concept. The set-aside eliminates the individual crop-by-crop controls that have been an integral part of the past programs and provides instead a single set-aside of acreage that a participating farmer must agree to hold out of production. The set-aside is the one important new feature of the Act of 1970, and it is a feature that leads to more total production and greater price fluctuation for farm products. In the name of giving more freedom to farmers (where the commodity programs are already voluntary), it permits the farmer to grow any amount of any crop, so long as he sets aside a designated parcel of land and holds it out of production. This program feature increases farm production by reducing the efficiency of controlling production and increasing the cost. It permits a farmer to both produce as much as his farm permits of his most productive crop and bring new land into production. Further, it permits wide swings in production among crop substitutes, and hence contributes to commodity price instability.

Other characteristics of the present program (common to both the 1965 and 1970 Acts) are: (1) high costs—gross government costs of commodity programs, together with related price, income, and disposal programs approximated $7.5 billion in the year ending June 30, 1970; and (2) high income payments to large producers of certain commodities with virtually nothing to assist hired farm workers.

Some analysts believe that the place to begin to solve these problems is with the size of payments made to producers. But before accepting a ceiling limit for commodity payments,[4] one should recognize two important characteristics of those payments. First, most payments are small—less than 5 percent of all payments received by farmer participants were over $5,000 in 1968. Second, payments are made for essentially two purposes: to control production and to supplement income, although these different purposes were not overtly recognized in the legislation. It should nonetheless be possible to eliminate extremely high individual payments and reduce program costs, at least modestly, by placing a ceiling on payments to farmers without seriously damaging the supply management aspects of the programs.

It should be noted that to achieve the cost reduction and equity objectives of the payment limitation provision, the government would need to administer the provision with care and vigor in order to prevent large operating units from being divided into smaller units under some new ownership status, wherein the newly divided and now smaller units became eligible for the full payment rate. Clearly, if the latter were permitted to occur, the equity and savings objectives of the payment limit provision would be circumvented.[5]

The Agricultural Act of 1965 is silent on the question of protection for hired farm workers, as is the Act of 1970, and all previous pieces of farm legislation dealing with price and income protection for farm producers. This is not because the problems have not been recognized. President Johnson's Food and Fiber Commission argued that: "Rural workers should have protection equal to that of urban workers in such important areas as workman's and unemployment compensation, Social Security, collective bargaining and minimum wages."[6] This could be achieved with legislation including the following provisions:

1. That farm workers not be denied by federal or state exemptions the benefits of policies and standards that are deemed to be in the interests of other wage earners.
2. That farm workers be included under the provisions of the National Labor Relations Act to the extent feasible, and wherever necessary, to achieve equivalent personal and social protection for those workers.
3. That farm workers be covered under minimum wage legislation.

Because it seems likely that prices of vegetables, oilseeds, beans and peas, livestock, and livestock products will follow grain prices downward in the domestic market as world grain prices declined, it would seem wise to consider other means for assisting farmers to stabilize those product

---

[4]The Act of 1970 contains a payment limitation of $55,000 per commodity per farm.

[5]Stories are circulating that the spirit of the $55,000 payment limitation on the 1971 crop was circumvented through the breaking up of large farms into smaller legal entities.

[6]*Food and Fiber for the Future*, Report of the National Advisory Commission on Food and Fiber (Washington D. C., July 1967), p. 119.

prices. In this connection, marketing orders might well be reexamined and promoted with producer groups whose products are destined primarily for the domestic market (for example, fruits and vegetables, eggs, pork, potatoes). Along this same line, further legislation to assist farm groups to form bargaining associations should be given serious consideration. The policy trick here is to grant a designated group of farmers sufficient market power to enable it to bargain efficiently, and not so much power that the farm group ignores the interests of consumers and established marketing organizations. Such conditions are separated by a fine and not easily discernible line.

Marketing orders and bargaining operations have definite limitations. They cannot control production over long periods of time. But they can regulate the flow of supplies to market during a particular production period and thereby help regularize the operation of a market and help stabilize prices. Thus, wisely used marketing orders and bargaining associations can assist farmers to market their products and bargain for price and handling advantages.

The Possibility of More Radical Changes in Commercial Policy

The section above is concerned with specific modifications to existing farm legislation that might occur in the normal political process. But any one of the forces discussed earlier, or a combination of those forces, might give rise to a situation in which more radical changes in commercial policy were forced onto the farm sector. The reordering of federal expenditure priorities, in which more funds were directed to the solution of urban problems and less to farm problems, could force an important shift in commercial farm policy. An extended world grain surplus with serious price-depressing effects for American farm products could also force a significant change in commercial farm policy. Or the pursuit of a policy of stringent environmental controls might require a radical shift in program mechanics—toward the more extensive use of land and away from the intensive use of certain inputs (for example, commercial fertilizer). Any one, or combination, of these forces, taken with the dwindling political influence of farmers in the Congress, could lead to some radical changes in commercial farm policy. Almost certainly the direction of such changes would involve:

1. Less emphasis on price support above equilibrium price levels.
2. Less emphasis on acreage controls.
3. Reduced expenditures (relative or absolute) on farm commodity programs.

The general features of a commercial farm policy that might emerge from such confrontations are not likely to satisfy most farm groups. Neither are they likely to satisfy most urban-based groups. Hopefully, they would represent a compromise intended to provide a reasonable degree of price and income protection to commercial farm enterprises and to assist disadvantaged persons and groups in agriculture, while at the same time moving in the direction of the aims and goals of an urban-oriented society. This is not an easy compromise to achieve. However, the general features of such a compromise might include actions to:

1. Support farm prices, through nonrecourse loans, at the average level of world prices of the five years preceding the inception of this policy. (Thereafter, the level of price support might be a five-year moving average of world prices.)
2. Control production, to the extent possible, in quantity terms (for example, in bushels and pounds) through voluntary programs, with payment limitations per farm operator.
3. Attach controls to the farm operator, not the landowner, and make those control rights negotiable.
4. Employ Agricultural Conservation Payments (ACP) to protect the ecosystem by inducing farmers to follow practices that do not pollute the environment.
5. Tax those input items that are determined to be persistently polluting the ecosystem (for example, commercial nitrate fertilizers). Input items that are directly injurious to the health of human beings should, of course, be banned by law.
6. Enact legislation that enables farm producing groups to bargain effectively with large processors and handlers of agricultural products.
7. Guarantee farm workers the same degree of social benefits and economic protection now provided nonfarm workers.
8. Negotiate the mutual reduction of trade and tariff barriers with foreign governments.
9. Continue storage programs for basic commodities to (1) make price support programs under point one operational, and (2) provide adequate reserve stocks to protect American consumers and help meet international food contingencies.
10. Provide training and relocation payments to farm operators and farm youth who are forced to seek nonfarm employment as the result of further development of commercial agriculture.
11. Convert the Department of Agriculture into a Department of Agricultural and Rural Affairs to deal with the issues raised in this and previous sections, as well as in the section on rural development that follows.

What are the implications of a farm policy including the actions outlined above? Taken as a unit, these actions would have the explicit objectives of:

1. Providing price and income protection and support to farm operators and farm laborers at reduced cost to the government.
2. Improving the efficiency of the operating farm economy, hence increasing the real product of the national society.

3. Humanizing the development process in agriculture by assisting individuals made surplus by the development process to find new and productive employment.

The program features listed above, then, would not benefit the large commercial farmers primarily, as is now largely the case. The program features listed above are intended to deal with the more critical problems confronting *people* now trying to earn a livelihood in agriculture, or who are in some way dependent on agriculture. Whether, in fact, the society of the United States will move in the directions implied by the above set of actions remains to be seen. But it is possible that the forces discussed earlier in this chapter might nudge society in these directions.

Problems of Rural America[7]

In this section, we turn away from the unique problems of commercial farmers and focus on the problems of rural America.[8] We will be concerned with the problems of people living in small towns, subsistence farmers, part-time farmers, nonfarmers living in the open country, and, of course, commercial farmers. In 1970, some 54 million people lived in rural America, and interestingly their absolute numbers have held almost constant over the past two decades while the urban population increased by 52 million persons and the farm population decreased by 13 million.

There are many desirable aspects to rural living: the air is clean and there is elbow room for the individual. But rural America is confronted with many difficult economic and social problems. Per capita incomes are low; unemployment and underemployment are commonplace; social and economic services are both lacking and of poor quality; and the incidence of poverty is high. On the average, the level of living is low and the quality of life poor in rural America.

Annual per capita income for metropolitan areas in 1968 stood at $3,811 in comparison with $2,614 in nonmetropolitan areas. In other words, per capita incomes in nonmetropolitan areas averaged only 70 percent of those in metropolitan areas in 1968.

One important reason for low average incomes in nonmetropolitan areas is the scarcity of productive jobs in those areas. The President's Commission on Rural Poverty estimated in 1967 that some 800,000 rural adults were unemployed, and of those who had jobs, some 18 percent were underemployed. The lack of productive jobs is the curse of rural America.

---

[7]Persons interested in the problems of rural America may wish to refer to the "Rural Development Chartbook" published by the Economic Research Service of the U.S. Department of Agriculture, October 1971.

[8]*Rural America* includes incorporated places with populations of 2,500 or less and all open country.

Per capita expenditures of local governments for selected services were as follows in 1966–67:

Service	Metro	Nonmetro
Education	$150	$136
Health and hospitals	18	14
Police protection	17	7
Roads	21	27
Fire protection	10	3
Sanitation	16	7
Welfare	24	12

Except for the category "roads," expenditures by local governments for social services in nonmetro areas are consistently below those in metro areas. And because of the greater costs of delivering social services over long distances in rural areas, the quality of social services in rural areas is lower than that implied in the expenditure differentials presented above. Space, distance, and sparse population greatly increase the costs of providing social services in rural areas over those in urban areas.

Although the number of substandard housing units in nonmetropolitan areas declined dramatically between 1950 and 1970, there still remain some 2.6 million substandard housing units in 1970 in these areas compared with 1.8 million such units in metro areas. Stated differently, 41 percent of all substandard housing units are located in metro areas and 59 percent in nonmetro areas, even though the population of nonmetro areas is just about half that of metro areas.

The incidence of poverty[9] is much greater in nonmetro areas than metro areas. In 1969, there were 12.0 million persons living in poverty in nonmetro areas and 12.3 million in metro areas. But the total population of the nonmetro areas was 69.8 million, and that for the metro areas was 130.0 million. The incidence of poverty in nonmetro areas is almost double that of metro areas.

In sum, by almost any standard of comparison that one chooses, the level of living is lower and the quality of life poorer in rural areas than in urban areas. There are many reasons for this: decades of poorer educational opportunities in rural areas; the distance factor in providing social services; almost total lack of economic and technical services for the nonfarm sector of rural America; and the failure of the agricultural industry to prosper outside of wartime for five decades. But the most important cause has been the inability of rural areas to generate productive enterprises and jobs to employ the people it has produced. Human labor has been surplus in rural America throughout the 20th century. Thus, rural areas have been in a

[9]As defined by the Social Security Administration and adopted by the Federal Interagency Committee in 1969.

chronic state of depression with much unemployment and underemployment, low wage rates, low average incomes, and widespread poverty.

How can this state of economic affairs be turned around? It cannot, through the development of the commercial agricultural sector alone. We have already observed the propensity for agricultural production to exceed demand, and the surplus problems that beset the agricultural industry as it enters the 1970s. In this context, there is no room for small, unproductive subsistence farms to grow into large, productive commercial farms, or for a large number of unemployed workers in rural areas to find jobs in commercial agriculture. Agriculture has been and will continue to be a contracting industry in terms of employment opportunities.

A prosperous agriculture would contribute to improved economic welfare in rural areas, but it would not solve the basic income-employment problem. The solution to the latter problem must be searched out along two separate but perhaps complementary routes. And the phrase *searched out* is used advisedly here, because the routes are hidden by the lack of technical knowledge, the inability and unwillingness to support needed local services, and an antiquated system of beliefs and values.

One route must be concerned with creating new enterprises and business undertakings that in turn create new, additional productive jobs. It must be concerned with economic development. In one sense, then, the route is one of economic development that is sought in both urban and rural areas to reduce unemployment and eradicate poverty in both areas. Hence, it could be argued that this economic development route should involve *one* national program to deal with the same kind of problem in both areas.

But there is one big difference: we really do not know how to achieve satisfactory rates of economic development in rural areas. In the past, economic development in rural areas has always involved agriculture, forestry, or mining. When those industries did not provide the desired rate of economic development, where and to what did you turn? There are monuments to manufacturing and distribution enterprises that have failed in the form of empty buildings in every little town. Economic development in rural America that does not involve agriculture, forestry, and mining is a poorly understood phenomenon.

Perhaps the place to begin is with a technical extension service to nonfarm rural America comparable to that of the agricultural sector. Perhaps, some hard planning at the local or county level can provide the guidance to enterprise creation that is required. Perhaps the integration of local enterprise with regional or national business firms can provide the operational guidance that is required. Certainly a government program of cheap credit sprayed indiscriminately across the rural countryside is not the answer. The answer must be *searched out,* making use of established research organizations, a technical extension service still to be created, local planning initiative, and past experience.

The second route that must be followed is concerned with the improved delivery of social and economic services to rural people by government. Here, we have in mind the following: improved quality of education, improved and more readily available health services, the availability of employment services, assistance in local development planning, available development credit, as well as continued technical and economic program services for farmers. This route is not shrouded in the same mystery as the economic development route for rural areas, but travel along it has been hesitant and faltering, except in connection with commercial agriculture. The *will* to provide social and economic services in rural areas has simply been lacking at almost every level of government.

The improved delivery of social services to rural areas will in itself improve the quality of life in rural areas. And the improved delivery of economic services should complement efforts to develop new enterprises and create new jobs by providing the information base, the technical base, and the credit base required by modern economic enterprise. The inadequacy of these services, except in commercial agriculture, may be *one* important reason, if not *the* important reason, that economic development in rural areas outside of agriculture has faltered so badly in the past. The informational, technical, and credit infrastructure provided agriculture has been completely lacking in nonfarm rural America—hence, the latter has failed to develop economically.

Some Conclusions

The problems of commercial agriculture and rural America are, of course, interrelated because commercial agriculture is one part of rural America. But the problems are different, too. In one sense, commercial agriculture has been the development showcase of rural America. Technological advance has been rapid in commercial agriculture, increases in worker productivity have been great, and the total commercial plant has produced a wondrous abundance.

But in another sense, commercial agriculture has not been a success story. It has been a contracting industry for six decades in terms of providing employment; the working force in agriculture declined from 13.6 million in 1910 to 4.5 million in 1970. In addition to this decline in the absolute level of employment in agriculture, there have been the untold millions of young people who left farming during this period because there were no jobs for them in agriculture. The nonfarm rural sector thus became the first dumping ground for displaced farm people—young and old. And from there, millions migrated on to the city. But, important for this discussion, the nonfarm rural sector has been burdened by displaced farm workers, surplus labor, and heavy unemployment for decades.

It should, therefore, be clearly recognized that successful development of the farm sector of rural America does not necessarily contribute to the development of the nonfarm sector. Such activities as the distribution of nonfarm production goods (for example, farm machinery) and the handling of farm-produced products (for example, grain and livestock) do contribute to development in the nonfarm rural sector. But the continued absorption of surplus agricultural workers acts as a drag on the development of the nonfarm rural sector. Programs of economic development and improved delivery of social and economic services must recognize this. The nonfarm rural sector needs comparable, but not the identical, kinds of creative and sustained help that the farm sector has received for a hundred years or more. And the nonfarm sector needs this help doubly because it has been the dumping ground for surplus workers from agriculture for sixty years or more.

Finally, commercial agriculture is going to be confronted with some monumental product surplus and resource adjustment problems in the 1970s. Once, it had the political muscle to acquire from government the assistance it needed and the arrogance to stand alone on these matters. But all this is changing, and farm people are being forced to learn how to live and operate in a world of reduced political power. In this changed state of affairs, it is to the advantage of the city man to help farm people develop and enact programs that provide price and income stability for agriculture and thereby contribute to the continued abundant production of food and fiber products at all times. Chronic food abundance is better, far better, than a chronic deficit for the city man, even if he must share in the cost of carrying the surpluses involved.

Index